Towards a History of Literary Composition in Medieval Spain

Colbert Nepaulsingh has written a new kind of history of medieval Spanish literature, one based on hermeneutic principles derived from such literary theorists as Hans-Georg Gadamer. Through a close and original reading of selected major texts such as *Razón de amor* and *Libro de buen amor*, he answers some of the fundamental questions about how literary works were composed during the medieval period.

Professor Nepaulsingh brings into clear focus the evolution of a series of sophisticated compositional techniques over three centuries. In early thirteenth-century texts, stringing and juxtaposing techniques predominated; at the end of the thirteenth and through the fourteenth century a more dialectical method of composing texts became more dominant; in the fifteenth century the most popular compositional device was the wheel of Fortune. Nepaulsingh deftly places these developments in the wider context of the biblical and apocalyptical traditions that overwhelmingly dominated medieval Spanish literature.

Students of medieval Spanish literature, and of literature in general, will appreciate the originality of the author's approach and the breadth and depth of his scholarship.

'Superb ... it will become a landmark in medieval Hispanic studies.' James Burke, University of Toronto

COLBERT I. NEPAULSINGH is an associate professor of Hispanic and Italian studies, State University of New York at Albany. He is the author of *El dezir a las syete virtudes y otros poemas*.

COLBERT I. NEPAULSINGH

Towards a History of Literary Composition in Medieval Spain

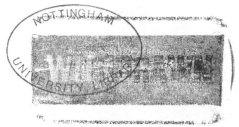

UNIVERSITY OF TORONTO PRESS
Toronto Buffalo London

© University of Toronto Press 1986
Toronto Buffalo London
Printed in Canada

ISBN 0-8020-2570-6

University of Toronto Romance Series 54

323379

Canadian Cataloguing in Publication Data

Nepaulsingh, Colbert I.
Towards a history of literary composition in
medieval Spain

(University of Toronto romance series,
ISSN 0082-5336 ; 54)
Includes bibliographical references and index.
ISBN 0-8020-2570-6

1. Spanish literature – To 1500 – History and criticism.
2. Spanish language – To 1500.
3. Literature, Medieval – History and criticism.
4. Spanish literature – Cricitism, Textual.
I. Title. II. Series.

PQ6058.N46 1986   860'.9'001   C86-094271-6

This book has been published with the help of a grant from the Canadian Federation for the Humanities, using funds provided by the Social Sciences and Humanities Research Council of Canada. Publication has also been assisted by a grant from the State University of New York at Albany.

To Alan Deyermond

❧ CONTENTS

✎ PREFACE

This book was completed between July 1981 and August 1982 with the generous help of a grant from the John Simon Guggenheim Memorial Foundation and with sabbatical-leave privileges from the State University of New York at Albany. I should like to thank these institutions for their support during what turned out to be a very rewarding academic year for me. Parts of the book – chapters 1, 4, and 6 – were completed earlier with financial help from the National Endowment for the Humanities and the State University of New York Research Foundation; two of these chapters were released earlier for publication in order to test scholarly reaction to the project from my colleagues. I should like to thank the editors of *Neophilologus*, the *Revista Canadiense de Estudios Hispánicos*, and *Acta* for permission to reprint this material.

When I write, I try to think of people who have done some kindness that has touched upon what I am writing. This is why every chapter of this book is dedicated to some person, and why the entire book, more than the sum of its parts, is dedicated to Alan Deyermond, the kindest scholar I know.

Since its completion in August 1982 and acceptance for publication in May 1984, this manuscript has benefited from the detailed comments of seven expert readers: three readers whose anonymous comments were passed on to me by the University of Toronto Press recommended the typescript for publication; Professors Alan Deyermond; David Hook (chapters 1, 2, and 3 only); Alicia de Colombí-Monguió, who read the typescript at my request; and Professor Keith Whinnom, who was kind enough to send me his comments on chapter 5.

I am deeply grateful to all of these readers for their kind remarks and helpful suggestions. They recommended many important minor changes, mainly of a stylistic and bibliographic nature, but fortunately no extensive revisions. The chapter for which they suggested most rethinking was chapter 2, in which three readers found the presentation more rigid than was necessary. Thanks to these readers chapter 2 now seems much less intolerant of other possible interpretations and much closer to what I sought to communicate in the first place. Of course I am to be blamed for the errors that remain in the text: the readers encouraged me to say better what I wanted to say; they did not seek to correct my mistakes or make my text their own.

I should like those who will read my book to know that, in my opinion, the Inter-Library Loan Department at the State University of New York at Albany, under the direction of Ms Sally Stevenson, is among the finest in the world. Without the assistance of the department's staff there would be no book. Sra Emilia de la Cámara y de la Torre, of the Biblioteca Nacional, Madrid, was very helpful in acquiring for me some material on Abraham Ibn Ezra not easily available. Ms Ronaline Dyson is an extraordinary typist, a very pleasant person, and some kind of unofficial handwriting expert to be able to decipher my longhand letters. My wife, Stephanie, has made me gifts of books that I never thought I would have reason to use in the preparation of this study, and that, I now humbly admit, were crucial to some of the solutions I would not otherwise have found. I have learned that one should not always be disdainful of sources that apear on the surface to be trivial and unacademic, especially if one seeks to understand the works of great artists who, though they were very learned, show signs in their writings of being also very humble, ordinary human beings. Finally, many other people have helped me in this project; the names of some of them are given in the Notes.

This book has been published with the help of a grant from the Canadian Federation for the Humanities, using funds provided by the Social Sciences and Humanities Research Council of Canada. Publication has also been facilitated by a grant from the offices of Professor Paul Wallace, Dean of the College of Humanities and Fine Arts, and Professor John Shumaker, Vice-President for Research and Educational Development of the State University of New York at Albany. My special thanks are due to Mary E. Willmot of the University of Toronto Press who added to my text a kind of expert editorial order that I respect but am not patient enough to deliver.

Colbert I. Nepaulsingh
Albany, New York

Towards a History of Literary Composition
in Medieval Spain

Introduction

FOR MARIO VALDÉS

This book is the work of a beginner. It can claim to be nothing more than the result of an elementary close reading of certain Spanish texts, with a view to answering some basic questions about literary composition during the medieval period; it is, in other words, a beginner's exercise in literary history and criticism. Yet, beginnings can lead to new directions if the neophyte, keenly aware of his limitations, is forced to avoid those areas fully explored by experts, and concentrate on questions that are simple enough to have been left unasked or incompletely answered.

As a beginner I do not aspire to summon up the powers of synthesis and organization that result in the histories of literature written by expert Hispanists like Alan Deyermond and Juan Luis Alborg.[1] Nor do I seek to collect in a single volume scintillating essays (like those of P.E. Russell, Dámaso Alonso, and Joaquín Gimeno Casalduero) that spark countless ideas in the minds of generations of scholars.[2] I have set myself a much more modest task, taking a cue from a book for beginners written (in part) by one of the greatest literary critics or our time: René Wellek.

Almost forty years ago René Wellek wrote that 'most leading histories of literature are either histories of civilization or collections of critical essays. One type is not a history of *art*; the other is not a *history* of art.'[3] From Wellek's remarks I deduced that it would be worthwhile to conceive of a literary history that would concentrate on the major elements of literature: titles, plots, characterization, settings, language, points of view, mythological or philosophical content, and structure. For me to attempt such a literary history would, of course, be ambitious and unnecessary. So I decided to choose one of these elements – structure – and to further limit my efforts to one aspect of this element, composition, which I understand to mean, simply, how parts of a work are put together.

Even within this limited range I have tried very hard not to encroach upon those areas of composition in which other Hispanists have demonstrated superior skills. I have left problems of versification, for example, in the hands of experts on linguistics and prosody, and have listed in the Conclusion other areas omitted that would be better treated by appropriately qualified experts. The most important word in the title of this book is therefore, in my opinion, 'Towards': I did not aim to write the literary history I had conceived; my more modest goal was to make a beginner's contribution towards it, building upon the many books and articles that have been written about the composition of individual medieval Spanish works.

To mention René Wellek in the age of Geoffrey Hartmann and Harold Bloom is tantamount to raising suspicions, in the minds of many avant-garde readers, about the vintage of one's theoretical approach to literary history and criticism. Let me therefore describe the theoretical bias I selected in order to approach the texts I discuss in the following chapters. I find myself most comfortable with a hermeneutical approach to literature and specifically with the kind of hermeneutics described by theoreticians like Hans-Georg Gadamer. Of course I do not claim to have understood Gadamer, nor can I pretend to practise a kind of criticism of which he would approve; but I believe I understand enough of Gadamer's theoretical views to feel completely at home with the flexibility he offers.

My preference for Gadamer was confirmed by a recent reading of a book by David Couzens Hoy, *The Critical Circle: Literature, History, and Philosophical Hermeneutics*.[4] Hoy's book is, in my opinion, a brilliant defence of Gadamer's work against criticism by most of the major contemporary theoreticians, including E.D. Hirsch, Jacques Derrida, Roland Barthes, Habermas, and Bloom. Hoy demonstrates that whereas the rigidity of some aspects makes the approach of most theoreticians brittle, Gadamer builds his approach with a kind of flexibility that seems to be presumably capable of accommodating all situations in criticism without degenerating into meaningless relativism.

I did not read Gadamer and Hoy before setting out to write this book, but having read their works I found support for most of the practices I had adopted in the preparation of these chapters. For example, I had decided not to approach the texts I would read as though they were remote medieval objects that could be isolataed and entirely devoured, as it were, by my powers of comprehension; in the medieval sense, that is, that gave Peter Comestor his famous name because he was perceived as capable of devouring biblical texts. Rather, I thought that I should treat these texts, as far as possible, as equals, and engage them in inter-subjective dialogue in which there would be two subjects, and not a perceptive critic as subject and an antiquated petrified text as object.

I was delighted to find the kind of approach I was taking approved by Hoy, who describes two conflicting conceptions of hermeneutics: the objectivist (represented by critics like Hirsch), which claims that the text is an object that the reader must come to *know*; and the historicist (represented by Gadamer), which claims that the reader does not reach out and know the text, but fuses with it in order to understand it. 'There is a clear difference between the questions, "Do you know the poem?" and "Do you understand the poem?"'[5] One can know a lot about a poem without understanding it. Consequently, this was the main precondition (and, I should like to think, the only one) that I am conscious of having set before my close reading of these texts: I would engage them in inter-subjective dialogue about how their main parts were put together.

Now that I have attempted to record the results of my dialogue, I notice certain tendencies that are attributable to my own limitations as a critic. For example, I tend to avoid pinpointing sources, and instead talk repeatedly of traditions. Clearly this is because it is often easier to glimpse the broad tradition in which a work is composed than to identify a precise source. So, in the following chapters I discuss the tradition of rosaries and psalters, the tradition of the Song of Songs, the apocalyptic tradition, logic and the liturgical tradition, the tradition of the wheel of Fortune, and the tradition of bookmaking.

I did not ask myself, 'What traditions are discernible in medieval Spanish composition?' and then proceed to identify them. I started with questions about the composition of each work in its turn, and to my astonishment and at times against my will, the texts directed themselves, as it were, to different traditions. The second chapter illustrates what I mean by 'to my astonishment and at times against my will.' For instance, I had assumed from previous readings that the *Razón de amor* would fit neatly into the apocalyptic tradition as a kind of body-and-soul narrative. But once I reread the *Razón* with more detailed information in my mind about the apocalyptic tradition, the text of the *Razón* told me clearly that it belonged elsewhere. The lesson that I learned from this is a simple one that I should have known before: texts are composed not *in vacuo* but in discernible traditions that they themselves identify.

Frankly, I felt a little less than sane when I thought about talking to texts and having them talk back to me; but then I read Hoy's statement that 'in a sense a text does speak; that is, it shows a meaning that claims our attention by addressing us in a manner relevant to our concern with our particular situation.'[6] So I calmly let the texts suggest to me to what traditions of composition they belonged.

Of course, I may have misunderstood some texts, or misread them, but I do not now believe that I have erred seriously in identifying the traditions that they indicated. I feel somewhat confident of this because, fortunately, I am not in the unenviable position of having to be the sole advocate for the existence of any of these traditions. As I mention in the respective chapters, Salvador Martínez noted the importance of the psalter tradition; Alicia C. de Ferraresi (now Alicia de Colombí-Monguió) and Alan Deyermond know the importance of the tradition of the Song of Songs; Burke and others are well aware of the vastness of the apocalyptic tradition; critics like Otis Green have discussed the tradition of 'sic et non'; Russell and Gilman are keenly aware of the tradition of magic and the wheel of fortune; and critics like Morreale know the importance of biblical texts, commentaries, and glosses hidden between and inserted into other texts.

I did not invent these traditions. I merely begin to discuss them conveniently within a single binding. Such a beginning has its advantages as well as its pitfalls. Since all readers are expert in some areas and beginners in others, I take advantage of the fact that I can at all times captivate the interest of some beginners, but I must also always avoid the risk of irritating experts. The advantage and the risk invite me to examine the question of validity in interpretation.

I rarely underline the books I read; when I do, it means first of all that I own the book, and second that I am anxious to arrive at a consensus with its author, but that his or her text abruptly cuts my attempts short before it can accommodate my point of view. E.D. Hirsch's *Validity in Interpretation* is one of the most heavily underlined books I own. I did not fully understand why this was so until I read Hoy's critique of Hirsch: 'Hirsch and others are apparently misled by a false antinomy ... [which] depends on picturing the past as one closed circle and the present as another. The question of how one can get out of one circle or horizon into the other can never be adequately answered because the picture itself is abstract and false.'[7]

I am anxious to agree with Hirsch when he distinguishes between validation and verification: 'I now prefer the term "validation" to the more definitive-sounding word "verification." To verify is to show that a conclusion is true; to validate is to show that a conclusion is probably true on the basis of what is known.' But for Hirsch, validation and truth, by means of an objective changeable consensus, are attainable at any given time: 'The aim of validation is to give objective sanction to a particular interpretive hypothesis and thereby to provide the only possible foundation for a consensus omnium with regard to the text ... such a consensus may, of course, be quite temporary since the wit of man is always devising new guesses, and his curiosity is always discovering new relevant information.'[8]

I can never hope that any of my interpretations will ever reach a consensus omnium. My interpretation will 'of course, attempt to assure its own legitimacy by striving to fulfill conditions that would lead to a consensus (although not necessarily a contemporary consensus, since we may reject the standards of colleagues and peers).' To argue, however, as Hirsch appears to, that such a consensus is attainable is, according to Hoy, to misunderstand history. In the chapters that follow I do not assume that any given text has one true, objective, transcendental meaning which exists somewhere outside it and which must be attained by the interpreter via a consensus omnium. Rather, I posit that what I claim to be true about a text is 'what any rational being in that particular situation would think.'[9]

When I submit, for example, that the *Razón de amor* is a single unit of composition, partly because what is said about wine in the second part of the narrative applies equally well to what can be said about love, I intend that this claim is valid only in so far as any rational reader would agree that the text permits my interpretation; but I entertain no hope of attaining consensus for this claim. Similarly, when I write throughout my text statements like 'this is what the author seems to have in mind,' I do not mean that I have succeeded in objectifying the author's intent and captured it with my knowledge; rather, I mean that I have come to understand one way of expressing one of the author's meanings as represented by the text and by the tradition in which the text was composed; it would be awkward to have to spell this out in its longer form every time I am unable to resist making statements like 'what the poet seems to have in mind.' Those of my readers who can feel comfortable with my claims might tolerate this use of the abbreviated form; those who cannot agree with me will, I am sure, find a more precise way to validate the claim. In either event, the aims of valid criticism will have been served.

How close should one stay to the text's surface meaning? How literally should one read it? These are questions capable of sending some Hispanists into camps representing a range of opinions. There are scholars, for example, who would staunchly support Ian Michael's extremely cautious approach to the *Alexandre*: 'Even in cases where one finds apparent ellipses in argument or motivation in a medieval literary text, great caution is necessary ... The text of the *Alexandre* does not support any religious typology.' These Hispanists would also agree with Roger Walker's insistence, in his criticism of the *Zifar*, on not 'having recourse to the over-sophisticated techniques of allegorical interpretation' since 'romances at least usually have no significance beyond the literal level, and their unity is demonstrable, if at all, in descriptions of self-evident relations.'[10]

In Gadamer's opinion, the modern tendency to rely heavily on the literal meaning of texts is related to Lutheran reforms of scriptural principles. 'Luther's position is more or less the following: scripture is *sui ipsius interpres*. We do not need tradition to reach the proper understanding of it, nor do we need an art of interpretation in the style of the ancient teaching of the fourfold meaning of scripture, but the text of the scripture has a clear sense that can be derived from itself, the *sensus literalis*. The allegorical method in particular, which had formerly seemed indispensable for the dogmatic unity of the teachings of scripture, is now legitimate only where the allegorical intention is given in scripture, itself.' A similar categorical disregard for allegorical interpretation of the *Razón de amor* is expressed by Olga Tudorica Impey: 'A lo largo de la primera parte de la *Razón de amor* no hay ningún indicio que justifique la interpretación alegórico – religiosa ... Es una lástima que Jacob haya enterrado estas valiosas observaciones en el montón de la alegoría religiosa.'[11]

In a different camp are scholars who would admire Burke's blatantly allegorical study of the *Libro del cavallero Zifar*. These Hispanists might also wonder silently why Thomas Hart's *La alegoría en el 'Libro de buen amor'* has met with such deafening silence after María Rosa Lida de Malkiel's review of it.[12] Of course, the authors singled out above (unfairly, but for constructive convenience) possibly no longer hold the views published many years ago under their names; and, of course, many other Hispanists would refuse to be identified with either hypothetical camp.

In the chapters that follow, as I try to decide how literally to interpret the text and when to ask what it implies besides the surface meaning of its words, I am reminded always of my favourite quotation from the Talmud: 'He who translates [read "interprets"] a verse with strict literalness is a falsifier, and he who makes additions to it is a blasphemer.'[13] I aim to be neither a falsifier nor a blasphemer. I refuse to be paralysed by caution when it is valid to inquire beyond the literal meaning, because I believe that 'there is no doubt that speech can also perform acts, and that these acts have a meaning that is not confined to the meaning of the words. A child's statement that he is hurt can just as easily be a request for sympathy as a real report of pain.'[14]

Like Keightley, I am aware that 'the dangers inherent in allegorical approaches to medieval texts in general are strikingly presented by Jean Misrahi, "Symbolism and Allegory in Arthurian Romance," *Romance*

Philology, 17 (1963–4), 555–69.'[15] But if, by citing Misrahi, Keightley means that to look beyond the literal level in the *Zifar* is 'as much an act of devotion as one of literary criticism or scholarship,'[16] then I cannot agree. Misrahi does not talk about 'medieval texts in general,' but about Arthurian romance in particular, and I do not believe that the *Zifar* can be best defined as an Arthurian romance. And although I appreciate Misrahi's useful distinction between symbolism and allegory, I am not impressed by the claim that because numerous medieval theologians sounded repeated warnings against a certain phenomenon, that phenomenon was either very scarce or did not exist at all.[17]

Misrahi writes: 'We are explicitly and especially warned by any number of medieval theologians against injecting hidden allegories into secular texts ... Of symbolism there is much in medieval romances ... but of allegory there is very little, and that little is almost always apparent on the surface or else it is explicated in the text itself.'[18] Would theologians, medieval or modern, sound such repeated warnings about a phenomenon that was so rare? Clearly, in the medieval period, as in any other, many texts (like the *Corbacho* and the *Libro rimado del palacio*) took great pains to spell out repeatedly, on the surface, the specific meaning that they intended; the repetition itself is an indication of the author's realization that it is never easy to limit a text to one specific meaning. But many other texts, like the *Zifar*, insist on departure from the literal level. I do not call the *Zifar* an allegory, and I am not sure it is a romance, but I am sure that it is an apocalyptic narrative that invites the reader to go beyond its cortex to decipher the symbolic meanings at its core.

I leave the text, therefore, when its surface meaning demands a symbolic interpretation. But some direct significant reference in the text itself should warrant such a departure, and the resulting interpretation must be tested against the entire text. For example, I am not persuaded by Alfred Jacob's arguments for Christian symbolism in the *Razón* nor by Spitzer's arguments for classical symbolism in the same work, because neither of these critics justifies departure to the symbolic level with direct significant reference to the text of the *Razón*; and neither Jacob's nor Spitzer's symbolic interpretation fits the text as a whole. I propose that the invocation to the *Razón* ('Sancti spiritus adsid nobis gratia amen') and its second line ('Qui triste tiene su coraçon benga oyr esta razón') are direct significant references to the tradition of the Song of Songs; and since the Song of Songs is at the very core of allegory in Western literature, departure from the literal level of the *Razón* is justified; further, the resulting allegorical or symbolic interpretation seems to fit the text as a whole.

Since by chance or by design a document that was surely intended to be taken literally has been attached to the *Razón*, and since this literal-minded document has certain themes in common with the *Razón*, I take the liberty to reconstruct how two kinds of medieval readers of both document and narrative (a literal-minded reader and a more subtle one) might have interpreted the *Razón*.

When I disagree with learned scholars, like Spitzer, I may be thought to sound more like an impertinent upstart than a beginner. Let me step out of my text – in parentheses, as it were – to try to explain the difference between my own attitude to all critics cited and what is expressed in this book. As I state in chapter 4, the most important lesson I have learned in literary criticism is that all critics must be treated seriously; invalid interpretations help to foster valid progress to consensus. Wherever it states disagreement, my text almost always conveniently omits the wider area of agreement upon which the apparent difference of opinion is based. This is especially true about those critics from whom I have learned most, some of whom I name here.

In the subtext of chapter 1 are critics like Karl-Ludwig Selig. He is cited only once, but by a happy coincidence I was writing the chapter when we were reading together the *Decameron*, the *Canterbury Tales*, and the *Heptaméron*. What he said about these works, and what he has written about rosaries in the *Quijote*, gave me confidence at an appropriate moment of the preparation of the text for my first chapter.[19] In the subtext of chapter 2 are critics like Alicia de Colombí-Monguió. My intent was to express complete agreement with her well-known contributions to the understanding of the *Razón*, but when I sat down to do this, my text did something more.

Although I am indebted to many critics for the separate sections in chapter 3, I can blame no Hispanist but myself for the general discussion of the apocalyptic tradition. In 1966, when I started work on Francisco Imperial, I noticed that his two longer poems are apocalyptic. I set about then to learn about apocalypticism in Spain; I did not know that such an undertaking would take me from Apringius of Beja to Christopher Columbus and after. In search of a reason why I did not tire of this exploration of apocalypticism, I have found only the memory of my maternal grandfather who used to put me on his knee and 'cipher from the Bible' about the End of things.

In the subtext of chapter 4 are critics like Otis Green, Leo Spitzer, and María Rosa Lida de Malkiel (for the *Libro de buen amor*) and Erich von Richthofen (for the *Corbacho*). In the subtext of chapter 5 are critics like P.E. Russell, Stephen Gilman, Bruce Wardropper, and Keith Whinnom;

and in that of chapter 6, R.S. Willis (for *cuaderna vía* and Juan Ruiz) and
Margherita Morreale (for her work on Spanish Bibles).

No other single critic has influenced my entire book as has Alan
Deyermond. He is, in my opinion, the most important contributor to
Hispanism in our time; so much so that statements like 'I should like to
thank Alan D. Deyermond' have now become a *topos* of Hispanic literary criticism. I have tried to sketch the tradition of criticism from
which this book solicits consensus. Readers should know that I hold
this tradition always in the highest esteem; if ever my book should
represent anything other than this esteem, it is simply that as a
beginner I have not learned to make my text say always everything I
want it to mean.

Having stepped out of my own text in order to sketch briefly the tradition to which I think it belongs, let me return to my suggestion that it
is valid to leave a text in justified search of an appropriate symbolic
interpretation if the diversion is demanded by some direct significant
reference in the text. I also think it valid to depart from a text in order
to understand the tradition of composition suggested by the text. For
example, while I was reading in preparation for chapter 1, the text of
Alfonso's *Cantigas* suggested rosaries to me. About rosaries I knew as
little as most people know. So I left the text to begin to find out about
rosaries; as a consequence I learned an enormous amount about gardens
and psalters, bead craft and book craft. This information served me in
good stead for not only chapter 1 but also chapter 6, which deals with
book craft.

When I returned to the *Cantigas* with this newly acquired knowledge,
I was able to answer questions about its composition and ask other questions about the composition of works like Berceo's *Milagros* and, to my
surprise, the *Cantar de Mio Cid*. I was able to conclude that these three
works are composed, like books on a string, within what I have called
the psalter tradition; further, I was able to suggest that stringing is such
an ancient and polygenetic mode of composition that it might very well
embrace much of early Spanish lyric as well as non-Spanish works like
the *Canterbury Tales*, the *Decameron*, and the *Heptaméron*. This does
not mean that these works must henceforth be discussed only within
the psalter tradition; clearly works of subtle artistry like the *Cantar De
Mio Cid* cannot be confined to any single tradition of composing literature. I use the psalter tradition, and other traditions, merely as heuristic
tools which I am prepared to discard as soon as they have exhausted
their hermeneutic purpose.

Why begin with the psalter tradition? Since this book claims to be a contribution towards a literary history, to what concept of history does it subscribe? This book, first of all, is intended to complement, not compete with or replace, other literary histories that are ordered conventionally by centuries, genres, generations, and 'isms.' Indeed, it might be classified as a variant of some of these categories: it moves, although not in strict chronology, from the thirteenth century in chapter 1 to the end of the fifteenth century in chapter 5. For some readers, the word *tradition* in the chapter headings might just as easily be replaced by -ism; for example, psalterism, apocalypticism. But this book does not aim at an eclectic variation of existing categories of literary histories: no literary history of medieval Spain has done that as skilfully as has Alan Deyermond's; the tables of contents of both his literary histories are chapters in themselves, innovative lessons in literary historiography. I do not aim as high. I do begin, however, to search for different tools of ordering.

Chronology will always be a useful tool, and so will genre; but by letting the texts suggest other tools, new possibilities of ordering begin to emerge. For example, when a number of disparate texts suggest the same apocalyptic tool, chronology takes on symbolic significance, and genre recedes in importance almost entirely. One begins to wonder if it is more than accidental that apocalyptic texts emerge more forcefully around the turn of centuries, especially since in one of them the concept of the jubilee year takes on functional significance as an element of composition. (In criticism of modern Spanish literature I have noticed recently an increasing use of *apocalypse* as the year 2000 approaches.) Again, when the texts like the *Disputa del alma y el cuerpo*, which are usually discussed under 'verse' or 'poetry' or 'debate forms,' can be discussed with validity and usefulness in the same category (apocalyptic narratives) as the *Zifar*, then genre, in that particular situation, is not an important concept. The way apocalyptic writers order and reorder time forces the literary historian, in turn, to reorder conventional categories and see a different pattern of history; different, but not new.

This book does not begin with the psalter tradition in the belief that the psalter tradition is the one that antedates the others, and the one from which the others evolve. It is tempting to assume, since stringing is such a primitive and universal manner of arranging, that it must have preceded a more literate and sophisticated form, like apocalypticism, for example. But this does not necessarily follow. If primitive artists were clever enough to chant prayers while counting the beads they strung, surely they were clever enough to think apocalyptic thoughts. The period covered by the book is so relatively brief (a mere three hundred years) that forms of composition cannot be seen to evolve in any accelerated way. But a simultaneous co-existence of mutating forms is perceptible throughout the period. For reasons dictated by contemporary circumstances and also by the way the evidence has survived, one mutated form appears to take precedence over others at different times. For example, the texts suggest a preoccupation with fortune and its mutations throughout the medieval period; but not until the fifteenth century does fortune predominate in literary composition, because of the tenor of the times.

This pattern of history (in which elements co-exist, receding and advancing in mutation at different times) is not new, but its application to Spanish literary historiography is, as far as I know, very recent:

> Perhaps the most serious impediment to a history of literary form has been the subsistence of the notion of unchanging universals as the only basis for classification. The profound breakthrough of Charles Darwin's populational schema seems to have made no inroads among literary historians. In Darwin's terms an organic species is not a permanent entity defined by unchanging essential characteristics, but neither are the members of a species associated by an arbitrary decision of convenience. In Darwin's schema and in our own, species or literary class is an historical entity. By this statement I mean that each class is an individual group whose component elements – all of them – are at all times subject to diversification, but that the group is also one within which selective factors are continually eliminating ill-adapted innovations and accepting others .... The issue is how to establish a record of change and of mutation in the literary form.[20]

This book is a search for ways to begin to record the changes and mutations in literary composition during the medieval period in Spain.

The search does not really begin at any fixed point, nor will it ever end (although I certainly will). My text says that I begin with the psalter tradition and end with the tradition of bookcraft. I say that I fused at a given point in time first with Imperial's text, in a tradition of criticism of that text which began long before my time; as a result of this initial dialogue I recorded certain observations about apocalypticism that made me want to, among other things, examine other texts; or did I fuse first with classical apocalyptic texts upon my grandfather's knee?

My text is forced to acknowledge at its conclusion that other texts must be examined and reexamined, and models changed, and tools discarded. Thus, I try hard to avoid mistakes, but I have no rigid fear of error nor am I needlessly oppressed by any desire to be definitive; however, I recognize the need to rein in, with aims at consensus and with validation, this self-imposed phenomenological flexibility. Likewise, it is tempting to say that my method is to begin with strict formal analysis of the text and end with hermeneutical interpretation, that is, in the manner often described as Ricoeur's hermeneutical arch.[21] But I am persuaded by Hoy's title that, to be more precise, there can be no objective beginning, no definitive end to what is, in effect, a critical circle. My text says, at its beginning in this introduction, that I am a beginner. I now say: I am not even that, since my so-called beginning is inseparably attached to countless others that preceded it.

1 Books on a String

My main concern in this chapter is simple: I should like to suggest that three medieval Spanish works – the *Cantar de Mio Cid*, (*Cid*) the *Milagros de Nuestra Señora* (*Milagros*), and the *Cantigas* of Alfonso el Sabio – are composed according to the primitive and universal principle of stringing things together. But I am forced by the evidence to adopt a very roundabout approach to illustrate this idea. Because the evidence is conclusive for only the *Cantigas* and the *Milagros*, I must go to extreme lengths and into areas of knowledge on which I am not an authority in order to show what the *Cid* might have to do with stringing. This means that I must first explain how in a large part of Europe and elsewhere, not just in Spain, books came to be related to beads and rosaries and the Virgin Mary; much evidence about this relationship is found graphically and more easily in paintings and in miniatures than in texts, so I talk a lot about beads, art, and other books before I can get to the books I want to analyse.

I suspect that a lot of the Spanish evidence that might have made it easy for me to state my case has disappeared. The *Cid* is such a polished work of art that one is led to believe that it is the unique survivor of a long tradition of such works. To compensate for this lack of suitable Spanish texts, I decided to analyse here only three well-known non-Spanish works in which the composition is easy to demonstrate as 'strung.' I chose an Italian work, Boccaccio's *Decameron*; a French work dependent on Boccaccio's, the *Heptaméron* of Marguerite de Navarre; and an English work, Chaucer's *Canterbury Tales*. I mean to suggest by this arbitrary, anachronistic selection that since stringing is not only universal but also polygenetic and transmitted, books could have been composed this way in Spain as in Italy, France, and England. But I choose Boccaccio somewhat more deliberately, because a great deal has been written about his influence on the 'novela sentimental' in Spanish literature in the fifteenth century. So what I say about Boccaccio in this chapter has reference to the *Cid*, *Milagros*, and the *Cantigas*, and especially the works discussed in chapter 5.

I ask the reader to bear in mind, therefore, that this chapter will not be as conclusive as those that follow, but that the simple point it tries to make is worth attempting for the sake of the rest of the book. In one sense, the suggestive nature of this first chapter is characteristic of all histories: in order to begin at a beginning that is obviously not a real beginning, one seems forced to speculate about unknown factors that might have accounted for the beginning that has survived. This speculation in no way impinges upon other research efforts to establish the specific origins of works like the *Cid*. Whether such origins turn out to be French or Spanish, what is said in this chapter about the text of the *Cid* (my main concern) should remain essentially intact.

It is well known that the stringing of things like beads and amulets is one of the most ancient crafts practised by human beings. 'The use of beads in Egypt dates back to the Neolithic period, that is from about 12,000 to 7,000 years ago. The earliest beads are in the form of small, natural objects such as bones, pebbles, seeds, shells and teeth ... worn around the neck, arm, ankle, or waist.'[1] It is also well known that this practice was/is world-wide (archaeologists have discovered evidence of bead craft on all continents), and that its significance was both practical and religious: beads have been used in all civilizations to both count and charm. In Spain the oldest beads yet found belong to the Late Neolithic and Early Bronze Ages.[2]

What is less well known and little explored is the relationship between bead craft and book craft – between the art of stringing things and the art of literary composition. It is obvious how some practitioners of book craft – the scribe, the illuminator, and the bookbinder – would have been compared with other craftsmen. For example, the frontispiece to a twelfth-century edition of the works of St Ambrose contains a miniature that shows a monk as painter surrounded by fifteen other monks, four of whom are praying while the other eleven are engaged in book-related activities; here the painter is in the company of the scribe, the teacher, and the smith who, with hammer raised above the hinge of a clasp on an anvil, is at work on a luxurious binding for a book.[3] But there is no clear indication that any of these craftsmen is an author and not exclusively a scribe, bookbinder, teacher, painter, or smith.

When Alfonso el Sabio mandated that clerics 'no deven ser menestrales si no en cosas contadas assí cuemo en fazer libros et escriptorios et arcas et redes et cuévanos et cestas,'[4] it is clear that scribes and those who worked in scriptoria were considered craftsmen; but it is not clear that those who composed books were also so considered: 'fazer libros' normally means 'componer libros,' but it can be argued that the phrase in Alfonso's command means to copy and manufacture books, not to write or compose them. We know that Alfonso is not using the word for craftsmen carelessly here because elsewhere he makes a clear distinction between the craftsman ('menestral') and the 'labrador':

> Et obras son aquellos que los homes facen estando en casas o en lugares cobiertos, así como los que labran oro et plata, et facen monedas, o armas, o armaduras, o los otros meesteres que son de muchas maneras que se obran desta guisa; ca maguer ellos trabajan por sus cuerpos, non se apodera el tiempo tanto dellos para facerles daño como a los otros que andan de fuera: et por ende a estos llaman menestrales, et a los otros labradores.[5]

According to this distinction writers, like smiths and others who work indoors, ought to be craftsmen; and it is precisely in the sense of craftsman 'menestral' with a 'mester' that the author of the *Libro de Alexandre* conceived of himself when he wrote: 'Mester trago fermoso, non es de joglaría / mester es sen pecado, ca es de clerezía.'[6]

To place the maker of beads and the composer of books in the same broad category of craftsman is merely to begin to explore the relationship between bead and book crafts. Both the beads themselves as well as the string that threads them together have been closely connected with literary composition for so long that it is easy to lose sight of the relationship. We refer in everyday usage to a *well-knit* discussion (in Spanish, 'un discurso bien enhilado'); we lose the *thread* of an argument ('perder el hilo'); to *weave* ('tejer') is also to compose, and a *text* ('texto') is something woven (from Latin, *texere, textus*). Medieval monks, like the one in the frontispiece to the works of St Ambrose, knew how to bind books by sewing together quires of paper or parchment.

Jews in Spain and elsewhere have always taken literally the command in Deuteronomy 6:4–9 to bind the words of the Lord to their hand and forehead. In this practice the straps of the tephilin are of animal hide and are not threads; nevertheless, the basic association is maintained between strings and words of a text since the straps are knotted to form letters, and are made to bind boxes containing scrolls of parchment upon which four passages from the Bible are written.[7] A closer association between threads and texts is made by the Jewish custom of wearing the tallith, or prayer shawl, in accordance with the commandment in Numbers 15:37–41 to make fringes in the borders of

garments in order to 'remember all the commandments of the Lord.'
The eight threads of the four corners of the tallith are made into five
double knots, which, when added to the numerical value of the word
for fringe (tsitsis), total six hundred and thirteen, or the number of
laws of the Torah. 'The thirty-nine windings that go into the making of
each of the four fringes equals the numerical value of the Hebrew
words for The Lord is one.'[8]

The ancient relationship between threads and literature is explained
succinctly by Eithne Wilkins: 'The thread on which the beads are
strung is literally a guiding thread. One can see why the Sanskrit word
sutra, from a root that gives us "suture" and "sew," means both a spun
thread and a sacred rule or book, a life-guiding statement of wisdom.'
As far as the relationship between the beads themselves and literature
is concerned, one might begin by pointing out that the Spanish word
for bead ('cuenta') is etymologically related to the word for story
('cuento'). In the *Libro de buen amor* the old women who wear large
beads around their necks also know many stories or fairy tales ('viejas /
que andan las iglesias e saben las callejas, / grandes cuentas al cuello
saben muchas consejas').[9] My colleagues who are linguists assure me
that Spanish is by no means unique in having lexical items that mean
both to count and to relate. Louise Fainberg, in particular, has drawn
to my attention several such relationships in Hungarian, German, and
English: (be)számolni, (er)zählen, and tell(er), for example.

In medieval European art beads and books are often found in the
same paintings, and saints and other pious persons are depicted holding prayer beads in one hand and a book in the other. One remarkable
French example, 'Sts Paul and Anthony Fed by a Dove' – a miniature in
the 'Belles heures' of Jean, Duc de Berry – shows St Anthony shading
his eyes with his left arm and clutching a string of beads in his right
hand, and St Paul, seated on the other side of the fountain between
them, reading a book. I know of at least three Spanish examples: in a
fourteenth-century *retablo* in the cathedral of Barcelona, Santa Clara
holds a book in her left hand and a rosary in her right; the 'Madonna of
Humility,' a fourteenth-century retablo in the Muntadas collection in
Barcelona, shows in the lower left panel a female saint holding a book
in her left hand and a rosary in her right; the Virgin Mary seems to be
holding a rosary as she dictates the gospel to St Luke, in a panel of a
fourteenth-century retablo of the Valencian Guild of Carpenters.[10] In
this last example St Luke is writing the gospel on a scroll, and there is
no way of verifying what book St Paul is reading in the French miniature; but in the two other examples cited, as in many others like them,
the book that is held in one hand is almost certainly a psalter. A brief

examination of the history of the rosary can explain why a psalter is often held in one hand and a rosary dangles from the other.[11]

The history of prayer beads can be traced back to prehistoric India, where they were used by devotees of the god Shiva, the great goddess Kali, and the goddess Arundhati. From India the use of prayer beads spread to Tibet, China, Japan, Persia, and Arabia. It is tempting to speculate that the prayer beads entered Europe from India via Arabia, that is, by a route similar to that of collections of short stories like the *Panchatantra*. But, with a phenomenon so widespread as the religious use of beads, polygenesis is at least as likely as transmission, and so it is possible that the use of prayer beads in Europe originated without Indian or Arabian influence.

The Christian hermits of the Egyptian desert in the third and fourth centuries devised a method of counting their prayers by shifting pebbles from one spot to another. In this period St Anthony is said to have devised a means of counting more convenient than moving small stones (*calculos*) from one place to another: he made knots in strings of wool. Among the prayers and chants that these early Christian monks needed to keep count of, perhaps the most popular were psalms. Irish monks were credited, as early as the fifth century, with dividing the 150 psalms into three convenient sets of fifty (*na tri coicat*). But not all monks were literate enough to memorize and recite the psalms in Latin. Consequently, it was permissible for an unlearned monk to substitute the paternoster prayer for a psalm, so that instead of reciting fifty different psalms, he would repeat the paternoster fifty times.

In the eleventh century the Ave Maria prayer became as popular as the paternoster, and it was common to repeat the Ave Maria fifty times. At about this time writers, like St Anselm of Canterbury, began composing Marian psalters, that is, hymns in praise of the Virgin Mary, which consisted of 150 stanzas. When such a hymn contained fifty instead of 150 stanzas it was called a *rosarium*, because Mary was called the 'rosa mystica.' Rosarium also meant a garland or wreath made of roses, and with increasing frequency from the twelfth to the fifteenth centuries, the word was used to refer to the beads themselves. The shifts in meaning of rosarium from flower garden to book collections of flowers, garland of flowers, and garland of beads is more easily understood if one keeps in mind that in classical and medieval literature collections and anthologies of writings were called *florilegia* (literally, gatherings of flowers); that beads have been made in India and Spain from petals of roses;[12] and that an Italian 'coronario' is a person who makes both wreaths of flowers and prayer beads.

In sum, the above examination reveals that the histories of certain

books (psalters) and certain beads (rosaries) are closely intertwined.
The Davidic psalter, consisting of 150 hymns, gave rise to a similar
number of hymns in the Marian psalter, which, by virtue of Mary's
association with rose gardens and garlands, came to be called a rosarium, which in turn lent its name to the string of beads used to count
the hymns and prayers of the psalter; and these associations are
reflected in many medieval works of Christian art that depict books
and beads in close relation to each other.

   If medieval painters related books and beads to each other, would
not their fellow craftsmen, medieval writers, have done likewise? A
strong case can be made that running a common thread through
things is a basic structuring principle of medieval artists and writers.
In art the running pattern was frequently ornamental only, as illustrated by Lucia N. Valentine in her glossary *Ornament in Medieval
Manuscripts*. But the pattern sometimes performed an intrinsic and
controlling function in the composition, as in the frontispiece of the
works of St Ambrose already referred to, in which the medallions sur-
rounding the central portion of the miniature are strung together on
the common theme of *scriptorum opus*, the work of the scribes.
Another fine example is folio 246 of the thirteenth-century *Bible
moralisée*, which consists of two parallel columns of four medallions
linked to each other and interspersed between two corresponding
columns of text. In the last medallion, in the bottom right column, an
artist is portrayed illuminating a book that itself is composed of
medallions.[13]

   After the form of the rosary was fixed and popularized by the
Dominicans in the late fifteenth century, baroque sculptors and
artists composed works that looked like rosaries: the 'Rosary Fresco'
by Weilheim unter der Teck, the 'Rosary Altarpiece' by Michael and
Martin Zirn, and the engraved 'Rosary Rose-tree in an Enclosed
Garden.' In this engraving and in many other works of art (like the
'Virgin of the Fountain' by Jan van Eyck, or 'The Little Paradise Garden'
by an anonymous master of the late-fourteenth and early-fifteenth centuries) the enclosed garden (*hortus conclusus*) is a rebus representing
the Virgin Mary herself, the Church, or the Marian psalter.[14]

   Some writers of the time, as stated above, composed books called
'rosaria' which were usually collections, or anthologies. The most
famous medieval example is the *Apparatus ad Decretum*, better known
as the *Rosarium* of Guido de Baysio, archdeacon of Bologna. This
work, consisting of a collection of canonical glosses not contained in
Gratian's *Decretum*, the standard text, itself became, immediately
after its publication early in 1300, an indispensable tool for all stu-

dents of canon law.[15] I should like to suggest that two other immortal collections, the *Canterbury Tales* and the *Decameron*, were influenced in their composition by the rosary.

Chaucer states his intention in line 24 of the Prologue to the *Canterbury Tales*, of having thirty pilgrims (Chaucer himself and 'Wel nyne and twenty in a campanye,' each tell two stories on the way to Canterbury and two on the way back ('That ech of you, to shorte with your weye, / In this viage, shal telle tales tweye, / to Caunterburyward, I mene it so, / And hom-ward he shall tellen othere two.'[16] This would have made a total of 120 stories, but as is well known, for whatever reason, Chaucer did not complete all of them. Chaucer also seems to have had in mind a prologue or connecting link to the stories of each of the thirty narrators, which would mean that at some time early in the conception of the *Canterbury Tales*, he must have planned a composition of 150 major units: 120 main stories and thirty main prologues. One hundred and fifty, as we have seen, is a number closely associated with the rosary, and it can be no accident that the most authentic portraits of Chaucer (the Hoccleve portrait, the Harvard portrait, the British Museum Add. MS 5141 portrait, and the National Gallery portrait) show him holding a rosary in his left hand. Furthermore, in all four portraits Chaucer is wearing around his neck (that is, where many medieval people wore their rosaries) a writing tool, either a penholder or a knife used for erasing manuscripts. In three of the portraits the English poet clasps the tool in his right hand, but in the fourth portrait he holds nothing in that hand, presumably because the artist wanted to make Chaucer's right index finger point to the words 'I have heere his lyknesse' in Hoccleve's text.[17]

By drawing both the writing tool and the rosary in the portraits, the artists, not unlike those medieval illuminators who placed a book in one hand and a rosary in the other, seem to be emphasizing the point that Chaucer, the teller of tales, was also a teller of beads. For those who might overlook the relationship between the rosary and Chaucer's text, Hoccleve's stanza 713 (preceding the one at which Chaucer points his finger) serves as reminder that Chaucer as writer was devoted to the Virgin Mary:

> As thou wel knowest, O blessed virgyne,
> With loving herte and hy devocioun
> In thyn honour he wroot ful many a lyne.
> O, now thy help and thy promocioun!
> To God, thy Sone, mak a mocioun
> How he thy servaunt was, mayden Marie,

And lat his love floure and fructifye.
(Hoccleve *Governail of Princes*)[18]

Canterbury, after all, was one of the principal medieval centres of worship to the Virgin Mary, and some of the earliest and most popular
Marian psalters were composed there by its archbishops: St Anselm
(d. 1109), St Edmund (d. 1240), and St Stephen Langton (d. 1228).

In critical discussions of the structure of the *Decameron* several key
words have recurred: hexameron, frame, cornice, for example, are a few
of them. Seldom, if ever, has the word *rosary* been mentioned. And yet
a clear case can be made for the composition of the *Decameron* as two
fifties or ten decades, depending on whether one views the time the
narrators spend as two weeks of actual time elapsed or as ten days of
story-telling time;[19] both concepts, two weeks/two fifties and ten days/
ten decades, are accommodated in the concept 'rosary.' Further, we can
be certain that Boccaccio is composing within the tradition of the rosarium because gardens and garlands form important links in the structure of the *Decameron*.[20] It was Filomena's idea to weave a garland that
would serve the group as a crown and move from head to head on successive story-telling days: 'E Filomena, corsa prestamente a uno alloro
(per ciò assai volte aveva udito ragionare di quanto onore le frondi di
quello eran degne e quanto degno d'onore facevano chi n'era merita-
mente incoronato), di quello alcuni rami colti, ne le fece una ghirlanda
onorevole e apparente; la quale, messale sopra la testa, fu poi mentre
durò la lor compagnia manifesto segno a ciascuno altro della real sig-
noria e maggioranza.'[21] The reference is clearly to a garland of not
Christian roses but classical laurel branches, and, as we shall see from
the quotation below, Boccaccio is very conscious of the Christian and
classical traditions he is artistically altering.

Before the start of the second day of stories, the narrators wander
leisurely through the gardens making garlands ('tutte le donne e i tre
giovani levatisi ne'giardini se ne entrarono, e le rugiadose erbe con
lento passo scalpitando d'una parte in un'altra, belle ghirlande facen-
dosi, per lungo spazio diportando s'andarono' (p. 73). On the third day
of story-telling the brigade moved to a walled garden that Boccaccio
clearly intended to be a variation of the Christian *hortus conclusus*
traditionally identified with the Church, the Virgin Mary, the rosary,
and the earthly paradise:

> Appresso la qual cosa, fattosi aprire un giardino che di costa era
> al palagio, in quello, che tutto era da torno murato, se n'entra-
> rono ... Le latora delle quali vie tutte di rosa' bianchi e vermigli

> e di gelsomini erano quasi chiuse … Nel mezzo del quale … era
> un prato di minutissima erba … Nel mezzo del qual prato era
> una fonte di marmo bianchissimo e con maravigliosi intagli …
> nel mezzo di quella … gittava … acqua verso il cielo … Il veder
> questo giardino … tutti cominciarono a affermare che, se Para-
> diso si potesse in terra fare, non sapevano conoscere che altra
> forma che quella di quel giardino gli si potesse dare. (p. 180)

The wall, the white and red roses, the fountain, the water spouting
at the heavens, the comparison with paradise are all motifs common to
the Christian tradition of the rosarium in art and literature. And lest
the reader should miss the deliberate variation he intends, Boccaccio
writes in his conclusion that the stories were not told in a church,
that is, not in an allegorical garden but in a real one; not in a classical
school of philosophers, but in a humanistic garden of mature individuals ('appresso assai ben si può cognoscere queste cose non nella chiesa
… né ancora nello scuole de' filosofanti … né tra cherici né tra filosofi
in alcun luogo ma ne' giardini,' p. 718).

This insistence on avoiding the church setting reminds the reader
that the seven ladies first met in a church where they were saying
their paternosters. ('Le quali … in una delle parti della chiesa adu-
natesi, quasi in cerchio a seder postesi, dopo più sospiri lasciato stare
dir de' paternostri … cominciarono a ragionare,' p. 17). It was at Pampinea's suggestion that they decided to stop telling their beads and start
telling their stories. We can be certain that Boccaccio intended to
compare beads or paternosters with stories because he wrote elsewhere about women who sit nervously in churches fondling their
beads when in fact their real beads are nothing but French chivalric
stories and Italian love poems:

> Giunta adunque nella chiesa … incomincia, senza restare mai, a
> faticare una dolente filza di paternostri, or dell'una mano nell'al-
> tra, e dell'altra nell'una trasmutandoli, senza mai dirire niuno
> … Ma io così fidatamente ne fallevava, per ciò che saper mi
> parea, e so, che le sue orazioni e i suoi paternostri sono i
> romanzi franceschi e le canzoni latine, ne' quali ella legge di
> Lancellotto e di Ginevra e di Tristano e d'Isotta.[22]

The women Boccaccio is describing are, therefore, very like Chaucer's
Prioress in the Prologue to the *Canterbury Tales*:

> Of smal coral aboute hir arm she bar

A peire of bedes, guaded al with grene;
And there-on heng a broche of gold ful shene,
On which ther was first write a crowned A,
And after, *Amor vincit omnia* (ll. 158–62)

Much later, towards the middle of the sixteenth century, one of Boccaccio's best-known imitators, Marguerite de Navarre, makes Parla-
mente, a character in her *Heptaméron*, reveal a plan for offering one
hundred stories instead of one hundred paternosters:

Entre autres, je croy qu'il n'y a nulle de vous qui n'ait leu les
cent Nouvelles de Bocace nouvellement traduictes d'ytalien en
françois ... Et, à l'heure, j'oy les deux dames dessus nommées,
avecq plusieurs autres de la court, qui so delibberent d'en fair
autant. Sinon en une chose different de Bocace: c'est de n'escri-
pre nulle nouvelle qui ne soit veritable histoire ... Et s'il vous
plaist que tous les jours depuis midy jusques à quatre heures
nous allions dedans ce beau prè le long de la rivière du Gave ...
là assiz a noz aises, dira chascun quelque histoire qu'il aura
veue ou bien oy dire à quelque homme digne de foy. Au bout de
dix jours aurons parachevé la centaine; et, si Dieu faict que
notre labeur soit trouvé digne des oeilz des seigneurs et dames
dessus nommez, nous leurs en ferons present au retour de ce
voiage, en lieu d'ymaiges ou de patenostres.[23]

The passage indicates that many sixteenth-century readers of the
Decameron were well aware that Boccaccio compared his stories to
paternoster beads. In fact, a contemporary version of the *Heptaméron*
adds immediately after the word 'patenostres': 'vous asseurant qu'ilz
auront ce present icy plus agreable.'[24] This remark means that the
sixteenth-century author of these words, maybe Marguerite de Navarre
herself, upon reading the prologue to the *Decameron*, understood that
Pampinea was encouraging her fellow members of Boccaccio's 'lieta brigata' that it was more profitable under the circumstances to tell stories
than beads. It is more difficult to determine whether or not Marguerite
de Navarre was also thinking of two fifties and ten decades, since she,
like Chaucer, did not complete her project. But according to one of the
critics of the *Heptaméron*, the first fifty stories of the collection form
an identifiable structural unit.[25]

Cantar de Mio Cid

In Spain the idea of stringing together parts of a literary work is clearly expressed by Prudentius in his *Peristephanon Liber*, one of the most widely read books in the Middle Ages ('Ast ego serta choro in medio / texta feram pede dactylico').[26] Prudentius's title means literally book of garlands or crowns (from the Greek, *stephanos*, a crown or garland), and since the work is a collection of hymns dedicated to the early Christian martyrs, the implication is that the reward for martyrdom is a heavenly crown. Every hymn is, therefore, a garland, which is why the entire collection was entitled 'book of garlands'; and as the quotation makes clear, every garland or hymn is woven or strung together by the dactylic measure of the lines.

The idea of singing hymns in praise of martyrs and religious heroes is somehow related to epic poetry. Experts in the field do not agree precisely how, – whether hymns to religious heroes gave rise to epic songs about secular heroes or vice versa, or whether they result from a mutual influence of religious and secular elements, both rooted in mankind's fondness for singing praises to great leaders. The precise historical sequence fortunately is not germane to this study; nor is it necessary to establish a direct relationship between hymns and epic poetry. What concerns us here is the fact that epic poetry, like Prudentius's *Peristephanon Liber*, consists of a series of units 'laisses,' or 'tiradas' leashed or tied together.[27] This does not necessarily mean that hymns are related to epic poems; it means simply that hymns and epic poems share a technique of composition. It cannot be accidental that the word *laisse* is etymologically linked, through the Latin *laxare*, to the word *leash*. Moreover, it is clear that a significant number of Spanish epic poems, lost or extant, are related in some way to monasteries, churches, or martyrology.[28] And at least one important episode of a Spanish epic poem, the 'Afrenta de corpes' in the *Cantar de Mio Cid*, belongs to the same martyrological tradition as Prudentius's collection.[29]

I do not mean to suggest a direct link between the *Cid* and the *Peristephanon*, nor am I suggesting a simple solution for the origins and development of Spanish epic poetry. These are not my concerns in this chapter or in this book. Rather, I am pointing to one technique of composing different kinds of books, not necessarily related to each other, that might also have been used in the *Cid*. Since one section of the *Cid* is composed in the same martyrological tradition as the *Peristephanon* of Prudentius, and since both works seem to use the technique of stringing in their composition, I conjecture that works like the *Peristephanon* (and who knows what other kinds of works?) might have formed part of a tradition of composition that preceded the *Cid*. I ask the reader to accept, on the basis of this tiny bit of evidence, only a very tiny point: that stringing is a technique of composition used before and, therefore, maybe also in the *Cid*. Anything else is peripheral to my main concern. If I had had more texts before the *Cid*, I could have been more conclusive and less suggestive. As it is, I must settle for Prudentius and guess that other popular and learned heroic songs of joy and praise, weddings, work, and warfare, like the Psalms, were sung in Spain just as they were in all societies of the world.

It cannot be claimed that the *Cid* shows any direct influence of the psalter tradition: there are no explicit references in the poem to psalms, rosaries, or Marian psalters. There are, however, indications that the all-pervasive nature of the psalter tradition did leave remote traces of indirect influence on the epic material concerning the Cid, Ruy Díaz de Vivar. The opening lines of the *Cid* (as it has come down to us) establish what subsequently becomes a major theme of the poem – deliverance from personal enemies – when the Cid prays to God about the injustice that has been done to him: '¡Grado a Ti, Señor, Padre que estás en alto! / Esto me an buelto mios enemigos malos.'[30] These enemies of the Cid are referred to again, explicitly and implicitly, in the middle and towards the end of the poem (ll. 1836, 1859, 2042, 3112, 3113); there can be little doubt that a major theme of the poem is the victory of the Cid over his personal enemies.

The theme would have reminded any medieval Christian, including the author of the poem, of the Psalms, since so many of them deal precisely with deliverance from personal enemies.[31] Psalm 119 of the Vulgate version especially reminds one of the *Cid*, since it is the prayer of a man, exiled from his native land, for deliverance from his enemies. Like any medieval Christian familiar with the Psalms, the author of the *Cid* would have thought that verses 2 and 5 of Psalm 119 were applicable also to the Cid: 'Domine, libera animam meam a labiis iniquis et a lingua dolosa ... Heu mihi, quia incolatus meus prolongatus est! Habitavi cum habitantibus Cedar.' And when these enemies are said to be the cause of the Cid's profuse weeping ('De los sos ojos tan fuertemientre llorando,' l. 1), any medieval Christian would have been reminded not so much that weeping was a well-known epic formula but especially that it belonged to the Psalms: 'Lavabo per singulas noctes lectum meum; lacrymis meis stratum meum rigabo. Turbatus est a furore oculus meus; inveteravi inter omnes inimicos meos' (Psalm 6: 7–8).

When the king finally invites the Cid to sit next to him at court and promises him justice in the presence of his enemies ('Venid acá ser, Campeador, / en aqueste escaño quem' diestes vós en don' / maguer que algunos pesa, meior sodes que nós ... que rreçiba derecho de infantes de Carrión / Grande tuerto le han tenido, sabemóslo todos nós,' ll. 3114–16, 3133–4), one cannot but think of Psalm 109 ('Dixit Dominus Domino meo: sede a dextris meis, donec ponam inimicos tuos scabellum pedum tuorum … Dominare in medio inimicorum tuorum. Dominus a dextris tuis; confregit in die irae suae reges. Iudicabit in nationibus,' vv. 1–2, 5–6). We will have reason to refer again to this passage from the Psalms, in connection with the last page of the *Cid*.

Another major theme of the Psalms is victory over, or deliverance from, national enemies (Vulgate 17, 19–20, 43, 59, 73, 75, 78–9, 82, 84, 88–9, 107, 109, 123–4, 128, 136, 143). This theme is, of course, also a major one in the *Cid*, in which so many scenes involve battles with the Moors. Several battle scenes in the *Cid* have a psalmodic ring to them. One good example is the relentless pursuit of the Moorish king, Búcar, by the Cid, which ends when the latter, with one sword-stroke, splits the body of the Moor down to the waist.

> Siete migeros conplidos duró el segudar
> Mio Çid al rrey Búcar cayol en alcaz
> …
> Buen cavallo tiene Búcar e grandes saltos faz,
> mas Bavieca el de Mio Çid, alcançándolo va
> Alcançólo el Çid a Búcar a tres braças del mar
> arriba alçó Colada, un grant colpe dádol' ha
> las carbonclas del yelmo tollidas ge la ha
> cortól' el yelmo e, librado todo lo ál
> fata la cintura el espada llegado ha. (ll. 2407–8, 2418–24)

This passage must have sounded to medieval Christian listeners as a fulfilment of Psalm 17: 38–9, which reads, 'Persequar inimicos meos, et comprehendam illos; Et non convertar donec deficiant. Confringam illos nec potuerunt stare; Cadent subtus pedes meos.'

The Cid's prowess in battle is often portrayed in the poem with the imagery of doors and gates, as Deyermond and Hook have correctly shown.[32] Perhaps the best example of this image is when the Cid and his company, attired in full glory, make their splendid entry into Toledo where King Alfonso rises to meet them and declares that the Cid is superior to him: 'A la puerta de fuera descavalga a sabor, / cuerdamientre entra Mio Çid con todos los sos' (ll. 3070–116, here quoted at 3104–5). This glorious entry of the Cid in regal splendour through the gate is reminiscent of the famous verses 7 and 8 of Psalm 23: 'Attolite portas, principes, vestras, et elevamini, portae aeternales, et introibit rex gloriae. Quis est iste rex gloriae? Dominus fortis et potens, Dominus potens in praelio.'[33]

The purpose of this grand entry of the Cid ('potens in praelio,') into Toledo, was to seek redress against his enemies, the Infantes de Carrión, who had almost 'martyred' his daughters ('Mártires seremos nós,' l. 2728) and left them for dead to be eaten by wild birds and beasts:

> rronpíen las camisas e las carnes a ellas amas a dos
> limpia salié la sangre sobre los çiclatones
> ...
> e a las aves del monte e a las bestias de la fiera guisa
> Por muertas las dexaron, sabed, que non por bivas. (ll. 2738-9, 2751-2)

This common martyrological motif is strikingly similar to, and can be said to be ultimately rooted in, Psalm 78: 2-3: 'Posuerunt morticina servorum tuorum escas volatilibus caeli, carnes sanctorum tuorum bestiis terrae ... Effuderunt sanguinem eorum tanquam aquam in circuiter Ierusalem, et non erat qui sepeliret.'

Another important theme of the *Cid* is the wedding. After their disastrous marriage to the Infantes de Carrión, the daughters of the Cid are sought after as queens by the future kings of Navarre and Aragon, and the poem culminates with news of these happy weddings:

> Piden sus fijas a Mio Çid el Campeador
> por ser rreinas de Navarre e de Aragón
> ...
> ¡Ved quál ondra crece al que en buen ora nació
> quando señoras son sus fijas de Navarra e de Aragón!
> Oy los rreyes d'España sos parientes son, a todos
> alcança ondra por el que en buena ora nació. (ll. 3398-9, 3722-5)

The news of these royal weddings must have brought to the minds of medieval Christian listeners, as must have occurred to the author of the scene himself, the psalm for royal weddings, Psalm 44, especially verses 17 and 18: 'Pro patribus tuis nati sunt tibi filii; constitues eos principes super omnem terram. Memores erunt nominis tuis in omni generatione et generationem. Propterea populi confitebuntur tibi in aeternum, et in saeculum saeculi.' This royal-wedding psalm also contains a command from the Psalmist for the king to gird on his sword ('Accingere gladio tuo super femur tuum, potentissime,' v. 4) that is reminiscent of one of the popular epithets for the Cid ('el que en buen ora çinxo espada' ll. 58, 78, et passim).

In addition to these common themes (personal enemies, national enemies, martyrdom, royal weddings), the language and style of the Psalms is also reflected in the instances of parallelism and contrast throughout the *Cid*. H. Salvador Martínez, commenting mainly on the Latin *Poema de Almería*, which mentions the Cid, has noted that Doña Ximena's prayer reflects the parallelism of the Bible, especially the Psalms; and he asks rhetorically if it is necessary to propose that a Castilian 'juglar' so steeped in the Psalms would look elsewhere for inspiration for his epic songs.[34] Salvador Martínez's solution may very well be extreme, but he is, nevertheless, one of the few critics to point to the Psalms as one of the possible sources of Spanish epic. In addition to the lines he quotes from the *Cid*, other lines too numerous to list here are parallel in structure, like 'Mucho pesa a los de Teca e a los de Terrer non plaze' (l. 625). This parallelistic construction is also characteristic of the Psalms, for example: 'Extraneus factus sum fratribus meis et peregrinus filiis matris meae ... Quoniam exaudivit pauperes Dominus, et victos suos non despexit.' (Psalm 68:9, 33)

A.D. Deyermond has correctly pointed to the frequent occurrence in the *Cid* of lines whose hemistichs form a contrast to each other,[35] but he makes no mention of similar constructions in the Psalms. Contrast in the lines quoted by Deyermond is found also in verses like Psalm 29:6 ('Ad vesperum demorabitur fletus, et ad matutinum laetitia'), which in turn sounds very much like Minaya Alvar Ffánez's words of encouragement to the Cid ('Aún todos estos duelos en gozo se tornarán,' l. 381).

Turning now to another element of the psalter tradition – the Virgin Mary – one finds that her role in the *Cid* is far more significant than has been noted by the critics of the poem.[36] Reference is made to the Virgin at least nineteen times in the poem: either to churches named in her honour (ll. 52, 215, 822, 1462, 1475, 2237, 2645), or in formulaic prayers like 'Plega a Dios e a Sancta María' (ll. 282, 1267, 1637, 1654, 2274, 2782), or especially to her alone (ll. 221, 273, 281, 333, 1668, 2524). Although they might seem stereotyped and insignificant to the twentieth-century reader, these references serve as evidence of the popular cult of the Virgin Mary which was expanding rapidly at the time that the poem was composed between the late-twelfth and early-thirteenth centuries.

Upon leaving Castile to go into exile, the Cid makes a solemn vow to the Virgin Mary (ll. 215–25) that if things go well for him, he will make rich gifts to her altar and arrange for a thousand masses to be said in her honour. This is a vow the poet does not permit the Cid to forget (l. 822). As the Cid is about to leave his wife and daughters, Doña Ximena asks his advice 'Por amor de Sancta María' (l. 273), and the Cid prays in reply that the Virgin Mary should permit him some day to marry his daughters with his own hands (l. 282). This prayer is one of the most important elements of the plot of the poem: the Cid reminds the treacherous Infantes (l. 2524) that it is on account of the Virgin Mary that they have enriched themselves after marriage to his daughters; when the Infantes abuse their wives they are in fact showing disrespect for the Virgin. It should be regarded as just one of the Virgin's many favours to her devotees when the Infantes are punished and messengers appear as if miraculously to request new marriages for the Cid's daughters to the kings of Navarre and Aragon. The Cid's nephew, Félez Muñoz, had prayed to the Virgin Mary for the punishment of the Infantes (l. 2782); as already noted, the Cid himself had prayed to Mary that he might give his daughters into marriage with his own hands.

It would be wise to reiterate at this point that evidence of influence of the psalter tradition in the *Cid* is remote and indirect. And yet this indirect evidence is extensive enough to suggest that the division of the *Cid* (into about 150 laisses, or tiradas, and three identifiable 'cantares')may be deliberately related to the psalter. Admittedly, no cantar has fifty laisses (the first has sixty-three, the second forty-eight, and the third forty-one). It should also be admitted that a complete text of the *Cid* is lacking, and that the existing version may be a variation of the original. Nevertheless, two other apparently insignificant details ought to be considered: on the bottom half of folio 74V[0], at the end of the unique manuscript copy of the *Cid*, are inscribed in a fourteenth-century hand, the first two verses of Psalm 109 and the first two words of the third verse, a copy of the Paternoster prayer, and a copy of the Ave Maria prayer;[37] and in the *Estoria de España*, at the end of the account of the life and death of the Cid, the following passage occurs: 'Et quando esto oo dicho Ruy díaz el noble varón dio a dios la su alma et sin manziella. Esto fue en la era de mill et C. xxxij annos en xv días andados del mes de mayo. Et agora dezit sendos paternostres con su ave maría que dios depare qui lo diga por vos.'[38]

Now there may be absolutely no relationship between these two details and the composition and/or content of the *Cid*. It may simply be that the manuscript of the *Cid* is an example of scribes testing their pens on the last blank page of a manuscript, as Ian Michael suggests.[39] An equally reasonable explanation is that the references to psalms and prayers at the end of accounts of the Cid's life in the *Cid* and the *Estoria de España* are like those made after someone dies, especially someone who has been a powerful benefactor to monasteries and cathedrals. For example, when a benefactor of Canterbury died in the eleventh century, each cleric was ordered to sing two 'fifties' for his soul, and each priest to sing two masses.[40] This explanation means that the possibility should not be entirely ruled out that a copy of the *Cid* earlier than the extant unique copy, and earlier also than the *Estoria de España*, contained references to the Psalms, paternosters, and Ave Marias in either the text of the poem itself or marginal and end notes to the text.

The practice of reciting psalms upon the death of a powerful benefactor could conceivably account for the indirect reminiscences of the Psalms in the *Cid*, as well as the quotation from the Psalms at the end of the poem. But it cannot be determined beyond all reasonable doubts whether these direct and indirect references to the Psalms were originally intended or made by the author of the poem, or whether they were merely a consequence of the impressions created by the author's work upon the minds of a reader or scribe. Nevertheless, it is possible that at least one fourteenth-century reader of the *Cid* was urged to copy the first verses of Psalm 109, verses that, as has been suggested above, are reflected in lines 3114 to 3116 of the poem in which King Alfonso invites the Cid to sit beside him.[41] It is also possible that thirteenth- and fourteenth-century readers of accounts of the life of the Cid were urged to recite the rosary in its early form of alternate paternosters and Ave Marias. For these reasons, and for reasons prompted by the indirect reminiscences of the Psalms, the composition of the *Cid* may be considered within the literary tradition of the psalter and the rosary. With respect to composition, the *Cid* and the Psalms are both works made up of units that are strung together.

Milagros de Nuestra Señora

If the evidence for the composition of the *Cid* within the psalter tradition is mainly indirect, clear and incontrovertible evidence does exist for supporting the *Milagros de Nuestra Señora* by Gonzalo de Berceo. In *Milagros* Berceo refers to the Psalms directly in at least six stanzas: 165, 262, 372, 602, 709, and 847.[42] In three of these stanzas Berceo follows his Latin source, but in the remaining three he refers to the Psalms, although his source might have had no such references.

These three instances of apparent originality are worth recounting because they serve to remind us twentieth-century readers of the constant presence of the Psalms in the daily life of Berceo and his contemporaries. The first example of these three psalter references occurs in the story of the shipwrecked man miraculously saved by the Virgin (miracle no. 22) in which the man's companions, seeing doves fly from

the water up to the sky and assuming that the doves are the souls of
their drowned shipmates, shout, 'Ya sodes "per ignem et per aquam"
passados,' (stanza 602, line b), a reference to Psalms 62:12, 'Transivi-
mus per ignem et per aquam.' The second example is found in the
famous Faustian story of Theophilus (miracle no. 24). Berceo, wanting
to emphasize how well Theophilus did his job as assistant to the
bishop, writes that, with Theophilus's help, the bishop had nothing to
do but say mass and recite the psalter ('Non avie el obispo embargo nin
lazerio / fuera cantar su misa e rezar el salterio,' st. 709ab). The third
psalter reference is in the anti-Jewish story of the little Jewish boy
who was thrown into the fire by his father (miracle no. 16) and is
miraculously saved. Berceo makes the Christians rejoice when the
father is in turn thrown into the oven and burnt to death; they do not
sing for the dead man's soul but shower curses upon him:

> non dizién por su alma salmos nin oraciones
> mas dizién denosteos e grandes maldiziones.
> Diziénli mal oficio, facienli mal ofrenda
> dizién por 'Pater noster,' 'Qual fizo, atal prenda.' (sts. 372cd–3ab)

This last example, like the first, is yet another illustration of the
almost automatic tendency of medieval Christians to think of the
Psalms when contemplating someone's death, a fact that might well
have influenced the composition of the *Cid*, as suggested above. It is
significant too to note in the third example that Berceo, only a few
lines before referring to the Psalms, compares the miracle of the little
Jewish boy, as well as other miracles, with 'cantares de gesta': 'Can-
taron grandes laudes, fizieron rica festa / metieron est miraclo entre la
otra gesta (st. 370cd).[43] The proximity of the references to the Psalms
and the Paternoster to Berceo's statement about the recording of epic
deeds is a clear indication that elements of the rosary tradition were
uppermost in the minds of epic poets, or, at least in the minds of a
reader (and imitator) of epic poetry.

In Berceo's *Milagros*, and in his Latin source, we find another element of the rosary tradition: the number *five*. Historians of the rosary
explain its frequent division into fives and tens as two successive
stages: the natural basic tendency to divide into fives and tens because
the beads were counted on the fingers; and the importance of five in
Marian lore (the five letters of the name Maria, the five joyful mysteries, the five wounds of Christ that redeemed mankind's sensual sins,
the five petals of the rose) also helped the division into fives.[44] In Berceo's fourth 'milagro,' 'El Galardon de la Virgen,' there is a passage, five
stanzas long (sts. 118–22), about a cleric who learned five lines of an

antiphon to the Virgin, which sang about her five joyful mysteries, which in turn are related to the five wounds Christ suffered (st. 120a); and Christ's five wounds in turn redeem mankind's sins committed on account of the five senses of the human body.

Some critics of Berceo's *Milagros* have pointed to the number five as a structural basis of the work, including the fact that there are twenty-five 'milagros' in Berceo's collection.[45] This is a feasible argument but not if it is taken to mean that Berceo's collection consists of five times five milagros. Berceo did not group the miracles in fives: those numbered five, ten, fifteen, twenty, and twenty-five are not distinguishable as markers from the rest. And yet, as far as is known, Berceo's Latin source contained twenty-four of 'his' miracles (in more or less the same order Berceo adapted them), to which he added a twenty-fifth; he chose not to use three miracles included in his source. He did not limit himself to twenty-five for any lack of other miracles, because he tells us twice (sts. 235, 412) that it would take years to recount a mere one tenth of all the miracles of the Virgin. Therefore, he probably chose the quantity twenty-five for a specific reason.

Berceo himself provides what could be a clue to his reason in the introduction to the *Milagros*, in which he identifies the Virgin Mary with a meadow ('prado'):

> En esta romería avemos un buen prado
> en qui trova repaire tot romeo cansado:
> La Virgin gloriosa madre del buen Criado,
> del qual otro ninguno egual non fue trobado. (st. 19)

Berceo goes on to explain, inter alia, that each miracle of the Virgin is like a tree in that meadow. His collection is therefore a meadow or garden with twenty-five trees. This meshes with two aspects of the history of the rosary: first, with the identification of the Virgin Mary as the garden itself, the *hortus conclusus*, as explained earlier; and second, as early as the eleventh century, with the practice of composing a hymn, called a *rosarium*, consisting of fifty stanzas. Berceo's collection of twenty-five miracles is half a rosarium. It is only half a rosarium probably because Berceo was concerned about its length: ('Non querré, si podiero, la razón alongar / ca vos avriédes tedio, yo podría peccar,' st. 704ab).[46]

Cantigas de Santa María

The relationship of Alfonso's *Cantigas de Santa María* to the rosary tradition is even clearer than that of Berceo's *Milagros*. Whereas Ber-

ceo composed half a rosarium, Alfonso arranged to have every tenth
cantiga be distinguishable as a song of praise ('loor'), from the preceding and succeeding nine. This arrangement fits neatly in the rosary
tradition. In some surviving medieval rosaries the tenth bead is larger
than the preceding and succeeding nine: on a monumental slab (dated
1273) of Frère Gerars, Knight Templar, the knight is portrayed with
such a rosary. Thurston explains that 'while it is obvious that the *pat-
enôtre* was meant to count tens ... it was in this case thought sufficient to mark the end of the decades, not by inserting extra and
superfluous beads, but by making every tenth bead larger than the
rest.' Again, out of the Irish practice of praying with the arms out-
stretched like a cross ('crossfigil') grew the practice of inserting in
some Marian psalters instructions to the reader to genuflect for nine
stanzas and stretch the arms out while reciting the tenth. So, although
Alfonso's arrangement differs from the modern rosary, it does resemble
rosary patterns of the thirteenth century and before.[47]

Apart from the division at the tenth song or bead, all the elements of
the psalter tradition already mentioned are found also in Alfonso's
Cantigas: direct reference to the Psalms (especially upon death), garlands, identification of Mary with roses and gardens, the Marian psalter, and the important number five. I shall elaborate on each of these
elements separately.

The Psalms are referred to directly in connection with death on at
least four occasions in the *Cantigas*. When the lustful cleric realizes
that he is about to drown in the River Seine he starts to recite matin
prayers and psalms ('Avia começado / madodyos e rezado / un salm');[48]
as a consequence, when he does drown, his soul is saved from the
Devil by the Virgin. When a friar dies after twice changing colour mysteriously, an order is given that those of his fellow friars who know the
entire psalter should recite it at once ('Disseron: "Rez" ora quen rezar
souber / o salterio todo, porque sen falir / nos saber Deus faça u este
fez ir' (c. 123, ll. 33,35); in consequence, the dead friar appears before
his live colleagues and assures them that his soul is not where they
feared but in a good place. A woman, who was once sterile and whose
son was dead for four days (because she broke her vow to the Virgin),
places her son's corpse on an altar and recites many psalms and litan-
ies over it (c. 347, l. 43); miraculously, the dead body comes to life. In
Alfonso's version of the Assumption, eleven of the Apostles begin
chanting Psalms when the Virgin tells them that she is about to leave
the world (c. 419, l. 77). These examples from the *Cantigas* of the close
association in the medieval mind of the Psalms with death lend support to the hypothesis that an epic poet, like the author of the *Cid*,

may well have had the Psalms in mind as he contemplated the death of his epic hero; they also help to place Alfonso's *Cantigas* firmly within the psalter tradition.

One of Alfonso's 'cantigas' serves as an explanation of how the garland of flowers fits into the psalter tradition. 'Cantiga 121' tells of the gentleman who promised to make for the Virgin every day a garland of roses. He was searching for roses in a valley one day when his enemies encountered him, and he fell on his knees and started to say Ave Marias. The Virgin appeared to aid and protect the gentleman from his enemies, who stood amazed and watched her weave the Ave Marias from his lips into a garland of roses. This miracle provides additional justification for placing Boccaccio's *Decameron* within the psalter tradition, not only because the members of the 'lieta brigata' weave garlands of laurel, but especially because they were persuaded to substitute stories for their paternoster prayers. Alfonso's 'Cantiga 121' has been quoted by leading historians of the rosary because in one German version every tenth rose the gentleman used was brighter and redder than the preceding and succeeding nine.[49]

It is no accident that the gentleman used only roses ('que lle guerlanda faria de rosas toda, non d'al,' c. 121, l. 8), because Mary was identified with both the rose (*rosa mistica*) and the garden (*hortus conclusus*); Alfonso's famous 'cantiga de loor' describes Mary as 'Rosa das rosas e Fror das frores' (c. 10, l. 1). Like Berceo, Alfonso uses the word *prado* instead of *orto* or *huerto* for garden, perhaps because it is an easier rhyme. In the *Cantigas* the Virgin appears to devotees several times in a 'prado' (c. 42, l. 15; c. 105, l. 39; c. 276, l. 1), and at least once she is clearly identified with a garden: 'e desto fez un miragre a que e chamada orto / dos viços do parayso' (c. 357, ll. 6–7).

The paternoster and Ave Maria prayers were easy enough to memorize and recite, but the more elaborate Marian psalters had to be read, because the variations interspersed between the set prayers were difficult to remember. For this reason we can be certain that Alfonso was acquainted with Marian psalters, because one of his cantigas tells of a nun who read her prayers to the Virgin out of a book: 'E fillava lazeiro / en loar muit' a Virgen, / ca un gran livr' enteiro / rezava cada dia, como nos aprendemos, / de grandes orações sempre, noites e dias. / E sen esto rezava ben mil Ave Marias' (c. 71, ll. 11–15).

Alfonso was aware of the importance of the number five to the Virgin: he composed one of his cantigas (c. 70) about the five letters of the name María, and his 'Cantiga 56' is about the miracle of the monk in whose mouth there appeared, when he died, a garland made of five roses because he used to recite in honour of the Virgin five psalms spe-

cially chosen so that the first letters of each psalm spell an anagram of
the name Maria:

> Quen catar e revolver
> estes salmos, achará
> 'Magnificat' y jazer,
> e 'Ad Dominum' y á,
> e cabo del 'In conver-
> tendo' e 'Ad te' está,
> e pois 'Retribue ser-
> vo tuo' muit' omildoso. (c. 56, ll. 35–42)

In this single cantiga are united several of the elements of the psalter
tradition: direct reference to the Psalms (which upon death are
replaced by roses), the garland, and the number five.[50] There is no
doubt that Alfonso's contemporaries were aware that he composed his
Cantigas in the psalter tradition because one of his biographers, writing in the thirteenth century, said that his songs to the Virgin were
written in the Davidic style: 'More quoque Davitico etiam, [ad] preco-
nium Virginis gloriose multas et perpulchras composuit cantinelas.'[51]
It is also certain that Alfonso was acquainted with rosaries, not only
because guilds of paternosterers had been formed by the end of the
thirteenth century in all major European cities,[52] but especially
because in the fourth panel of the miniatures for 'Cantiga 172' a rosary
is included among the objects miraculously saved after a violent storm
at sea.[53]

It will be necessary to refer again to the captioned miniatures that
accompany the *Cantigas* of Alfonso, but first I should like to examine
a linking device used throughout the *Cantigas*, not because it is peculiar to the psalter tradition but because the device is one of the simple
polygenetic means of composing by stringing things together. The cantigas are composed in a 'zejelesque' structure in which the rhyme of
the refrain is dropped and then taken up again before the refrain is
repeated: *aa bba aa*, for example. The *zéjel* was invented in Spain,
birthplace also of its learned antecedent called *muwashshah*, a poem
usually of five stanzas written in Arabic or Hebrew with an ending
(usually in two or four lines) called a *kharja*, written usually in vulgar
Arabic but sometimes containing words in Spanish mozarabic dialect.
The *muwashshah* is significant for the literary technique of stringing
things together because it is by definition 'a poem in which rhymes
alternate in the manner of a "wishah," i.e., collar formed by two lines of
pearls of different colours.' The word *kharja* means an exit, so that the

kharja at the end of a *muwashshah* is like a clasp at the end of a neck-
lace; and necklaces are referred to in at least three *kharjas*.[54]

Jewish poets of medieval Spain are known to have imitated these
Hispano-Arabic models. Todros Abulafia, for example, a Jewish poet in
the Christian court of Alfonso X at the time that the cantigas were
composed, explained in the preface to his collection of *muwashshahs*:

> When days and nights were keeping faith, and there was no
> uproar, and time was generous and full of sweet reason, I
> planted some gardens for myself, and *recited songs inlaid with*
> *necklaces* and more precious than the stars of the skies: above
> each of them I indicate the models, and there will be found none
> but Arabs when the patterns are mentioned, since all of them
> are built on Arabian foundations.[55]

There was, obviously, in thirteenth-century Spain much multicultural
encouragement for writers to compose works, as it were, on a string.
The psalter tradition, the cult of the Virgin, the *zéjel*, and the *muwash-*
shah were all at their peak, and the itinerant rabbi Moses of Coucy
was preaching to Jewish communities a revival of devotion to the
tephilin and tallith. It is, therefore, not surprising that *leixapren* (literally, 'put down and take up') is one of the most popular poetic devices
of the period. In Alfonso's *Cantigas* rhymes are dropped and picked up;
in the profane cantigas lines are dropped and picked up; in the *Cid*,
laisses (note the similarity in meaning between *laisse* and *leixa*) are
dropped and picked up, in Berceo's work words, hemistichs, lines, and
stanzas are dropped and picked up.[56]

The refrain repeated between the stanzas of Alfonso's *Cantigas* is
not found in the *muwashshah*. Instead of repeating lines and rhyme
verbatim like the cantiga's refrain, the *muwashshah* repeats only the
rhyme between stanzas, and there are different names for what corresponds to the refrain. The first and last 'refrains' of the *muwashshah* are
called *matla* (prelude) and *kharja*, respectively, and the 'refrains'
between the *matla* and *kharja* are called *simt* (string). Clearly, therefore, the *simt* strings the poem together, and the *matla* and *kharja*
open and lock it. In this sense, Alfonso's refrains can be said to open,
string, and lock his cantigas in place. Alfonso's refrain and the *kharja*
are also similar in that both serve as captions, or expressive outlets,
for the emotional lyricism built up in the rest of the poem. A less significant similarity is that both *kharja* and refrain are usually two or
four lines long.[57]

Alfonso's technique of stringing his cantigas together and then illustrating them with captioned miniatures seems to have influenced only slightly the composition of the *Conde Lucanor*, the best-known work of his nephew Juan Manuel. Juan Manuel divided his *Conde Lucanor* into five main parts: part one consists of fifty-one *exempla*; parts two, three, and four contain one hundred, fifty-one, and twenty eight *sententiae*, respectively; and part five explains how souls can be saved by devotion to the sacraments of the Roman Catholic faith. In the whole work very little can be said to fall within the psalter tradition, except perhaps some slight adherence to the numbers five and fifty. There is in the *Conde Lucanor* very little reference to the Virgin Mary, the Psalms, or to paternosters, Ave Marias, garlands, and rosaries. People die in the *Conde Lucanor* but no psalms are sung.

This lack of reference is remarkable in a writer who had access to the work of Alfonso X, who had contacts with Jews and Arabs, and who (alas, for proponents of the Dominican invention of the rosary) founded a Dominican monastery at Peñafiel. The composition of the *Conde Lucanor* bears only a slight resemblance to that of the *Cantigas*. In the first part of his work Juan Manuel begins each exemplum with a formula that includes the words 'fablava el conde Lucanor con Patronio ... et el conde le rogo quel dixiesse commo fuera aquello,' which serves as a kind of prose refrain, or *simt*, that threads through the *exempla*. Juan Manuel also ends each exemplum with a sort of moralistic caption that, like the cantiga refrain and the *kharja*, usually consists of two or four rhyming lines. After these rhyming lines come the words 'Et la ystoria deste exemplo es ésta que se sigue,' which give the impression that, like the cantigas, each exemplum was designed to be followed by an illustration ('ystoria'). But neither the moralistic caption nor the illustration is peculiar to the psalter tradition. In Spain miniatures with moralistic captions go back at least as far as Prudentius, and they were, of course, found in illustrated Bibles.[58]

So, in the work of Juan Manuel in the second half of the fourteenth century, the psalter tradition, which flourished in the thirteenth, is either dead or dormant. This is not to say that all reference to the elements of the psalter tradition disappears in the fourteenth century. At the end of the thirteenth and the very beginning of the fourteenth century, Arnald of Vilanova (1240–1311) called his chemical treatise *Rosarium Philosophorum* because for it he culled quotations from other philosophers: 'Porro hunc librum nominavi Rosarium: cum in compendium ex philosophorum libris ipsum contraxerim, quoad melius per me hoc fieri potuit.'[59] Towards the middle of the fourteenth century, Juan Ruiz, archpriest of Hita, selected a verse from Psalm 31 ('Intellectum tibi dabo,' v. 8) for the prose prologue/sermon to the *Libro de buen amor,* and in stanza 438 (see p.18) made passing reference to old women who wear beads and tell stories. Around the end of the fourteenth century, Bernabé de Módena painted a long string of beads in front of Juan Manuel in the 'Retablo de Santa Lucía.'[60] Much later Diego de San Pedro and Fernando de Rojas experimented with different kinds of linking, and Cervantes played with chains and rosaries.[61] But these are all faint echoes, mere glimpses of a strong tradition of literary composition, the psalter tradition, which in terms of major works, blossomed and decayed in thirteenth-century Spain.

In the conclusion to this book I will begin to find answers for the recession of the psalter tradition when I consider it in the light of the traditions discussed in the other chapters. In the mean time, I shall summarize some of the points of this chapter that will recur in different form in subsequent chapters. I have attempted to establish here that gardens, psalters, and the Virgin Mary are elements that identify Berceo's *Milagros* and Alphonso's *Cantigas* as works composed within a tradition of stringing, which I have conveniently called the psalter tradition. I have suggested that since the *Cid* shares two of these elements with *Milagros* and the *Cantigas* – namely, direct significant reference to the Virgin Mary, and repeated indirect but significant references to the Psalms – the *Cid* ought to be considered as belonging to the psalter tradition. This does not mean that the psalter tradition is the key to understanding the composition of the *Cid*; it does mean that it seems to be one of several possible keys. I should have liked the evidence about the *Cid* to be more conclusive, but it is not. I can suggest, therefore, only very tentatively that *Milagros* and the *Cantigas* are later variants within the same psalter tradition: they stress one element – the Virgin Mary – differently, and with a greater emphasis than does the *Cid*.

The textual evidence I can muster in support of this suggestion is slight and inconclusive: Berceo, in his story about the Jewish boy, seems to compare his method of composition with that of epic poems like the *Cid* when he writes, 'Metieron est miraclo entre la otra gesta'; and a contemporary of Alfonso el Sabio, Gil de Zamora, describes the king's work as Davidic 'cantinelas.'[62] Since I do not know precisely what Berceo means by 'gesta' and what Gil de Zamora means by 'cantinelas,' I am still left to guess at the types of composition that preceded the *Cid*. I know, however, that before the composition of the *Cid*, stringing was a form of composition used by Jewish and Arabic poets in cultures that shared geographic space with the culture that produced the *Cid*. This places within the realm of possibility the hypothesis that stringing was used also by the composer of the *Cid*. At the very least, it is clear that stringing, as a tradition of composition, existed in Spain at the time of the composition of the *Cid* and before. But it was not the only existing tradition of composition in Spain at that time. In the next chapter, I shall analyse another masterfully composed work, *Razón de amor*, which uses elements of the psalter tradition – the garden, the Virgin in the garden – in a very different way from the *Cid*.

2 The Song of Songs and the Unity of the *Razón de amor*

por razones de amor y poesía

The previous chapter included a discussion of how the Virgin Mary came to be represented by a garden – the *hortus conclusus* of the Song of Songs – and a proposal that this conception of her affected to some extent the composition of the *Milagros*, the *Cantigas*, and maybe even the *Cid*. But the garden in the Song of Songs was by no means the only one that impressed its symbolism upon the minds of medieval writers. The garden of Ave in the Song was frequently compared with the garden of Eva in Genesis, or, as Alfonso el Sabio of Spain put it in his 'cantiga de loor': 'Ca Eva nos tolleu / o Parays' e Deus / Ave nos y meteu.'[1] In Spain there also existed knowledge of the luscious gardens described in the Koran, a veritable paradise through which flowed magic rivers of water and of wine. And there were other literary gardens, gardens of song, like the one described by Todros Abulafia as a preface to his book of poems (see p. 37), and the one described by Moses ben Jacob Ibn Ezra:

> Kol iš dᵉweh lᵉb̲ā̲b̲ umar ṣoreḥa al-yehemeh libᵉkha wᵉyēānēḥa
> boā lᵉgan-širay wᵉtimᵉṣa-lakh sᵉrî āṣbakh
> wᵉ sam tagîl kᵉron poṣeḥa
>
> nopet lᵉmul taᵉmam lᵉpeh yemar wᵉgam reyḥam
> lᵉmulo mar-dᵉror soreḥa
>
> Bam šamᵉu herᵉšim wᵉilgîm dibᵉru wayeḥezu
> iwᵉrim wᵉras piseḥa
>
> Bam yisᵉmᵉḥu nik̲ᵉim wᵉneᵉ ṣabim wᵉgām kāl-iš
> dᵉweh lᵉb̲ā̲b̲ umar ṣoreḥa
>
> All who are sick at heart and cry in bitterness
> Let not your soul complain in grief.

Enter the garden of my songs, and find balm
for your sorrow, and sing there with open mouth.

Honey compared with them is bitter to the taste,
And before their scent, flowing myrrh is rank.
Through them the deaf hear, the stutterers speak,
The blind see, and the halting run.
The troubled and grief-stricken rejoice in them,
All who are sick at heart, and cry in bitterness.[2]

The countless earthly gardens where ordinary mortal lovers held
their trysts and ordinary workers sought, from the heat of the noon-day
sun, the shade of a brook-watered tree were, of course, commonplace
in Spain as anywhere else in the world. Toss these elements into the
air a thirteenth-century Spanish poet breathed and, with the help of
twentieth-century hindsight, it should be not unexpected that out of
Ave, Eva, magic wine and magic water, lustful song and ordinary
debate, should arise a poem of consummate medieval artistry – the
Razón de amor. All the details of *Razón de amor* cannot be made to
coincide with those of the Song of Songs or with the garden of Eve in
Genesis, or with any other garden of either courtly literature or folklore where 'boy meets girl'; but the Song of Songs is such an important
locus classicus for all such details, including ideas about courtly literature (King Solomon's court), that it would be worthwhile to examine
how works far removed from it vary its contents.

The composition of the *Razón de amor* has been a subject of much
debate ever since A. Morel-Fatio published the work as two separate
poems in 1887. In 1905 Ramón Menéndez Pidal argued convincingly,
in the introduction to his edition and facsimile reproduction of the
manuscript, that the two parts of the poem constitute a unit. In 1950
Leo Spitzer declared that Menéndez Pidal's arguments for unity were
definitive, and he added to those arguments his own aesthetic reasons
for believing that the work was one single, complete poem composed
on the medieval principle of the harmony of contraries, *sic et non*.
Nevertheless, as recently as 1974, it has been correctly pointed out
that literary historians and anthologists remain divided in their opinions about the unity of the work, a fact that is reflected in the failure
to drop the second part, 'Denuestos del agua y el vino,' from the bipartite title normally used for the work.[3]

The search for the unity of the *Razón de amor* has led many able
critics into several interrelated sources of information. Spitzer argued
for Roman mythology, and other critics have tried to show how Chris-

tian symbolism, cathar heresy, grail legends, troubador poetry, linguistics, folk lyrics, and structural analysis can be used to prove or disprove the unity of the poem. All of this critical material includes many convincing insights about the lyrical tradition to which the *Razón de amor* belongs, and yet no single source that has been cited, nor any eclectic combination of those sources, can claim to have satisfied the critical queries that have arisen out of the search for the unity of the poem. There are missing links.[4]

I should like to suggest that one of these missing links is the Song of Songs, which is mentioned only in passing in the critical material on the *Razón de amor*, except by Alicia de Colombí-Monguió, who states explicitly that 'ningún clérigo-escolar pudo ignorar nunca el *Cantar de los Cantares*. Cierto es que, de darse algún eco suyo en el *Razón de amor*, se da tan quedo que debe llegar de muy lejos. Pero la posibilidad de su presencia ayudaría a explicarnos ese manzanar-malgranar, árbol de la fecundidad, de la unión amorosa, del paraíso terrenal y de la salvación.'[5] I shall not claim that the Song of Songs is a direct source for the composition of the *Razón*. Rather, I hope to illustrate that many of the problems left unanswered by searches elsewhere, including the problem of unity, can be resolved by a careful reading of the Song of Songs and its commentaries.

I shall attempt to justify my reference to the Song of Songs by listing some of the main motifs that it has in common with the *Razón de amor*. On the basis of this justification I shall then discuss the question of unity. By listing common motifs I do not mean to suggest exact relationships between the Song of Songs and the *Razón*. My point is that from the widespread tradition of the Song, the poet had available to him many motifs that could be repeated exactly, or altered, to suit artistic purposes. In other words, my emphasis is on identifying the tradition itself correctly, not on finding exact parallels. I am convinced that mutations take place constantly within the same tradition, and I do not believe that medieval artists were capable of only imitating a source exactly.

I should also make clear from the outset that if it can be established satisfactorily that the *Razón* was composed in the tradition of the Song of Songs, the ambiguities in the *Razón*, to which critics like Colombí-Monguió have correctly referred would be adequately explained. Scholars of the Song have always omnilaterally conceded its inherent ambiguity, and there has never been universal agreement among biblical scholars that the Song should be included among the canon of holy books. Advocates of its holiness, like Rabbi Akiva and St Bernard, were keenly aware of the erotic qualities of the work, but considered it holy in spite of, even because of, its erotic content. Other scholars, of course, have refused to concede any divine content to the Song, choosing to consider it simply as a collection of erotic wedding songs. So a similar debate about the content of the *Razón* helps to confirm its composition within the tradition of the Song.[6]

It has been noted that the invocation to the poem ('Sancti spiritus adsid nobis gratia amen') is different from the invocations in the works of other medieval Spanish authors.[7] But its appropriateness becomes clear if this invocation is interpreted within the context of medieval attempts to understand the Song of Songs. The invocation to the *Razón de amor* is most probably a direct reference to the Book of Wisdom: 'Spiritus enim sanctus disciplinae effugiet fictum.'[8] Because Solomon was believed to be the author of both the Book of Wisdom and the Song of Songs, this verse was used by commentators to explain how Solomon was divinely inspired to write the Song of Songs. St Bernard cites the verse from the Book of Wisdom in his sermon on the title 'Song of Songs,' and Abraham Ibn Ezra makes oblique reference to it in his interpretation of the title: 'Quoniam autem testificatur contextus scripturae Dominum Salomoni bis apparuisse, quid eum mirum est vaticinatum de re futura, cum praesertim afflatu Spiritussancti hunc librum fuderit.'[9] I shall have reason to return to the invocation when I discuss the unity of the *Razón*. At that time I will also explain how the second line of the poem ('qui triste tiene su coraçón benga oir esta razón') is related to the Song, and how that relationship helps to clarify the problem of unity.

In line 3 the motif of a perfect composition ('razón acabada') is clearly linked to interpretations of the title of the Song of Songs. Abraham Ibn Ezra, for example, in his commentary on the title refers to the excellence of the Song of Songs above all other songs of Solomon, and to its perfection ('Hoc enim sive carmen sive canticum dignius excellentiusque est caeteris … Itaque cum sit suis numeris perfectum, illud exposui tribus modis.'[10] St Bernard also refers to its excellence in his sermon on the title. The idea that this perfect composition was 'feyta d'amor' (l. 3) is one that medieval poets associated with the Song of Songs seem to have known; a twelfth-century French version of the Song of Songs explains in its introductory lines 'Quar d'amor est li livres faiz.'[11]

In line 4 the author of the *Razón* is described in terms that apply as well to the author of the Song of Songs: Solomon was well known as one who 'siepre dueñas amó.' In the context of 'loving women,' if the word *tyrança* in line 5 has a negative connotation (meaning trials, tribulations, or bad dealings), the author of the *Razón* shares this motif with that of King Solomon: 'Rex autem Solomon adamavit mulieres alienigenas multas, filiam quoque Pharaonis, et Moabitidas, et Ammonitidas, Idumaeas, et Sidonias, et Hethaeas: de gentibus, super quibus dixit Dominus filiis Israel: Non ingrediemini ad eas ...' (1 Kings 11:1–2). In spite of differences in geographical locations (Lombardy, Moab), the tradition is discernible in the *Razón*: Solomon's court was considered to be a court of love and wisdom, and it must have been, ultimately, one of the models for other students of courtly love, like Andreas Capellanus.[12]

The spring motif in line 7 ('en el mes d'abril') echoes one of the most famous passages of the Song of Songs: 'Iam enim hiems transiit; imber abiit et recessit. Flores apparuerunt in terra nostra' (2:11–12). In the same line of the *Razón* the motif of the noonday meal ('depués yantar') is reminiscent of 'Indica mihi, quem diligit anima mea, ubi pascas, ubi cubes in meridie' in the Song of Songs (1:6).

The olive tree, named in lines 7 and 54 of the *Razón*, is not found in the Song of Songs, but the apple tree and its shade are mentioned twice in a manner that reminds one of lines in the *Razón*; ('Sicut malus inter ligna silvarum, sic dilectus meus inter filios. Sub umbra illius quem desideraveram sedi ... Sub arbore malo suscitavi te' 2:3, 8:5). By referring to the olive tree the poet probably seeks comparison with the great songwriter David, who described himself as an olive tree growing in the house of God: 'Ego autem sicut oliva virens in domo Dei' (Psalms 51:10). The likelihood of this comparison increases if it is noted that St Bernard refers to this verse of the Psalms in his sermon on Song of Songs 1:3. In addition, the olive was probably more common in Spain at the time of the poem's composition than were the palms and pomegranates and other exotic trees mentioned in the Song of Songs. Impey suggests that the olive is the tree of wisdom, as in the *Siervo libre de amor*.[13]

The motifs of the wine, water, 'dueña,' and their special qualities appearing in lines 9 to 17 of the *Razón* are central to, and will be treated in, the discussion of unity. The siesta mentioned in line 18 is echoed in Song of Songs 1:7, a verse one modern commentator explains in this way: 'The violent heat of noonday compels people in the East to desist from labour, and recline in some cool part of the house. Shepherds especially, being more exposed to the burning rays of the sun, lead their flocks under some shady tree near wells and streams. We have beautiful descriptions of the same custom by Greeks and Romans.'[14] The motif of disrobing is common to both works, but in the *Razón* both lovers disrobe – the man in the heat of the siesta (l. 19), and the woman in heat of passion at the sight of her lover (l. 66); in the

Song, only the woman disrobes, not in a siesta but after she has gone to sleep ('Ego dormio, et cor meum vigilate ... Exploliavime tunica mea, quomodo induar illa' 5:2–3).

The *locus amoenus* of the *Razón* (ll. 20–8) with its fountain, flowers, and aromatic herbs, belongs clearly to the tradition of the *hortus conclusus* described in the Song (4:12–16). The description of a beautiful woman, from the top down, in this *locus amoenus* is also common to both works (ll. 29–39; 4:1–5), although the descriptions differ in detail. It has been noted that the 'doncela' of the *Razón* is like most other medieval women except that she wears a hat to shield her from the sun (l. 38).[15] There is a curiously close relationship between this descriptive detail of the beautiful white doncela of the *Razón* and the fact that the famous woman of the Song of Songs is beautiful but black because she had been scorched by the sun in the vineyards she had tended ('Nigra sum, sed formosa ... Nolite me considerare quod fusca sim, quia decoloravit me sol. Filii matris meae pugnaverunt contra me; posuerunt me custodem in vineis,' 1:4–5).

Several motifs in the song sung by the doncela in the *Razón* (ll. 41–50) are found also in the Song of Songs. The doncela's song expresses the desire of a woman to be with a lover about whom she has heard much but whom she does not know (ll. 41–4); similarly, the ancient commentators described the entire Song of Songs as the desire of a wife (Israel) to be united with her husband (God) whom she has long forsaken and now knows only through the sayings of her forefathers. In line 45 the doncela sings that she would rather be with her lover than be queen of Spain; she repeats a similar choice in line 75 ('no vos camiar por un emperad-'). With regard to the doncela's preference, at least one medieval Spanish commentator of the Song of Songs noted that the story concerned a love triangle in which the woman chose her shepherd lover instead of King Solomon.[16]

The doncela of the *Razón* has one fear resulting from her jealousy of another woman who is said to be deeply in love with the same lover (ll. 46–9); but in spite of her jealousy she is confident that the lover will choose her (l. 50). This combination of jealousy and self-confidence is found also in the Song of Songs where the woman first acknowledges that other women love her lover; but towards the end of the book she is described as a confident winner by her lover ('Oleum effusum nomen tuum; ideo adolescentulae dilexerunt te ... Sexaginta sunt reginae, et octoginta concubinae, et adolescentularum non est numerus. Una est columba mea, perfecta mea ... Viderunt eam filiae, et beatissimam praedicaverunt; reginae et concubinae, et laudaverunt eam' (1:2; 6:7–8).

The motif in line 51 of the *Razón* – of the woman who goes into a garden to work and is surprised there by a man – is found also in the Song of Songs ('Descendi in hortum nucum, ut viderem poma convallium, et inspicerem si floruisset vinea, et germinassent mala punica. Nescivi: anima mea conturbavit me, propter quadrigas Aminadab,' 6:11–12). Because the woman in the *Razón* has never seen her lover she cannot describe him precisely. Nevertheless, her description of him as intelligent and circumspect (ll. 56–9) fits the more detailed description of the lover in the Song of Songs: 'Dilectus meus candidus et rubicundus; electus ex millibus ... Guttur illius suavissimum, et totus desiderabilis' (5:10–16). The fact that the lover has made expensive gifts to the woman (ll. 60–9) is yet another motif found in the Song of Songs ('Murenulas aureas faciemus tibi, vermiculatas argento, 1:10). Finally, the kiss in line 66 of the *Razón* and the long time the lovers spend savouring their love reflect motifs in the Song. 'Osculetur me osculo oris sui ... Ut inveniam te foris, et deosculer te ... Adiuro vos, filiae Jerusalem ... ne suscitetis, neque evigilare faciatis dilectam, quoadusque ipsa velit' (1:1; 8:1; 2:7; 3:5).

Thus far I have commented on the *Razón de amor* line by line, and in the first seventy lines of the poem I have found very few sections that are not echoes of the Song of Songs. These echoes do not necessarily mean that the poet was working with a version of the Song of Songs in front of him; many of the motifs I have mentioned are ordinary themes that the author could have culled from numerous sources. Yet, by going directly to a mother lode of sources for medieval love lyrics, I believe I have been able to demonstrate that half of the *Razón de amor* belongs to the tradition of the Song of Songs. If it can be demonstrated that the second part of the poem, which has come to be known as the 'Duenestos del agua y el vino,' is also related to the Song of Songs, another reason will have been added to those arguments already made for the poem's unity. It does not much matter now when such a unity may have been conceived and executed, and by whom, whether by one poet before the composition of the entire poem or by another poet who attached a second part and reworked an earlier poem. The question is whether or not the poem in its present state is an artistic unit, and more specifically, whether or not the Song of Songs can help to clarify such thematic unity.

The second part of the *Razón* consists of three main elements, all of which can be related to the Song of Songs: the actions of a dove, a debate between wine and water, and the superiority of wine over water mainly because of wine's relationship to Christ. The dove is mentioned in several passages in the Song of Songs, and its behaviour in *Razón*, as represented by the spirit of wisdom, is clearly connected with the tradition of the Song of Songs. The idea that wine and water are adversaries and should be made to debate with each other can be derived from the Song of Songs. Wine is repeatedly compared with love in the Song ('Quia meliora sunt ubera tua vino ... Memores uberum tuorum super vinum ...Pulchriora sunt ubera tua vino ... Guttur tuum sicut vinum optimum,' 1:1,3; 4:10; 7:9).[17] In the Song of Songs wine is the favoured drink of lovers ('Bibi vinum meum cum lacte meo. Comedite, amici, et bibite; et inebriamini, carissimi,' 5:1), and water is placed in an adversary position to love ('Aquae multae non potuerunt extinguere charitatem,' 8:7). The narrative unity of the *Razón* seems to be based on a question implied by the poet: Which substance leads to true love ('fin amor'), water or wine? The protagonist drinks water and immediately experiences an amorous encounter which, though pleasant enough while it lasts, leaves him sad and almost kills him (ll. 76–7). A dove then appears to the poet and in a debate teaches him the wisdom of choosing wine over water.

The wise choice of wine over water is based on both wine's relationship to Christ and the equation found in commentaries on the Song of Songs that love is equal to wine because Christ is the true vine. We can be certain that medieval readers associated love with a special kind of wine because St Bernard, in his sermon on the Song of Songs verse beginning 'Introduxit me in cellam vinariam' (2:4), says explicitly that love is wine: 'Respondit mirum minime esse, si vino aestuaret, quae in cellam vinariam introisset. Et secundum litteram ita. Secundum spiritum quoque non negat ebriam, sed amore, non vino, nisi quod amor vinum est.'[18] St Bernard's interpretation cannot be surprising since it is common in Christian commentaries that Christ is the bridegroom in the Song of Songs. If, therefore, in the *Razón* there are indications that love is equivalent to wine, the equation that love is wine (because of Christ) and water is the enemy will be seen as common to the Song of Songs and the *Razón*.

The language of both halves of the *Razón de amor* indicates that, in the mind of the poet, love is equivalent to wine. Wine is described in the first half of the poem as 'fino' (l. 9), and this is the same adjective used to describe love ('fin amor,' l. 29). Moreover, it is evident that the courtly-love concept of *amor purus* and *amor mixtus* is based on an analogy to pure and mixed wine. This and many other courtly-love concepts are rooted ultimately in the Song of Songs.[19] It is even easier in the second half of the *Razón de amor* to demonstrate that love is wine, because here everything that is said about wine applies equally to love. It can reasonably be said that love dislikes to be weakened by bad companions (ll. 88–90); love does strange things to people's heads, making good people sceptical and wise ones mad (ll. 95–8); love has no hands or feet and yet it has the power to conquer valiant men even as it conquered Sampson (ll. 113–18); a table set without love is worthless (l. 117); any rustic Romeo, giddy with love, will, if unassisted, stumble and fall (ll. 120–2); love alters perception (ll. 123–5); love is always stored as an honourable possession (l. 132); and that love works miracles, making the blind man see, the lame man walk, the dumb man speak, the sick man well, just as it says in the Bible that Jesus Christ, the source of love, worked miracles (ll. 133–7). There can be no doubt that in the second half of the *Razón de amor* love is wine. Since, in the same section of the poem, water is engaged in verbal combat with wine, it follows logically that water is enemy to love.[20]

Once it has been demonstrated that the equations that love is wine (because of Christ) and water is the enemy are common to both the tradition of the Song of Songs and the *Razón*, the thematic unity of the *Razón* can be considered established. The entire poem, not just the first half, is a 'razón acabada feyta de amor' – a title that reflects the title Canticum Canticorum Salomonis, The Song of Songs, which is Solomon's. The poet captures the full meaning of the biblical superlative with his 'acabada,' and uses the same enigmatic genitive that kept medieval commentators wondering whether the Song was written by Solomon, about him, or both. The title 'Denuestos' could be dropped, and the poem could be called *Razón* (compare Song), *Razón acabada* (compare Song of Songs), or *Razón de amor* (compare Song of Solomon).

With the wine-love-Christ equation in mind, a number of difficulties that have plagued previous interpretations of the poem can be clarified. Again I comment line by line, highlighting those lines that have not been sufficiently explained in the first part of this chapter. I do not intend interpretations that precede or follow as definitive readings of *Razón*; nor do I mean to suggest that *Razón* must henceforth be understood always in the tradition of the Song of Songs. As Alicia de Colombí-Monguió has correctly pointed out, ambiguity in *Razón* is a necessary poetic device without which much of the work's artistry would be lost.[21] I use the tradition of the Song of Songs throughout this chapter only as an heuristic tool to help explain the poem's unity, but other meanings and interpretations are surely elicited by this polysemous text. What follows, therefore, is a test to see if a reading of *Razón* in the tradition of the Song of Songs can be sustained justifiably throughout the poem.

Some editors follow Morel-Fatio and omit the invocation in line 1 entirely ('Sancti spiritus adsid nobis gratia amen'); others, after Menéndez Pidal, include it, but apart from the rest of the poem. But there seems sufficient reason to follow London's edition[22] and count the invocation as the first line of the poem. The poet writing in the tradition of the Song of Songs chooses an appropriate invocation closely related to King Solomon. King Solomon asked God for wisdom (1 Kings 3:6–9), and in return he received divine inspiration to compose his works, including, according to the medieval commentators, the Song of Songs (1 Kings 4:29–32). Likewise, the poet of the *Razón* invokes the presence of the Holy Spirit and by implication, like Solomon, appeals for wisdom. Since both wisdom and the Holy Spirit are represented in the poem, this invocation, in so far as it foreshadows the appearance of wisdom and the Holy Spirit, ought to be considered an integral part of the whole work.

A careful analysis of the invocation alerts the reader to the fact that what seems commonplace in the poem might be of greater aesthetic significance. This is certainly true of line 2 of the poem, which on the surface seems to be a minstrel's stereotyped invitation to listeners. In fact, this line is a direct reference to the text in the Psalms beginning 'Et vinum laetificet cor hominis' (103:15), and is appropriate in the *Razón* for two reasons. First, the text was quoted by commentators on the passages about wine in the Song of Songs; St Bernard, for example, quotes it in his sermon on the third verse of the first chapter of the Song. Second, the same text forms a part of the literary tradition of the debate between wine and water; it is found, for example, in one of the Hebrew wine-and-water debates.[23] The poet has therefore told careful readers in the second line of the poem exactly what the outcome of the *razón* will be: they should drink wine if they are sad at heart because 'wine makes the heart glad.' There is, in the second half of the poem, a similarly subtle use of cliché when the poet makes wine say 'placem de coraçó' (l. 112); it is fitting, according to Psalm 103:15, that wine should say that it is pleased at heart.

The poet promises in lines 3–6 to tell from experience why those who are lovesick should drink wine; not any kind of wine (note 'qui de *tal* vino,' l. 13), but a special kind of clear, red, fine wine that he once saw in a silver vessel, covered from the heat, in the bough of an apple tree; it had been placed there by the lady who owned the garden. Now these details do not make complete sense if they are to be taken only literally. How could the poet see what was inside a vessel in the bough of a tree if he was under another tree ('so un olivar,' l. 7)? Either he had prior knowledge of the contents of the vessel and of how it got on the bough, or his words are not to be taken only literally. If the poem was composed in the tradition of the Song of Songs, and it is accepted that this tradition is at the very core of allegory in Western literature, it can be safely assumed that the poet means these words to be taken figuratively as well as literally, as appropriate. What then do the apple tree, the covered silver vessel of wine, and the lady of the garden represent on the figurative level?

The apple tree is like the tree of knowledge of good and evil mentioned in Genesis 2:9–17. By choosing the tree from the book of Genesis the poet has not left the tradition of the Song of Songs. It was accepted medieval practice to compare the gardens of the Song of Songs with the gardens described in Genesis; and more importantly, when Solomon asked for wisdom he asked to be able to choose between good and evil ('Dabis ergo servo tuo ... discernere inter bonum et malum,' 1 Kings 3:9).

The 'señora del huerto,' like the bride in the Song of Songs, is, in a Christian context, like the Church. In the Song of Songs she prepares a special wine for her lover ('Et dabo tibi poculum ex vino condito,' 8:2), and therefore was identified, by commentators on the Song,[24] with wisdom who, in Proverbs 9:1–5, invites all to partake of her specially mixed wine: 'Sapientia aedificavit sibi domum ... miscuit vinum, et proposuit mensam suam. Misit ancillas suas ut vocarent ... "Venite ... ... et bibite vinum quod miscui vobis."' The wine in the silver vessel therefore is the good fruit placed on the apple tree of knowledge of good and evil; it is the wine of wisdom, the wine prepared by the Church. Note that the vessel of wine does not grow naturally on this tree but has been placed there (l. 11). The poet affirms that whoever drinks of this communion chalice every day while taking the host ('quan comiesse,' l. 13) shall never again fall ill.[25] The poet probably knows this at first hand as a result of the experience about to be narrated; the words in lines 11–14, like those in the opening and closing lines (ll. 1–6, 145–6), refer to the moment of narration and must be distinguished from words referring to the events that occurred before the moment of narration (for example, ll. 7–10, 15–144).

The passage about the cup of water (ll. 15–29), like the one about wine, must be interpreted figuratively as well as literally because it is not explained how the poet could literally see the contents of the cup; it is not important to decide whether or not the poet fell asleep after line 19 and experienced in a dream what is related after that line. The entire passage is figurative as well as literal. So is the rest of the poem, for that matter, since wine and water cannot be understood, literally, to have debated with each other.

The cup of water represents the evil fruit on the tree of knowledge of good and evil. But water is not always evil. Since it is born of the tree of good as well as of evil water sometimes serves good purposes. For example, water nurtures the very tree on which it was born; it feeds the miracle-working aromatic herbs and flowers around the fountain (ll. 20–23); it makes the long-dried-up mother vine pregnant again (ll. 105–10); it cleans up dirty places (ll. 127–31); and it is used in the sacrament of baptism to give new life to Christians (ll. 139–44). But in spite of its good life-giving qualities, this water represents evil and is associated with death (note 'encantado,' l. 17, 'omne muerto,' l. 26, and 'muerta,' l. 118) because in Genesis 2:17 God promised man that if he ate of the evil fruit, he would surely die. Water is also associated with nakedness and with sex or carnal knowledge, because Adam realized his nakedness after he ate the fruit and 'knew' his wife, Eve. In this carnal sense, this water gives new life, in the form of sexual potency, to 'dead' lovers, a potency that, in terms of some common interpretations of Genesis, is the ultimate cause of death among mankind. Note that, unlike the vessel of wine, this evil fruit grows naturally on the tree ('en el mançanar s-nacía,' l. 16).

The water cup itself is not described as being of a precious metal, as is the silver vessel of wine, and wine later reminds water of this: 'C'a mi siepre me tiennen ornado de entro en buenna cubas condesado' (l. 132). The cup of water, unlike the vessel of wine, is uncovered, naked like Adam after he had eaten the fruit. So when the man (l. 19) and the woman (l. 66) disrobe, they align themselves symbolically with the cup of nakedness and carnal knowledge. For all these potentially evil reasons, the cup of water is described as being farther away from man's reach than the wine ('arriba del mançanar, l. 15), not simply, as some have supposed, to facilitate the spilling of the water into the wine; if the water were below the wine, the dove – if it flew upwards out of the water – would still have been able to spill water into the wine.

There are, it seems, two fountains: one that rises out of the apple tree of knowledge of good and evil (l. 16), and another that feeds the herbs and flowers (ll. 20–8). This interpretation of two fountains is later supported by lines 81–2 in which the dove avoids one fountain and flies to another, but the meaning of the text here is not as clear as it might be. These fountains, if there are two, are alike, since both contain a special kind of cold water (ll. 16 and 21–2) which is to be compared with the two kinds of fountain waters described in the Song of Songs: the well of living waters (4:15), and the waters associated with death that cannot quench love (8:6–7). As with the tree of good and evil in Genesis and the waters of life and death in the Song, the waters of the fountains in the Razón can serve a double purpose. When the fountain is a baptismal font the purpose is good and the water gives new spiritual life to a spiritually dead person. But when the fountain is used for ordinary purposes, the water acts as an aphrodisiac which, through the smell of the flowers it feeds, arouses a sexually inactive man ('a omne muerto Ressucytarya,' l. 26) without being able to quench his thirst for love.

It is crucial to the understanding of the *Razón de amor* to note that the man, an 'escolar,' does not use the water of the fountain for good, baptismal, purposes. Clearly, since he is a 'clergyo' (l. 57), he is already baptized. When he *drinks* of the water, ignoring the special wine of the church, he uses the fountain for ordinary purposes and the consequences of this use are immediately predictable. First of all he suffers a thorough chill (l. 27). (This is what biblical scholars and clerics described as the 'chill of Satan.'[26]) Then he takes a flower in his hand. The smell of this flower, under good, baptismal circumstances, would have given him a spiritual resurrection and he would have then been able to sing of 'fin amor.' Instead, he is unable to sing of 'fin amor' (l. 29) because the sight of the 'doncela,' the most beautiful woman he has ever seen, sets his carnal waters flowing; the 'fin amor' this woman represents is unable to quench the escolar's thirst for love.

This beautiful 'doncela' is, like her surroundings, not all evil; some of her qualities are like those of the wine: her complexion is clear and ruddy (ll. 31–2, 35), and she is clothed. But she also possesses some qualities of the evil fruit: her face is as fresh as an apple (l. 32), reminiscent of the apple with which Eve tempted Adam, and her eyes are black and smiling (l. 34), not unlike the water described later in the poem as 'muerta Ridiendo' (l. 118). It becomes clear from the woman's song, and especially from her repeated use of the verb *conocer*, that the love she represents is not a spiritual 'fin amor,' but the carnal, perhaps illicit, love for a cleric. She is, in fact, Scientia, and she must be distinguished from Sapientia, the 'señora del huerto.' Scientia is not wisdom, which is probably represented by her rival, the 'dueña cortesa e bela e bona' (l. 47); she is worldly, carnal knowledge that comes but does not linger (compare 1 Corinthians 13:8), the noonday devil to whom St Bernard dedicates an entire sermon on verse 6 of the first chapter of the Song of Songs.[27] Scientia, like the waters of the Song, cannot quench love's thirst, and, as a consequence, leaves the love-sick cleric as sad ('desconortado,' l. 76) as the listeners to whom he appeals in line 2, and almost dead (l. 77).

It is a well-worn theme in medieval literature that someone who has come very close to death experiences a visionary insight into truth. Such an experience is often described as taking place in the twilight

world between sleep and wakefulness, which is why the cleric explains
that he really wanted to sleep ('por verdat quisieram adormir,' l. 78).[28]
Because of the visionary nature of this experience, the dove and its
actions should be interpreted both literally and figuratively.

The dove is mentioned several times in the Song of Songs (1:15, 2:14;
4:1; 5:2, 12; 6:9), but the verse that fits most closely the scene in the
Razón is the one in which the lover's eyes are described as doves,
bathed in milk, beside streams of water ('Oculi eius sicut columbae
super rivulos aquarum, quae lacte sunt lotae, et resident iuxta fluenta
plenissima,' 5:12). The motifs of whiteness (l. 79) and bathing (l. 82) are
present also in the *Razón*. In order to understand what the dove represents on a figurative level, one must note that, on the literal level, the
dove's behaviour is exactly the opposite of that of the doncela. The
cleric is certain that the doncela, although she does not know him,
will not flee when she sees him (l. 52); but this is exactly what the
dove does ('en la funte quiso entra mas quando a mi vido estar / etros'
en la del malgranar,' ll. 81–2). The fact that the dove flees from the
cleric makes it easy to identify the bird on the figurative level. In
Solomon's Book of Wisdom, in the sentence before the one to which
the invocation of the *Razón* refers, the wisdom of the Holy Spirit is
described as refusing to enter a sinful body or soul and fleeing from
deceit ('Quoniam in malevolam animam non introibit sapientia, nec
habitabit in corpore subdito peccatis. Spiritus enim sanctus disciplinae effugiet fictum').

The dove, therefore, is the wisdom of the Holy Spirit, which rejected
the sinful cleric when he was a disciple of water and taught him to be
a disciple of the right wine. The dove does not attempt to *drink* the
water of evil. It enters the fountain/cup and, like the poet, feels or pretends to feel the chill of cupidity (l. 85), but it flies out immediately
('festino,' l. 86), shaking the water from its body on to the wine of wisdom. The dove thus gives a graphic lesson to the cleric about how he
should behave, and the lesson is further impressed upon the cleric's
mind by wine's victory in the debate with water.

Before some points in the debate are clarified, it would be well to
examine closely two 'mistakes' attributed to the poet or to the scribe.
It has been noted that the vessel of wine is never uncovered; at least
one critic believes that this detail is an error because, if the vessel
remained covered, the water could not have been spilled into it.[29] But
we have already shown that the vessel of wine remains covered for
very sound aesthetic and symbolic reasons related to the nakedness of
Adam and Eve. Clearly the wine must have been covered with a fine
porous cloth (like a ritual corporal) through which water would pass as

easily as through a sieve. The poet is also supposed to have erred in lines 82–3 in which 'malgranar' should have been 'mançanar.' Since this passage is not only repeated but also garbled, there is good reason to suppose the cause was either scribal error or the poet's bad memory. However, the poet might have deliberately used 'malgranar' for at least two valid reasons: first, pomegranates are mentioned three times in the Song (4:12, 7:12; 8:2), twice juxtaposed with reference to wine; second, the Latin name for pomegranate (*malum granatum*) describes a kind of apple that, because of its first syllable in Spanish (mal-), connotes evil.

We have seen how the subtlety of the debate between wine and water lies mainly in the facts that everything said about wine applies equally well to love, and everything said about water belies its dual function as a fruit on the tree of knowledge of good and evil. As early as the poem's second line, we have seen a subtle anticipation of the outcome of the debate, namely, that those who are sad at heart should drink wine, not water. Not everyone will agree that this is the outcome of the debate. Some will want to agree with Spitzer that the outcome of the debate is a reconciliation between two warring elements, a *concordia discors*: 'C'est comme si l'auteur, fine mouche, nous disait, "L'eau est aussi nécessaire que le vin – donnez-moi *donc* du vin!"'[30] Others may want to claim that water has won the debate because it seems to have the last word. This claim rests on the assumption that the extant version is complete, which is not necessarily true. It remains to be demonstrated, therefore, even in spite of all that has been said about the wine of wisdom and the water of evil, precisely how water has been made to concede defeat.

Water's final claim (ll. 139–44) is characteristic of its duplicitous nature throughout the poem: what seems like a solid defence and victory is, in fact, a self-defeating argument. It seems conclusive for water to imply that since baptism is essential in Christianity, wine must be baptized (hence watered down) in order to be called a child of God – a very clever argument on the surface.[31] But wine does not need to reply to this argument because water has already conceded, in line 106, that everybody knows that wine *is* the child of God ('que no a homne que no lo sepa que fillo *sodes* de la çepa'); everybody knows that Christ is reported to have said, 'I am the true vine' (John 15:1); so everybody also knows, as water admits, that wine, the fruit of the vine, is the child of God.

Wine does not need to repeat itself because it has already said precisely that it is the child of God in its much misunderstood climactic argument in line 137 ('asi co dize en el scripto de fazem' el cuerpo de iesu Xo'). This line is normally assumed to refer directly to the sacrament of Communion, but this cannot be, because in this sacrament wine becomes the *blood* of Jesus, not the 'cuerpo de iesu Xo' (Matthew 26:26–8).[32] The subject of 'fazem' is 'el cuerpo de iesu Xo,' not 'el scripto.' So the meaning of the line is, 'just as it tells in the Scripture about the body of Christ making me,' not 'where it [the Scripture] makes me the body of Christ.'[33]

It is clear that the poet intends to refer vaguely to Communion with the well-known phrase 'cuerpo de iesu Xo,' but he means to refer specifically to instances where the body of Christ associates itself with wine. The most memorable of such instances is at the wedding at Cana where Jesus worked the miracle of changing water into wine (John 2:1–11). We can be certain that line 137 refers to this miracle because it comes at the end of references to other miracles Christ performed – making the blind see, the lame walk, the dumb speak, and the sick well (ll. 135–6).[34] Another memorable instance where Christ associates himself with wine is when he says, in John 15:1, 'I am the true vine.' So line 137 must be interpreted to mean 'just as it tells in the Scripture about the body of Christ, the true vine, making me, wine.' In other words, since the body of Christ, the true vine, made wine, everybody knows that wine is the child of God, which is exactly what water concedes in line 106 ('que fillo sodes de la çepa').

The poet's ending of the debate after water's self-defeating argument is, therefore, by no means abrupt. What water says in lines 138–44 not only has no effect on wine's argument but also proves wine correct, *quod erat demonstrandum*. Similarly, what water says in lines 138–44 not only has no effect on the narrator's experience, but also proves the decision artistically correct to end the debate and call for wine in line 145 ('Mi razón aqui la fino e mandat nos dar vino'). What water says about baptism convinces the narrator that he should end the debate and call for wine because he knows that when he drank the water he could not possibly have been thinking about baptism. Baptism is a sacrament usually performed only once, and not only was he, a cleric, already baptized, but (if Jacob is right about a Lenten setting) baptism was forbidden during Lent.[35] The narrator is forced to concede that water and baptism, though essential, are not sufficient to cure his lovesickness, because even though baptized, he drank water and ended up sick again ('desconortado,' l. 76). This is theologically sound in a Christian context: baptism is essential for salvation, but is not sufficient to guarantee it. Spitzer is therefore not correct in asserting that the poet orders wine because, since both water and wine are essential, either will suffice. The poet orders wine because he has learned that water will make him sick again, and that only wine can cure his illness, as claimed in lines 14 and 136 of the poem.

Line 146 offers further proof of why the narrator orders wine. In the light of how subtly the poet has used stereotyped expressions throughout the poem, it would be unwise to treat this line as a mere cliché typical of an explicit. Like the invocation, which also reads like a cliché, the explicit is an integral part of the poem. When the text says, 'Seper cum Domino bibat,' the poet is not just punning ('bibat' for 'vivat'), nor does the text mean, 'May he drink [either water or wine] forever with the Lord.' Instead he is referring specifically to the promise Christ made to his disciples that they would drink wine with him in the Kingdom of Heaven: 'Dico autem vobis: non bibam amodo de hoc genimine vitis usque in diem illum, cum illud bibam vobiscum novum in regno Patris mei' (Matthew 26:29). The key word in this text, 'vobiscum,' is what causes the poet to write 'cum Domino.'[36]

It would be equally unwise to dismiss the signature of the poem ('Lupus me fecit de moros') as simply the name of a poet from a town, in Saragossa, north of Ateca.[37] There is ample reason to suppose that even if Lupus de Moros were a real person, the name also alludes to the fact that the poem thus signed is an attack on Moorish customs, written by a wolf among the Moors. It is well known that Muslims are prohibited from drinking wine on earth, and a poem that urges the drinking of wine on earth obviously flies in the face of a Muslim religious precept. It is also well known that although Muslims are prohibited from wine on earth, they are repeatedly promised wine in Paradise. (Indeed, numerous passages of the Koran sound much like the scene in the *locus amoenus* of the *Razón de amor*.) Here are three typical examples:

> The righteous shall surely dwell in bliss ... They shall drink of a pure wine, securely sealed ... a wine tempered with the waters of Tasnim, a spring at which the favoured will refresh themselves. (83:22–8, p. 50)

> Allah ... will reward them for their steadfastness with robes of silk and the delights of Paradise. Reclining there upon soft couches, they shall feel neither the scorching heat nor the biting cold. Trees will spread their shade around them, and fruits will hang in clusters over them. They shall be served with silver dishes, and beakers large as goblets; silver goblets which they themselves shall measure: and cups brim-full with ginger

flavoured water from the Fount of Selsabil. (76:12–17, p. 18)

> They shall recline on jewelled couches face to face, and there
> shall wait on them immortal youths with bowls and ewers and a
> cup of wine (that will neither pain their heads nor take away
> their reason); with fruits of their own choice and flesh of fowls
> that they relish. And theirs shall be the dark-eyed houris, chaste
> as hidden pearls: a guerdon for their deeds. (56:15–23, p. 116)[38]

The pure wine securely covered, the springs, the special water, the
silver vessels, the heat and cold, the shady trees, the dark-eyed houri,
all are reminiscent of the *Razón de amor*. As well, the Koran has a passage about disrobing at noon: 'Believers, let your slaves and children
ask your leave when they come in to see you before the morning
prayer, when you have put off your garments in the heat of noon, and
after the evening prayer' (24:57, p. 219).

The Koran alludes to the twofold function of water – as the original
good substance from which all life was created, and as the dirty substance in carnal love: 'Are the disbelievers unaware that the heavens
and the earth were one solid mass which We tore asunder, and that We
made every living thing of water? (21:31, p. 298) ... 'Let man reflect
from what he is created. He is created from an ejected fluid, that issues
from between the loin and the ribs' (86:57, p. 38). The descriptions of
Paradise in the Koran are filled with streams of pure water. Since water
is such an important substance in the Muslim pre-prayer ritual
(wudu), one wonders whether the references in the *Razón* to water and
baptism are not also attacks on Muslim ablutions, which have been
compared to Christian baptism. It is important to note that these quotations from the Koran are by no means a departure from the tradition
of the Song of Songs. The descriptions of Paradise in the Koran are
either directly dependent upon the Song of Songs and its parallel in
Genesis or, if not directly dependent, at the very least were written in
the same Semitic tradition.[39] The *Razón de amor* could hardly have
been written other than in Spain where Jews, Christians, and Muslims
scrutinized each other's religious practices for centuries.

To sum up: the *Razón de amor* is a Judaeo-Christian poem written
(perhaps in an environment in which there were many Moors) to warn
clerics against the sin of *luxuria*. Additional circumstantial support
for this claim exists in the document attached to the poem and written in the same hand. This document on the Ten Commandments was
attached to the *Razón de amor* probably because both works are aimed
at the instruction of priests and both sets of instructions deal mainly

with luxuria. The *Razón de amor* tells priests how to avoid luxuria themselves, while the attached document tells priests how to deal with luxuria when they hear the confessions of their parishioners. Consequently, although the general tendency in *Razón de amor* criticism has been to ignore the attached addendum, this document merits a more careful examination to see if it reveals how a priest who read it might have interpreted the *Razón*.

The document can be divided into two parts. The first part lists the Commandments one by one and explains how sins are committed against each one, in order that the priest will know how to question the confessant concerning each commandment. The second part instructs the priest how to probe the confessant about sins committed through the five senses, on the job, with the body, mind, and soul, through omission, and with one's wife. This second part also reminds the priest that sins are of three kinds (against God, against one's neighbour, and against oneself), and explains how to exact proper penance for sins, to process serious sins, to dismiss the confessant, and lastly, how to pray for the scribe who wrote the work.

It is not surprising to read in this document that the priest is instructed to probe for luxuria in the commandments against fornication and coveting a neighbour's wife. But it is revealing to observe that luxuria is discussed even under a commandment like 'keeping the Sabbath holy,' where the priest is told to ask if the confessant 'canto cantares luxoriosos en vigilias.' Luxuria is also implied in the commandment against murder: 'E quinto es: *Non mataras*. En este peca qui mata de feito o de voluntat o por mal exemplo, o, si, pudo, que no liuro de muerte a so cristiano, o si mato nino chiquielo [en] el vientre de so madre, o ensenno erbas con que lo matasen o dieu erbas a alguno con que mories.'[40]

It is well to remember that instructions like these were written partly because they were ignored. Nevertheless, since the medieval Christian world was made up of confessors and confessants in constant contact with each other, it is easy to imagine an ordinary priest who took his job seriously wondering, as he read the *Razón de amor*, if the doncela ever sang lustful songs on the Sabbath, or if she had anything to do with the special water her lover drank that almost killed him, or if she collected special flowers and herbs for purposes of abortion. If he were a more learned priest, he would, of course, understand the tradition of allegorized lust in which the poem was written.

In the second part of the document an entire paragraph is devoted to lust, even lust between husband and wife. Here the priest is instructed that the third category of sin (against oneself) is committed 'por comer e por beber e por luxuria,' that the penance for this category is fasting, flagellation, and pilgrimage, and that the sin of lying with a virgin is serious enough to be referred to the bishop.[41] But the most revealing passage of this part is the one about the five senses:

> E deve demandar el preste al pecador si va veder fornicaciones o las mulleres, como non deviese bolver sos ollos a la vanidat, e demandel si vaveder lo[s] juegos los dias domingos o de las fiestas; el del odor: si porta con si musco [o] otras odores; del odir: si ode buenaminetre cantares o otros omnes que dicen paraulas feas, que los pecadores enújan se de odir la misa e las paraulas de Dios, e de los cantares de la[s] caçurias non se enuyan e beven el vino puro e las carnes calentes e muytas por raçon de luxuria e beven huevos por exa raçon, ed es mayor pecado que si quebrantas la quaresma: del taner: si toco muller en las tetas o en otro lugar de vergonça.[42]

Again it is easy to imagine a literal-minded priest wondering, as he read the *Razón*, if the *locus amoenus* where the lovers disrobed was a favourite spot for voyeurs, if anything in the garden smelled of lustful musk oil, if the cleric enjoyed listening to the doncela's song as much as he enjoyed listening to mass. He might also wonder where the cleric touched the doncela, and, especially, if the cleric drank pure wine for lustful aphrodisiac purposes.

The priest would probably classify the cleric's offence in the category of sins against oneself (since it involved eating, drinking, and luxuria), and would have either ordered the confessant to fast and flagellate (but not go on pilgrimage since that is where he seemed to have met a lot of dueñas). For lying with a virgin, the priest would have referred the poet to the bishop. The bishop, a more learned reader, would probably have been pleased that the poet had either confessed his sin or invented a cleric who could narrate a subtle and learned autobiographical testimony for the benefit of other clerics; he would have probably reminded the poet of how God punished King Solomon for his lustfulness, and urged him to continue taking Holy Communion daily to either avoid recidivism or prevent his autobiographical fiction from ever becoming fact.

As far as the Moorish environment is concerned, the evidence in the document on confession is as slight as it is in the *Razón de amor*. This evidence is implied in the translation of the biblical *neighbour* in the first part of the document on confession. The Vulgate uses 'proximus' for 'neighbour,' and the author of the document was aware of this because he used 'próximo' twice in the second part, in the paragraph about the three kinds of sins. But in the first part of the document 'neighbour' is translated as 'cristiano' (for example, 'que no livro de muerte a so cristiano,' 'Non cobdiciaras ren de to cristiano,' and 'Non cobdiciaras de to cristiano la muller').[43] The implication is that the author was probably writing in a context in which one's neighbour was not necessarily Christian.

In the history of literary composition in medieval Spain, the document on confession is, of course, more important to the study of works that are arranged around the Ten Commandments and the five senses (like Talavera's *Corbacho*) than to the study of the *Razón de amor*.[44] Nevertheless, the document does demonstrate that luxuria was a subject important enough to cause a prosaic tract on confession to be copied in the same manuscript in the same hand as a subtle allegorical poem written in the tradition of the Song of Songs. This juxtaposition adds support for the working hypothesis that questions posed from a European perspective about Christian symbolism, Cathar heresies, grail legends, troubadours, classical traditions, and goliards, though often essential, are not always sufficient without questions about luxuria and the biblical tradition in the composition of certain medieval Spanish works. This is not to say that in the rest of Europe confession is incompatible with lust, but simply to suggest that in medieval Spain the universal debate about wine, women, and song (common to both the document on confession and the *Razón de amor*) sometimes has a special biblical and Semitic flavour.

The pagan paradise described in the *Razón de amor*, although resembling the *locus amoenus* of world literature, has a greater affinity with the Koran than with European literature; this is the negative paradise that later evolved in Spain into the 'infierno de los enamorados' so popular with Santillana and his fifteenth-century contemporaries. After the *Razón de amor*, medieval Spanish writers did not forget the exegetical tradition of the Song of Songs. Santillana, for example, refers to the Church, in one of his sonnets, as 'la sancta esposa'; he quotes the Song directly in his 'Goços de nuestra Señora'; in his 'Canonización de los bienaventurados sanctos' he dresses the Virgin Mary in the words of Solomon; and he begins his 'Triunfete de amor' with a noonday vision.[45] In fact it can be said with fairness of Santillana and his contemporaries that their constant reference to classical literature is in large measure a superficial varnish, a thick 'fermosa cobertura,' for their fundamental commitment to biblical themes, and especially to the Song of Songs, which the Spanish love lyric imitates.[46] Even in *Celestina*, in which there is so much Petrarch, the prime mover of the story is that Calisto has dared to transform the *hortus conclusus* and the Virgin Mary of the Song of Songs into his own church/garden and god ('Melibeo so e a Melibea adoro e en Melibea creo e a Melibea amo ... Por Dios la creo').[47] But although the Song and its motifs remain present in medieval Spanish literature, they do not predominate aesthetically and artistically after the *Razón de amor* until, of course, the work of the mystics in the sixteenth century, beyond the medieval period.

In the light of this strong reliance in Spain on the Bible, it is not surprising that the references in the *Razón de amor* are, in its first part, to the Old Testament, and in its second part to the New Testament, and that events in the first part prefigure those in the second part. The bipartite composition, which has caused critics to consider it two poems, is therefore precisely what lends it unity, a unity reflected in the composition of the Christian Bible and its exegesis. This method of composition remains faithful to the tradition of the Song of Songs because Christian exegetes have interpreted Christ, the true vine in the New Testament, to be prefigured as the bridegroom in the Song.

3 The Apocalyptic Tradition

FOR HENRY SLINGER AND
GEORGE AND OMEGA NEPAULSINGH

The *Razón de amor* is a narrative about a man who has come very close to death, and who has benefited from the actions of a white bird and from an ensuing debate. It is possible to argue that the bird represents the man's soul, and critics have proposed this.[1] But all indications in the text are that the bird comes from afar towards the man, not out of him and away towards the opposite direction ('volando *viene* por medio del uerto,' ll. 79-80). The white bird could have been made to represent the man's spirit of wisdom that, in a moment of weakness, leaves him; that is, something like a mid-thirteenth-century illustration to 1 Samuel 16:14-19 that shows a white bird flying up and away from King Saul, and the accompanying legend explains that 'qualiter spiritus bonus recedit a Saul.'[2] But the poet of the *Razón* chooses to compose his material otherwise: he intends to have the bird fly towards the man and, with the help of its bell, fix his attention upon the lesson it is about to teach him.

The poet also disregards other options for composition available to him with material very similar to what he uses. For example, the woman who appears to the man, instead of being a kind of noonday devil that brings him close to death, could have been Death herself; instead of disrobing and kissing him, she could have invited him to dance; he could have died, and the white bird, as his soul, could then have engaged his body in debate instead of causing wine and water to debate. If the poet had chosen to compose his material in this way, he would have written an eschatological or, more precisely apocalyptic narrative of the kind analysed in this chapter. But the poet of the *Razón* was more inclined to compose a narrative about the theology of gardens, wine, women, song, water, and lust than about eschatology.

Eschatology is a phenomenon common to all religions and cultures. Tribes in precolonial Brazil are known to have made long migrations in search of the Land without Evil, and their ritual practices were conducted in order to save them from the destruction of the world. Other primitive religions derive their concepts of right and wrong from nature, which is presumed to be perfect; their eschatological hope is to be united, in the end, with nature, unaffected by time and season.[3] Oriental religions tend to stress an eschatology that finally frees the individual from repetitive time into some form of eternal nirvana-like existence. Greek and Roman cultures offer many variations of eschatological beliefs, prominent among them the idea that time is conquered, and immortality achieved, through fame.

Apocalypticism is a particular form of eschatology rooted perhaps in Zoroastrianism and peculiar to Hebraic religions – Judaism, Christianity, and Islam. In the Zoroastrian end of time, the forces of evil will be vanquished in battle by the forces of good, the dead will be resurrected, and a perfect age will be established forever in a new world. Judaic apocalypticism is distinguishable from the period of the Jewish prophets, although it is certainly heralded by their works, especially those of Jeremiah, Ezekiel, Isaiah, and Zechariah. Judaic prophecy was an oral tradition: the prophets delivered their messages by word of mouth, and their words were later written down; these prophetic messages were usually exhortations to the people to change their behaviour in order to avoid disaster. The Judaic apocalyptists, unlike the prophets, were literary artists: they wrote down their messages for the last days, pretending to be some well-known personality of the past; the apocalyptists therefore were usually engaged in reinterpreting past events in such a way that their enlightened contemporaries would perceive analogies with current events and have their beliefs confirmed in an eschatological future.

Scholars do not agree on a comprehensive list of Judaic apocalyptic works, but most lists would include those of Ezekiel and Daniel, the three Books of Enoch, the Book of Jubilees, the Testaments of the Twelve Patriarchs, the Sibylline oracles, the Psalms of Solomon, the Assumption of Moses, the Life of Adam and Eve, the Apocalypse of Ezra, the Apocalypses of Baruch, the Ascension of Isaiah, the Apocalypse of Abraham, and the Testament of Abraham.[4] To these works Christians added the Little Apocalypse of the Gospels (Matthew 24, 25; Mark 13; and Luke 21) and the classic apocalyptic work, the Book of Revelation; and Islam added the revelations to the prophet Mohammed about the Last Days of Judgment referred to frequently in the Koran.

Many of these apocalyptic works would have been known to medieval scholars in Spain, especially those works included in the Jewish, Christian, and Islamic Bibles. Since apocalypticism is a cornerstone of Judaism, Christianity, and Islam, and since the apocalyptic tradition has left an indelible mark upon medieval Spanish literature, it is worthwhile listing some of the most characteristic elements of the apocalyptic works mentioned above, so that some conclusions may later be made about how these elements affected the composition of certain medieval Spanish works. Among the most-repeated elements of apocalyptic literature are the following:

(a) A preoccupation with precise dates, usually at the beginning of chapters (for example, in Ezekiel 1:1 'in trigesimo anno, in quarto, in quinta mensis,' and throughout Ezekiel and Daniel, at the beginning of Baruch)

(b) The division of history into spans of time, and the allegorical interpretation of time (for example, in Daniel 2:36–45, Daniel's interpretation of Nebuchadnezzar's dream; Ezekiel 4:5, in which 390 days are equivalent to as many years; the reference in Revelation 12:14 to a time, and times, and half a time; and the Book of Jubilees, in which history is divided into periods of seven times seven years)

(c) A visionary journey in which Heaven is seen, or Hell, or the throne of God, or a new Kingdom (for example, Ezekiel 3:14, 8:1; Revelation 4:1, 19:20, 20:1; the journey of Enoch through the heavens; the ascension of Isaiah; and the night journey of Mohammed)

(d) The idea that, in preparation for the Last Judgment, individuals of all estates of society should confess their sins, repent, cultivate virtues, and shun vices in accordance with God's commandments (for example, Daniel 9:4, 20; Ezekiel 9:4, 11:12, 18–21; and Revelation 2:23)

(e) Reference to esoteric books (for example, Daniel 7:10, 10:21, 12:1; Ezekiel 2:8–3:3; and Revelation 3:5, 5:5, 10:2, 10:8, 13:8, 17:8, 20:12, 20:15)

(f) A messianic hope for a perfect ruler

(g) The idea that in past and current events there are eschatological signs, and that before the end of time there will be more signs, which those who are wise will interpret correctly (for example, Mark 13; Daniel 12:10; Ezekiel 3:27; and Revelation 2:11, 2:17, 2:29, 3:6, 3:13, 3:22, 13:9)

(h) The idea that the dead will be resurrected and judged (for example, Ezekiel 37; Daniel 12:2; Revelation 2:11, 11:18, 20:5, 20:12, 20:13)

This list is neither comprehensive nor sacrosanct. It is meant as an heuristic tool to help in the analysis of the composition of the works discussed in this chapter. It is hoped that any critic who has read the classic apocalyptic works mentioned above will agree that these eight elements are found repeatedly in them. Nothing else is claimed for these eight elements; I am not attempting to establish a genre. I have not admitted or excluded works from discussion on the basis of their symbolic or hypothetical relation to these elements. Rather, I look for direct significant reference in the text to apocalypticism; if such reference is present, I ask if these eight apocalyptic elements are arranged in the work, and if so, how.

There is ample evidence that the apocalyptic tradition captivated the imagination of writers in Spain throughout the Middle Ages. As early as the sixth century, Apringius of Beja wrote a commentary on Revelation; in the seventh century, Julian of Toledo, Valerius of Bierzo, and Isidore of Seville wrote works about apocalyptic matters; and in the eighth century Beatus of Liébana wrote one of the most widely used commentaries on Revelation. From the twelfth century only one anonymous sermon, 'De adventu Domini,' has survived, but certainly many more like it must have been written and delivered. In the thirteenth and fourteenth centuries St Martin of León, Arnald of Villanova, and Ramón Llull were among the well-known writers who treated apocalyptic themes. This list does not aim to be exhaustive but merely to illustrate how firmly the apocalyptic tradition was established in medieval Spain.[5]

In addition to these Latin works, written no doubt for learned audiences, others have survived that were composed in the vernacular. The rest of this chapter will be devoted to a discussion of how the apocalyptic tradition affected the composition of Berceo's *Signos del Juicio Final*, writings that involve discourse between the body and soul, the *Libro de Alexandre*, the *Poema de Fernán González*, the *Libro del cavallero Zifar*, the *Danza general de la Muerte*, two poems in the *Cancionero de Baena*, the *Libro rimado del palacio*, and the *Laberinto de Fortuna*.

Signos del Juicio Final

It should not be necessary to demonstrate that Berceo's *Signos del Juicio Final* belongs to the apocalyptic tradition: the title of the work is evidence enough, as is its contents.[6] I tend to agree with James W. Marchand that the title by which this work is commonly known is imprecise, and that 'Berceo might have called it something like *Del Juicio Cabdal*.'[7] The work consists of seventy-seven cuaderna vía stanzas, the first four of which name the author's source and introduce the topic. Stanzas 5 through 21 describe fourteen of the fifteen signs that herald that Last Judgment; the signs occur on successive days, one sign per day. In stanza 22 the final (fifteenth) sign is described as taking place on the Day of Judgment itself, and the next fifty-two stanzas of the poem (sts. 23–74) describe the awesome events of that long day (l. 68a), including the sentencing of the blessed and the damned and their respective rewards and punishments. The poem ends with a prayer (st. 74) that Christians be spared the punishments, and an exhortation (sts. 76–7) that they better their lives by doing penance and praising the Virgin Mary in order to avoid such punishment.

Marchand and Dutton have pinpointed the kinds of sources Berceo had at his disposal for the poem's first twenty-two stanzas, but sources for the remaining stanzas have not as yet been found.[8] It is possible that either Berceo had a single source (or various sources) for all seventy-seven stanzas, or he himself elaborated the last fifty-five stanzas, based on his knowledge of the Little Apocalypse of the Gospels and of Revelation. In any event, Berceo's work reveals his acquaintance with most of the eight apocalyptic elements listed above:

(a) He is not describing his own vision, so he does not give the precise dating typical of Ezekiel and other apocalyptic works

(b) He studiously avoids predicting when the Last Judgment will occur, perhaps because, as he states, basing himself on Matthew 24:36 and Mark 13:32, 'La cuyta del Judicio sera muy desguisada / por omnes nin por angeles nunca sera asmada'

(c) When the blessed journey to heaven (st. 50), they have a clear unobstructed view of the entire world (st. 55)

(d) It is stressed that penance can compensate for sins (sts. 70, 76)

(e) There is reference in the first four stanzas to the esoteric books from which, according to Berceo, St Jerome derived his information about the Last Judgment

(f) The final judge is described as a perfect ruler, 'Rei de los reyes, alcalde derechero' (st. 49)

(g) The poem's emphasis on the fifteen signs is obvious

(h) It is stated clearly that the dead will be resurrected for judgment (l. 20c, sts. 22–4).

Berceo's arrangement of these apocalyptic elements is basically chronological: first he declares his source; then he explains, day by day, the events of the last fifteen days of the world, with special emphasis on the final, fifteenth day – the long Day of Judgment; finally he exhorts Christians to avoid punishment on that final day by doing penance. With respect to the number of stanzas, Marchand has posed this intriguing question: 'Is it significant that there are exactly seventy-seven cuadernavías?' He suggests that 'seventy-seven expresses the number of sins and also the abundance of divine remission of sin.'[9] Berceo gives no precise reason for his choice of seventy-seven stanzas, but it is true that he devotes seven stanzas (sts. 1–4, 75–7) to his prologue and epilogue, leaving the remaining stanzas for the body of his work. It is also true that the number seven was so frequently associated with sin and its remission that one thirteenth-century writer,

Alain de Lille, basing himself on Isidore, sought to explain 'quare poenitentiae sub septenario numero frequentius injunguntur.'[10] It might be accidental that Berceo stops at seventy-seven stanzas, or the number of stanzas might simply be attributable to the length of his source material. However, if his number of stanzas is symbolic, it should be remembered that the number seven occurs repeatedly (for example, seven churches, seven candelabra, seven seals, seven vials, seven angles, seven horns, seven eyes) in Revelation, a book that is cited frequently in the Signos.

Body-and-Soul Narratives

Whereas Berceo's poem concentrates on the last fifteen days of the world and on the judgment of all souls, another trend in apocalyptic literature concentrated on the judgment of individual souls, that is, on what one writer has termed 'individual eschatology.'[11] In medieval Spanish literature several works deal with individual eschatology: the Disputa del alma y el cuerpo, the Visión de Filiberto, the Disputa del cuerpo e del ánima, the Revelación de un hermitaño, and the Tractado del cuerpo e de la ánima. Traditionally these works have been effectively discussed in histories of literature as debate poems, because they contain dialogue between the body and the soul about which of them is to be blamed for the sentence to be passed on the individual after death. However, information can also be gathered about the composition of these works if they are studied as apocalyptic literature, quite apart from the debate form.

The debate between body and soul was so popular and has survived in so many versions that it has not been possible to trace its evolution definitively. One plausible history of the development of the debate suggests that it is rooted in two ancient stories: one about the vision of Alexander, a disciple of St Macarius, and the other about a vision attributed to St Paul.[12] In both these ancient legends, once death has occurred and the soul has left the body, only the soul (and not the body) is able to speak. As the legends increased in popularity elements of the visions of St Macarius and St Paul were combined. Then it must have been realized that there was no reason why in a vision a corpse could not be imagined to speak, and the corpse was permitted to engage the soul in debate; later, all mention of a vision was dropped, as, for example, in the Provençal poem 'De l'arma e del cors.' What remains constant throughout this evolution is the strong apocalyptic element. The earliest and the latest versions of the story mention the Last Judgment, specific dates, visionary journeys to Heaven or Hell, penance, books, God as a perfect ruler, and the resurrection of the dead. As one historian of the topic states succinctly, 'The Body and Soul theme offered a dramatic way of bringing home the eventual fate of man, the terrors of the Last Judgement, the pains of hell and the joys of heaven.'[13] And the body-and-soul narratives of Spain are just as firmly rooted in the apocalyptic tradition as those from other countries.[14]

The composition of these Spanish works becomes comprehensible when they are viewed as attempts to answer this apocalyptic question: What happens to the soul after death? As a first step to answering this question, all the Spanish works explain that a response is possible because of a vision that came to either the poet (*Tractado, Disputa*) or St Philbert (*Visión, Revelación*). The next step is to answer the question: When did this vision occur? All the Spanish texts answer this question specifically but in different ways. The *Visión* specifies, in the tradition of the *Dialogus inter corpus et animam* that it was in the deep silence of a winter's night when St Philbert was slipping tiredly between sleep and wakefulness. The *Tractado* drops the reference to winter but keeps the idea of slipping tiredly between sleep and wakefulness ('Dormiendo en un lecho velando cansado.')[15] Both versions of the *Revelación* stay firmly within the apocalyptic tradition of precise dates by stating the time, the date, and the year ('Después de la prima la ora pasada / en el mes de enero la noche primera / en CCCC e veynte durante la hera'; in this way they maintain the idea of winter and nightly silence, and in the next few lines they keep the idea of being unable to sleep. The *Disputa* has by far the most interesting response to the question of the time of the vision ('un sábado esient / domingo amanezient.' It is a precise time, which also reflects a tradition found in the *Visio Pauli* that as a result of Paul's intercession, souls were granted permission to visit their bodies once a week between Saturday night and Monday morning.[16]

After the time has been established, the next question is: What happens at that particular time? All texts answer that there was an encounter between a dead body and its soul. The variations here are slight: the *Disputa* says only that the corpse lay on a new sheet and the soul was naked like an infant; the *Visión* just states that the body was lifeless ('syn espirito'; in both versions of the *Revelación* is a description of the putrid state of the body before the soul speaks, and the soul takes the form of a white bird; the *Tractado* describes the corpse simply as very cold and stiff ('muy frío tendido.')[17] In all versions the soul weeps or laments, and in all versions the soul speaks first, lending plausibility to the hypothesis that the topic evolved from a monologue of the soul to a debate between body and soul. In all versions the soul blames the corpse for having sinned, and the soul takes advantage of the body's putrid state to deploy the 'Ubi sunt' theme.

The *Disputa* fragment ends before the soul completes its speech, but in the missing portion, if we are to judge by a similar French version, the body did respond to the soul. The essence of the body's reply in all other versions, includng the French, is that the soul was given control over the body by God, and so the soul must bear the responsibility of sinfulness. The soul's counterpoint to the body's reply is incomplete in the *Visión*, because of a missing folio, but judging from versions of the *Revelación* and the *Tractado*, the soul countered with the claim that it was deceived by the world, the devil, and (in the *Tractado* only) the body itself. After the exchanges between the disputants, all texts begin a transition from debate to some form of judgment or resolution. The transition is most artistic in the *Visión*: the body is made to ask the soul if there is any way out of their predicament, a bribe perhaps.

The variations in the judgment are interesting. The Paris *Revelación* ends with the body claiming victory because after death it has found its place, namely, earth, whereas the soul is doomed never to find its place. The Escorial *Revelación* defers judgment to God, and when an awesome devil comes to claim the soul, it is saved by an angel of God. In the *Visión* two monstrous devils grab the soul away, and there is a morbid description of how it is treated in Hell. In the *Tractado*, an angel of God appears, scroll in hand, and sentences both body and soul to damnation, whereupon a devil throws the soul into a deep ditch.

All three versions that extend beyond the judgment include moral conclusions drawn from the vision. In the *Visión* and the *Tractado* the visionary awakes and denounces the world, making specific reference to current affairs. In the Escorial *Revelación*, however, there is a curiously delightful twist when the soul, which had recently been denounced as sinful by the body and had been salvaged by an angel, is made to denounce the world. When studied in the light of the apocalyptic tradition, therefore, the composition of the Spanish body-and-soul narratives shares a strikingly logical movement from vision to encounter and debate to judgment to moral conclusion. These narratives are not simply debates; they are, more precisely, apocalyptic narratives that contain, among other elements, an eschatological debate.

Danza general de la Muerte

The *Danza general de la Muerte* (*Danza*) is another form of apocalyptic narrative clearly and logically related to the *Signos* and to the body-and-soul narratives. A great deal has been written about the *Danza*, about its country of origin, its text and author, its artistic imagery, and its reflection of contemporary society.[18] In much of this critical writing there is often a realization that the *Danza* is somehow related to the apocalyptic tradition. Thus Pedro Bohigas, in his review of Whyte's book, writes that 'en ningún período de la Edad Media encontraríamos tal vez un ambiente que mejor armonizase con el espíritu de la *Danza de la Muerte* como en aquel final de siglo, en pleno cisma, época llena de pesimismo, en que hallaban favor las profecías más gratuitas sobre transformaciones catastróficas y el próximo fin del mundo'; and Eisler noted that 'all the Dance of Death pantomimes, pictures and verses [are] not unlike the medieval works of art representing the Last Judgment and showing popes and bishops, kings and nobles among the damned swallowed by the maw of hell.'[19] Yet, in spite of this realization, the *Danza* has not been analysed as part of the apocalyptic tradition, an analysis that is certain to shed light on its composition.

The *Danza* consists of a prose introduction of three sentences, followed by seventy-nine stanzas of *arte mayor* rhyming *ababbccb*. In the first seven stanzas Death introduces herself and the subject matter (sts. I–IV), and permits the Preacher to confirm her initial statements (sts. V–VII).[20] In the next seventy stanzas (sts. VIII–LXXVII), the main part of the poem, Death calls upon thirty-five persons, including two women, from various walks of life (for example, ecclesiastics, noblemen, merchants) to join the dance of death. The final two stanzas (sts. LXXVIII–LXXIX) are a general invitation to all those not mentioned previously to join the dance.

In the body of the poem, Death permits each person, except the two women, to make a statement consisting of one full, eight-line stanza. In each of the stanzas that follow a statement Death replies for seven lines and then, in the eighth line, calls upon the next person. Thus Death's replies consist always of seven lines. The first conclusion to be drawn from a most cursory examination of its composition is that the *Danza* shares with the *Signos* of Berceo what seems to be an apocalyptic use of the number seven. Berceo's work has seventy-seven stanzas, the *Danza* has seventy-nine, divided into seven introductory, seventy main, and two final stanzas, slightly fewer than half of which (thirty-three) are subdivided into seven lines plus one. As has already been noted, the number seven is used at least fifty-four times in the classical apocalyptic work, the book of Revelation.

In addition to the use of the number seven, other elements of its composition link *Danza* more firmly to the apocalyptic tradition. Florence Whyte isolated and analysed 'three principal elements' in what she called 'fully typical Dances of Death': 'the arrangement of characters by estate,' 'dancing,' and 'the imminence of Death.'[21] Whyte was not concerned, however, with the relationship of these elements to the apocalyptic tradition. Criticism of the injustice of members of the powerful estates is perhaps the central element of all apocalyptic literature, and this injustice is what led to messianic hopes for a just ruler. Thus Ezekiel, for example, made plain how the powerful priests, elders, kings, and princes would be judged on Doomsday: 'Ecce dies, ecce venit ... Requierent pacem et non erit ... et lex peribit a sacerdote, et consilium a senioribus. Rex lugebit, et princeps induetur moerore ... Secundum viam eorum faciam eis, et secundum iudicia eorum iudicabo eos' (7:10, 7:25–7).

Because the societies that the prophets of apocalyptic literature satirized were rigidly hierarchical, the medieval apocalyptic tradition manifests a tendency to divide society into vertically structured estates, especially since medieval society was at least as hierarchical as that of the ancient biblical world. This tendency was by no means limited to the apocalyptic tradition: as Florence Whyte summarizes, 'the impulse to enumerate such fixed ranks of society was widespread in medieval literature.'[22] Much of this impulse to enumerate society's ranks stemmed from meditation on the biblical story of Creation, according to which all mankind, rich and poor alike, became subject to death as a consequence of the eating of the apple.

One of the earliest-known elaborations of this theme is the poem 'Vado Mori,' which states clearly, 'Pauperis et regis communis lex moriendi / ... Gustato pomo nullus transit sine morte.'[23] 'Vado Mori' lists people from various estates, but since the poem makes no specific reference to the Last Judgment, it seems reasonable to propose that other poems about the levelling power of death across all ranks existed before the apocalyptic element was added to form poems like the *Danza*. But this sequence is not necessarily the only possible evolution of these forms. What makes this proposed evolution slightly more acceptable, however, is the fact that in the apocalyptic works already analysed that antedate the *Danza*, the theme of the levelling power of death is used, even if the estates are not elaborated upon as in the *Danza*. So, in Berceo's *Signos* we read that 'morran todos los omnes, menudos e granados'; in the *Visión* the conclusion drawn from the vision is to renounce all wealth and power because they cause men of great estate to oppress others ('que por dineros son tornadas las voluntades de los juyzios a declinar del derecho e de dar falsas sentencias';

and the Escorial *Revelación* concludes with remarks about the powerful types who are affected by their estates: 'Veo que rreyes e enperadores / Papas, maestres e cardenales, / sus magnificencias e santificales, / todos fenecen en vanos sabores. / Condes, duques, obispos, priores, / segund obraren, ansy gosaran / e los letrados entonce veran / los malos juysios tornar en sabores.'[24]

Although the surviving evidence seems to support the hypothesis that the *Danza* is an elaboration of earlier literature about death in general and, more specifically, an elaboration of the estate motif found in earlier apocalyptic works, the reverse is also conceivable, namely, lost antecedents of the *Danza* were whittled down in later literature about death. It would be wiser to posit that various apocalyptic elements co-existed from which forms like those of the 'Vado Mori,' the *Signos* , the body-and-soul narratives, and the *Danza* could have emerged and reemerged at various times, as circumstances dictated. In oppressive hierarchical societies throughout the period in question, the explanation of death according to Genesis co-existed with Christ's repeated assertion about the rich man, the camel, and the needle's eye; and this co-existence always had the capacity to generate a variety of literary forms at any given time.

Part of the apocalyptic vision of justice is that men from powerful estates, like all others, will be judged according to their own deeds. A typical example from classical apocalyptic literature is the statement from Ezekiel 7:27: 'Secundum viam eorum faciam eis, et secundum iudicia eorum iudicabo eos.' This is an apocalyptic cliché repeated, for example, in Revelation 2:23 ('et dabo unicuique vestrum secundum opera sua'). Berceo expresses this cliché in stanzas 41–6 of the *Signos* by making 'the punishment fit the crime' in such a way that, for instance, false witnesses hang by the tongue, kings and emperors are ruled by servants, in a reversal of roles, coveters of wealth have their mouths stuffed with gold, and workers who cheated are forced to give fair labour for false rewards. The Escorial *Revelación* states simply, 'Segund obraren, ansy gosaran.' The motif is so common that few readers would have difficulty understanding the following passage from the *Visión* even though words are missing in the manuscript: 'Propia justicia e verdadera que aquella ley es ally que ordeno nuestro sennor dios el qual da a cada una syn falla su [] segund lo merece.'[25] It is this apocalyptic cliché that underlies the imagery of the *Danza*, and that some scholars have described as the topos 'world upside down.'[26] In the *Danza* those who took vain pride in their physical beauty are made hideous, those who lived in fine palaces are given homes in stinking tombs, those who ate fine food are eaten by worms; the motif is stated as early as the tenth stanza of the poem.

It is not as easy to demonstrate convincingly the relationship of the dancing element of the *Danza* to the apocalyptic tradition as to account for the element of the estates. Florence Whyte argued that the dancing element was introduced by means of dancing songs, like 'Ad Mortem festinamus,' which were designed to lure the faithful away from more attractive secular songs and dances. But this argument did not convince critics like Pedro Bohigas; who commented that 'podríamos considerar este poema como un punto de partida de la *Danza de la Muerte* si en su *texto* descubriésemos un atisbo de la situación que constituye la esencia de esta obra y que más arriba hemos enunciado: la Muerte invitando a danzar con ella a los diferentes estados sociales. Faltando este elemento en el texto del *Ad Mortem festinamus*, resulta impropio hablar de su "dancing element."' Robert Eisler argued that the dancing element was a contribution of Jewish burial societies from which the word *macabre* derives. But Felix Lecoy rejected Eisler's etymological suggestions and concluded 'qu'il aura du mal á convaincre qui que soit que la *Danse de Morts* est, en réalité et à l'origine, une "danse des fossoyeurs."' Fehse had suggested in 1907 that the dance element has its origin in a belief that the dead leave their graves at night and persuade the living to dance with them. Eisler seemed to agree with him, but Whyte was not entirely convinced. Leo Spitzer proposed a combination of the belief in the dancing dead and of legends of the 'Wild Hunt,' but Hans Sperber found problems with this idea. More recently Deyermond has argued that epidemic hysteria and the medieval world view about the dance of the cosmos may have contributed to the origin of the dancing element in the dance of death.[27]

In the face of this richly varied constructive counterpoint, it is neither easy nor necessary to attempt a definitive solution to the question of the origin of the dancing element in the dance of death. Dance is such a natural and universal human reaction to the life cycle that its origin needs, and perhaps can have, no satisfactory detailed explanation. In addition to the death dance in medieval Europe cited by Deyermond, more recent examples attest to the universality of dance as a reaction to apocalyptic beliefs about death. Black Americans have sung, and often danced to, the Negro spiritual about the connection of the bones of the human skeleton, which is based on the apocalyptic passage in Ezekiel 37 about the valley of dry bones. Towards the end of the nineteenth century American Indians created a ghost dance which was rooted in their ancient messianic belief but prompted by a contemporary apocalyptic message that they would regain the lands they had lost to white settlers.[28]

In the light of the universality of dance as a reaction to crisis, it is not at all unexpected that the author of the *Danza* has the preacher announce, without explanation, that Death is about to hold a dance. The author would assume that the audience would find nothing strange about such an announcement; the fact that twentieth-century critics bother to search for the origins of such a dance is a telling statement about the sedentary nature of our profession. Yet, although it is unnecessary to explain the origin of the dance, the author is somewhat specific about its nature: this is to be a 'dança esquiva,' an unwelcome dance that will cause most people to recoil. The author also repeats several times that no one will escape this dance, which means much more than the fact that everybody must die at some time or other; since the dance is 'general' and not many individual dances, the reference here is to the apocalyptic belief that in the Last Days all persons will die at the same time at the hands of the Angel of Death. In other words, the third element of *Danza* is not what Whyte called 'the imminence of Death.'[29] More precisely the third element is the apocalyptic death described in Revelation 14:13–20 and elsewhere; it is the death Berceo described as happening on the thirteenth of the last fifteen days of the world ('Del trezeno fablemos, los otros terminados. / morran todos los omnes, menudos e granados / mas a poco de termino seran resucitados, / por venir al Judicio justos e condenados'). In terms of the history of literary composition, therefore, *Danza* can be described as a variety of apocalyptic narrative that elaborates on the belief summarily expressed in the twentieth stanza of Berceo's *Signos*.

Once the apocalyptic nature of *Danza* is admitted, at least four elements of its composition seem to yield greater meaning. It is clearer, first of all, that the preacher introduced by Death at the beginning of the poem plays the important role of the apocalyptic prophet who, like John in Revelation, is commanded to warn the people of the imminent end of the world and describe a vision of that end. Second, it is not accidental but part of the apocalyptic tradition that Death engages the victim in conversation. Death could have come silently, as in the famous poem by Antonio Machado upon the death of his wife, in which Death comes like a thief in the summer night and with surgical fingers, like Atropos, cuts the umbilical cord of life, robbing the poet of his precious jewel, the apple of his eye, without giving him a single word of explanation.[30] But in *Danza* Death calls upon the victims and answers their queries, in the apocalyptic tradition of Jewish and Christian accounts of the deaths of Moses and Abraham and of the Islamic account of the Malak 'l Mauti.[31]

Third, Death comes with a musical instrument in *Danza* (elsewhere she carried a sickle), partly because the most popular apocalyptic passage upon which this final reaping is based (Revelation 14) begins with the description of a loud sound of music ('Et vocem, quam audivi, sicut citharoedorum citharizantium in citharis suis. Et cantabant quasi canticum novum ante sedem,' vv. 2–3).[32] That only the select hundred and forty-four thousand who were singing this 'new song' could ever learn it is made explicitly clear ('Nemo poterat dicere canticum, nisi illa centum quadraginta millia, qui empti sunt de terra,' v. 3). This is probably why the rabbi in *Danza* is made to say, 'Mandad-me que dance, non entiendo el son.'[33] Although the passage in Revelation makes no specific mention about dancing, it is easy to understand that a poet would assume that the song and musical arrangement were accompanied by a dance, the dance of the blessed.

Fourth, classic apocalyptic literature offers a possible explanation for why members of the powerful estates are prominent among those invited to dance by Death. This explanation is based on the fact that the verses in Revelation 14 describing the awesome 'new song' are immediately preceded by an account about the making of the image of a beast which is worshipped by members of all estates ('Et faciet omnes pusillos, et magnos, et divites, et pauperos, et liberos, et servos habere characterem,' Revelation 13:16). This text was automatically compared with a popular apocalyptic text in Daniel in which King Nebuchadnezzar calls upon members of all the powerful estates to worship his image ('Tunc congregati sunt satrapae, magistratus, et iudices, duces et tyranni, et optimates qui erant in potestatibus constituti, et universi principes regionum, ut convenierent ad dedicationem statuae quam erexerat Nabuchodonosor rex,' Daniel 3:3).[34] In both biblical texts the righteous who failed to worship images were threatened with death. In Daniel 3:4–7 the signal for worship was sound from all manner of musical instruments, and the punishment was death in a fiery furnace.

What we seem to have in the *Danza*, therefore, is a typical apocalyptic composition in which the punishment is made to reflect the nature of the crime. In other words, the members of the powerful estates who had been guilty of responding to the music of idol worship are called upon to respond to a new and different music they cannot understand, and ultimately, like the usurer, they are to be tossed into a 'fuego infernal.'[35] Those who are likely to be saved, like the monk, welcome the new sound. Specific references to these apocalyptic passages were probably included in earlier versions of the topic, and may have been omitted from versions like the *Danza* for reasons similar to those that may have dictated the omission of reference to the preacher in the version of the *Danza* printed in Seville in 1520. Even if the conjecture about the estates were proved incorrect, the apocalyptic composition of the *Danza general de la Muerte* would still remain intact.

Libro de Alexandre

We have seen thus far that within the apocalyptic tradition, mention may be made briefly of the various estates of society, as in Berceo's *Signos* and the body-and-soul narratives, and that the various estates may be treated more elaborately, as in the *Danza*. Another obvious variation of the theme of the estates would be to isolate and develop one of the estates. Three notable examples of this variation, which have not been analysed as apocalyptic works, are the *Libro de Alexandre* (about the demise of an emperor), the *Poema de Fernán González* (about a famous Castilian count), and the *Libro del cavallero Zifar* (about a 'cavallero de Dios'). I hope to show how most, sometimes all, of the common apocalyptic elements help dictate the composition of these three works.

The composition of the *Libro de Alexandre* (*Alexandre*) has been carefully analysed by several scholars, some of whom will be mentioned. One of the best and most recent summaries explains that the work's 2,675 cuaderna-vía stanzas reveals 'a basic linear development, the narration of the life of Alexander the Great, but the poet has incorporated a second linear narrative, the story of the Trojan war, as well as other digressions of varying length and purpose. The result is not a simple structure but a composition of considerable complexity.'[36] Willis had noted correctly, and Michael has documented in detail, that key elements in the composition of *Alexandre* are the author's christianization and moralization of the source material.[37] After Michael's detailed documentation was published, Bly and Deyermond demonstrated conclusively that 'the supposed digressions ... [have] structural compatibility with the remainder of the poem ... and thematic importance. It is significant that in all but one of the cases where the poet goes beyond the normal Alexander tradition for his material, he does so in order to foreshadow the fate of his hero either by *figura* or by moral commentary: this is true of the Trojan story, of the Bestiary material, and of the moralizing on the state of the world.... The exception is the catalogue of precious stones with their properties (1468–92) included in the description of Babylon.'[38]

Bly and Deyermond need not have made an exception of the description of the precious stones of Babylon as moral commentary that foreshadows Alexander's fall: if they had been studying *Alexandre* as an apocalyptic work, they would certainly have noted that the fall of wealthy Babylon is one of the most popular apocalyptic themes found in, for example, Jeremiah and Revelation. The discussion of the properties of precious Babylonian stones in *Alexandre*, although possibly derived from Isidore's *Etymologiae*, is ultimately an elaboration of the description of the wealth of Babylon (including its precious stones) found in Revelation 18:10–20. *Alexandre* criticism has thus far established that Christianization and moralization are important elements of the poem's composition, but it has not as yet satisfactorily explained why the poet was attracted to Alexander the Great as a topic for Christianization and moralization when there were other topics that, at first glance, would have seemed more suitable. An immediate answer to this crucial question is that the Spanish poet was attracted to the topic because he was well aware of the importance of Alexander the Great as an apocalyptic figure.

Throughout the Middle Ages Alexander the Great was an important apocalyptic figure because his deeds were referred to in apocalyptic passages in the sacred writings of Judaism, Christianity, and Islam, and because these passages were constantly reinterpreted in order to make them suit apocalyptic needs at different times. The texts in question are found in Daniel 8:5–26, in which the prophet has a vision of a he-goat which is identified with Alexander; 1 Maccabees 1:1–8, in which Alexander's life and exploits are summarized; and the Koran 18:83–110, in which Alexander is identified as Dhul-Qarnain, who encloses Gog and Magog between two mountains. Related sacred texts are found mainly in Ezekiel 38–9 and Revelation 20:7–10, which discuss Gog and Magog. From these sacred texts and commentaries upon them, Alexander emerges in three main apocalyptic roles: first, as the person who encloses the tribes, either of Gog and Magog or of the Jews, that are to be temporarily loosed upon the world before the end of time; second, as a kind of devil, or Antichrist, who precedes the second coming of Christ; third, as an example, type, or figure of the Last World emperor who goes to Jerusalem to pay homage to God. These three roles were deliberately mixed by apocalyptic writers as historical circumstances changed.[39]

We can be certain that the author of *Alexandre* was fully aware of Alexander's apocalyptic role because he refers specifically on four occasions to the passage from Daniel (sts. 1145, 1339–40, 1536, 1800–1) and once to Judas Maccabeus (st. 1756); he takes great care to include the episode in which Alexander encloses the Jews (st. 2098–116); he repeatedly compares Alexander with a kind of devil (sts. 799, 1186, 1725, 2327, 2550), who is also a precursor of Christ (sts. 2441–2, 2664); and because he makes detailed reference to the visit of Alexander to Jerusalem during which he pays homage to a high priest who he believes is a messenger of God (sts. 1131–63).[40]

It will be argued that these references are also in the author's sources. In reply to this argument it should be pointed out that the author could have omitted any references he thought were insignificant; one of the references (to Judas Maccabeus, st. 1756) is original; and in two important instances (the visit to Jerusalem and the enclosing of the Jews) the author had to search for material outside of his principal source. For two apocalyptic passages (the enclosing of the Jews and the description of Babylon) the author takes care to tell the reader that he is making an extra effort to find material outside of his main source: 'Pero Galter el bueno en su versificar / sedia ende cansado e queria escansar / dexo de la materia mucho en es logar / quando lo el dexo quierolo yo contar' (st. 2098), and 'Ça Galter non las pudo mager quiso conplir / yo contra el non quiero nin podria venir / Pero fincan estas que non son de dexar' (sts. 1501–2). Yet, in spite of these indications of the author's special care to include apocalyptic material, not everyone will be convinced of apocalyptic intent in *Alexandre* unless such intent is found in the little material deemed to have originated with the Spanish author.

The evidence for apocalyptic intent in the ninety-one stanzas of *Alexandre* invented by the Spanish poet is, in my opinion, impressive.[41] These original stanzas are woven smoothly into the fabric of the composition at eight crucial points of the narrative:

(1)   At the beginning, to introduce the material (sts. 1–6)
(2)   To describe Alexander's education for the formidable tasks he is to perform (sts. 38–47)
(3)   To describe Alexander's physical appearance and record Darius's first reaction to it (sts. 145–59)
(4)   To describe the moral conclusions Alexander draws from the major ancillary episode – the Trojan War (sts. 762–72)
(5)   To note the moral conclusions made by the Spanish poet in reaction to the death of Darius (sts. 1805–30)
(6)   To describe the Queen of the Amazons (sts. 1872–9)
(7)   To provide an appropriate Spring setting for Alexander's marriage to Roxanne (sts. 1950–4)

(8)   To draw final moral conclusions after Alexander's death (sts. 2668–75).

In addition to these eight major original insertions, a passage of ninety-one stanzas (sts. 2334–424), although not entirely original, does contain much original material concerning the description of hell.[42]

The longest, and in many respects, most important, original passage in *Alexandre* (sts. 1805–30), after Darius's death, is unequivocally apocalyptic , as shown by the specific reference to 'el dia del juyzio' (st. 1820). These stanzas share with the body-and-soul narratives apocalyptic motifs pertinent to the death of a person of high estate. A debate or battle between body and soul, is hinted at in stanza 1809 ('Es de la carne señora el espíritu vencido'); the smallness of the grave, in stanza 1812, is found also on page 51 of the *Visión*, in lines 55–6 of the Paris *Revelación*, and in line 31 of the *Tractado del cuerpo e de la ánima*. The motif of contempt for the world expressed in these *Alexandre* stanzas is also an apocalyptic commonplace in the body-and-soul narratives, as noted earlier in this chapter. *Alexandre*'s long original section also shares with the apocalyptic literature discussed above, and especially with the *Danza general de la Muerte*, the denunciation of society by estates. There is a listing, between stanzas 1817 and 1828, of labradores, menestrales, bufones, usureros, reyes, príncipes, clérigos, calonges, monges, vasallos, señores, cavalleros, abades, and obispos.

The same (actually, the fifth) original section of *Alexandre* also provides valuable clues for the understanding of the apocalyptic undertone in the Spanish poet's other original insertions. For example, in stanza 1824, when the poet chides clerics like himself for lack of liberality ('en prender somos agudos en lo al perezosos'), we are given to understand more clearly the apocalyptic import of stanza 1, his first original stanza ('Señores sy queredes mi servicio prender / querryavos de grado servir de mi menester / deve de lo que sabe ome largo seer / sy non podría en culpa e en yerro caher'; note 'prender' in both quotations). For the Spanish poet, 'clerecía,' especially when it is 'syn pecado' (sts. 1–2, 4), is a powerful apocalyptic 'menester'; without 'clerecía' as many as ten generations might be condemned ('Non demandan hedat nin sen nin clericía / ... recúdeles la sangre bien a dies generaciones,' sts. 1825–7). In this light, therefore, the second original section – Alexander's description of his education as 'clerecía' (sts. 38–47) – also has a strong apocalyptic undertone: with the help of his 'clerecía' Alexander is able to see the plight of earlier generations ('entendió sus ahuelos qual cueyta pasavan,' st. 21), but is not completely successful in reversing their plight because his 'clerecía' is not 'syn pecado.' As will ˻ ˻

demonstrated later in this chapter, the idea of educating a perfect messianic prince to atone for the sins of the forefathers was well developed by apocalyptic writers.

The fourth original insertion, Alexander's moral conclusions on the Trojan war (sts. 762–72), the sin of the Greek forefathers is blamed on a woman ('los nuestros visahuelos por solo un pesar / por una mala fembra que se dexó forçar,' st. 768), and their effort to undo this sin is explained as a desire for either vengeance or fame ('por vengar su despecho o por prescio ganar,' st. 768).[43] Probably this ambivalence between vengeance and fame is what leads the author to describe Alexander's moral conclusions as strange ('estraños motes,' st. 763). On the one hand, vengeance would certainly not be compatible with apocalypticism unless it was God's (as, for example, in Isaiah 34:8, in which the Day of Vengeance is described as the Lord's: 'Quia dies ultionis Domini'), and the poet had expressed in Alexander's own voice, not many stanzas earlier, disapproval of vengeance 'Fiso con el despecho una grant crueldat / por vengarse de la ira olvidó piedat,' (st. 713). Fame, on the other hand, in the sense of doing good works that would be recorded, remembered, and ultimately judged, is one of the keystones of apocalyptic belief. In this fourth original insertion Alexander is shown to have practised the art of 'clerecía' ('es costunbre de los predicadores / en cabo del sermón adoban sus sermones,' st. 763), but his art, in the opinion of the Spanish poet, is strangely flawed on apocalyptic grounds.

The third, sixth, and seventh original passages, being simple descriptions, ought to have nothing to do with apocalyptic matters, but even here the Spanish poet finds a way to attach some apocalyptic remarks. In his original description of Alexander (sts. 145–59) he includes the different colours of the emperor's eyes ('El un oio ha verde e el otro bermeio,' st. 150), a detail that can be traced to an apocalyptic commentary on Daniel 8:5: ' "Et ecce hircus veniebat ab occidente, et non tangebat terram." Hic est Alexander quasi volans, per invia quaeque gradiens, ut hircus, ut ab hircis oculorum, quod diversi coloris habuit.'[44] In his original, even if stereotyped, description of Thalestris, Queen of the Amazons, the Spanish poet worries about causing others to sin ('a christiano perfeto torlía la pereza / ... temo fer alguno de voluntad pecar,' sts. 1876, 1879). And after his original May song for Alexander's wedding, the poet adds that songs like the ones sung by the ladies at home in Greece will be repeated 'fasta que venga Elías' (st. 1967), an apocalyptic reference to the popular Christian belief that Elias (Elijah) and Enoch will reappear in the last days to help battle the Antichrist.

The work's eighth and final original section (sts. 2668–75), after Alexander's death, for obvious artistic reasons includes some of the same apocalyptic motifs found in the longest and most important original insertions after Darius's death (sts. 1805–30). In stanzas 2672 and 1812 there is a reference to the smallness of the grave; manuscript O only refers, in stanzas 2675 and 1820, to the Day of Judgment;[45] and there is an interesting variation of the reference to the battle between body and soul in stanza 1809, which in stanza 2668 becomes a battle for survival between the body and fame ('sy murieron las carnes ... non murió el buen prescio'). The implication seems clear: Alexander's 'buen prescio' is what survives him, not his soul. The implication is reinforced by the use of 'alma' in stanza 2670 in a manner that indicates that Alexander might not have saved his soul because he was 'pagano de vida tan seglar' (st. 2667c), he placed too much trust 'en este siglo,' (st. 2670b) and on 'la gloria deste mundo' (st. 2671a), and his emphasis on worldly power was so excessive 'que en mares nin tierra non podie caber' (st. 2672ab). The repetition of words having to do with earth, as opposed to heaven ('seglar,' 'siglo,' 'gloria deste mundo,' 'mares,' 'tierra'), seems to imply that Alexander might have earned 'buen prescio' on earth merely to lose his soul to hell ('el peor lugar,' st. 2671d).[46]

The Spanish poet takes care to conclude in a manner clearly consistent with his apocalyptic beliefs, not with the 'contrarios motes' with which he believed Alexander had concluded (st. 763). He chooses his final words with careful symmetry. The 'Criador' is 'rey de gloria' (st. 2669), and Alexander is 'rey de grant poder' (st. 2672). The 'Criador' 'lives' y regna en complida victoria' (st. 2669); Alexander is dead in a small grave, defeated by 'la gloria desti mundo' that has thrown him in 'el peor lugar' when he thought he was most secure (st. 2671), as a 'buen rey' (st. 2669) with 'buen prescio' (st. 2668). Much that has been written about 'buen prescio' in *Alexandre* documents the concern with fame but omits the overriding concern with apocalypticism.[47] When the text says, for example, that 'qui muere en buen prescio es de buena ventura / que lo meten los sabios luego en escriptura' (st. 2668), the credited sources are not only writers like Gauthier de Châtillon, but especially apocalyptic writers like Daniel and the author of Maccabees who, for the poet, must have carried greater authority; 'escriptura' in stanza 2668 includes the biblical sense in which 'escripto' is used a few stanzas earlier ('como dis el escripto de Dios nuestro senor,' (st. 2664).

If we are to judge by the inclusion of some apocalyptic references in all eight passages deemed to have originated with the author of *Alexandre*, we should conclude that the topic attracted the poet not simply because of Alexander's chivalresque 'buen prescio,' but especially because of the belief in his role as an apocalyptic instrument of God, a role in which he appears in the sacred writings of Jews, Christians, and Muslims.[48] Alexander, in the eyes of the Spanish poet, achieved 'buen prescio' because he was an instrument of God, but in spite of this he lost his soul because, like Lucifer, he challenged God with pride ('nunca mayor sobervia comidio Lucifer,' st. 2327). God's judgment of Alexander is like judgments in which the punishment is made to fit the crime, which we have seen in other apocalyptic works: 'El sopo la soberbia de los peces judgar / la que en sý traxo non la sopo asmar / ome que tantos sabe judicios delibrar / por qual juysio dio por tal deve pasar' (st. 2330). The emperor who ruled all the world is himself ruled by 'sobervia,' the empress of all the vices ('de los vicios enperadris,' st. 2407).

The reference to pride as empress of the vices appears in the long passage that is not completely original with the Spanish poet (the stanzas between 2334 and 2424). This passage combines the third and fourth of the eight most common apocalyptic elements listed early in this chapter: the journey to Hell, and virtues and vices. With respect also to the latter element, it should be noted that passing reference is made in stanza 200 to journeys to Rome for pardons, and that Darius's prayer in stanzas 1703–9 is a confession. Alexander, however, never confesses; his last words constitute a sermon (st. 2622) and a testament (st. 2634) which are full of pride but not of contrition. Of the first two elements, precise dates in connection with visions or prophecies are found in only stanza 1338, and allegorical interpretation of time occurs only in stanza 1799. Attempts have been made to use this stanza to date the poem's composition, but the stanza is garbled in both manuscripts, because either a scribe erred or the writer, like Berceo, did not wish to attempt to solve the secrets of God, a sin for which he condemns Alexander. The elements concerning esoteric books and eschatological signs are covered by the esoteric references to Daniel. The final element, the resurrection and judgment of the dead, is referred to in stanza 1813.[49]

The messianic hope for a perfect ruler is of course the element in 'Criador que es rey de gloria / que bive e rregna en complida victoria,' but I should like to speculate about another possibility. Whatever the story of Alexander was in the sources he used, the Spanish poet composed out of it an apocalyptic narrative about a king who inherits a kingdom from his father, liberates it from the Arabs, and subjugates the Jews. After he has restored his country's independence, the king remains dissatisfied. When he attempts to make himself emperor of not only the world but the entire universe, the king loses his life and soul. Since apocalyptic writers sought to reinterpret history in such a way that perceptive readers could apply contemporary circumstances to past events, it is tempting to speculate that the Spanish poet intends a comparison of Alexander with Alfonso el Sabio.[50] Alfonso was called El Sabio because, like Alexander, he pursued knowledge zestfully, and, like Alexander, he also inherited a kingdom from his father – Fernando el Santo – who had begun to liberate Spain from the Moors. In 1256, a brief four years after he was crowned and before he had completed the reconquest, Alfonso began to nurture ambitions of becoming Holy Roman Emperor.[51] The Spanish poet, who makes Alexander favour Spaniards over other peoples (st. 2609), probably considered Alfonso a Spanish Alexander, perhaps the Last World emperor who would precede the Antichrist in preparation for a messianic age.

    This analysis of the composition of the *Libro de Alexandre* has made reference to the entire work, but has concentrated particularly on the few stanzas (182 out of 2675) that contain long original passages by the Spanish poet. However, a careful edition of the entire poem would yield other apocalyptic references.[52] Two such examples chosen at random are the reference in stanza 2533 to the apocalyptic valley of Jehosaphat mentioned in Joel 3: 1–12; and the motif, in stanza 2646, of the corpse being thrown on the ground when the soul leaves the body, a motif found in at least one other apocalyptic narrative and probably implied in others.[53] This ritual treatment of a corpse is a custom rooted in Jewish eschatological beliefs and appropriated by medieval Christians; it has little or nothing to do with humility, as claimed by María Rosa Lida de Malkiel, and less to do with a 'regal way of dying,' as proposed by Michael.[54] These two examples, in addition to those cited earlier, indicate that apocalyptic references are found throughout the poem. Even if the hypothesis about Alfonso el Sabio as a Spanish Alexander be proven unfounded, there are grounds, nevertheless, for claiming apocalyptic influence on the composition of the *Libro de Alexandre.*

Poema de Fernán González

A recitation of the deeds of Alexander the Great would have been one excellent way to remind thirteenth-century Spaniards of apocalyptic acts against the Moors. But since Alexander was neither Christian nor Spaniard, an even more efficient way would have been to recite the deeds of a Spanish hero who could be compared, accurately or not, with Alexander. This is what the anonymous author of the *Poema de Fernán González* (*Fernán González*) seems to have had in mind.

Fernán González has survived incomplete in a codex belonging to the Escorial, and exactly how much of the poem has been lost cannot now be ascertained. Some 736 cuaderna-vía stanzas, in whole or in part, are copied in the Escorial version; another thirty-two stanzas are believed to have been omitted by the copyist from the body of the poem, and an unknown number of stanzas have been lost at the end of the manuscript.[55] The contents of the lost stanzas can be reconstructed to some extent from the *Primera crónica general*, which used *Fernán González* extensively from stanza 171 to the end. Although the incomplete nature of the text has hampered analysis of the poem's composition, studies have noted a tripartite structure.[56] Part 1 (sts. 1–190) summarizes the history of Spain from the Gothic kings to Fernán González; Part 2 (sts. 191–573) tells how Fernán González defeated the Muslims and the Navarrese; and Part 3 (st. 574–end) tells mainly how Fernán González liberated Castile from León. At least two interesting questions remain about the composition of *Fernán González* in spite of the studies completed thus far. If the poem is about the count, Fernán González, then why does the poem include such a long introductory section about the Gothic kings, and does it end with the liberation of Castile from León, or with the death of the count? Some advances can be made towards definitive answers to these and possibly other questions if the composition of *Fernán González* is analysed in the light of the apocalyptic tradition.

Direct explicit reference to classical apocalyptic literature is almost nonexistent in *Fernán González*. However, it is possible, with editorial intervention, to read in stanza 15 of the manuscript a significant reference to the apocalyptic Gog in 'Venieron estos godos de parte de oryente ... del linaje de godos vyno aquesta gente.' Editors, from Marden on, have corrected the second 'godos' to read either 'Magog' or 'Gog,' based on the fact that the chroniclers understood the Goths to be descendants of Gog and Magog. The chroniclers, of course, derived this information directly or indirectly from commentaries on the apocalyptic books of Ezekiel and Revelation. In Spain Isidore of Seville and Apringius of Beja are among the writers who identified Gog and Magog with the Goths.[57]

For Apringius, who is cited by Isidore as one of the foremost authorities on the subject, the passage from Ezekiel and Revelation were intimately linked, and they had specific reference to Spain ('quia Mosoch Cappadociam significat, Thubal autem Hispaniam').[58] Since these apocalyptic passages prophesy the downfall of Gog and Magog, Apringius, in quintessential apocalyptic style, probably intended his commentary as a political attack upon the Goths who had invaded his country approximately a century and a half before he wrote his work.[59] More than seven hundred years later, that is, after Apringius's interpretation had come true, the anonymous poet of *Fernán González* seems to remember the biblical prophecy. For him the Goths were not nearly as heretical as for Apringius ('non fueron estos godos de comienço cristianos / ... Fueron de sancty spyritus los godos espyrados / ... Quando los rreyes godos deste mundo pasaron / fueron se a los cielos gran rreyno eredaron,' sts. 16, 20, 25). Their descendants, however, in the eyes of the author of *Fernán González*, were guilty of grievous error, which is why the biblical prophecy came true and they were defeated by the Moors ('por nuestro mal sentydo en gran yerro caymos. / Sy nos tales fuesemos como nuestros parientes / non avryan poder aquestas malas gentes,' sts. 98–9).

Stanzas 98 and 99 imply that the prophets referred to in stanza 77 ('ca les fue de los profectas esto profetizado') must be Ezekiel and John of Patmos. The line is not likely to refer to Muslim prophets, as some editors have claimed, because the fiercely Christian poet, who would not have attributed such divine prophetic accuracy to Muslims, makes it clear that God arranged the downfall ('Era la cosa puesta e de Dios otorgada / que seryan los de España metidos a espada,' st. 80).[60] These two stanzas also imply that stanza 80, with its reference to destruction by the sword, is probably a reference to Ezekiel 39:23 ('et ceciderint in gladio universi') from which the idea 'universi' is captured by the poet in 'moryeran los cristianos todos,' st. 83). The melting of the Gothic weapons in a huge fire (st. 63) probably echoes Ezekiel 39:9 ('et succendent et comburent arma'), and the shaking of the earth and the heavens in stanza 82 ('e las tierras e los cielos semejavan movydos') recalls an event in Ezekiel 38:19–20 ('Quia in die illa erit commotio magna super terram Israel ... et subvertentur montes cadent sepes').

In the passage from Ezekiel it is clear that the prophet understands the land inhabited by the descendants of Gog and Magog to be Israel. Later apocalyptic writers therefore had to understand Israel, symbolically, to mean the people chosen by God, for only in this way could Ezekiel's prophecy be applied to their own lands. This symbolic application is precisely what the poet does: in *Fernán González* Spain becomes Israel and the Castilians are God's chosen people. Spain, like Israel, is a promised land full of the best of everything (sts. 145–6), and of Spain, Castile is the best region (st. 157), the centre, as is Jerusalem of Israel (Ezekiel 5:5). Spain, like Israel, has judges (like Nunno Rasura, st. 165), kings (like Pelayo, st. 115), prophets (like Fray Pelayo, st. 236), and great warriors (like Bernaldo del Carpyo, st. 132, and especially Fernán González, who fights like a Spanish David against the Moorish Goliath, st. 267, and parts the waters miraculously like Moses, st. 359). The kings of Spain, like those of Israel, sometimes forget God (st. 399), and the people of Spain sometimes complain to their leaders (st. 423, among others) as did the Israelites to Moses and Joshua. As he did for the great leaders of Israel, God shows his displeasure miraculously when Fernán González surrenders (sts. 604–5); and God's grace makes Fernán González invincible before Moors and Christians (st. 768).

Not everyone may be convinced by these links between the text of *Fernán González* and classical apocalyptic literature: some may reject reading 'Gog' for 'godos,' and others may prefer to argue that the references to Ezekiel and Revelation are imposed upon rather than invited by the text of *Fernán González*. Let such doubtful readers consider that the strongest argument for placing *Fernán González* firmly within the apocalyptic tradition is the anonymous author's interpretation of past events in such a way that intelligent readers will realize their application to current affairs. In this regard several critics have demonstrated that *Fernán González* has more to do with thirteenth-century Spain than the time of Fernán González.[61] It is difficult not to deduce, from María Eugenia Lacarra's conclusions, that the author of *Fernán González* has shaped historical details about the count's dealings with the Moors, the Navarrese, and the Leonese in such a way that his poem is less a chronicle of Fernán González's rule than a political program for Alfonso X. This technique is common among apocalyptic writers.

Two other interrelated factors link *Fernán González* to the apocalyptic tradition: the poem's relationship to the *Libro de Alexandre*, and Fernán González's attitude towards death. About the first point there can be little doubt: several scholars have pointed to the many textual similarities between *Fernán González* and *Alexandre*.[62] Alexander is one of several heroes with whom Fernán González is compared in the poem (sts. 351, 357, 437), and it is hardly likely that the staunchly Christian poet of *Fernán González* would not have been aware of Alexander's apocalyptic role as outlined in the books of Daniel and Maccabees; the last line of stanza 357 ('de Judas el Macabeo fyjo de Matavyas') sounds like a paraphrase from memory of 1 Maccabees 3:1 ('Et surrexit Iudas, qui vocabatur Machabeus, filius eius [i.e., Mathathiae]'). Another possible apocalyptic link between *Fernán González* and *Alexandre* is the legend that fire fell from heaven on Alexander's army.[63] In *Fernán González* (sts. 471–86) the Castilians see in the sky a serpent that spits fire upon their camp. They awaken the sleeping Fernán González, who interprets the portent, without having seen it, as the work of the Devil who will try in vain to help the Moors. In *Alexandre* the legend seems to take the form of a dream that Darius had, which he later relates to his men in order to assure them of victory over Alexander (sts. 951–3). These stanzas from *Fernán González* and *Alexandre* are reminiscent of John's vision of the apocalyptic beast (Revelation 13:13) that has the diabolical power to spout fire on earth.

At first glance it seems that Fernán González's attitude towards death is similar to Alexander's. The topos that death spares no one, found in all the apocalyptic narratives discussed so far in this chapter, is expressed also in *Fernán González* (sts. 210, 313, 355) and *Alexandre* (sts. 72, 771). In both poems the leader urges his men to fight without fear of death since to die while doing good works is desirable. Yet when they hear how they will die, both Alexander and Fernán González do not welcome death bravely but seek to prolong life. Alexander asks the tree of the moon for details about his assassination so that he might avoid it (st. 2492), and Fernán González chooses prison over death in the face of García's ultimatum (st. 604). Indeed, God's displeasure (shown when the church's altar is rent in st. 604) may be expressed at Fernán González's less-than-brave decision as well as García's treatment of the count. His choice of imprisonment is the only instance in the poem when Fernán González openly avoids death. Part of the reason for this avoidance, of course, is the fulfilment of Fray Pelayo's prophecy, although Fernán González could have been taken captive while fighting; instead he is made to surrender, explicitly, to save his life, when he had previously condemned to Hell anyone who had made such a treacherous decision (sts. 449–50).

The mention of Hell in stanzas 449–50 might not be without consequence for the composition of the work. On the whole, the Castilians under Fernán González suffered much greater loss of life than did the Greeks under Alexander. This greater loss has lead María Eugenia Lacarra to conclude that the poet of *Fernán González* was not attempting to incite the Castilians to war against the Moors, who were no longer a serious threat by the time of the poem's composition around 1275.[64] This conclusion, though understandable, is at least open to question, because it does not take into account the apocalyptic factor stated clearly in *Fernán González*. There is much death among the Castilians because, on the one hand, being taken prisoner through fear of death meant being condemned to Hell for treachery (sts. 450–1) and, on the other hand, dying on the battlefield meant entering paradise 'Todos los mis vasallos que aqui son finados / serian por su senor este dia vengados / todos en parayso conmigo ayuntados,' st. 559). The main difference between the attitudes towards death in *Alexandre* and

Fernán González is illustrated by Alexander's promising his men only 'buen prescio' (st. 2668) and Fernán González's apparent ability to guarantee his men salvation in a Christian paradise. The sine qua non for such salvation in all apocalyptic literature is confession or some form of penance, the fourth apocalyptic element listed earlier in this chapter. It is no accident that proud Alexander never confesses, whereas Fernán González and his men are carefully described as doing so 'Levantaron se todos misa fueron a oyr / confesar se a Dios sus pecados descrubrir,' st. 487).[65]

In the light of these apocalyptic details, it should now be possible to attempt to answer the two questions posed earlier about the composition of *Fernán González*. Analysis of the poem as an apocalyptic narrative reveals that the long introductory section about the Gothic kings, the subject of the first question, becomes an essential part of the composition, which documents how the ancestors of the apocalyptic hero caused the divine disfavour that is to be remedied. In other words, the episode about Rodrigo and the Gothic kings is to *Fernán González* what the episode about the Trojan War is to *Alexandre*. This conclusion is not at odds with the suggestion that the introduction makes *Fernán González* resemble chronicles that aim to begin at the beginning: many apocalyptic works, because of their pretensions to historical accuracy, read like chronicles.[66] In the light of the apocalyptic attitude towards death in the poem, the answer to the second question lies in the likelihood that *Fernán González* ends with not the liberation of Castile from León but the death and judgment of Fernán González. In other words, *Fernán González* probably ends in a manner not unlike the end of *Alexandre*, but with the important difference that of Fernán González, as of his early Gothic ancestor, Vanba, the poet might well have written, 'En paraýso sea tan vuen rey eredado' (st. 32).[67] This answer would confirm, with apocalyptic arguments, what Lacarra concluded from an examination of the *Primera crónica general*: 'Terminar el poema con el entierro de Fernán González era más lógico y coherente con los planes del autor.'[68]

It would be helpful to reiterate at this point the nature of the relationship of the *Poema de Fernán González* with the apocalyptic tradition of literary composition in Spain. One key to understanding that relationship is the *Alexandre*. The poet of *Fernán González* knew the *Alexandre*, and judging from his references in stanzas 351, 357, and 437, he interpreted Alexander's role in an apocalyptic manner. He also knew that Alexander and his country were pagan. He sought, therefore, to describe the apocalyptic deeds of a Christian, Spanish Alexander. The choice of Spain is fitting in an apocalyptic context because for many writers (Isidore, Apringius, Augustine, among them), Spain is the country referred to in the apocalyptic passages of Ezekiel 38:1–3 and Revelation 20:7–8 in which Gog and Magog (the Goths and the Moors) will be defeated in final apocalyptic battles.

Since it is based on common knowledge, this hypothesis does not have to be supported explicitly in the text of *Fernán González*, although, in my opinion, it is, if one agrees that 'las primeras profetas' (l. 12a) are Ezekiel and John and that 'godos' (l. 15c) should read 'Gog or Magog.' Even if one does not accept direct reference in the text to Gog or Magog and to Ezekiel and John, it is still clear from the text that Spain becomes the new Israel with which, through a new Moses, God makes a new covenant to set free his people who, because of the sins of their forefathers had fallen into the hands of their captors. In other words, *Fernán González* is not simply an epic, like the *Cid*, although it obviously has epic elements; more precisely, it is an apocalyptic work patterned after apocalyptic passages in Ezekiel and Revelation and after another apocalyptic work, the *Alexandre*. Perhaps the case would be easier to make if the entire text were available, but, in my judgment, the text as it survives identifies itself adequately with the apocalyptic tradition.

Libro del cavallero Zifar

As I write this section I note (tongue seriously in cheek) that it has been about ten years since I first laid siege to the impenetrable *Libro del cavallero Zifar* (*Zifar*). After ten years my critical faculties, like Zifar's horse, seem to have fallen dead beneath me, just when I need them most. What is left of my critical instinct tells me that the full subtlety of this work will be appreciated only when a generation of Hispanomedievalists has been trained to be at home with the sacred writings, liturgy, and hermeneutics of Judaism, Christianity, and Islam. The reader is invited, therefore, to read in the interrogative 'mood,' not the indicative (proper punctuation notwithstanding) what I write about *Zifar*.

What does *Zifar* have to do with apocalypticism, and how can the apocalyptic tradition help us to understand the composition of *Zifar*? In an initial attempt to answer this question it can be stated that key ideas in *Zifar* are traceable to apocalyptic sources, and that these ideas dictate the structure of *Zifar*.

The author, in order to explain the lineage of Zifar, uses an apocalyptic text as his main source: the tenth chapter of the book of Genesis. Genesis 10 is an important apocalyptic passage partly because it mentions Magog in its second verse and partly because the chapter was also considered a messianic passage that links all the nations of the earth (Genesis 10:32) as one family. It is clear that the author of *Zifar* does not rely on Genesis alone for details but also on commentaries about Genesis. He includes, for example, opinions of Jewish authorities ('e otrossy dizen los judios,' p.37, l.11) which contrasts with Christian beliefs, ('pero los cristianos dezimos,' p.37, l.14), and states emphatically that a certain detail cannot be found in any source whatever, thus indicating that he might have access to other sources ('porque se non falla en escriptura ninguna que ...' (p.39, ll.25–6).[69]

These textual clues suggest that all the right places have not been sought for valuable source materials for *Zifar*. Such a search is not within the scope of this study, but all biblical passages with any connections to Genesis 10 should be examined, and especially all related medieval commentaries, including, of course, Aramaic commentaries in the Talmud and the Midrash, especially the Midrash Haggada. Only thus can the author's reference to a Chaldean source be fully verified. About whether or not scholars in Spain knew enough Aramaic to translate from that language, it should be noted that from the end of the tenth century onward and throughout the Middle Ages, Spain became the most important centre in the world for Judaic studies, including Aramaic and, of course, Old Testament studies.[70] At the time of the composition of *Zifar* there was much reason in Spain for interest in Aramaic. Alfonso X, el Sabio, had begun his *General Estoria*, which draws extensively upon the Old Testament, and at about the same time the *Zohar*, the bible of the Cabbalists, was being written in crabbed Aramaic. At about the same time in Christian circles a plan was being discussed for widespread instruction in Aramaic, which led at the Council of Vienne (1311–12) to the establishment of chairs in Hebrew, Greek, Arabic, and Chaldean at the University of Salamanca.[71]

Ferrán Martínez, the most likely candidate for authorship of *Zifar*, was a scribe in the Spanish court from 1274 (during the reign of Alfonso X to at least 1295.[72] Since the author of *Zifar* refers to extrabiblical details about the curse of Ham and Canaan (p.37, ll.11–16), it would not really be unexpected if Aramaic commentaries yielded more information about Zifar's strange curse. But even without the help of Aramaic sources, minor details about *Zifar* become clearer if greater attention is paid to Genesis 10 and related biblical passages. For example, the city of Safira, mentioned in the last chapters of *Zifar*, seems to take its name from the biblical Sephar (Genesis 10:30), which was written as Çafira and Çaafara in medieval Spanish Bibles.[73] The 'tierras de Çin,' which Walker claims 'is a clear reference to China, for which the

Arabic name is *sin*,' could be either of two places mentioned in Exodus 16:1 and 17:1, Numbers 13:21 and 33:11–12, Ezekiel 30:15–16 (some versions only), and Joshua 15:3.[74] More importantly, since both Zifar and Abraham were descendants of Shem, then the King Tared in *Zifar* (p.36, l.4) might be none other than the father of Abraham, Terah. Terah is written as Thare in the Vulgate and as Tareh and Taré in medieval Spanish Bibles (Genesis 11:31). In Joshua 24:2 we are told that Terah 'served other gods,' which corresponds with the statement in *Zifar* that Tared lost his kingdom 'por malas costumbres' (p.36, l.4). Whether or not Terah, the father of Abraham, is Tared the ancestor of Zifar, it remains clear that Abraham and Zifar share the same ancestry, which increases the likelihood that Zifar's journey from his homeland is meant to be a figure for Abraham's famous journey from Ur of the Chaldees.

This comparison with Abraham explains why Roboán's son, Zifar's grandson, is called Fijo de Bendición (p.514, l.24) and why Roboán's empire is called Tierra de Bendición (p.515, l.26), because God promised Abraham a blessing ('bendición') when he said, 'Go from your country and your kindred and your father's house to the land that I will show you. And I will make of you a great nation, and I will bless you, and make your name great, so that you will be a blessing. I will bless those who bless you and him who curses you I will curse; and by you all the families of the earth shall bless themselves' (Genesis 12:1–3). Roboán's achievement, therefore, and Zifar's, fulfil a messianic dream, not just for their family, but for 'all the families of the earth,' which is one reason why the sun does not set for seven days when the family is reunited at the story's messianic end (p.515, l.17).

A central theme in *Zifar* is that the sins of past generations can be redeemed by the good deeds of one member of a family. This is a key apocalyptic idea that, as has been discussed, appears in *Alexandre* and *Fernán González* and is operative as well in the excerpts about Abraham. The idea falls under what James F. Burke defines as the 'sermonic theme' of *Zifar*: '*redde quod debes* which means that every man must repay what he owes – to God as well as to his fellow man.' But Burke was convinced that *redde quod debes* was 'not a biblical verse', and he despaired of relating *Zifar* to the apocalyptic tradition: 'Due to an incomplete understanding of the social message of Lull and Villanova, not to speak of Joachim, it is impossible to exactly relate those elements of messianic thinking present in the *Zifar* to the tradition preceding it.'[75]

There is no pressing need to refer to Ramón Llull, Arnold of Villanova, or Joachim of Flora, since the author of *Zifar* leaves little or no doubt that he is thinking of Ezekiel 18. This classic apocalyptic chapter is one that the author of *Zifar* knew very well, as the following excerpt should indicate:

> If a man is righteous and does what is lawful and right – if he does not eat upon the mountains[76] or lift up his eyes to the idols of the house of Israel ... does not oppress anyone, but restores to the debtor his pledge [Vulgate: pignus debitori reddiderit], commits no robbery ... covers the naked with a garment ... executes true justice between man and man ... he is righteous, he shall surely live ... If he begets a son who is a robber, a shedder of blood, who does none of these duties ... does not restore the pledge [pignus non reddentem] ... he shall surely die ...
> But if this man begets a son who sees all the sins which his father has done, and fears, and does not do likewise, who does not eat upon the mountains ... exacts no pledge [pignus non retinuerit] ... he shall not die for his father's iniquity; he shall surely live. (Ezekiel 18:5–17)

What Burke calls *'redde quod debes'* is more correctly rendered as 'non tardabis reddere' (Deuteronomy 23:21), since Ezekiel 18 is based on the laws repeated in Deuteronomy 23 and 24, especially 24:16.

We can be sure that the author of *Zifar* has Ezekiel 18 in mind because he paraphrases the proverb cited in the second verse of the chapter ('The fathers have eaten sour grapes, and the children's teeth are set on edge') in two places at a key portion of his text. About those who have been traitors once, he writes, 'Ca los omnes que comieron agrazes con dentera fincan' (p. 328, ll. 14–15), and a few pages later he describes the Jews with the same proverb, 'Ca los sus auuelos comieron el agras e en ellos finco la dentera de la fealdat contra los fijos de Iesu Cristo' (p. 332, ll. 4–5). This last reference to Jews in terms of Ezekiel 18:2 is essential to the apocalyptic composition of *Zifar*, as will be explained later.

The passages in Ezekiel (and in other apocalyptic writings) that describe the punishment for disloyalty and disobedience are themselves derived from the book of Leviticus, which gives in greater detail the punishment that apocalyptic works merely summarize. Thus, Ezekiel 14:21, which lists apocalyptic punishment as 'four sore acts of judgment, sword, famine, evil beasts, and pestilence,' is a statement in brief of the famous 'tokaha' passage (Leviticus 26:14–45, restated in Deuteronomy 28) that elaborates upon the nature of the deterrents against disobedience: sickness, loss of food, beasts, siege, and diaspora.[77]

Zifar is composed in such a way that Zifar must overcome similar obstacles in order to redeem his family's inheritance. Leviticus describes the sickness as 'sudden terror, consumption, and fever that waste the eyes and cause life to pine away' (26:16). Zifar is not stricken with terror, consumption, or fever, but he does 'pine away' for a long time about his predicament (p. 16, ll. 23–4) before his wife persuades him to share it with her, because she had never before seen him in that state ('Çertas nunca vos vy flaco de coraçon por ninguna cosa que vos ouiesedes, sy non agora,' p. 15, ll. 25–6). The 'strength' of Zifar is 'spent in vain' (Leviticus 26:20) in the service of his king, and as a consequence he is unable to sustain himself ('La desventura corre comigo en me querer tener pobre y querer me enuilescer con pobreza,' p. 14, ll. 28–9); he is fed by a hermit and by the 'ribaldo' before he redeems himself (pp. 120, 123, 124, 135).

Leviticus 26:22 states clearly: 'And I will loose the wild beasts among you, which shall rob you of your children'; and Zifar lost his son Garfin to a lioness (p. 85). Leviticus 26:25 describes a terrible siege 'And if you gather within your cities I will send pestilence among you, and you shall be delivered into the hand of the enemy'; Zifar is not impeded by pestilence, but he is obliged to lift sieges against Galapia and Menton. Finally, Leviticus 26:33 describes a diaspora ('And I will scatter you among the nations'), and Zifar's family, like Abraham's, representative of a nation, is scattered among other nations before it is reunited in Menton.

The parallels are by no means exact, and I should make clear that I am not claiming here that Leviticus (or Genesis or Ezekiel) is a source for *Zifar* in the sense of an exact one-to-one relationship. Rather, I seek to demonstrate that the author of *Zifar* is moulding his source material around these biblical passages for the same apocalyptic reasons that the author of *Alexandre* Christianized and moralized the story of Alexander. We can be certain that the author of *Zifar* has Leviticus in mind because he writes, 'E dixo Dios que quien se desuiase del bien, desuiarse-ha el bien del' (p. 318, ll. 2–3), which paraphrases the central theme in Leviticus ('And if [you] walk contrary to me, then I also will walk contrary to you,' Leviticus 26:23, 27).

Once it is realized that the author is using Leviticus, other major and minor details about the composition of *Zifar* fall into place. It is in Leviticus 25:8–55, for example, that details about the jubilee year are found, and it is partly on this passage that the Pope derived his authority to reinstate the practice referred to in the prologue to *Zifar* (p. 1, ll. 3–13). The author emphasizes that this apocalyptic concept of a jubilee year, in which penance is made and pledges are redeemed, is a key element in the structure of his work, one that should serve as an example to its readers: 'E porende el trasladador de la estoria que adelante oyredes ... puso e ordeno estas dos cosas sobredichas en esta obra, porque los que venieren despues de los deste tienpo, sera quando el año jubileo a de ser, porque puedan yr a ganar los bien aventurados perdones que en aquel tienpo son otorgados' (p. 6, ll. 13–19). In Leviticus 25:2-7 is found the concept of the sabbatical year for the land, to which the author of *Zifar* makes brief but important reference when the 'ribaldo' tells his master: 'E non sabes tu que a canpo malo le viene su año?' (p. 123, l. 4). The entire episode in which the 'ribaldo' liberates himself from his master, the fisherman, is related to the apocalyptic idea of freeing slaves in the jubilee year, as explained in Leviticus 25:46–55.

It is also very important to understand that the two exempla about testing friends, which Zifar tells his wife in chapters 5 and 6, belong to a tradition of stories that were told in order to explain Leviticus 19:18, a verse that, for many, is the most important in the entire Bible (partly because it occurs at the very centre, the heart, of the Pentateuch): 'Thou shalt love thy neighbour as thyself.' The ancient rabbis often debated the limits to which this 'golden rule' should extend. Thus, in the oldest rabbinic commentary on Leviticus, the Siphra, is found the example of two friends who are stranded in the desert. One friend has enough water for one person to reach safety; should he share the water with his friend, which would mean that both would die? One rabbi, Ben Petura, thought the friend should share the water. But Rabbi Akiba ruled that in such a crisis one's own life is more important than the life of one's neighbour, or else the text would have read: 'Thou shalt love thy neighbor *more* than thyself.'[78]

It is precisely in the tradition of similar debates that the author of *Zifar* places the conversation between Zifar and his wife about whether one should share a problem with one's friends. Zifar at first thinks not, because he loves his wife more than himself: 'El cauallero, quando vio a su muger que amaua mas que a sy ... dixo: "¡Por dios! señora, mejor es que el vno sufra el pesar que muchos"' (p. 15, ll. 27–30). But his wife persuades him to confide in her, and Zifar then tells her two important exempla about knowing when to share and with which friend or neighbour. The versions of these exempla in *Zifar* preserve their connection with apocalypticism because the first account (about the 'medio amigo') takes the form of elders' instructions to a son, and the second (about the 'amigo entero') shows the murderer repenting when he thinks about 'el dia del juyzio' (p. 29, l. 19).

The golden rule was important enough to the structure of *Zifar* to

make the author return to the New Testament version of it in the
second section of the book when Zifar is defining charity to his sons:
'Ca caridat es amar ome su proximo verdaderamente' (p. 281, l. 17). The
author also weaves the golden rule into the fabric of the book by giving the 'ribaldo' the sobriquet 'Cavallero Amigo,' and making of him a
true friend who repeatedly risks his life (though not always gladly) for
his masters, Zifar and Roboán.

Another important link between Leviticus and the composition of
Zifar has to do with leprosy. Chapters 13 and 14 of Leviticus contain
the law of leprosy, and from this law was derived the concept of leprosy as an outward sign of a moral disease; the worst kind of moral disease was considered to be slander or treachery. Zifar is slandered by
his enemies at court in his native land (p. 12, ll. 2–7), and he later compares treason with leprosy: 'Onde sy los omes quesieren parar mientes
a saber que cosa es traycion, fuyrian de ella como de gafedat' (p. 222, ll.
1–3). Count Nason is punished like a traitor: he is maimed like a leper
before being burnt.[79]

Yet another minor but important connection between Leviticus and
the composition of Zifar is concerned not just with the lifting of
sieges, but especially with doing so with far fewer men than the enemy's forces. Zifar is usually outnumbered, as, for example, when he is
faced with having to lift the siege at Galapia 'con ciento caualleros de
buenos cuydaria acometer con la merced de Dios mill caualleros de
non tan buenos,' p. 51, ll. 2–4). His son Roboán, who also fights with
inferior numbers, 11,000 against the 15,000 of the king of Grimalet
(pp. 403–4), similarly credits his victory in such impossible circumstances to the help of God ('Nos non tenemos esperança que nos venga
acorro de ninguna parte, saluo de Dios tan solamente e la verdad que
tenemos,' p. 404, ll. 29–30). When Zifar and Roboán rely on God's help
they rely as well on the promise in Leviticus 26:8 that 'five of you shall
chase a hundred, and a hundred of you shall chase ten thousand; and
your enemies shall fall before you by the sword.'

The most important link between Zifar and the apocalyptic tradition is that the author of Zifar, like the authors of Alexandre and Fernán González, is commenting upon contemporary circumstances in
Spain even as he pretends to be telling a story that occurred in the
past. He expects intelligent readers to hold a mirror up to his story
and draw conclusions about their own circumstances: 'Asy como los
padres santos fezieron a cada uno de los sieruos de Iesu Cristo ver
commo por espejo e sentir verdaderamente e creer de todo en todo que
son verdaderas las palabras de la fe de Iesu Cristo, e maguer el fecho
non vieron ... E porende el que bien se quiere leer e catar e entender lo

que se contiene en este libro sacara ende buenos castigos e buenos enxiemplos' (p. 10, ll. 16–24). The reference to the mirror is, of course, reminiscent of Paul's first letter to the Corinthians, 'for now we see in a mirror dimly, but then face to face,' (13:12). But it is pertinent to remember that Paul's reference is based on Numbers 12:8, which exemplies leprosy as a punishment for slander.

Francisco Hernández has succeeded in unveiling some of the thirteenth-century concerns over which the author of *Zifar* has thrown a subtle 'fermosa cobertura.' Hernández documents convincingly that the exemplum in chapter 170 of *Zifar* about an 'emperador desheredado' fits similar circumstances in the reign of Alfonso x as well as it applies to *Zifar*; that chapter 171 of *Zifar* reflects contemporary concerns about the office and duties of the chancellor of Castile; that chapter 154 of *Zifar* is written in such a way as to make an analogy with the minority reign of the grandson of Alfonso x, Fernando IV; and that there were Jews whom Ferrán Martínez had reason to resent. These associations are not simply an example of the author's environment seeping its way through, naturally and casually, to the fabric of his composition; they represent, rather, a deliberate use of the apocalyptic technique that we have seen at work in *Alexandre* and *Fernán González*.[80]

The authors of the latter works drew upon past historical accounts: the life of Alexander the Great and the exploits of Fernán González, respectively. The author of *Zifar* notifies his readers that he deliberately chooses an account that many will consider fictitious, but he warns against disregarding the serious moral implications of his choice: 'E porque este libro nunca aparesçio escripto en este lenguaje fasta agora, nin lo vieron los omes nin lo oyeron, cuydaron algunos que non fueran verdaderos las cosas que se y contienen, nin ay provecho en ellas ... Pero commoquier que verdaderas non fuesen, non las deuen tener en poco nin dubdar en ellas fasta que las oyan todas complidamente e vean el entendimiento dellas' (pp. 9–10). In *Alexandre* and *Fernán González* the veiled apocalyptic message was to defeat the Moors, as Alexander and Fernán González had done. In *Zifar* the Moors have disappeared as a significant threat, and the apocalyptic instruction is to beware of the internal threat of treachery as exemplified in the Jewish advisors to the king.

The composition of the entire work is woven around this message. At the very core of Zifar's advice to his sons is a chapter (155) 'de commo se deven de guardar los reys de poner sus fechos en poder de judios nin de otro estrano de ley'; this is the fruit hidden inside the shell of the book ('Ca atal es este libro para quien bien quisiere catar por el, commo la nuez, que ha de parte de fuera fuste seco e tiene el fruto ascondido dentro,' p. 10, ll. 7–8).

The warning against treacherous Jewish advisors at the core of the 'Castigos del rey de Mentón' has important parallels in the other two sections of *Zifar*. Nasón, the traitor in the first section of the book, gets his Jewish name from 'the leader of the people of Judah' mentioned in Numbers 2:4.[81] Farán, the traitor in the third section of *Zifar*, gets his Jewish name from a leader of the Pharisees, according to the author ('Ca los fariseos tomaron el nonbre de Farán,' p. 330, ll. 19–20). Farán does not go to Mass, and engages in other unchristian activities (p. 494, l. 30).[82] The author takes care to establish the apocalyptic connection: Nasón's ashes are thrown into a 'lago solfareo' (p. 225, l. 9), that is, the kind of lake of fire and brimstone (sulphur) featured prominently in the apocalyptic book of Revelation (14:10, 19:20, 20:15, 21:8). Again on an apocalyptic note, Farán causes the 'ribaldo' to be sold into servitude (p. 492), from which he had already redeemed himself when he left his former master, the fisherman (p. 122).

The strong anti-Jewish content of *Zifar* is based in part on a misinterpretation of an apocalyptic cliché: the description of Israel by the prophets as a stubborn, rebellious people. Thus, the prophet Ezekiel, for example, is told: 'I send you to the people of Israel, to a nation of rebels, who have rebelled against me; they and their fathers have transgressed against me to this very day. The people also are impudent and stubborn' (Ezekiel 2:3–4). Later the author of Revelation varies the cliché in a manner that suits the apocalyptic purpose of the author of *Zifar*, for whom the Jews are Antichrist: 'I know your tribulation and your poverty (but you are rich) and the slander of those who say that they are Jews and are not, but are a synagogue of Satan' (Revelation 2:9). It is characteristic, therefore, that Nasón and Farán rebel against their lords.

After the studies of Scholberg, Walker, Burke, and Keightley, no serious question can arise about the aristic unity of *Zifar*.[83] In terms of the history of literary composition one question follows logically: what kind of artistic unit is *Zifar*? The evidence just presented should demonstrate that this thirteenth-century opus cannot be adequately described as an interlaced sermon, although, like many other medieval works, *Zifar* does contain interlacing and preaching modes of composition.[84] *Zifar*, it seems to me, is more aptly described as an apocalyptic narrative.

In terms of composition it would be more revealing to analyse how the author has arranged the apocalyptic elements that *Zifar* shares with Berceo's *Signos*, with the body-and-soul narratives, and with the *Danza, Alexandre,* and *Fernán González.* It is, of course, more closely aligned with the last two works than with the first three. With the *Signos,* the body-and-soul narratives, and the *Danza, Zifar* shares an emphasis on penance and confession, virtues and vices.[85] It is concerned with precise dates (the jubilee year 1300), allegorical interpretation of time (the seven nightless days at the story's end), description of an other-world (Islas Dotadas and the Enchanted Lake), reference to esoteric books (Chaldean sources), messianic hope for a perfect ruler, and eschatological signs in current political affairs. *Zifar* also takes for granted that the dead will be resurrected and judged. But obviously *Zifar* and the other apocalyptic narratives show important differences in composition. *Zifar,* like *Alexandre* and *Fernán González,* concentrates on what a person can do throughout life in order to insure a certain kind of afterlife; whereas the *Signos,* the body-and-soul narratives, and the *Danza* are concerned mainly with what happens when a person dies and afterward. Also, the messianic ruler in the *Signos,* the body-and-soul narratives, and the *Danza* is God himself, whereas in *Zifar,* as in *Alexandre* and *Fernán González,* the messianic ruler is a human being used by God as his instrument. Consequently, the criticism of current affairs in the *Signos,* the body-and-soul narratives, and the *Danza* is general; in *Zifar, Alexandre,* and *Fernán González* there are specific, though veiled, historical reasons for certain choices.

For example, the name Roboán was probably chosen because Rehoboam's father, Solomon, was called, like Alfonso X, the 'Wise King'; the choice of name seems to be a deliberate invitation to compare Zifar, his two sons, and his grandson (the 'fijo de bendición') with Alfonso X, his two sons (Sancho IV and the Infante Don Juan), and his grandson Fernando IV. The apocalyptic hope implied in this selection is probably that Fernando IV would inherit and maintain a redeemed 'tierra de bendición.' These emphases in the structure of *Zifar,* if it were to be an artistic success, called for a different arrangement of contents than that of the other apocalyptic narratives. With *Zifar* it was not a question of a day-by-day description of the last fifteen days of the world or of the separation of the soul from the body, a debate between the two, a judgment of both, and a moral conclusion; nor was it a question of listing the estates by rank and inviting each to dance with Death. Further, since the author of *Zifar* chose to discard the historical model used in *Alexandre* and *Fernán González,* he gave himself both the challenge and the opportunity to find a fictional model for his composition that would achieve an equally effective apocalyptic aim.

It remains to be verified whether the author found or invented the fictional model that supports the composition of *Zifar*. At present it can be stated that he used a fictional model that resembles the legend of Placidus and similar oriental tales, and that he moulds this material around the archetypal model of the biblical story of Abraham, who left Ur of the Chaldees and became a 'caballero de Dios' in order to redeem his family. The journey of Zifar, like that of Abraham, leads him from the hell of 'malas costumbres,' through the ups and downs of purgatory, to paradise. We can be certain that the author of *Zifar* intended this Dantesque arrangement because one of the most-repeated motifs throughout the entire work takes a form something like: bad beginning, mixed (good and bad) middle, and good end, or good beginning, mixed middle, and better end.[86]

We can be certain that this is not a simple Aristotelian arrangement of beginning, middle, and end because the 'ribaldo' explains its eschatological significance: '"Cavallero," dixo el ribaldo, "asy va ome a parayso, ca primeramente ha de pasar por purgatorio e por los lugares mucho asperos ante que alla llegue. E vos ante lleguedes a grant estado al que auedes a llegar, ante avedes a sofrir e a pasar muchas cosas asperas"' (p. 133, l. 10). Each of the principal characters (Zifar, Grima, Garfin, Roboán, and Ribaldo) makes a journey similar to the one the ribaldo describes, and the author invites readers, and Spain as a whole, to journey likewise by citing as an example in the prologue his own trying experience of redeeming, for Spain, from Rome the body of an important Spanish cardinal. The king of Spain, in particular, is invited to redeem the country by punishing its treacherous Jewish advisors.[87] In order to insure the maintenance of such a redemption, it is necessary that future kings be properly educated. This requirement is why the carefully written second section ('Castigos del rey de Mentón') is so crucial to the structure of the whole book; in this second section future Spanish kings pass through the refining fire of purgatory in order to learn about virtues and vices in order that they may later become perfect, messianic rulers.

Indeed, were it not for its fatal anti-Jewish flaw, *Zifar* might have been said to be the most beautifully composed work of medieval-Spanish literature. But lamentably, in the last analysis, the author of *Zifar* could be judged as he himself dispensed judgment: he accused the Jews of slander and treachery, but he himself treacherously slandered the Jews, using an apocalyptic technique of composition invented by them. Even as he accused the Jews of 'sotileza' and 'maestria' (p. 334, ll. 2, 5), the author's own subtlety and skill destroyed the artistic beauty of *Zifar*. But then, could any medieval Spaniard, whether Christian, Moor, or Jew, no matter how intelligent, have been expected to escape his circumstances and do other than condemn his neighbour of competing faith? From a twentieth-century point of view the artistry of the composition of *Zifar* can be understood, even if the book itself should not be condoned with praise.[88]

Libro rimado del palacio

Less than one hundred years after the appearance of *Zifar*, historical circumstances provided fresh and unexpected reason for a renewed interest in apocalypticism: in 1378 Robert of Geneva was elected pope while Pope Urban VI still reigned. 'The scandal of two popes competing for the leadership of Christendom could not but seem a confirmation of apocalyptic warnings concerning the approaching End ... The Schism bulks large in almost every apocalyptic text of the period after 1380.'[89] The chancellor of Castile, Pero López de Ayala, played an active role in trying to find an end to the schism, although he died before the matter was resolved. Ayala left a long work, the *Libro rimado del palacio* (*Rimado*), which falls indubitably within the apocalyptic tradition. The composition of this work has defied satisfactory explanation partly because it has never been analysed as an apocalyptic narrative.

Rimado has survived in two main manuscripts, neither of which is complete. From them can be reconstructed some 2,120 stanzas (mainly cuaderna-vía) of a work which can be divided into two main parts: stanzas 1–921, which consist of a rhymed confession, statements about current affairs, and a number of prayers and songs to the Virgin Mary; and stanzas 922–2170, which is an adaptation from the biblical book of Job and St Gregory's commentary on that book, the *Magna Moralia*.[90] Joset has been one of the first scholars to put forward a cogent argument for the unity of the entire work: 'La lectura del *Libro* enseña, de inmediato, una ley de composición básica, que es la alternancia entre *experiencia* y *doctrina* ... La ley de alternancia *experiencia-doctrina* se verifica al nivel global de la obra. En efecto, las coplas 1–921 corresponden, globalmente, al informe que da un hombre sobre su vida, y las coplas 922 y siguientes, a la doctrina fundada en la experienca'.[91] Without detracting from Joset's analysis, it is possible to improve upon it by explaining what *Rimado* has to do with apocalypticism.

Rimado justifies discussion of apocalypticism because the text makes significant direct reference to the Day of Judgment (repeatedly; for example, in stanzas 35, 144–51, 270, 304, 307, 570, 1015, 1018,

1195, 1265, 1412, 1582–3, 1687, 1692, 1694–6, 1805, 1813, 1826, 1998),
the Little Apocalypse of the Gospels (st. 147), and the Antichrist (sts.
1613–15, 1962). Armed with this justification, one may proceed to
examine the major elements of the composition of *Rimado*: a confession, statements about current affairs, a 'cancionero' to the Virgin
Mary, and, as already mentioned, an adaptation of material from Job
and Gregory's *Magna Moralia*. All of these four major elements serve
the author's apocalyptic aims, leaving little or no doubt that the author
intended to compose a unified apocalyptic narrative.

Confession is one of the most important of the list of elements of all
apocalyptic literature, and it has been seen as operative in all the
Spanish works discussed in this chapter as apocalyptic narratives. But
none of these works treats confession with the same attention to form
and detail that Ayala employs in *Rimado*. In the *Signos*, the body-and-
soul narratives, and the *Danza*, a confession is strongly urged upon
readers by example of the punishment meted out to those who did not
confess. It is possible to assume, from what the text of *Alexandre* says,
that Alexander lost his soul partly because his pride did not permit
him to confess; Fernán González, unlike Alexander, confessed repeatedly and saved his life. And the author of *Zifar* wrote the important
middle section of his work, the 'Castigos,' so as to have Zifar impress
upon his sons, and thus upon all readers, the inestimable value of confession. At the beginning of his 'Castigos,' Zifar tells the story of a
physician who gave to a king a recipe to cure sins; the recipe includes
the Ten Commandments, virtues and vices, and control over the body's
five senses.[92]

In none of these works has this element taken the form of a general
confession as outlined in manuals (like the one, described in chapter 2,
attached to the *Razón de amor*) written for the guidance of clerics and
parishioners; it is in this form of a general confession, however, that
Ayala chose to arrange the first important section of *Rimado*, setting a
tone, it would seem, that resounds throughout the entire work. Stanzas
7–190 are the rhymed confession of a 'yo' (not necessarily Ayala himself) who repents for having sinned against the Ten Commandments,
for having committed the seven mortal sins, neglected the works of
corporal and spiritual mercy, and indulged the body's five senses. This
arangement is an important development in the history of Spanish
literary composition, and there will be reason to refer to it again in the
chapters dealing with the *Corbacho*, the *Libro de buen amor*, and the
so-called sentimental novel.[93]

The next major section of *Rimado* is a statement about current
affairs (sts. 191–728), divided into affairs of the Church (sts. 191–233),

and affairs of state (sts. 234–728). Criticism of current affairs is a key element of apocalyptic literature, and this section of Ayala's work exemplies many of the clichés discussed earlier: *contemptus mundi* (st. 547), ubi sunt (st. 566), the idea that death spares no one (st. 554), the value of advice from elders and from young people (st. 691), dangers of a young king (st. 665),[94] anti-Jewish sentiment (sts. 245, 393, 404), the education of princes (st. 638), cardinal virtues (sts. 373–83), and a need for justice (especially stanzas 343–72). The structure of the section on current affairs has a faint resemblance to the structure of the *Danza* although in *Rimado* the estates are not ranked as rigidly. A case can be made for the following loose arrangement of the estates in *Rimado*: the pope (st. 193), cardinals (sts. 203, 229), prelates (st. 217), priests (st. 221), bishops (st. 230), the king (sts. 234, 236), princes, emperors, dukes, counts (st. 234), tax collectors (st. 243), knights (st. 260), advisors (sts. 272, 276), merchants (st. 298), learned officials like lawyers (st. 315), warmongers (st. 338), judges (st. 356), mayors (st. 364).

The main theme of the section on current affairs is the absence of justice in affairs of church and state, so, after the estates are listed and condemned, there is a section on the cardinal virtues that are necessary if justice is to be achieved (sts. 372–84). Following the section on virtues a long prayer (sts. 385–422) fits neatly into the section on worldly current affairs because it is a plea for deliverance from the perils of the world ('que aya conpasión de me querer librar / de peligros del mundo,' (st. 422). This prayer also serves to link the section on the cardinal virtues to the section on confession since it repeats a request for mercy to the sinful ('que ayas piedat del flaco pecador,' st. 397) and at the same time anticipates the next sections on the Virgin Mary ('Pongo por abogada a tu madre Santa María,' st. 402) and Job ('por provar su paciencia, al santo Job tormentaste,' st. 390).

The prayer for delivery from the perilous injustices of the world is followed by final documentation of such injustice in the form of what the narrator himself experienced at court ('Grant tienpo de mi vida pasé mal despendiendo,' sts 423–730). The apocalyptic treatment of current affairs in *Rimado* differs, therefore, from that in *Alexandre*, *Fernán González*, and *Zifar* in that Ayala does not choose to tell an ancient story in order to illustrate the apocalyptic significance of what is happening in his own time. One possible reason for Ayala's choice might be that the Schism itself was such a potent apocalyptic sign that there was no need to search for analogies from the past. Yet, in a very real sense, it can be claimed that Ayala applied the ancient story of Job to contemporary circumstances.

The next major section of *Rimado* consists of a songbook of prayers

to God and to the Virgin Mary (sts. 731–921), written in different verse
forms and linked by cuaderna-vía stanzas. The apocalyptic nature of
this section is obvious since it is couched in terms of appeals to God
to be merciful in his apocalpytic judgment of the sinner ('Señor, si Tú
has dada / tu sentencia contra mí, / por merced te pido aquí / que me
sea revocada,' st. 732). Many of these appeals in song are made through
the Virgin Mary because she is the narrator's advocate before God
('ayudadora e abogada mía,' st. 752). Ayala confirms the apocalyptic
role of the Virgin by referring to her in terms of the well-known apocalyptic passage in Ezekiel 44:2: 'Tú eres puerta cerrada / de quien dixo
Ezechiel / que non sería otoragada / sino a Dios e al fijo d'El,' st. 878).
But in this section the author also takes care to weave references to
the other three major sections: stanzas 741–2 summarize the structure
of a general confession; stanzas 824–68 are devoted to the effect of the
Schism on current affairs; and stanzas 792–808 refer to Job and a
prayer that anticipates the section on Job.

Ayala might have come upon this weaving, or interlacing, technique
as he sought to make one large unit of various smaller works he had
written over a period of many years. In the first section confession is
the dominant pattern in the weave, but there is also a background
pattern, with passing references to Job (st. 156), the Virgin Mary (st.
83), and current affairs (for example, sts. 75–82, on avarice). In the
second section the dominant pattern is current affairs, but, as described above, the background pattern includes references to confession
(st. 397), the Virgin Mary (st. 402), and Job (st. 390). In the third section
the Virgin Mary is the dominant pattern, and in the background pattern are references to confession (sts. 741–2), current affairs (sts. 824–
68), and Job (sts. 792–808). In the fourth section Job provides the dominant pattern, which is interwoven with references to confession (sts.
1281–5) and current affairs (sts. 1962–8). References to the Virgin
Mary are lacking in the surviving text of this last section, but that she
might have been mentioned in the lost final stanzas cannot be ruled
out.

The suspicion of weaving might be, of course, groundless: Ayala
might not have thought of weaving at all as he put together the various parts of his book. What definitely is on his mind in every part of
Rimado is the apocalyptic judgment of God, which is why he chooses
to adapt material on Job for the last and longest section. The selection
of Job as the theme for the final section of Rimado is most appropriate
in apocalyptic terms. Job is significantly mentioned in classical apocalyptic works, as, for example, in Ezekiel 14:12–20, in the Apocalypse of

Paul, and in the apocalyptic passages in James 5:7–11. Job 'is the principal biblical figure in the fully developed Office of the Dead of the High Middle Ages and after,'[95] which explains why the narrator of *Rimado*, as he contemplates his own death, thinks so much about Job.

Job is also a superb example of the belief repeated throughout *Rimado* that God's judgments, though just, are incomprehensible to human beings: 'Señor, en estas cosas non quiero más fablar, / ca son fechos secretos que fueste Tú guardar / en el tu santo seno' (st. 652).[96] Job, a righteous man, is, with God's permission, subjected to an ordeal, thus prompting the logical question also repeated in *Rimado*: Why do the righteous suffer while the wicked seem to prosper (sts. 1179–95)? Ayala also chose Job, and specifically Gregory's commentary on Job, because through Gregory's commentary he could arrive at an explanation for what was happening to the Church in his time. Just as God mysteriously permitted the saintly Job to be afflicted, so too He must be permitting the Church to pass through the bitter trials in the Schism. This correlation between Job and the Church is found between stanzas 1948 and 1973 (esp. 1958–9): 'Por tal príncipe dezía Job en este lugar: / "La su saña contra mí este quiso demonstrar," / ... los dientes d'este enemigo son malos perseguidores / que despedaçan la Eglesia.'

In the section on Job Ayala inserts other clichés of apocalyptic literature discussed earlier: a description of the rewards of Paradise and the punishments of Hell (sts. 1188–95, 1734–40; and earlier at 571–6), the lot of the descendants of a sinner (st. 1225), a debate about the nature of the resurrection of the dead (sts. 1669–90), and reference to the beginning and the end of an undertaking (st. 1936), the importance of covering the nakedness of one's father (st. 1744), and the levelling power of death (sts. 1824–5).

In the light of the direct significant allusions in *Rimado* to apocalypticism, and since the four major sections are made to serve apocalyptic ends, there can be little doubt that *Rimado* is indeed a unified apocalyptic narrative. While contemplating his impending death and the state of current affairs, Ayala is moved to create a narrator, not unlike himself, who confesses his sins, appeals to the Virgin Mary, laments the Schism in the church as a sign of Antichrist, and remembers the example of Job, all in preparation for the final judgment of God.

Dezir a Juan II and *Dezir a las syete virtudes*

Pero López de Ayala was by no means the only writer of his time to be concerned with apocalypticism. Roger Boase, in his study of the troubadour revival in late-medieval Spain, has demonstrated that messianic ideas were uppermost in the thoughts of many of the approximately nine hundred (a conservative estimate) court poets of fifteenth-century Spain: 'Attempts to resuscitate a courtly and chivalrous past coincided with messianic expectations and predictions.'[97] It will not be practicable to discuss here all the apocalyptic poems found in the anthologies of Castilian fifteenth-century courtly verse. Instead, I will comment on two long poems by Francisco Imperial for arbitrary reasons: partly because Imperial might well have helped to introduce a special kind of Dantesque apocalypticism to Spanish literature, and partly because the idea for this chapter on the apocalyptic tradition occurred to me while I was preparing an edition of the poems of Imperial.[98]

The two long poems of Francisco Imperial – the *Dezir a Juan II* (*Juan II*) and the *Dezir a las syete virtudes* (*Syete virtudes*) – are subtly composed apocalyptic narratives. Both are visions that occurred to the narrator between sleep and wakefulness. *Juan II* is a description of a miraculous vision about the birth of a perfect, messianic prince, and *Syete virtudes* is a vision of paradise of the kind not unlike the insight into truth that is said to be given to righteous people who are about to die. Thus, Imperial's two poems are related to body-and-soul narratives because they deal with the entry of a soul into a body at birth, and with the kind of experience that is believed to accompany the exit of a soul from a body at death.

In *Juan II* there is a direct significant reference (l. 6) to the apocalyptic passages on childbirth in Revelations 12:1–6, and the psalm referred to in line 78 is a well-known messianic psalm. Lines 449–50 of *Syete virtudes* contains a direct significant reference to an apocalyptic passage used at baptismal ceremonies (Isaiah 41:17), because the narrator experiences a kind of new life after death, as catechumens are said to experience after baptism (pp. lxxxviii–lxxxix, cii–cx). But Imperial's narratives are not composed like the body-and-soul narratives discussed earlier. Although they share the detail of a vision that occurs between sleeping and waking on a precise date, the earlier body-and-soul narratives deal with death and are based on ancient legends about the soul, whereas Imperial's narratives deal with birth and with death-like experiences like baptism, and are based more on medieval astronomy than ancient legends.

Juan II is a poem about the birth of a prince (later King Juan II) to Enrique III of Castile and his queen Catalina of Lancaster. The poem consists of 408 lines divided into fifty-one eight-line stanzas which rhyme a b a b b c c b. The whole narrative may be divided into three main parts. The first part tells in thirteen stanzas (ll. 1–104) how at daybreak on the first Friday of March in 1405, the narrator, who does not know if he is asleep or awake, hears the cries of a woman in childbirth; he opens his eyes and finds himself in a *locus amoenus* which he describes in detail; following the direction of voices in the meadow, he comes to a fountain in the shade of a pine tree, where he sees a lioness enter seated on a bull; then he sees, on the faces of maidens, eight planets – Saturn, Jupiter, Mars, Sun, Venus, Mercury, Moon, and Fortune – who are about to hold a conclave. The second part of the poem transcribed in thirty-five stanzas (ll. 105–384) the speeches of these eight planets, who bestow their special gifts on the creature before he is born. What makes this birth miraculous is that Fortune, which does not normally agree with all the other planets (ll. 353–60), sanctions their gifts in this special instance and adds gifts of her own. The third part of the poem begins after Fortune's speech. In this part the poet sees the lioness (the queen) with the new-born baby, to whom he attempts but is unable to pay his respects because he is expelled from the garden (ll. 385–408).

Juan II is composed according to the belief that the planets influence the character of human beings before they are born; a perfect human being would thus be one who receives the best gifts from all the planets. To emphasize this idea Imperial makes the second part of his poem of symbolic length: the speeches of the planets last for 280 lines, that is, one line for each day of the nine months of pregnancy from the thirtieth of May to the day of birth on the sixth of March. The *locus amoenus* carefully described in the first part of the poem is the abode of Fortune, whose speech dominates the second part of the poem; the narrator is ejected from this realm in the third part of the poem, so Fortune is a key unifying element in the composition of the narrative.

The narrator's expulsion from the *locus amoenus* is symbolic of not only the narrator's misfortune but also the indiscretion of the king of the realm, represented by the 'ortelano' who ejects him (ll. 407–8). The narrator's misfortune is perhaps based on an historical occurrence: the poet himself had recently failed to be appointed admiral of Castile, a position in which he had acted and for which he must have sought confirmation (pp. xvii–xx). Since it describes the birth of a perfect prince and does not extol the virtues of the reigning king, the poem can be construed as an indictment against the king. Further, since Discretion invites the narrator to pay homage to the prince, calling the narrator 'amigo e fiel' (l. 405), the king is made to act indiscreetly and disloyally when he expels the narrator from the realm of Fortune.

Enrique III died in 1406, when the perfect prince whose birth is described in *Juan II* was still an infant. The king's death gave Imperial the opportunity to compose an apocalyptic narrative about a kingdom ruled by a young king, in which vice has taken hold, virtues are absent, and injustice prevails. *Syete virtudes* is such a narrative. The poem consists of fifty-eight eight-line stanzas (totalling 464 lines), rhyming *a b a b b c c b*, and can be divided into two main parts: an introduction (to a vision) five stanzas long (ll. 1–40), and a description of that vision in the remaining fifty-three stanzas (ll. 41–464). The introduction begins with a reference to Dante's *Divina commedia*, and tells how the narrator went to a fountain just before dawn to wash his face, how he was overcome there by a deep sleeplike state in which he was able to stay awake to see an other-world vision, and ends with an appeal to Apollo to give the narrator the ability to describe the vision accurately so as to inspire others in Castile.

In the vision itself, the narrator enters a paradisiac garden at a precise time on a precise day of the year – just before dawn on the day that the sun rises in the constellation Aries, that is, on the anniversary of what was believed to be the first day of the creation of the world (p. xcviii). The garden, with its fountain and walls of trees, is like an outdoor church, of the kind painted by fifteenth-century landscape artists like the Van Eyck brothers (p. cv). Since churches were built directed towards the constellation of Aries, the narrator is made to enter not merely a paradise on the first day of Creation but also a church at Easter (pp. cv–cvi). When the sun rises in Aries at Easter during the spring equinox, four circles are said to form three crosses (ll. 41–2, and p. xviii), and these circles and crosses were believed to represent the four cardinal and three theological virtues.

Before the narrator enters the garden/church he perspires profusely, a medieval symptom of death (l. 85, and pp. 129–30); and as soon as he crosses the threshold, as it were, he experiences a kind of purification process (ll. 86–8) whereby his clothes become white and he becomes aware of all of his sins. In the garden/church the narrator is conducted by a special guide, the poet Dante, who instructs him in the nature of the seven virtues and the seven vices. The highlight of this instruction is the apocalyptic denunciation by the guide, Dante, of a noble city (presumably in Castile) that harbours all of the seven vices and to which justice will return when its child-king comes of age (ll. 353–400). This denunciation calls to mind Dante's denunciation of Florence in *Purgatorio* 6:127–44, as well as the denunciation of Babylon in

Revelation. At the end of the vision the narrator awakes and finds in his hands a copy of one of Dante's books (ll. 457–64). Thus, Dante and his *Divina commedia* are the main unifying elements of Imperial's narrative composition. Imperial makes some reference to the *Divina commedia* in most of the fifty-eight stanzas of *Syete virtudes*, and uses Dante's judgment of Florence as a model for an apocalyptic denunciation of a major city in Castile.

As far as the history of literary composition in Castile is concerned, Imperial's direct reference to Dante might well be an innovation, but similar forms of composition were certainly not unknown in Castile before Imperial's time. As our study of the *Libro del cavallero Zifar* has shown, a Castilian author had composed, around the turn of the fourteenth century during the reign of another child-king, an apocalyptic narrative based on a symbolic journey through purgatory to paradise.

Laberinto de Fortuna

Dante's apocalyptic *Divina commedia* became increasingly popular in fifteenth-century Castile. We know, for example, that the poet Juan de Mena refers readers of his commentary on his own poem *Coronación o Calamicleos* to Benvenuto Rambaldi da Imola's commentary on the *Divina commedia*.[99] And we know that Mena's *Coronación*, although it includes 'no verbal reminiscence' that can be indisputably traced to Dante's works, does contain an 'architectonic reminiscence' that can be correctly regarded as Dantesque apocalypticism: the description of a visionary journey from a kind of hell to a kind of paradise.[100] But surely Mena did not need to rely solely on Dante for ideas about apocalyptic composition; and others of his works reveal Mena to be a writer steeped in the apocalyptic tradition that attracted many writers including Dante. Post explains correctly that Mena's unfinished poem *Debate de la Razón contra la Voluntad* is a 'composition ... to be classed within the same tradition as the category of sins in the *Alexandre*, the series of debates of Body and Soul, or particularly, the debates of just such personifications as Reason and Desire in the works of Ruy Paes de Ribera.'[101]

If Mena's *Debate* belongs firmly to what is described in this chapter as the apocalyptic tradition, another poem attributed to Mena, *Razonamiento con la muerte*, is written in the apocalyptic tradition of the dance of death; and even if it should later be proved that the *Razonamiento* or any other poem mentioned above was not composed by Mena, nevertheless from the fifteenth century onward Mena was believed to be a writer of apocalyptic narratives.[102] The purpose of this section is to demonstrate that Mena's best-known work, the *Laberinto de Fortuna* (*Laberinto*) is also an apocalyptic narrative.

The structure of *Laberinto* attracts attention to itself because of its conspicuous complexity, and as a consequence has been the subject of several excellent critical analyses. Briefly, the poem tells in 297 eight-line stanzas (rhyming a b b a a c c a, except for the first stanza which rhymes a b a b b c c b) how the narrator is guided by Providence through the realm ('casa') of seven planets where the great potential future of Spain and its king as well as the deceitful ways of Fortune are revealed to him.[103]

María Rosa Lida de Malkiel devoted several sections of her study of Mena to the question of the structure of *Laberinto*. For Lida de Malkiel *Laberinto* is related in its structure not to classical or renaissance epic but the oriental novel, which entered Europe with the *Disciplina clericalis* and reached a high point with the *Decameron*. These works, acording to Lida de Malkiel, consist of a narrative frame that encloses an indefinite linear series of fixed situations, or episodes, linked only by the fact that they are all experienced by the same ego. She lists thirteen of these episodic situations and attempts to pinpoint their sources more accurately than had other scholars, like Post, Menéndez-Pelayo, and El Brocense.[104] For Lida de Malkiel, Mena's manner of referring to the canonized doctors of the Church, noting more the morality of their comportment than their intellectual prowess, reveals 'una desatención a las formas hondas de la vida espiritual'.[105] Rafael Lapesa later noted correctly that the work also displays a strong moral element.[106]

Joaquín Gimeno Casalduero divided the work into three main parts: introduction (sts. 1–60), the description of the poet's journey through the seven planets (sts. 61–267), and a final section, based upon the second, which guides the king of Spain towards a desired future (sts. 268–97). Gimeno Casalduero also noted the resemblance between *Laberinto* and Imperial's *Juan II* and the absence of Fortuna in a large part of the first half of *Laberinto*: 'Aunque en la segunda estrofa Juan de Mena alude a la Fortuna, y aunque más adelante la ataca, la invoca y la requiere, la diosa (ausente durante las ciento cuarenta y una coplas primeras) no responde a su llamada ... Cuando por fin el reino luminoso de la Providencia ha sustituido al confuso laberinto de Fortuna, la atención de Mena se dirige a las circunstancias de Castilla.'[107]

Clearly, Gimeno Casalduero understood 'reino luminoso de la Providencia' to be antithetical to 'confuso laberinto de Fortuna,' but, nevertheless, Philip Gericke argued that because they are antithetical they must be treated as separate units: 'No one has drawn the distinction between the development and significance of Circles I-IV, on the one hand, and Circles V-VII, on the other; they have been invariably treated as a single unit comprising the central part of the poem. Gimeno Casalduero ... notes ... the ascendancy of Fortune in Circle V, but he still treats the seven circles as one unit.'[108] Even if Gericke's views are correct (which I doubt, for reasons to be explained shortly), his reasoning is strange: he argues that thesis and antithesis cannot form a single unit in Mena's work. By this reasoning Mena's *Calamicleos* and many other medieval works are not single units of composition. About the *Calamicleos* Mena himself wrote that 'por que un contrario puesto sobre otro o cabe otro más claramente es alunbrado, segund dize el philosopho; ansí que en este lugar parescerá mayor gloria puesta cabe la miseria y mayor miseria puesta cerca de la gloria.'[109] (In fact, contrary to what Gericke implies, the aesthetic of contraries is one of the principal building blocks of medieval Spanish literary composition, as I shall explain in the next two chapters, where the quotation from Mena's *Calamicleos* will be juxtaposed with references to medieval methods of composition.)

Dorothy Clotelle Clarke devoted a book to discussing *Laberinto* as a classic Aristotelian epic which is, at the same time, a variation of the *mester de clerecía*.[110] Clarke's book and the critical material on the structure of the *Laberinto*, though they have increased our understanding of the composition of *Laberinto*, can be made even more precise if *Laberinto* is analysed as an apocalyptic narrative.

Direct significant reference to apocalypticism in *Laberinto* has been overlooked, probably because it occurs in the form of an allusion to classical literature. Detailed reference to the sibyls in stanzas 28, 121, and 122 of *Laberinto* is by no means casual but crucial to the apocalyptic structure of the work. 'The Sibylline books that have come down to us, fourteen in all, are of Jewish and Christian origin, though they undoubtedly contain pagan material as well. They represent an interesting fusion between pagan and Judaeo Christian notions of prophecy and ... are the apocalyptic of Hellenistic Diaspora Judaism.... They were also a witness to the universality of revelation: the Sibyls were thought to have performed the same functions for the pagan world that the prophets had in the case of Israel – to testify to the true God, to call sinners to penance, and to announce God's plans for the coming age. "Teste David cum Sibylla" ... as a thirteenth-century poet put it, was no idle remark.... The Sibylline Oracles were treated with great respect by the Christian Fathers from the second century, a respect that was not to decline until the time of the Enlightenment.... Augustine himself, generally so opposed to any form of apocalypticism, not only quoted the Sibyl but also included her among the members of the City of God.'[111]

Mena's *Laberinto* is, essentially, not just a vision or an apocalypse, but a revelation about the nature of revelations, and the importance of distinguishing the true revelations from the false. I will elaborate upon this point shortly, but for the moment note that when Mena compares his guide, Providencia, with the Cumaean Sibyl in the sixth book of Virgil's *Aeneid* (st. 28), and when he places in the heaven of the sun ten different sibyls, all of whom he knows by name (sts. 121–2), he gives notice in his text that he is well aware of the apocalyptic role of the sibylline oracles as sanctioned by Christianity. Direct reference to the sibyls in *Laberinto* is significant enough to justify asking if the eight apocalyptic elements listed earlier function in Mena's best-known work.

For Gericke, 'the concept of a developmental narrative structure was not a part of Mena's inherited poetics. One can view the *Laberinto* as falling within the tradition of episodic, linear narrative compositions which abound in Romance literature well past Mena's time; it is logical to treat it within that tradition.'[112] Gericke does not explain what he means by 'developmental' as opposed to 'episodic, linear' narrative compositions, but he seems to assume that in history the latter precedes the former and that Mena could not have inherited a narrative structure that was both 'developmental' and 'episodic, linear.' It can certainly do no harm to study *Laberinto* in 'the tradition of episodic, linear narrative compositions,' to which Gericke, following Lida de Malkiel, refers;[113] but I do not know if that is the tradition of narrative composition in which *Laberinto* can best be analysed. I do know, however, that the text of *Laberinto* indicates that Mena is acutely aware of the tradition of apocalyptic narrative in which he is composing. As I will demonstrate shortly, all eight of the listed elements of the apocalyptic tradition function significantly in the composition of *Laberinto*.

Before I discuss these key apocalyptic elements in *Laberinto*, let me make an important, if small, distinction between the procedure in Clarke's book and the one that I have developed. For Clarke, Mena's *Laberinto* should be studied in the tradition of classic Aristotelian epic and the *mester de clerecía*. Clarke's approach has a great deal of merit, especially since she attempts to link Aristotle to the *mester de clerecía*. We know, for example, that Aristotle is injected into the apocalyptic tradition at least as early as the composition of *Alexandre*, if not before. But by jumping to Aristotle without direct significant justification from the text, Clarke misses an opportunity to focus on an apocalyptic tradition that embraces Aristotle.

Clarke seems to argue that since Mena uses Virgil as a model, and since Virgil's classic epic, like all classic epics, can be discussed in terms of Aristotle's *Poetics* (which Mena must have known), it is valid to analyse *Laberinto* in terms of Aristotelian theories of composition. But, in spite of the section on 'Aristotle and Mena,'[114] Clarke produces no convincing textual evidence that Mena has Aristotle or an Aristotelian tradition in mind. Aristotle is one of a standard list of philosophers mentioned by Mena (st. 118), but the Aristotelian schema drawn up by Clarke, though useful in many instances, is in the last analysis imposed upon Mena's *Laberinto*. Earlier I suggested that Mena's reference to the sybils justified an examination of *Laberinto* within the apocalyptic tradition; such a procedure would avoid difficulties inherent in Clark's approach. I shall now explain how the key apocalyptic elements – for convenience, in the same sequence as they were listed near the beginning of this chapter – affect the structure of Mena's long poem.

(a) *Precise times.* Towards the end of *Laberinto* the sun begins to rise and the narrator begins to wonder if the revelation he has experienced was a dream or real ('El lúcido Phebo ya nos demostrava / el don que non pudo negar a Phetonte / ... / pensé si los fechos de lo relatado / oviesse dormiendo ya fantasiado, / o fuesse verace la tal compañía,' sts. 268–9).[115] In other words, the revelation in *Laberinto* takes place during a state of 'duermivela' very similar to the states described in such body-and-soul narratives as the *Visión*, *Tractado*, and *Revelación* already discussed. In the *Disputa* the revelation occurs before dawn ('un sabado esient domingo amanezient'), which is when it happens in *Laberinto*, although not between Saturday and Sunday.

At least on one occasion the narrator of *Laberinto* secs a soul that has recently left its body ('E vi por lo alto venir ya volando / el ánima fresca del santo clavero, / partida del cuerpo del buen cavallero,' st. 208), but he does not take the opportunity to elaborate this apocalyptic element further along the lines of the body-and-soul narratives. Mena chooses to emphasize other apocalyptic elements. Precise time has a different symbolic significance in *Laberinto* from that in the body-and-soul narratives, a significance close to the symbolic time of Imperial's long poems, in which the relevation occurs before dawn and in a state between sleeping and awaking ('passando el aurora, viniendo el día / ... / non sé sy velava, ni sé sy dormía'; 'cerca la ora quel planeta enclara / al oriente, que es llamada aurora / ... vynome / ... un grave sueno, maguer non dormia.'[116] In Mena, as in Imperial, the precise time is symbolic of the dawn of a new age, a messianic age.

(b) *Division of history.* In *Laberinto* Mena divides history simply into past, present, and future. By so doing he chooses not to use apocalyptic devices like the Jubilee year (effectively used by the author of *Zifar*) and the seven ages of the world (used by other authors, like Pablo de Santa María in his *Edades del mundo*). Nevertheless, Mena's simple choice is quintessentially apocalyptic. Like the authors of *Alexandre*, *Fernán González*, *Zifar*, and *Rimado*, and like such classical apocalyptic writers as the authors of Ezekiel, Daniel, and Revelation, Mena makes analogies between the remote past and the present or recent past in order to predict and effect a desirable apocalyptic future. Providencia is made to clarify this approach to history before she reveals it ('de tres edades que quiero dezir: / passada, presentes e de por venir,' st. 58).

It is fitting that Providencia should make this clarification since her domain is not limited to the past, contrary to Gericke's claim, nor to any single time frame.[117] Providencia takes care to explain that her 'grand escelencia,' her divine attribute, consists of being able to fuse with all times in all places ('"Non vengo a la tu presencia / de nuevo, mas antes soy en todas partes,' st. 23); she orders the present, disposes the future, and reveals the past. Thus Mena's Providencia is more powerful than Fortuna, who has left impressions in the past and will leave impressions in the future, but can act only in the present, without necessarily dominating it.[118]

All of this rich interplay of time is reflected in the composition of the poem. The poem's broad outline tends to shift from an emphasis on the past in its first half (to about stanza 146) to an emphasis on the present in the second half (to about stanza 291), and ends with a faint glimpse of the future in stanzas 292–7 ('e mas abaxando su boç sabidora, / representava ya, como callando, / los tiempos futuros,' st. 292). But superimposed upon this general shift of emphasis in the narrative is a corresponding movement in the portion of the poem between stanzas 61 and 267.

Luis Beltrán demonstrates, with some imprecisions noted by Fainberg, that under each of the planets except Saturn, Mena starts by discussing the past and shifts to the present. Beltrán also notes that 'when at the end of every planet, Mena interrupts the continuity of the narrative to address his king, he does so in the present, of course, but it is to the king's future that he is looking.'[119] In the section of the narrative between stanzas 1 and 60, the intent to move from past to present is stated early: 'Fasta que al tempo de agora vengamos / de fechos passados cobdicia mi pluma' (st. 2). This section makes early mention of characters from the remote past, like the Cid, and the bulk of the section is devoted to a description of the world which is seen as if

peopled by ancient heroes and heroines. Towards the end of the section (st. 55) Providencia jolts the narrator out of his contemplation
of this remote ancient world and fixes his attention on his present
environment: 'Déxate deso, que non faze al fecho, / mas mira ... /
algo de aquello por que eres venido.' At the end of the section she
explains to the narrator why he can have only a glimpse of the future
(sts. 59–60).

Between stanzas 268 and 297 the narration moves from the remote
past of Spanish history, through the present, to a faint glimpse of the
future. Circumscribing these circles (of past, present, and future),
which keep fusing within specific parts of the narrative and around its
general frame, is the king, Juan II, who figures prominently at the
beginning, middle, and end of the poem (sts. 1, 142–6, 292–7). He
seems to have the potential for future divinity, to fuse like Providencia with all times, if he follows her guidance in the present (st. 297)
even as he gazes at the past glories sculptured on his throne (st. 143).
Thus, out of the simple apocalyptic device of drawing analogies from
the past to interpret the present and predict the future, Mena con-
trives a complex narrative of ever-fusing circles the composition of
which reflects that of the vision it describes. The divisions of the
poem are deliberately fluid, not fixed, in accordance with a corresponding fluidity between past, present, and future.

(c) Visionary journey. The narrator of Laberinto does not see God or
the throne of God; he sees one of God's ministers and the throne of
King Juan II. Nevertheless, the vision in Laberinto is written within
the apocalyptic tradition of similar visions described by Ezekiel and
Dante. Ezekiel's vision of God and the throne of God shares with the
vision in Laberinto a discussion of the north wind (Ezekiel 1:4; Laberinto st. 11), an extraordinary cloud (Ezekiel 1:4, 10:4; Laberinto sts. 18,
20), and wheels within wheels (Ezekiel 1:16 'rota in medio rotae,' 10:10;
Laberinto sts. 56, 67–8). There are, of course, important differences:
Ezekiel describes four wheels that move in four directions, and Mena's
narrator describes three wheels, two of which are stationary and one in
motion; Ezekiel's wheels have eyes (Ezekiel 10:12), Mena's assume
human forms. Nevertheless, the similarities are patent.

When Dante's narrator sees God at the end of Paradiso, he describes
three circles, of different colours, that fuse like rainbows reflecting
each other ('tre giri / di tre colori e d'una contenenza; / e l'un dall' altro
come iri da iri / parea reflesso, e l'terzo parea foco / que quinci e
quindi igualmente si spiri.' Dante's final image describes God as love
(presumably in three circles) that causes wheels to rotate around it
while the wheels rotate around themselves ('ma gia volgeva il mio disio

e'l velle, / si come rota ch'igualmente e mossa, / l'amor che move il sole e l'altre stelle.'[120] John Freccero has argued persuasively that this final image derives in part from Ezekiel and commentaries upon Ezekiel.[121] Thus, Mena's circles, spheres, and wheels cannot be proved to have been derived from Ezekiel and Dante, but they are described in the same apocalyptic tradition as those of Ezekiel and Dante.

Since Mena used Virgil as an important model for *Laberinto*, another possible source of inspiration for his wheels could be the well-known *rota Vergilii*. As described by John of Garland, Virgil's wheel can be conceived of as a globe circumscribed by three circles, one circle for each style – *humilis, mediocris, gravis*. Each circle contains six others, representing types and characteristics of each major style; thus, the entire globe consists of three sets of seven circles, not unlike Mena's three circles each with seven planets.[122] There were, then, many graphical representations of wheels, circles, and spheres, in addition to the ones pointed out by Post and others, that could have affected Mena's depiction of universal time and space. In fact, common theological belief that God transcends time (for example, Augustine's eternal *nunc*), coupled with any map of the heavens available to Mena, could account for the system of wheels in *Laberinto*.

In addition to the vision of one of God's ministers, Mena's visionary journey contains another cliché of apocalyptic literature that has not been recognized as such: the *mapamundi*. It will be remembered that in Berceo's *Signos*, when they journey to heaven, the blessed have a clear unobstructed view of the world ('Verán del mundo todo los cabos postremeros.'[123] Berceo chose not to describe a map of the world, but many other apocalyptic writers decided to do so, sometimes because it was natural to imagine that an extraterrestrial traveller would have a view of the entire world, and sometimes because apocalyptic passages (for example, the location of Gog and Magog) demanded geographical details. Thus, at the end of some Beatus manuscripts a map of the world is included,[124] and among the Spanish works studied in this chapter, *Alexandre* and *Zifar* contain descriptions of the world.[125] Mena's description of the world (sts. 34–55), whatever its direct source may have been, is therefore written in an apocalyptic tradition known to Berceo and used by the authors of *Alexandre* and *Zifar*.

Further research into the details of the rapture in *Laberinto* would certainly link the work to an ancient tradition of apocalyptic writings. For example, the location of the vision in a wilderness plain ('un grand desierto,' st. 14, as opposed to a mountain top) might well be connected, like Ezekiel's 'plana deserto' (Ezekiel 47:8), to Jewish apocalyptic reaction to false pagan mountain-top prophecies; and details like the winged chariot and the eagle (sts. 13–14) are of long apocalyptic standing: 'In the Adam Book (*Apoc. of Moses*) God rides in the cherubwagon when appearing to Adam ... And now we learn from the cuneiform documents that this heavenly ride upon the eagle to look down upon earth and heaven from immeasurable heights ... goes back to the giant Etan, of hoary Babylonian antiquity.[126]

(d) *Virtues and vices.* Important discourse on confession or virtues and vices has been shown to be a constant concern of the apocalyptic narratives examined in this chapter. In Mena's *Laberinto* the theme of virtues and vices is announced as early as the sixth stanza ('inmortal Apolo, / aspira en mi boca por que pueda sólo / virtudes e viçios narrar de potentes'), and is sustained throughout the work. Mena, like Imperial, chooses to treat virtues as something received by individuals from appropriate planets ('e todos de todas por esta manera / son inclinados a disposición / de las virtudes e costelaçión / de la materia de cada una spera,' st. 68). It is well known that towards the end of his discussion of each planet Mena addresses the king directly and defines some virtue or vice. Thus, under the planet Moon the king is addressed in stanza 81 and chastity is defined in stanza 84; for other planets the corresponding stanzas for addresses to the king and definitions are: Mercury, 98–9 (avarice); Venus, 114–15 (clean, Catholic love); Sun, 134, 137 (prudence); Mars, 212–13 (fortitude); and Jupiter, 230–1 (justice).

It is sometimes held that 'Saturn is the only planet where one finds no definition at the end.'[127] It would indeed be strange if Mena should disrupt his careful scheme without artistic reason, and Beltrán, in search of such a reason, has suggested that 'Saturn, being the outer one in a series of concentric circles, necessarily embraces all the others.... What we will find in it will not be, however, a long series of men representing one of the cardinal virtues, but one single man representing the four of them.'[128] Beltrán might well be right, but it is also true that Mena does not break, for Saturn, the pattern he had followed for the other six planets.

Because Saturn represents a high point of his narrative Mena begins by focusing on the king (st. 270). The narrator then addresses the king directly (st. 292). The poet proceeds according to his established plan and defines the virtue that corresponds to Saturn – Providencia herself. Naturally, a precise definition of her eludes him (sts. 293–7); for Mena, Providencia is to be distinguished from prudence which she dispenses ('la qual [i.e., Providencia] vos ministra por mando divino / fuerça, coratge, valor e prudencia,' st. 297). Mena's scheme is therefore the opposite of the one found in Cicero's *De Inventione*, according to

which providence is a part of prudence and not the reverse.[129] For
Mena, the distinction is clear: prudence is infinite knowledge of good
as well as of evil and the ability to always choose the better of the two
('Sabia en lo bueno, sabida en maldad, / mas siempre las vías mejores
acata,' st. 137). So in *Laberinto* prudence is knowledge of true and false
prophecies and the infinite ability to choose between them; Providencia, by contrast, is true prophecy, a concept that embraces prudence
while remaining distinct from it.

Mena's scheme is a variation of the one used by Imperial, who places
prudence in Saturn's sphere and makes her exert influence on Fortuna.
Imperial, however, does not distinguish prudence from providence.
The different treatments confirm the perception that whereas Imperial
lays emphasis on Fortuna in *Juan II*, in *Laberinto* Mena means to stress
prophecy (pro-videre). Imperial makes Fortuna say: 'E vos, la Prudencia,
en mi çirculaçion / más lugar avedes que donzella aya';[130] Mena invokes
Providencia, not Fortuna, because, in the realm of Providencia, Fortuna
has little sway ('a ti [Providencia], cuyo santo nombre convoco, / que non
a Fortuna, que tiene allí poco,' st. 25).

Once Mena's emphasis is appreciated, it becomes clearer that *Laberinto* is an apocalyptic work par excellence because it aims to demonstrate the distinction between true revelation as represented by
Providencia and false prophecy as employed by Fortuna. Providencia,
apart from representing true prophecy, has the prudence to reveal the
deceptiveness of prophecies associated with Fortuna ('las fechas
revelo'). Providencia reveals to the narrator how, under the fifth and
seventh planets, Mars and Saturn, respectively, false prophecies associated closely with Fortuna deceived people who were not able to
interpret them prudently. On Mars the Conde Niebla hears a prophecy
that advises him not to set out to war across the sea (sts. 163–7). The
count is deceived because he assumes that the prophecy – which mentions broken anchor cables and sail rigs, a mast that sways in calm
weather, and Palinurus – has to do with a storm at sea (a play on *fortuna*). The prophecy told to the Conde Niebla turns out to be accurate
(although it has nothing to do with a storm at sea) when Fortuna
arranges to have the count's boat sink in calm, shallow ('non fondas,' st.
160) water close to shore, under the weight of too many of his men (st.
184); accurate, but deceptive. Although he is deceived by Fortuna ('ves-
tido de engaño,' st. 160), the Conde Niebla and his men are rewarded by
Providencia and placed in the heaven of Mars.

In the seventh circle, Saturn, another deception is revealed after a
prophecy that Alvaro de Luna will be overthrown (st. 256). Believers of
the prophecy are deceived when Fortuna arranges to have a statue of

Alvaro de Luna overthrown; and it is explained to the believers that the prophecy was fulfilled accurately but that they had not paid careful attention to its words (sts. 263–5).

In between these two deceptive prophecies of the recent past on Mars and Saturn, the narrator sees King Juan II seated on a throne in a city surrounded by fire in the present heaven of the sixth planet, Jupiter (sts. 221–2). A similar vision is noted in the heaven of the fifth planet, Mars, where Juan II had been placed by Fortuna: Fortuna named Juan II king of not merely Spain but the entire world (st. 142). When the narrator sees him on Jupiter, the king is 'digno de reino mayor que Castilla' (st. 221). And about this vision Providencia prophesies, on Saturn, that the king will be king of kings ('será rey de reyes, señor de señores,' st. 271).

All these prophecies and visions are, of course, unfulfilled ('non son perfectas,' st. 296). In order that they be fulfilled, Juan II must know how to interpret them truthfully: he must use the attributes provided for him by Providencia ('fuerça, coratge, valor e prudencia,' st. 297) and defeat the Moors in order to gain glory in paradise. In other words, Juan II, with full knowledge of the prophecies of Fortuna and others, must prudently choose truthful Providencia as his guide: like Prudencia, he must be 'sabio en lo bueno, sabido en maldad, / mas siempre las vías mejores acata' (st. 137).

(e) Esoteric books. It is interesting that for the deceptive prophecies about Conde Niebla and Alvaro de Luna, Mena draws heavily from Lucan's *Pharsalia*, whereas for the more creditable prophecies of the sibyls he relies on Virgil's *Aeneid*. I do not believe that these selections are accidental or casual. The choice of the *Pharsalia* is appropriate because it deals with civil war, one of the main vices that Mena advises Juan II to eradicate; but the poet refrains from placing Lucan in the heaven of the Sun for fear that he should be accused of favouring a fellow native of Córdoba (st. 124). The choice of the *Aeneid* as the main model for *Laberinto*, however, must have been influenced by Mena's knowledge that Virgil, though pagan, was widely considered during the Middle Ages an *anima naturaliter christiana*. Mena's *Laberinto* is an apocalyptic reworking of Virgil's *Aeneid* in much the same way that *Alexandre, Zifar, Rimado, Fernán González*, and *Syete virtudes* represent reworkings of the *Alexandreis*, a 'Chaldean' book, Job, chronicles, and the *Divina commedia* respectively.

(f) Messianic hope. There can be no doubt that *Laberinto* describes Juan II as a perfect ruler of all the world, comparable to Jesus Christ. The first stanza of the poem extols Juan II as a potential ruler of the entire world: 'Aquél con quien Júpiter tovo tal zelo, / que tanta de

parte le fizo del mundo / quanta a sí mesmo se fizo del cielo.' At the
approximate centre of the work Juan II is depicted overpowering those
who seek him in antagonism, precisely as Jesus Christ is said to have
overpowered those who sought to arrest him in the garden at Gethse-
mane ('Bien como cuando repuso en el huerto el Sumo Maestro … ansí
en Medina, siguiendo tal ley / vista la cara de nuestro grand rey / le
fue todo llano e allí descubierto,' st. 156). The mention of Medina,
denoting a Spanish town but also connoting a sacred city of Islam, is
obviously not intended to be casual. And towards the end of the poem,
as the sun rises, symbolic of the risen Christ, Providencia announces
that Juan II will outshine all his predecessors ('Será rey de reyes, señor
de señores, / … qu'en su claro tiempo del todo serán / con él olvidados
sus anteçessores,' st. 271).

It is the injection of the messianic symbol of the rising sun that
leads critics like Beltrán to suppose unnecessarily that discussion of
the planet Saturn ends at stanza 267, and to conclude that there is no
definition of virtue or vice at the end of Saturn's section.[131] But since
the section on Saturn deals with great rulers (st. 232), the list of Spanish kings, including Juan II, falls also within Saturn's jurisdiction. And
although as the sun rises the narrator begins to question the veracity
of the vision (st. 269), the vision itself continues as long as Providencia
keeps speaking to the narrator (st. 291) and until she disappears (sts.
294-5). The question of veracity raised in stanza 269 is crucial to the
artistic composition of the work, as we have seen; and the rising sun
serves to not only symbolize the messiah but also lend veracity to the
vision, since stanza 269 seeks to confirm that although the experience
appeared to be a dream, the narrator was able to 'see the light' as
clearly as possible ('Yo, que las señas ví del claro día,' st. 269).

(g) Eschatological signs. The signs of the clear day that the narrator
sees in stanza 269 refer to both the sunlight described in the previous
stanza and the details of the vision itself ('los fechos de lo relatado,' st.
269). These signs refer, in other words, to the past and current events
described in the poem; the narrator interprets them as eschatological
signs that herald a clear, messianic day. One of the eschatological
signs is civil war, a noticeable portent caused by the inhabitants of the
infernal regions ('E por que fizieron las pazes [con los moros], asayan /
sembrar tal discordia entre castellanos / que fe non se guarden hermanos a hermanos,' st. 254). Civil war within Spain is what provides Juan
II, in the opinion of the narrator, with the opportunity to be a messianic leader by uniting his country ('quando veríamos el reino apacado,'
st. 293) and defeating the Moors to gain glory ('aya de moros puxante
victoria / e de los vuestros ansí dulce gloria,' st. 297).

It is interesting to note that in his eschatological interpretation of current affairs, Mena does not criticize the Jews directly, as had been done by earlier apocalyptic writers, notably Berceo, the author of *Zifar*, and Pero López de Ayala. The harshest criticism of Jews in *Laberinto* is a mild reference to their ingratitude towards God (in the person of Jesus Christ) who had liberated them from the wilderness ('A fijos de los que libró del desierto, / e como aquel pueblo cayó casi muerto,' st. 156). For the narrator of *Laberinto* the apocalyptic enemy is not the Jews, it is the Moors ('La ira, la ira bolved en los moros,' st. 255). Anti-Moorish sentiment in *Laberinto* is no more to be condoned with praise than anti-Jewish sentiment in *Zifar*. Yet, the intense hatred of Jews in *Zifar* is not paralleled in *Laberinto* with a similarly intense hatred of Moors.

(h) Resurrection and judgment. The text of *Laberinto* assumes, without need for elaborate explanation, that bodies will be resurrected, judged, and rewarded or punished. *Laberinto* does not include the kind of elaborate debate about resurrection that is found in Ayala's *Rimado*. Instead, it provides the reader with vivid details about the resurrection of a corpse by a witch at Valladolid (sts. 244–56). What the text does not say here might well be as significant as what it says: if a witch at Valladolid can resurrect dead bodies, the unstated implication is that such a feat is surely also within the powers of God, as explained in apocalyptic passages like Ezekiel 37. On the one hand, the text of *Laberinto* does make clear the kind of deeds judged worthy of reward on earth as well as in paradise: virtuous war against the Moors is described, in about the middle of the poem, as earning for Spaniards 'gloria en los cielos y fama en la tierra' (st. 152). This message is further emphasized when Pedro de Narbaes is rewarded with 'la corona del cielo e la tierra' for fighting valiantly against the Moors (st. 197). Civil war, on the other hand, brings no such reward in heaven or on earth ('La discordia del reino que anda / ... non gana ninguno corona,' st. 207).

The foregoing analysis of apocalyptic ideas in *Laberinto* reveals that all the important elements of the work – an appeal to a king, a rapture, a visionary journey, a map of the world, a discussion of planetary influence on virtues and vices, an examination of past and current events in terms of signs for the future, an interpretation (of mankind's fortune and misfortune) by a learned divine guide – are also important elements in the apocalyptic tradition described in this chapter. Thus, *Laberinto* can with reason be called an apocalyptic narrative, and its composition can be defined more precisely than it has been before.

It is not wise to fix the fluid divisions of the work as firmly as Gimeno Casalduero, Gericke, and Beltrán have attempted. It is possible and convenient to divide the work into three sections, as Gimeno Casalduero has done: introduction (sts. 1–60), journey through the planets (sts. 61–267), and guide towards the future (sts. 268–97).[132] But there are problems with this division if it is meant to be a rigid one. For example, although there seems to be a transition in the narrative between stanzas 60 and 61 ('Mas esto dexado, ven, ven tu conmigo'), nevertheless the narrator's journey can be said to begin as far back as stanza 13 ('quando robada sentí mi persona'); so the introductory stanzas can be said to 'end' at the end of stanza 12, in which the narrator requests an extraterrestrial journey. Likewise, there seems to be a transition in the narrative, where Gimeno, Beltrán, and others have indicated, between stanzas 267 and 268. But, contrary to what most critics claim, the vision of the planets does not end at the last line of stanza 267, because after this line the narrator asks for and receives a description of the heaven of Saturn ('Yo te demando, gentil compañera, / me digas del nuestro grand rey e fiel, / que se dispone en el cielo d'aquél,' st. 270).

The visionary journey ends somewhere after the last line of stanza 291, at which point Providencia's audible speech fades as she disappears. But it is perhaps clearer here than anywhere else in the poem that Mena does not prefer fixed divisions for his work; although Providencia's speech ends at the last line of stanza 291, in stanza 292 she is still speaking, although in a manner not intelligible to the narrator's human ears ('e más abaxando su boç sabidora, / ... como callando'). Therefore, one fairly precise way to describe the composition of *Laberinto* would be to say that the poem is divided into three main parts that are made to fuse seamlessly into each other: an introduction to a vision (sts. 1–12), a description of the vision (sts. 13–291), and a fading away of the vision (sts. 292–7).

In all three of these sections, but especially in the long middle section, are complex fluctuations between past, present, and future, as explained earlier. In the middle section, the narrator journeys through the domain of Providencia, during which his perception of past, present, and future is sharpened by her revelations. Therefore it is imprecise to claim, as Gericke does, that the domain of Providencia is limited to the first four circles (sts. 61–137), and the domain of Fortuna to the last three (sts. 138–268).[133] What Gericke calls the domain of Fortuna is described mainly in terms of the fortunes of warfare and civil strife, and the narrator states clearly that Providencia has dominion over such matters ('disponedora / ... de pazes e guerras, e suertes e fados,' st. 24). It is also imprecise to claim that 'the "labyrinth" of the poem is, figuratively, Mena's Spain.'[134] The labyrinth of the title is described more aptly as the infinitely complex domain of Providencia, that is, the universe consisting of earth and planets through which, in the opinion of the narrator, a person's body and soul must pass before birth, during life, and after death.[135]

The imprecise interpretation of the domain of Providencia leads Gericke to conclude that the composition of *Laberinto* reveals a dramatic progression in the understanding of the narrator: 'This initial view of the relationship between Providence and Fortune is modified considerably as the poem unfolds.'[136] In other words, Gericke believes that the narrator has one understanding of Fortuna at the poem's beginning, and he learns about Providencia for the first time when she appears to him and corrects his understanding of Fortuna. But this cannot be true. Before the narrator meets Providencia for the first time, he knows well what she does but he does not know what she looks like. The narrator's description of the duties of Providencia (st. 24) is clearly information he knew already, since it clarifies and adds to what Providencia hinted to him in stanza 23.

The so-called progression Gericke talks about is merely the face-to-face 'coloquio' with Providencia in stanzas 20–4. The element of surprise in the narrator's voice ('así que tú eres la governadora') does not mean that he used to believe that Fortuna controlled circumstances he now sees in Providencia's domain; it simply means that the narrator is pleasantly surprised to see, for the first time, someone (Providencia) with whom he has already been acquainted for some time. In other words, the emphasis in the line is greater on the word *tú*, which implies, 'so this is what you look like' than on the word *governadora* (implying, 'so this is what you do'), because the narrator already knows, and can explain after only a few hints, what Providencia does. Therefore, the guided visionary journey that constitutes the bulk of the narrative (sts. 13–291) does not mark a dramatic progression in the narrator's beliefs, as Gericke would have it. Rather, it provides divinely inspired confirmation of the narrator's old beliefs that, although Fortuna operates deceitfully in the present, Providencia reveals the past (exposing Fortuna's deeds), orders the present, and disposes the future. Providencia, therefore, not Fortuna, is the true divine apocalyptic guide, in the opinion of the narrator; she appears to him because he always calls for divine (not pagan) assistance 'siempre divina clamando clemencia,' st. 19).

This chapter has concentrated on some of the medieval Spanish works in which the composition has been seriously affected by the apocalyptic tradition. Of course, apocalyptic ideas can be found in almost every medieval Spanish work that has survived, just as ideas from each of the traditions discussed in this book can also be found in most medieval Spanish works. But apocalyptic elements of composition cannot be said to dominate in most other medieval Spanish works as they do in the works analysed in this chapter. Further, since the apocalyptic tradition seems to dominate throughout the medieval period, an opportunity is provided for the historian to record variations in the mutation of the tradition. In different works different apocalyptic elements are emphasized and varied, though all or most of the apocalyptic elements might be present. For example, apocalyptic signs are stressed in the *Signos*; resurrection and judgment, in the body-and-soul narratives and in the *Danza*; exemplary virtues and vices and their effect on current affairs, in works like *Alexandre, Zifar*, and *Fernán González*; confession and current affairs, in *Rimado*; the visionary journey and messianic hope, in Imperial's poems and in Mena's *Laberinto*.

These different emphases call for different ways of composing the same common apocalyptic elements. Thus, no two works discussed in this chapter can be said to be composed in precisely the same way, although they can all be said to belong to the same apocalyptic tradition. Even where proof exists that one work served as a source for another (as in *Alexandre* and *Fernán González*, and, possibly, in Imperial's poems and *Laberinto*), the composition of the sources varies markedly from that of the works they influenced. What is more, it would appear that much additional insight can be acquired about the composition of both the source and its dependent work if both are studied within the broader tradition to which they belong. Finally, it is particularly useful to study the question of sources and dependent works in the light of the apocalyptic tradition, because it was desirable practice for apocalyptic writers not to follow their sources slavishly but to reinterpret them, even to the point of distortion, to suit current apocalyptic needs.

4 Sic et Non: Logic and the Liturgical Tradition

FOR RAYMOND WILLIS AND
ERICH VON RICHTHOFEN

The dominance of apocalypticism throughout medieval Spanish literature has forced us to lose the semblance of chronology with which we started this literary history. Chapters 1 and 2 dealt with works composed in the thirteenth century, but the third chapter, if it was to have coherence, had to include works from the late-twelfth or early-thirteenth through to the late-fifteenth centuries, the entire period covered in this book. For no convincing reason other than to restore a semblance of chronology, this chapter will start more or less where the second stopped, and will analyse in its first section the fourteenth-century masterpiece by Juan Ruiz, the *Libro de buen amor* (*Buen amor*). Then, once more, chronology will be abandoned in the chapter's second part which will deal with a fifteenth-century work – Talavera's *Corbacho* – dating from approximately one hundred years after *Buen amor*. What links these works, written so far apart in time, is a technique of composition rooted in medieval philosophy, a topic that became increasingly popular in Spain as interest in university education became more widespread.

This technique of composition has to do with the use of contraries. The use of binary (positive and negative) forms of composition is certainly simple enough to be considered universal, and can be found in all the texts analysed in this book. We have already seen, for example, how some lines in the *Cid* are like passages in the Psalms that are constructed in a pattern that juxtaposes contraries ('Aún todos estos duelos en gozo tornarán').[1] It can even be argued that the composition of the *Cid* was influenced by the tendency of the poet, or 'juglar,' to give the listening or reading audience a sad theme followed by a happy one – for example, sad exile in the first 'cantar,' followed by joyful weddings in the second, followed by sad 'afrenta' in the third. We have also seen in the *Razón* how vulgar debate is juxtaposed with refined tryst and demotic

clichés are made to have hieratic connotations. By the time it reached
Mena at the end of the third chapter (and the fifteenth century), this
simple technique already had had more important philosophical consequences for literary composition: 'Porque un contrario puesto sobre otro
o cabe otro más claramente es alunbrado, segund dize el philosopho;
Ansí que en est lugar parescerá mayor gloria puesta cabe la miseria y
mayor miseria puesta cerca de la gloria.'[2]

The philosopher to whom Mena refers is most likely Aristotle, and
since the texts analysed in this chapter also refer to Aristotle, it will be
helpful to cite in some detail another text that elaborates upon the idea
expressed by Mena. But let us first turn to the thorny problem of analysing the structure of *Buen amor*. After the analysis I will cite the Aristotelian text (actually a translation by Hermannus Alemannus of the
commentary by Averroës of Aristotle's *Poetics*) that seems to support
my interpretation of the structure of *Buen amor*. Since Averroës is one
of several authorities cited by Martínez de Toledo, I will then analyse
the structure of the *Corbacho* in the light of the same Aristotelian text.

Libro de buen amor

One of the most intriguing challenges to Hispanic scholarship has
been the re-creation of the ordering principles that informed Juan Ruiz
in the composition of *Buen amor*. A.D. Deyermond, in an excellent
prologue to a much-needed reprint of *Recherches sur le 'Libro de Buen
Amor,'* has written two concise paragraphs summarizing the attempts
made by Hispanists, from Felix Lecoy to Oliver T. Myers, to solve the
problem of the structure of the book of the archpriest of Hita.[3] The following study does not seek or claim to be a definitive solution to the
problem, but its aims will have been achieved if it in some way com-
plements previous efforts and facilitates future more final appraisals of
the structure of *Buen amor*.

THE LECOY TRADITION

Felix Lecoy was, as Deyermond correctly described him, 'something of
a pioneer in his discussion' of structure, and his basic findings – that
essentially *Buen amor* consists of two principal parts, the adaptation
of *Pamphilus* (sts. 680–891) and the battle between Lady Lent and Lord
Meatseason (sts. 1067–314), around which are grouped minor satellite
episodes – are as sound today as when they first appeared in print in
1938.[4] Indeed, two recent and largely successful analyses of the book's
structure are variations of Lecoy's central idea. R.M. Walker concludes

that 'The *Lba* can be divided into two main parts, the first of which is a more or less straightforward Art of Love. The second part seems to be the presentation of the other side of the coin, the sinfulness of love and its ephemeral nature';[5] and Oliver T. Myers considers 'the work as composed of two principal divisions, separated by an interlude of divergent, contrastive character. The two divisions are (roughly) mirror images, the second reversing the structure of the first.'[6] Walker and Myers accept Lecoy's two main divisions, but whereas Lecoy asserted these divisions to be independent units, they posit a contrastive relationship between them. Myers admits that his views are close to Walker's and, not unlike Walker, concludes that 'the didactic message of Part 1 is that love is inseparable from life and stems unavoidably from our very existence. Part 2 teaches that love leads inevitably to death, and that there is no hope of lasting love on earth except for the love of God.'[7]

In so far as they rely on the absence of death in the first part, the arguments of Walker and Myers are not convincing. Walker goes so far as to declare that in contrast to the second, in the first part there is 'certainly no thought of death.' In fact death is referred to in numerous stanzas of the first part, the following among them: 182, 184, 197, 207, 222, 224, 232, 236, 254, 258–9, 267, 269, 273, 275, 281–2, 294, 297, 302, 307–9, 311–12, 315, 318, 335, 399, 406, 420, 505, 507, 520, 529, 540–1, 543, 547, 582, 584, 588, 590–1, 593–4, 602, 651, 662, 670, 701, 707, 759, 776, 783, 786, 789–91, 794–5, 832, 837, 839, 841, 843, 846, 855, 857–60. In so far as they attempt to improve Lecoy's explanation of the minor pieces as satellites grouped with haphazard artistry around the two main parts, Myers has much more success than Walker. Walker concedes that his 'attempt to find a unity of theme running through the *Lba* (like all such attempts) ... overlooks to a large extent the comic aspect: the bawdy burlesque of the serrana episode, the mock-epic parody of the battle between Carnal and Cuaresma, the satire of the procession of love, and the ubiquitous irony.'[8]

Myers, inspired by a remark in María Rosa Lida de Malkiel's *Two Spanish Masterpieces*, finds 'careful symmetry' between the satellites of the first and second parts. The satellites in the first part, according to Myers, lead up to the first main episode, the seduction of Doña Endrina, whereas the satellites in the second part fall away from the second main episode, the battle between Dame Lent and Lord Meat-season. Between parts one and two Myers places stanzas 950–1067 as a sort of mountain interlude, and thus is able to depict the structure of the entire book as a mountain, with parts one and two as ascending and descending slopes, respectively, and the serrana episodes as a type of plateau, or meseta. This is perhaps the most brilliant and certainly the most graphic illustration of the structure of *Buen amor*. It has, however, at least two minor but unfortunately fatal flaws. The first flaw is that since Myers's plateau, which he labels 'serranas,' extends from stanza 950 to stanza 1067, but the serrana episodes end at stanza 1042, Myers, is forced to include material that does not seem to fit the serrana episodes (a poem to the Virgin Mary and two poems on the passion of Jesus Christ, sts. 1043–66) into his plateau. The second flaw becomes apparent when, at the end of the descent of his mountain, Myers has to contend with the poems to the Virgin Mary that end the book. These 'gozos' seem to represent ascending, not descending, action, so Myers adopts the awkward solution of changing the direction of his mountain profile and separating the line that represents the gozos from the rest of the mountain.[9]

THE CASTRO TRADITION

The major problem with the structure of all episodes of *Buen amor*, satellite as well as central, is their shifting perspective: at times their tone seems didactic and sincere, at others it is blatantly sinful and ironic. If the solution to this problem eluded Lecoy, Walker, and Myers, Américo Castro and later María Rosa Lida de Malkiel offered solid contributions to the understanding of the structure of the book. For the latter two critics *Buen amor* has an open-ended structure typical of Semitic rather than Christian culture. Castro describes the work as an 'open arabesque in which beginning and end are not only lacking but impossible,' and Lida de Malkiel asserts that 'la forma cerrada, con acción central y andadura dinámica que Lecoy ... recorta en el *Libro* falsea incurablemente lo que Juan Ruiz de hecho escribió. No hay una primera parte (coplas 71–909) que desarrolle el aprendizaje amoroso, ya que el único triunfo es de don Melón, no del protagonista en primera persona, y al reaparecer éste reaparecen los fracasos, y no hay una segunda parte (950–1634), fiel al ritmo de la liturgia y de las estaciones, ya que las alusiones al calendario se limitan a las coplas 1067–1321, esto es, a menos de la mitad.'[10]

The backbone of this open-ended structure, according to Castro and Lida de Malkiel, is the *persona* of the narrator. For Castro, the narrator was of necessity following a Muslim rather than a Christian tradition:

> Since he was a Christian (even though imbued with Islamic tradition), he could not help revealing the contrast between the spontaneity of the senses and moral reflection. Not only his

writing, but he himself was Christian, and he could not speak in
the same breath as both sinner and moralist. The mingling of
such opposites, of course, the Archpriest had not only observed
among the Moslems but had read about in their literature ...
When Christians spoke in the first person of matters of morality, they did not at the same time express pleasure in the sensual charms of this world.[11]

Castro's assessment here of the Christian mentality is superficial.
When St Augustine confessed, he frequently admitted that his sins
were beautiful and charming even though later, as a convert, he perceived not only their beauty but their underlying distress:

> Was there no one to lull my distress, to turn the fleeting beauty
> of these new-found attractions to good purpose and set up a goal
> for their charms ... The eye is attracted to beautiful objects by
> gold and silver and all such things. There is great pleasure, too,
> in feeling something agreeable to the touch, and material things
> have various qualities to please each of the other senses ... For
> these earthly things, too, can give joy, though not such joy as
> my God, who made them all, can give ... I also fell in love,
> which was a snare of my own choosing. My God, my God of
> mercy, how good you were to me, for you mixed such bitterness
> in that cup of pleasure! My love was returned and finally
> shackled me in the bonds of its consummation. In the midst of
> my joy I was caught up in the coils of trouble.[12]

For St Augustine, as for any upright medieval Christian, it was not
simply, as Castro claims, a question of contrast between the sensual
and the moral; it was also a question of constant gradation between
earthly joys and heavenly ones. Both these joys co-existed inseparably
in man, who was himself God's creation. Moreover, it was the medieval
Christian view that although God did not create sin, no man was ever
without sin. Christians pointed to numerous passages in both the Old
and New Testaments to substantiate this view (Psalms 51:5, 130:3; Proverbs 20:8; 1 Kings 8:46; 2 Chronicles 6:36; Ecclesiastes 7:20; 1 John
1:8), and St Augustine himself summarized it thus: 'Hear me, o God!
How wicked are the sins of men! Men say this and you pity them,
because you made man, but you did not make sin in him. Who can
recall to me the sins I committed as a baby? For in your sight no man is
free from sin, not even a child who has lived only one day on Earth.'[13]
So, to agree with Castro that no Christian could simultaneously be

moralist and sinner is absurd, since every Christian, be he moralist or baby, was supposed to believe himself to be, simultaneously, a sinner.

María Rosa Lida de Malkiel may have had reservations about Castro's understanding of the Christian outlook, but she does agree with Castro, at Lecoy's expense, that there are no Christian precedents for the autobiographical structure of *Buen amor*: 'Lo que de veras demuestra este esfuerzo por hallar análogos a la autobiografía del *Buen Amor* dentro de la literatura cristiana, es que no los hay, y que al buscarlos en la literatura medieval no cristiana, la intuición de Castro es certera.'[14] She proposes, in place of medieval Christian works and the Arabic *Collar de la paloma* suggested by Castro, the Hispano-Hebraic *maqamat*. It was Lecoy who first documented in extensive detail the Christian European tradition to which *Buen amor* belongs, and in spite of Castro and Lida de Malkiel, many scholars have continued to consider the work within the Christian European tradition. One of the most persuasive arguments in Lecoy's favour is a well-reasoned article by Francisco Rico. Rico points out that the long Latin poem, *De Vetula*, to which Lecoy had referred, is an erotic autobiography of Ovid which offers 'fundamentales coincidencias con la de Juan Ruiz, de los prólogos en prosa y en verso a los loores de la Virgen como remate ... En estructura, propósito y tema (fuertemente ligados) no conozco nada más próximo al *Libro de Buen Amor*.'[15] Yet in spite of Rico's convincing arguments, his findings are of necessity not complete enough to describe the structure of the *Buen amor*: the structure of the model is not necessarily that of the work itself. It is helpful to say that the structure of *Buen amor* resembles that of the *Collar de la paloma* or the *Libro de las delicias* or the *De Vetula*, but these resemblances cannot adequately constitute a comprehensive analysis of the structure of *Buen amor*. The book must be made to reveal its own structure.

THE SPITZER TRADITION

The contention that Juan Ruiz's shifting perspective is Semitic is opposed by the argument, well represented by Leo Spitzer, that the archpriest's style is nothing but subtle Christian irony and laughter:

> Las burlas del Arcipreste quedan justificadas desde este trasfondo dogmático: esas burlas hay que insertarlas y justificarlas dentro del *ordo dei*. Por esto, no veo dificultad teológica alguna en que él, un sacerdote cuente historietas picantes: el *Libro de Buen Amor* cuenta locuras ... porque la necia conducta de los hombres entra también en el orden querido por Dios ... El Arci-

preste no necesita 'pasaporte' de ningún género para pasar del
reino de la frivolidad al de la decencia, por la razón de que no
había barreras que impidieran el paso de uno a otro.[16]

Otis H. Green echoes Spitzer's views closely: 'Juan Ruiz' *Libro de Buen
Amor* is, if I interpret it aright, primarily a manifestation of medieval
laughter and joy: of that medieval release from the awe of the sacred
which, for all its merriment, cannot quite escape the opposite emotion
– deep awareness of the sacred intensified by fear of the ultimate loss
of happiness through death.'[17]

Edgar Paiewonsky Conde varies the Spitzer/Green posture only
slightly when he argues that there were two didactic literary attitudes
in the Middle Ages – the sacred and the comic, and that the unique-
ness of Ruiz's work is that it oscillates between these two opposite
poles: 'El *Libro* del Arcipreste refleja la realidad oscilando entre los dos
polos que estructuran esa realidad, reproduciendo así el patrón rítmico
de la vida misma. Es una obra extraordinaria precisamente porque
refleja la realidad desde la perspectiva de un protagonista ordinario –
que sin ser permanentemente santo ni perdido, es ambas cosas conse-
cutivamente.'[18]

To the question of subtlety and ironic style A.N. Zahareas devotes
one of the longest chapters of his *The Art of Juan Ruiz*. Zahareas enti-
tles this chapter 'The Structure of the *Libro de Buen Amor*' and openly
places himself within the Spitzer tradition in a footnote to the effect
that 'Leo Spitzer has influenced all subsequent critics. His early views
concering the medieval and didactic character of the *Libro* have been
used, cited and expanded. He has given clearest and most elaborate
arguments of the relationships between medieval art, didactism and
the *Libro*.' Zahareas goes on, however, to give the impression that he
advances Spitzer's views: 'Spitzer leaves many questions unanswered
because I suspect he relies, here, on the long-established traditions at
the expense of the text.' For Zahareas the section between stanzas 44
and 70 'is the backbone of the *Libro*'s structure' because 'structurally,
the author's admonitions and *exemplum* presage the autobiography
proper and thus establish a pattern that will be paralleled in succeeding situations ... literally, the author's ironic play keynotes the
manner of his commentary while his technique indicates his artistic
preoccupations.'[19]

The key to the understanding of this ironic structure, Zahareas
explains, is the word *sotil* mentioned in line 656. It must be stated in
fairness that Spitzer had already underlined, though differently and
perhaps more adequately than Zahareas, the importance of *sotil* and

the ironic style: 'Así el propio Arcipreste, en el prólogo en prosa, glosa de
tres maneras un versículo de los Salmos y Sem Tob … emplea las palabras "sotil" y "glosa" en idéntica conexión que el Arcipreste de Hita
… La postura de complicada ironía la encuentra ya ante sí el poeta
medieval; pero es la suya una ironía a estilo del creador del mundo, que
contempla abierto ante sus ojos el libro del mundo como un texto de
múltiples reflejos y susceptible de muy variadas interpretaciones.'[20]

In summary, the contributions of the 'Spitzer tradition' are impressive. In so far as they demonstrate that laughter was an integral part of
the medieval Christian ethic, these contributions successfully debili-
tate the contrary claims of the 'Castro tradition.' The following paragraph, entitled 'Easter Laughter,' tends to support the well-founded
claims of Spitzer and Green:

> On Easter Sunday afternoon most people in the villages and
> towns of Central Europe come back to church for the solemn
> services of Vespers and Benediction. At the sermon that pre-
> ceded this afternoon service, a quaint custom was practiced in
> these regions during medieval times. The priests would regale
> their congregations with funny stories and poems, drawing
> moral conclusions from these jolly tales (Ostermarlein: Easter
> fables). The purpose of this unusual practice was to reward the
> faithful with something gay after the many sad and serious
> Lenten preachings. The reformers violently attacked the prac-
> tice as an abuse, however, and it was gradually suppressed by
> the Church during the seventeenth and eighteenth centuries.[21]

The 'Spitzer tradition' is also important in that it heralds a tendency
to rely less on sources and models and more on the text itself. Zahareas proclaims repeatedly his allegiance to the text over and above its
tradition or its sources because 'the meaning derived through traditional sources (Latin or Arabic) does not explain many of the central
elements in the *Libro*'; yet on the question of the *Libro*'s structure,
Zahareas's textual analysis leads only to a vague inconclusiveness that
by 'Side-stepping the Didactic Frame' … 'the *Libro*'s frame is the ironic
counterpart of the didactic frame.' Paiewonsky Conde's textual analysis
seems to be more formalistic than Zahareas's, and his conclusion
slightly more graphic and precise: 'El artista intercede entre el Arcipreste y el amante; lo estético entre lo ético y lo erótico.'[22]

In spite of its impressive contribution, the 'Spitzer tradition' does
not answer a fundamental question about the structure of *Buen amor*:

Granted that medieval laughter, medieval subtlety, and medieval irony are an integral part of the medieval Christian outlook, why is there so much more laughter, subtlety, and irony than serious and sincere sermonizing in Juan Ruiz's book? Laughter, subtlety, and irony might well be acceptable in a medieval Christian context, but excessive laughter, subtlety, and irony are not Christian virtues. It is not simply a question of oscillating, as Paiewonsky Conde claims, between the sinner and the saint, between 'lo ético y lo erótico'; it is, rather, a question of leaning heavily towards the decidedly sinful direction. The tendency in the text towards excess did not go unnoticed by Spitzer, even though he did not dismiss it satisfactorily: 'Puede parecer que el Arcipreste se detiene demasiado morosamente en el pecado de la lascivia, en vez de practicar el "guarda e passa."'[23] It is mainly because of the preponderance of sinful elements that the 'Lecoy tradition' described the work as goliardic and the 'Castro tradition' considered it Semitic. The remaining pages of this chapter will attempt to show that *Buen amor* is neither goliardic nor Semitic but eminently Christian, for structural reasons that are not those advanced by the 'Spitzer tradition.'

From the preceding account of attempts to solve *Buen amor*'s structure, the deduction, one that almost every Hispanist would accept, can be justly made that at least two ordering principles underlie the work: an autobiographical principle, and a principle based on the juxtaposition of contraries. About the first of these María Rosa Lida de Malkiel wrote in 1959: 'Así, pues, lo que da unidad estructural al *Libro* es la personalidad de su autor, que se expresa en forma autobiográfica.' Francisco Rico qualified this slightly in 1967 when he wrote that 'obviamente, el vínculo estructural del poema es una autobiografía: mas no una autobiografía cualquiera, sino, como se subraya desde el mismo título, constitutivamente, una autobiografía amorosa.' Deyermond, writing in 1974, was still able to state confidently in his introduction to Lecoy's *Recherches* that 'the question of structure cannot, of course, be wholly divorced from that of the autobiographical form.' About the second principle Ramón Menéndez Pidal pointed out in 1957 that 'el Arcipreste percibe la realidad toda como enigma indescifrable de elementos contrarios.' It is to this comment that Green, after Abelard, refers in 1968 as *Sic et Non*, and it is what Paiewonsky Conde calls in 1972 a 'polarización medieval.'[24] Any attempt to analyse the structure of *Buen amor* should therefore offer satisfactory replies to at least two questions: (1) What is the essential nature of the personality of the autobiographical narrator of the work; and (2) Why does the narrator constantly shift his perspective by juxtaposing, subtly, ironically, if you like, contrary with contrary?

THE PERSONALITY OF THE AUTOBIOGRAPHICAL NARRATOR

The narrator of *Buen amor* is a sinner. In the prayer that opens the book he prays for help as a sinner to the 'Gloriosa Madre de pecadores' (ll. 10d, 1046d), and in the prologue he reminds his readers continually that 'se non puede escapar de pecado' (p. 7), that 'la natura umana mas aparejada e inclinada es al mal que al bien' (p. 9), and that 'es umanal cosa el pecar' (p. 11).[25] Describing himself before his first amorous episode, the narrator writes: 'E yo, porque so omne, como otro pecador, / ove de las mugeres a vezes grand amor' (ll. 76ab); and before one of the final amorous episodes the same narrator yearns to be the sinner that would defile the nun Doña Garoça ('¡Ay Dios! e yo lo fuesse aqueste pecador,' l. 1501c). But the narrator is no ordinary sinner: he is a disciple of Don Amor and Doña Venus ('Quesiste ser maestro ante que discípulo ser,' l. 427a; 'Partióse Amor de mí e dexóme dormir. / Desque vino el alva pensé de comedir / en lo que me castigó; e por verdad dezir, / fallé que en sus castigos usé siempre vevir,' st. 576).

Don Amor is described by the narrator as a kind of devil ('manera as de diablo,' l. 405a), and throughout the narrator's diatribe against him, Don Amor is an agent who facilitates the work of the devil (sta. 184d, 197, 207, 222, 224, 232, 275, 293), causing people to lose both body and soul. Don Melón de la Huerta was sent to his encounter with Doña Endrina by Trotaconventos herself (ll. 872ab), but it was Don Amor and Doña Venus who had sent him to Trotaconventos in the first place; so when Trotaconventos says, '¡Don Melón, tiradvos dende! ¿tróxovos y el diablo?' (l. 875b), the reader can safely deduce from the irony of the situation that Don Amor, Doña Venus, and Trotaconventos are devils, or the devil's agents, since it was they who sent Don Melón to meet with Doña Endrina. But Don Amor is not merely a devil; he is, by reason of his relationship to Doña Venus, an Antichrist.

Doña Venus is the diabolical counterpart of the Virgin Mary. Archpriest Ruiz takes care to point out at the beginning and at the end of his book that the Virgin Mary is the beginning and end of all goodness ('Porque de todo bien es comienço e raíz la Virgen Santa María,' ll. 19ab; and 'Porque Santa María, segund que dicho he, / es comienço e fin del bien,' ll. 1626ab). The diabolical narrator uses the same terminology to describe Doña Venus, omitting the key word 'bien' that applies to the Virgin Mary ('Fuime a Doña Venus, que le levasse mensaje, / ca ella es comienço e fin d'este viaje,' ll. 583cd). Don Amor is described by the narrator as a Cupid who shoots his poisoned arrows at his most devoted followers ('enervolas tus viras; / al que mejor te sirve a él fieres quando tiras,' ll. 183bc); but both Doña Venus and Don Amor himself agree that the latter is the former's husband ('Pámfilo, mi criado ... con mi muger, Doña Venus, te verná a castigar,' ll. 574cd; and 'Ya fueste consejado del Amor, mi marido,' l. 608a). The implication is clear: just as the Virgin Mary is at once the wife of God (having conceived of the Holy Spirit) and the mother of God (having given birth to Jesus Christ), so too her devilish counterpart, Doña Venus, is at once the wife of a devil (Don Amor) and the mother of a devil, since Don Amor is depicted as Cupid (ll. 183bc). Don Amor is, therefore, the devilish counterpart of Jesus, or, in other words, an Antichrist; and the narrator of *Buen amor*, who confesses that he has lived all his life according to the commandments of Don Amor (st. 576), is not merely an ordinary sinner but essentially a disciple of a devil.[26]

Once the essential diabolical nature of *Buen amor*'s narrator has been revealed, many of the problems that have plagued critics of the work's structure can be reexamined. In the first place, the devil and his disciples were believed to have the ability to change into various forms at will. In one of the 'Milagros' of Berceo, for example, the devil appears to the drunken cleric in the forms of a bull, a dog, and a lion.[27] Likewise, the narrator of *Buen amor* changes his form at will from that of an archpriest to Don Melón de la Huerta (whose name means either melon or badger) and back to an archpriest.

In the second place, the narrator reminds his readers of something they often forget – that the Devil was once a most powerful angel in heaven ('primero muchos ángeles, con ellos Lucifer, / ... / de las sillas del cielo ovieron de caer,' ll. 233bd); as a direct consequence of his prior angelic state the Devil is no stranger to truth and goodness, which he knows how to use subtly in order to achieve evil ends. In a story that Don Amor, a devil in his own right, tells as an example to his disciple the archpriest (sts. 529–43), the devil uses a 'sotil engaño' (l. 529c) to deceive a hermit. 'Con sotileza' (l. 531c) the devil approaches the hermit piously ('¡Dios te salve, buen monje;' l. 531d); he then promises the hermit what the latter yearns for: a taste of the 'cuerpo de Dios' (l. 533c). As can be expected, what the hermit finally gets is not the body of God but the body of a woman whom he raped and killed in his drunkenness and for which crime he was executed. The important point is that in order to achieve the ruin of a holy man the devil assumes a pious stance and persuades him with the truth according to the dogma of the church, namely that wine is a holy substance because from it is made the true blood of God ('Non deves tener dubda que del vino se faze / la sangre verdadera de Dios: en ello yaze / sacramento muy santo; pruévalo, si te plaze,' ll. 534abc).

The irony of this exemplum is overwhelming: it is a story about the Devil told by a devil to a devil's disciple, and the first words the devil utters to the holy man are 'May *God* protect you.' This exemplum is no less intrinsic to the understanding of *Buen Amor*'s ironic structure than is the one about the Greeks and Romans (sts. 44–70); excessive subtlety and irony are not a reflection of 'una ironía a estilo del creador del mundo,' as Spitzer puts it, but, rather, a reflection of the subtle deceptive irony of the devil.[28] The diabolical narrator of *Buen amor*, to whom Don Amor teaches this exemplum, learns the lesson well: he not only refrains from wine, but he also changes his perspective subtly and ironically so as to confuse his inexperienced readers. At times the narrator, like the devil in the exemplum, adopts a perfectly orthodox religious stance, and though the moral of his stories, like that of the Doña Endrina episode, often seems to be religiously correct, much of this correctness stems ultimately from the fact that the narrator, like the devil, is no stranger to the doctrines of the church.

THE JUXTAPOSITION OF CONTRARIES

Juan Ruiz was able to conceive the structure of *Buen amor*, *De vetula* and other models notwithstanding, largely because he was, as a learned medieval man, accustomed to think in contraries. One of the most popular forms of writing in the archpriest's time, the lives of saints, consists in effect of biographies that contain reliable, pious third-person narrators who tell the spiritual deeds of holy men. By contrast the archpriest chose an unreliable, diabolical first-person narrator who tells the carnal deeds of a sinful man – the archpriest's book is not the life of a saint but the life of an anti-saint. The life of a saint was depicted as an imitation of the life of Christ (*imitatio Christi*); Ruiz's narrator follows the footsteps not of Christ but of Don Amor, an antichrist (*imitatio Daemonii*). The life of a saint is usually traced from his birth through his religious upbringing as a young man to his death in old age; when the saint dies, those who have assisted him live on to tell not only the miracles of his life but the miraculous deeds that occurred on his account after his death. By contrast, the narrator of *Buen amor* refers to his birth in one stanza only ('En este signo a tal creo que yo nací,' l. 153a), and the entire autobiography is devoted to one period of his life, youth. Before the Doña Endrina episode the narrator explains that he is acting as other young people do ('E porque es costumbre de mancebos usada / ... / tomé amiga nueva, una dueña encerrada'); Don Melón de la Huerta is described by Trotaconventos as a young man ('Es Don Melón de la Huerta, mancebillo de verdad,' l. 727c; ll. 730a, 738c, 758c); and in one of the final episodes of the book Doña Garoça is told by Trotaconventos that the archpriest is a young man ('Desque me partí de vos a un arcipreste sirvo, / mancebo bienandante,' ll. 1345ab; 1489a).

The training of this young man is not altogether religious and Christian, for he is a disciple of Don Amor and has learnt lessons about pagan books like those of Ovid, Virgil, and Aristotle. This youthful narrator does not die like a saint, to be survived by those who have served him; rather, those who serve him die (Trotaconventos, Doña Garoça); though they are no longer as impressive as before, the narrator's carnal 'miracles' continue after the death of Trotaconventos.

Because of his penchant for juxtaposing contraries, it is difficult to tell precisely where the book of the unreliable narrator begins and where it ends. He talks in lines 1626cd, for example, of not closing his book ('e con tanto faré / punto a mi librete, mas non lo cerraré'), but shortly afterwards, still referring to his book, he talks about 'closing up shop' ('por ende fago punto e cierro mi almario,' l. 1632c). Nevertheless, it is possible to decide on a beginning and an end for *Buen amor* if one reads stanza 1626 with care:

> Porque Santa María, segund que dicho he
> es comienço e fin del bien, tal es mi fe,
> fiz le quatro cantares, e con tanto faré
> punto a mi librete, mas non lo cerraré.

One may argue that 'quatro cantares' refers to the four songs to the Virgin Mary found between stanzas 1668 and 1684 of the Salamanca manuscript. But it seems a more attractive proposition to argue – because of the phrases 'segund que dicho he' (referring to a similar statement already made) and 'comienço e fin' (implying a division in two parts, one part at the beginning and a second part at the end) – that 'quatro cantares' refers to the four songs to the Virgin, two at the beginning between stanzas 20 and 43, and two at the end between stanzas 1635 and 1649.

Although the 'gozos' form a rather decisive beginning and end to the book, it is aesthetically important to respect Juan Ruiz's desire not to be confined to a single beginning and a single end. Other possible beginnings are to be found at line 1a, for the obvious reason that this is the first line, and at line 11a, where manuscript G begins the version of 1330. Other possible endings are lines 1684d, as already explained,

1634d in the Toledo manuscript, 1728 in the Gayoso manuscript, and 1709d where the Salamanca manuscript comes to a stop. The archpriest's book might thus be said to decisively begin at 20a and end at 1649d; beyond these stanzas are introductory material (sts. 1–10, the prose prologue, and sts. 11–19) and terminatory material (sts. 1650–728).

The aesthetic function of the introductory and terminatory material is to lend an air of indecisive formlessness to the whole work by detracting from, but at the same time highlighting, the structure of the more decisive intervening unit. So the structure of the entire work is carried out according to the principle of the juxtaposition of contraries, since it proceeds from indecisive unit (introductory material) to decisive unit (sts. 20–1649) to indecisive unit (terminatory material). This structure can be depicted graphically:

introductory

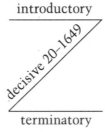

terminatory

It must not be supposed, however, that the apparent formlessness of the introductory and terminatory material indicates a deficiency in structure. I have demonstrated elsewhere that the prose prologue has a rhetorical structure based on contraries,[29] and that Ruiz preferred to juxtapose contraries because he believed that to be the way to build a solid edifice ('firme edificio,' p. 13). Both the prose prologue and the entire introductory unit, are built upon contraries since they move from poetry to prose to poetry in a manner similar to the major units of the work.

The terminatory material is an independent unit of separate poems linked by the common theme of supplication. As a unit it shares this theme with the introductory material, but there is also contrast between the two parts. In the introductory unit Archpriest Ruiz's supplication is directed to one Christian God and to his readers; to God for deliverance and inspiration, and to the intellect of his readers for understanding. By contrast, in the terminatory unit, although the plea for deliverance from prison is repeated, the supplication is less for nonsubstantial gifts like inspiration and understanding, than for material things like food for the scholars and blind beggars and carnal comfort for the clerics of Talavera who are threatened with the loss of their concubines.

In addition to its complementary and contrastive relationship to the introductory unit, the terminatory unit has the same structure as the entire work by reason of the direction of its supplications. Following the sensible order established by Willis in his edition, stanzas 1650–60 and 1710–28 are the supplications of scholars and blind beggars directed to individual human beings, stanzas 1661–89 are the supplications of one individual to two goddesses (as opposed to one God in the introductory unit), and stanzas 1690–1709 are the supplication of a group of clerics to one human being, the king of Castile, against another, the pope. The unit proceeds, therefore, in a structure similar to the one described above, from supplication of group to human beings to supplication of individual to goddesses to supplication of group to human being.

The decisive structural unit of *Buen amor*, consisting of all the material between lines 20a and 1649d, comprises the following elements:

(a) Four songs in celebration of the Joys of Mary
(b) Fourteen amorous episodes
(c) Thirty-five illustrative exempla (Willis counts thirty-three)
(d) Six doctrinal expositions on the dogma of the Catholic church: on deadly sins, the canonical hours, confession, the battle between Lent and flesh, the passion of Jesus Christ, and the virtuous arms of the Christian
(e) Three satirical pieces: on the powerful properties of money, small women, and death
(f) The triumph of Don Amor, including his victory parade and a description of his tent

There is in each of these elements much symmetrical building with contraries. Some of the contrast in the four songs (a) stems from the fact that the songs are a beginning and an end. In the amorous episodes (b) the description of the women and of the setting shifts from that of five beautiful and urbane ones to four ugly and rustic ones to five beautiful and urbane ones. Since the main function of the illustrations (c), 'is to illustrate a point of argument,' as Ian Michael has shown,[30] they frequently tend to proceed from point to counterpoint, building with contraries. The contrast in the doctrinal expositions

(d) stems in large part from the combative nature and tone of all the pieces except the passion of Jesus Christ, which has its own contrary function as will be demonstrated shortly. With respect to the satirical pieces (e) I have shown elsewhere that the poem on the properties of small women has the same zigzag structure of the diagram.[31] The contrary aspect of Don Amor's triumph is crucial and, therefore, deserves special treatment.

The triumph of Don Amor is intended as a deliberate contrast to the passion of Jesus Christ. It must be noted that the two passion poems between stanzas 1046 and 1066, as their titles imply, make no mention whatever of the triumph or resurrection of Christ; they emphasize his defeat. The poems lead immediately not to the triumphal resurrection of Christ, as would be expected in a Christian context, but to the battle between Don Carnal and Doña Cuaresma, which in turn leads directly to the triumph of Antichrist, the lord and master of the diabolical narrator. The diabolical narrator becomes at this crucial point in the book's structure, the most devoted disciple of Antichrist: he calls Don Amor 'mio señor' (sts. 1258, 1261, 1263), and whereas at the beginning of the book he sought to chase Don Amor from his home ('Si Amor eres, non puedes aquí estar,' st. 1826), the narrator now invites him to a magnificent banquet at his home (l. 1261d). When Don Amor accepts the invitation (st. 1262) in the face of so many others, the narrator becomes the chosen disciple of Antichrist. This change is significant since it prepares the narrator for his most diabolical amorous episode; only the most devoted, chosen disciple of Antichrist would attempt to seduce the bride of Christ, Doña Garoça. After his attempt to seduce Doña Garoça, not even a pagan Moorish woman will listen to proposals from the diabolical narrator, and he is finally denounced by his inept messenger, Don Furón.

It would be impractical here to analyse in greater detail each of the six elements of the work's decisive unit, but from the above analysis three deductions can be made. (1) Between the 'gozos' at the beginning and those at the end there is nothing that cannot be described as diabolical; even the most pious poem to the Virgin (sts. 1043–5) and the two poems on the passion of Jesus are made to serve a diabolical end. The devil, it must be remembered, knows how to deceive with piety. (2) Between the seduction of Doña Endrina at the beginning of the amorous episodes and that of Doña Garoça at their end, and between the rejection of Don Amor at the beginning and his welcome at the end, there seems to be a continuous step-by-step line of descent in the diabolical character of the narrator. Even when he seems to be climbing in the sierras, he is in fact descending a social ladder in his choice of women and setting; and when he seems to be climbing the social ladder with the choice of a nun, he is in fact descending a moral one. Those readers who are not convinced that an archpriest would confide in a devil and be influenced by him have only to read the description of the three devils on the tent of Don Amor (sts. 1281–5), especially stanza 1283:

> El segundo diablo remece los abades;
> arciprestes e dueñas fablan sus poridades
> con este compañón que les da libertades
> que pierdan las obladas e fablen vanidades

(3) Because they are 'de todo bien comienço e raiz' (l. 19a) and 'comienço e fin del bien' (l. 1626b) there can be nothing diabolical about the 'gozos.' Moreover, it is significant that there are fourteen 'gozos' (two sets of seven) at the beginning and fourteen at the end; these twenty-eight heavenly joys counterbalance and overpower the fourteen earthly joys as represented by the amorous episodes. Once again the structure of the large decisive unit zigzags from fourteen heavenly Marian joys to fourteen earthly venereal joys to fourteen heavenly joys.

STRUCTURE AND MEANING

If these deductions are in essence correct it would be justifiable to represent the structure of *Buen amor* as:

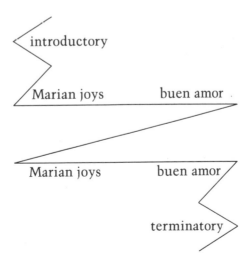

For more precision the above lines should be serrate rather than straight. One can be certain that many Hispanists have entertained similar thoughts about the structure of *Buen amor* and have seen no need to scribble it out ingenuously. In a sense the above study merely documents what Castro had in mind by 'continuous inner transition,' what Menéndez Pidal meant by 'este espejismo, siempre cambiante,' and especially what María Rosa Lida de Malkiel, who refers to Menéndez Pidal, intended by 'un zigzagueo de situaciones ofrecidas y súbitamente negadas.' Yet although these critics seemed to agree about what they thought regarding the structure of *Buen amor*, they could not agree on what the structure meant. Deyermond, whose insights and summaries are always valuable, explains the problem succinctly: 'A drawback to the latter approach is that the structure conveys different meanings to different critics: for Lecoy, it shows that *Buen amor* is an art of love, while for Walker it proves that this is ultimately a moralising work.'[32] However, if one examines the aesthetic to which Juan Ruiz subscribed, it is possible to extract meaning unequivocally from the structure of his work.

Underlying the archpriest's use of contraries is the belief that the truth of an affirmation is cemented unequivocally by negative reference to its opposite; this was one of the key rules of the art of preaching, as Robert de Basevorn and other theoreticians recommended.[33] There can be little doubt that the archpriest of Hita is preaching throughout *Buen amor*: the decisive unit is an extraodinary popular sermon (*divisio extra*) complete with ridiculous stories, not unlike the Easter Sunday afternoon sermons described above.[34] To emphasize the fact that he is preaching, the archpriest inserts a learned sermon (*divisio intra*) into the book's introductory material as a cementing contrary to the popular sermon that is the main part. Two questions arise: what truth is he preaching, and are there not too many diabolical stories?

The answer to both these questions is found in Ruiz's favourite literary device: *exsuperatio*. *Exsuperatio*, briefly, is overstatement to the point of absurdity; its function is to create suspicion by its very excesses, thus exposing the invalidity of the thing exaggerated.[35] *Buen Amor* is a moralizing Christian work *because* it contains, between brief affirmations of its Christian morality, a lengthy and absurd guide on an art of love. Because he dwells at such absurd length on 'loco amor,' the archpriest is affirming the truth of his belief in the 'buen amor' that is the beginning and end of all good works like his.

This study attempts to contribute to a clearer understanding of the meaning of *Buen Amor* by emphasizing, as has not been done before as far as I know, the role of the archpriest as devil.[36] Consequently, it is fitting to conclude this analysis by answering the question: Is it credible that a medieval archpriest would attempt to teach a Christian lesson by describing himself as, and playing the role of, a devil? The answer is a most emphatic yes.

On the medieval stage and in medieval life the Devil was by far the most important and perhaps the only conception that indelibly impressed on the mind of men at one and the same time fear, affinity, satire, and ridicule – fear of eternal damnation; affinity, because, as the archpriest repeats in his prologue, it was believed that man's nature as a sinner inclined him more readily towards evil than towards good; satire, because the Devil's acts exposed the wrongs of others; ridicule, because the Devil's pride was shown to lead to folly before the ultimate wisdom of God. As a dramatic didactic device the Devil, as Milton, for one, knew, is superb. When the archpriest inserts himself in the role of the Devil he acts as an exemplary Christian. He preaches the fear of eternal damnation, he wins the sympathy of his audience which has affinity with his own sins, and by exaggerating these sins, he makes his confession more dramatic – St Augustine, it may be remembered, exaggerated the magnitude of his sins by confessing even to those he may have committed as a baby. The archpriest satirizes not only the wrongs of society as a whole, but especially those of his peers, archpriests; and he makes his audience laugh with comic relief at the ridiculous excesses of his own diabolic performance.

Corbacho

The method of composition that I ascribe to *Buen amor* is explained in some detail in a philosophical treatise that was available to Juan Ruiz – the translation by Hermannus Alemannus of Averroës's commentary on Aristotle's *Poetics*:

> Et partes sermonis fabularis secundum quod est representativus due sunt. Omnis enim representatio aut imperat sibi locum per representationem sui contrarij et post permutatur ad suam intentionem, (et est modus qui dicitur apud eos circulatio) aut rem ipsam non faciens mentionem aliquam sui contrarii (et hoc est quod ipsi nominabant significationem) ... Et dico per circulationem imitationem contrarii eius quod intenditur ad laudandum, primitus ut ipsum respuat aut abborreat anima et ut deinde permutetur ab hoc ad imitationem ipsiusmet quod laudandum est: ut cum quis voluerit imitari seu representare felic-

itatem et ei pertinentes incipiat primo ab imitatione infelicita-
tis et ab illis qui ei pertinent deinde permutetur ad imitationem
felicitatis et ei pertinentibus. [Aristotle said:] And the elements
of fiction which make it representational are two. For all representation commands attention to itself either through representation of its contrary and is then changed completely to its real
intention (and this is the style which is called among those people circumlocution) or through the thing itself, not making any
mention of its contrary (and this is what the same people called
direct meaning) ... And [Aristotle said] I mean by circumlocution the imitation of the opposite of that which is intended to
be praised, so that the soul first spurns or abhors this [opposite]
thing and so that it may then be turned away from it towards
the imitation of the real thing which is to be praised. So that
when someone wishes to imitate or represent success and those
things pertaining to success, he may first begin from an imitation of failure and those things which concern failure, then he
may turn to the imitation of success and to those things concerning success.[37]

The above quotation explains the method of composition of Juan Ruiz
and also writers like Alfonso Martínez de Toledo, archpriest of Talavera. Juan Ruiz uses the aesthetic of contraries referred to above as
circulatio, to which he adds *exsuperatio*. I should like to demonstrate,
now, how Martínez de Toledo uses the method referred to above as *significatio*, and elsewhere in the same commentary as 'directio sive
directiva significatio.' But let me state clearly that it is not my intention to refer to the translation of Hermannus Alemannus and to the
Corbacho in terms of source and influence, nor do I mean to imply
that the contents of Averroës's commentary are not to be found in
other sources also available to Martínez de Toledo. I connect these
texts to show how one text refers to a system that is found in the other
text in a more elaborate form, not to show that one text influenced the
other.[38]

The commentary of Averroës on the *Poetics* was especially popular
among those Christian writers who sought to accommodate in an
orthodox manner those writings of Aristotle that were of doubtful
orthodoxy.[39] Averroës stresses the didactic function of literature:

Omne itaque poema et omnis oratio poetica aut est vituperatio
aut est laudatio (Boggess, p. 3) ... Et ex quo representatores et
assimilatores per hoc intendunt instigare ad quasdam acti....es

que circa voluntaria consistunt et retrahere a quibusdam, erunt necessario ea que intendunt per suas representationes aut virtutes aut vicia. Omnia enim actio et omnia mos non versatur nisi circa alterum istorum videlicet virtutem aut vicium (Boggess, p. 7; MP p. 43, l. 29: vitium). [Aristotle said:] And so every poem, every poetic utterance, is either praise or blame ... And since writers and imitators aim through this [method] to instigate [people] towards certain actions, which are found among things done of one's own accord, and to dissuade [people] from certain others, those things for which they aim through their representations will of necessity be either virtues or vices. For every action, every trait has to do with nothing but one or the other of these, namely, virtue or vice.

Both Juan Ruiz and Martínez de Toledo (the latter in the *Corbacho*) chose to encourage virtue by denouncing vice. The archpriest of Hita preferred the art of blaming vice through circumlocution (*ars vituperandi per circulationem*), whereas the archpriest of Talavera chose to denounce vice by direct means (*per directivam significationem*). In addition to dividing all fiction into the didactic arts of praising and blaming, Averroës emphasized the fundamental role of imagery in literary works ('Et sermones poetici sermones sunt imaginativi,' Boggess, p. 3) [Aristotle said:] And poetic utterances are imaginative utterances]. In fact, most of the commentary as translated by Hermannus is devoted to a definition and discussion of imagery, with examples. I shall refer below to this discussion of imagery in an attempt to understand the organizing principles of the *Corbacho*, first of the work as a whole, and then of its units.[40]

According to the *Commentary*, one of the ways of making images is by analogy, which is defined as 'concambium pro suo comproportionali videlicet quando fuerit alicuius proportio ad secundum proportio tertii ad quartum tunc permatatur [sic] nomen tertii ad primum et econtrario' (Boggess, p. 4; MP p. 24, l. 22 permutatur) [A trope as good as its proper coordinate, as for example, when the relationship of any one thing to a second thing is as the relationship of a third to a fourth, then the name of the third is substituted for the first, and vice versa.] A similar image from the science of logic is used by Martínez de Toledo when he wishes to emphasize the veracity of the *Corbacho*: 'Non es esto coronica nin ystoria de caualleria, en las quales a las vezes ponen c por b.'[41]

To substitute *c* for *b*, no matter how colloquial the expression might be, is tantamount to substituting the third letter for the second. It would be surprising if the archpriest of Talavera, who uses terminology from the science of logic throughout his book, was not thinking of the common analogy a is to b as c is to d when he wrote the phrase 'ponen c por b.' The archpriest seems to be differentiating his book from others that are ordered illogically. If this were so, it would imply that his own book is structured according to logic. Indeed, the *Corbacho* is divided into four main parts in such a way that the first part is related to the second in a manner similar to the way in which the third is related to the fourth ('E va en quatro principales partes diuiso: en la primera fablaré de reprobación de loco amor. E en la segunda diré de las condiçiones algund tanto de las viçiosas mugeres. E en la tercera proseguiré las complisiones de los ombres quáles son [o] qué virtud tyenen para amar o ser amados. En la quarta concluyré reprobando la común materia [manera] de fablar de los fados,' Prologue, p. 2; [PP]).[42]

The first part of *Corbacho* is a denunciation of the 'loco amor' of men and women in general; the second is a denunciation of some women in particular ('las viçiosas mugeres'); the third is a denunciation of all men in general but according to their four particular types; the fourth is a denunciation of those men and women who believe in fate and fortune ('muchas personas, asý omes como mugeres, que tienen que sy mal han, que non les viene synon porque de nesçesario les avía de venir, llamando a esto tal ventura, fado o fortuna,' p. 228). Not only is the first part related to the second in the same way (from general to particular) as the third is to the fourth, but the author states clearly that the third part should not be substituted for the second, that is, c must not be substituted for b:

> E por quanto el yntento de la obra es prinçipalmente de repro- bación de amor terrenal, el amor de Dios loando, e porque fasta aquí [i.e., during part 2, which can be called b] el amor de las mugeres fue reprouado, conuiene quel amor de los ombres non sea loado ... [i.e., in the next part, part 3, or c]. *E por quanto comunmente los ombres non son reprehendidos como las mugeres so reglas generales*, esto por el seso mayor e mas juyzio que alcançan, conviene, pues, particularmente fablar de cada uno segund su qualidad ... [i.e., what is to be done in the next part, c, is not normally done in the style of the previous part, b]. Por que algunos non digan que non faze esto tractar a propósyto de reprouaçión de amor, sy faze, e mucho, sy la consideran e aunque tal se[a] mismo de las mugeres. Pero generalmente ellas tienen otras condiçiones que los ombres [and hence demand treatment in separate sections] de las quales voluntariosamente

les plaze vsar e vsan, segund dalta ya dixe. (p. 190; brackets and italics mine)

In anticipation of what his detractors might argue (and, fortunately, he did have many detractors), Martínez de Toledo insists on justifying, in the above quotation, his reason for separating the second section of his book from the third. Because he reprehended some women in particular in the second section, he devotes a separate third section to denounce all men in general; but since men, being superior, are not to be reprehended as women normally are 'so reglas generales,' he does not lump together all men but treats them according to their four particular types, 'conviene, pues, particularmente fablar de cada uno segund su qualidad.' The ordinary treatment of vicious women in part 2 (or *b*) must not, according to the author, be confused with the particular treatment of men in part 3 (or *c*). It should cause no astonishment that the archpriest should select a structure from the science of logic for his book, since one of the major misinterpretations of the *Poetics* made by Averroës was to place literature as a theological science firmly within the realm of logic.[43]

It has been a source of some bewilderment that Archpriest Martínez calls the fourth part of his book the middle part ('media parte').[44] With regard to this phrase it should be noted that Hermannus translated Averroës's title as a 'middle commentary' (commentarium medium). Averroës wrote three types of commentary: long (commentarium magnum), middle (commentarium medium), and the compendium, or epitome. These three types were distinguished from each other by the ways in which they treated the original source being explicated. The commentarium magnum quoted from the original source extensively and carefully differentiated between text and commentary. The commentarium medium quoted the original less extensively and sometimes paraphrased before commenting on it. In the compendium little effort was made to separate text from commentary and the exact words of the original were alluded to only occasionally.[45] Thus the possibility emerges that when the archpriest of Talavera uses the words 'compendio' and 'media parte,' he might well have had in mind 'book' words that refer to special kinds of commentary.

The method used by Averroës to compose all of his compendia was 'to delve into Aristotle's works and to extract from them those scientific statements which govern his particular line of argument'; he then explicated each of these scientific statements.[46] The method is not unlike the one used by Martínez de Toledo in the *Corbacho*. Every chapter consists of a strong statement which is carefully explicated;

and the author describes his method in a manner similar to that of Averroës: 'Propuse de fazer un compendio breue en romance ... Por ende yo ... tomé algunos notables dichos de un doctor de París' (pp. 2–3). Moreover, Martínez de Toledo's treatment of sources in the 'media parte,' which most critics agree is unlike the rest of the book, is much more like a commentarium medium than a compendium. The use of the word 'romance' seems to imply that the archpriest was seeking to distinguish his work from Latin compendia.

With respect to a 'media parte,' a passage in the *Commentary* about the middle part of a work of art should be noted:

> Et ultimum est cum eis quibus est ultimum; neque est ante. Medium autem est ante et cum. Ipsum ergo melius est utrisque extremis, cum sit medium in loco qui est inter id quod est ante et inter id quod est post. Talem enim locum optinent in bello illi qui fortes sunt, scilicet locum medium inter locum timidorum et locum audacium seu protervorum. Et hic est locus medius, et hoc modo terminus bonus in compositione est medius, et est qui componitur ex extremis et ex quo non componuntur extrema. Neque oportet ut medium sit solummodo medium in compositione et ordine et loco sed in quantitate et bonitate (Boggess, pp. 24–5; MP p. 50, l. 7 obtinent). [Aristotle said:] The end comes attached to those things to which it is an end; and it does not come before. The middle, moreover, comes before and attached to. It is therefore better than both extremes since the middle is in the place which is between that which comes first and that which is last. Indeed in war those who are brave hold such a position, that is, the middle position between the position of the cowardly and that of the daring or the [excessively] bold. And this is the middle ground, and in this way the middle is a good location in composition, for it is that which is composed from the extremes and that from which the extremes are not composed. And it is not fitting that the middle should merely be middle in [terms of] composition and arrangement and position but in [terms of] quantity and beauty.

In the above passage the images are visual: the middle is to be visualized in relation to the extremes. In terms of location the middle comes before the end, somewhere between the end and the beginning (which does not necessarily mean midway between the end and the beginning); and the middle remains distinct from the extremes. In terms of ideological content the image is military: the middle group is

neither cowardly nor excessively bold, but brave, a position derived
from both extremes though entirely divorced from them. In terms of
quantity and beauty an organic image is used to explain that the middle must be of determinate length ('quantitatem determinatam,' Boggess, p. 25 MP p. 50, l. 16 terminatam) and natural shape ('non dicitur
de animali parvi in comparatione individuorum sue speciei quod sit
bonum seu pulcrum,' Boggess, p. 25 [it is not said of an animal that is
small in comparison with the individuals of its species that it is beautiful or fine]).

The archpriest of Talaver's 'media parte' fits these criteria. 'Media
parte' seems to mean 'the part inserted' anywhere between the two
extremes rather than at the point midway between them. This 'media
parte' remains distinct from the other parts. A passage in the *Corbacho's* 'media parte' both emphasizes Hermannus's 'voluntaria' and also
links the middle part of an action with its end: 'Pero asý traydos, el
byen que después fazen, voluntario le fazen e de grado; e sy el
comienço fue forçado, el medio e la fin son voluntarios de byen fazer'
(p. 230). In terms of ideological content Martínez de Toledo also uses a
military image to describe those against whom he is arguing: he describes people who speak 'osada e atreuidamente' (p. 242), which corresponds to the 'locum audacium seu protervorum' of Hermannus. The
archpriest's own position is that of the middle ground between that of
the 'letrados' and the 'symples e ynorantes' (p. 239) but closely allied to
the latter. In order to understand the image's military nature it is
necessary to refer to a passage at the end of the second part in which
Martínez de Toledo quotes St Augustine and then states his own position.

> E demás, por conclusyón, dixeron algunos grandes letrados san-
> tos de Dios escogidos, en especial Sant Augustín: 'Veemos unos
> violentos ombres que el mundo los aborresce e los tyene en
> estima de non nada por *symples, pobres e de poca ciencia* e auc-
> toridad, que roban e arrebatan los altos çielos por fuerça e con
> grand furia e violençia que non ay detenimiento en ellos. E
> nosotros, con todo nuestro saber e ciencia, somos çabullydos en
> los ynfiernos.' Asý, que non lo pongo en comparaçión esto por
> [yo] ser tal, nin uno de los violentos, por que me pesa; byen uno
> de los que poco saben e la merced de Dios esperan. (p. 188; quo-
> tation marks and italics mine [PP].

From this passage it can be deduced that Martínez de Toledo places
himself between the 'letrados,' who are not violent (and perhaps

occupy the *locum timidorum* described by Hermannus), and the 'symples, pobres e de poca ciencia,' who wage audacious war against the high heavens; but he is closer to the latter in his middle ground because he describes himself as 'uno de los que poco saben'; he differs from the 'atrevidos' with whom he allies himself in that, instead of waging war in ignorance, he awaits the mercy of God. The image of battle is sustained in the important epilogue, in which women who felt unjustly denounced in the second part call the author a 'loco atrevido' (p. 329) and attack him fiercely.[47]

In so far as the 'media parte' is supposed to be of, according to Hermannus, determinate length and natural shape, it should be noted that the principal parts of the book consist of two long sections of equal length: the first (101 pages in Pérez Pastor's edition) and the fourth (101 pages); and two shorter sections of unequal lengths: the second (76) pages and the third (34 pages). It might not be accidental that the entire book can be divided into three sections of approximately equal length: the prologue and part one (110 pages, mainly of doctrinal arguments), parts two and three (110 pages of reproof of men and women, separated into two distinct parts), and part four and the epilogue (104 pages, mainly of doctrinal arguments).[48]

In the light of the foregoing discussion of the overall structure of the *Corbacho*, it is reasonable to find that the archpriest of Talavera uses imagery from the field of logic at key points in each of the four principal parts of his book. We have already discussed the image in part one ('poner c por b'). In part two the author deems it wise, after rebuking women, 'que los términos e propusyciones se conviertan' (p. 187). At the end of his explanation of the four kinds of men in part three the author decides 'por ende todo esto dexado vengamos al propósyto e conclusyión (p. 201). In part four the author puts forward his best arguments in favour of free will, and then, with vocabulary from the field of logic, invites dissenters to debate with God himself if they remain unconvinced: 'Empero sy dizes que asý non es esto, dispútalo con El, e déxate de mí, que de los fechos de Dios non te puedo más certificar, que nin recibe argumento ynsoluble, nin sofisma, nin oblygatoria, nin terminus yn quem, nin argumento lulista, remonista nin sofista' (pp. 230–1).

Apart from the imagery from the field of logic which helps to elucidate the structure of the work as a whole, Martínez de Toledo uses surprisingly little imagery, partly because he chooses the direct method (*directio sive directiva significatio*) of describing the thing itself rather than finding an analogy or depicting it through its contrary: he sets out to condemn 'loco amor,' and that is what he does directly. Of course, since anything one does affects directly the contrary of that thing, according to medieval theory, the archpriest's direct reprobation of 'loco amor' implies praise of 'buen amor,' as he himself explains: 'Maldezir del malo loança es del bueno' (Prologue, p. 7). Because he usually describes the thing itself rather than an image of a thing, the relatively few images Martínez de Toledo uses tend to stand out; they themselves are as direct and as easy to understand as the things with which they are compared. The most frequent and important images fall into seven categories, each of which will be discussed: truth, rhyme, animals, the five senses, fire, women, sleep.[49]

Truth. One way of producing effective imagery, according to Hermannus Alemannus, is to emphasize its veracity. The author could achieve this result in any one of three ways or by a combination of any of these ways: (a) by describing something that the author had witnessed; (b) by describing so vividly that the subject of the description seemed to be visible to the very eyes of a reader or listener; (c) by describing those kinds of actions that are most likely to arouse pity and fear. Here are passages in Hermannus's translation that refer to the first way, the eyewitness account:

> Et altera est habitudo significans hominis credulitatem seu opinionem. Non est enim habitudo eius qui loquitur certus existens de re habitudo eius qui loquitur dubius existens (Boggess, p. 18).
>
> (Et Mutenebbii poeta probatissimus fuit in hac manerie representationis, prout apparet in eius poematibus. Ideoque refertur de ipso quod noleurit aliqua gesta describere regis Sceifi Addauleti domini sui quibus ipse non interfuerit cum ipso. Certius enim comprehenduntur a se ipso prospecta quam audito ab aliis. Optime ergo se habet quis ad referendum ea que ipse cum quibuslibet suis accidentibus et circumstantiis propriis per se comprehendit et quasi sensualiter conspexit) (Boggess, p. 57; MP p. 62/l. 29 voluerit; the sense seems to support 'noluerit'). [Aristotle said:] And another [kind] is the appearance [or attitude] which conveys the credulity or opinion of a man. For the appearance of one who speaks being certain of the topic is not that of one who speaks being doubtful.
>
> (And the poet Mutenebbii was excellent at this kind of representation, as is evident from his poems. Of this same poet it is said that he refused to describe any deeds of his lord, King Sceifus Addauletus, in which he himself had not taken part with the king. For those things which are witnessed by oneself are

understood more clearly than those which are heard from other witnesses. For one does best at relating those things which, together with their incidental particulars and attendant circumstances, one understands for oneself and which one contemplated as if sensually).

It is well known that Martínez de Toledo puts an emphasis in the *Corbacho* on things that he himself had experienced, as, for example, the story of Irazón the painter and his lover ('Dentro en Tortosa yo ví fazer justiçia de una muger que consyntió que su amigo matase a su fijo porque los non descubriese,' p. 71); or the account of Argentera ('Yo ví una muger, que se llamaba la Argentera, presa en Barcelona,' pp. 71–2); or the tale of Juan Orenga and the woman who bit off her husband's tongue ('Vý más en la dicha cibdad de Tortosa por ojo dos cosas muy fuertes de creer; pero, por Dios, yo las vý,' p. 72). At the end of the book's part one is the general affirmation 'que esto que dicho he, sabe que es verdad, e es dubda de faltar dello o de grand parte. E non pienses que el que lo escriuió te lo dize porque lo oyó solamente, saluo porque por prática dello mucho vido, estudió e leyó' (pp. 106–7). The archpriest's assertion that it would reflect doubt not to tell his story ('es dubda de faltar dello') recalls the statement in Hermannus's translation that fiction based on doubtful invention ('ab adinventione dubitabili') does not produce the desired effect.[50]

The second element of imagery based on truth, that is, vivid description, is discussed in the following two passages in Hermannus's translation:

Et oportet ut sit fabularis adinventio pavorosa dolorosa inventio quasi ante oculos constituta que quasi ex visu fidem habeat. Quando enim fabularis narratio ambigua fuerit et adinventa ab adinventione dubitabili non aget actionem que per ipsam intentam fuerat. Quod enim non crediderit quis non movebit eum neque ad timendum neque ad miserendum (Boggess, p. 42; MP p. 56/l. 25 intena) ... Et bonitas narrationis poetice et perventio in ipsa ad finem complementi est quidem quando poeta in relationibus et narrationibus suis sic certitudinaliter narrat ut rem narratam quasi presentem sub sensu et aspectu auditorum ponat, ita ut non solum rem narratam comprehendant sed etiam cointellectus contrariorum ipsius eos non pretereat (Boggess, p. 56; MP p. 62, l. 8 quo intellectus; p. 62 l. 9 perterreat). [Aristotle said:] And in order that fiction should arouse fear it is fitting that a pitiful invention be composed as if before the eyes, which would be as convincing as if seen. For when a narrative is ambiguous and composed of doubtful material it does not have the effect it was intended to have by itself. For what a person does not believe will not move him either to fear or pity. ... And excellence of poetic narrative, and the accomplishment by itself of a certain complementary goal, result when a poet narrates his accounts and stories so convincingly that he presents the thing narrated as if present before the perception and gaze of the listeners, so that not only may they understand the thing narrated but also a simultaneous understanding of the contraries of the thing itself may not escape them.

Most critics agree that vivid description is Martínez de Toledo's forte, and a few of his memorable portraits will suffice here: the proud lover who rides 'muy estirado sobre su silla' (p. 84); the lazy man who constantly procrastinates 'avosteçando e esperezándose, estendiendo los braços' (p. 93); and the portraits of Fortune and Poverty (pp. 185–6). One of the *Corbacho*'s portraits, that of an angry man, is found also in a discussion of imagery as an example of how vice can be detected in facial expression in Hermannus's translation:

Et hoc secundum diversitatem eius quod accidit in vultu iracundi: scilicet torvus aspectus, et angustia quedam, et quasi ignis stridor adversus eum qui ipsum provocavit (Boggess, p. 16). [Aristotle said:] And this is what happens in the face of an angry man in accordance with the change within him: namely the face is twisted and a certain meanness [appears] and a crackling like fire against the man who provoked him.

In his discussion of the sixth mortal sin the archpriest of Talavera describes angry men who 'se van mordiendo los rostros e los beços, apretando las muelas e quixadas, echando fuego de los ojos de yra e malenconía; ... toma yra tanta que cuyda rebentar, diziendo: ... quando le do, ándame alegre, quando nol do, el rostro [me] tuerce' (pp. 91–2; [PP]). The references to the twisted face, the crackling sound of the jaws, and fiery eyes of the angry man are, of course, clichés, but they constitute nevertheless another detail that the *Corbacho* shares with Hermannus Alemannus.

About the kinds of action most likely to produce pity and fear Hermannus's translation is very explicit:

Et huius sunt que accidunt amicis quibusdam a quibusdam amicorum suorum voluntarie, ut parentum interfectio et pericula et dampna et cetera consimilia nocumenta, non enim quod accidit inimicis quibusdam a quibusdam inimicorum suorum. Non enim contristatur quis neque leditur neque expavescit propter malum quod infertur ab inimicis quemadmodum contristatur et offenditur propter malum illatum ab amicis ... ut occisio fratris a fratre aut patris a filio aut filii a patre (Boggess, pp. 43–4; MP 57 l. 9 huiusmodi). [Aristotle said:] And of this type are those which are perpetrated by certain friends willfully on their own friends, like the murder of parents, threats and losses and other similar injuries, indeed not what is perpetrated upon certain enemies by some of their enemies. For one is not saddened nor hurt nor terrified on account of an evil deed which happens between enemies in the same way as one is saddened and offended by an evil deed committed between friends ... such as the murder of a brother by brother or of father by son or of son by father.

This is precisely the kind of tragic occurrence between friends and relatives that Martínez de Toledo emphasizes repeatedly in the *Corbacho*. In chapter 3 of part 1 the archpriest explains how love causes death: 'Vemos que vnos con otros han desamistades, amigo con amigo, hermano con hermano, padre con fijo ... e demás muchas muertes ... se syguen' (p. 13). In chapter 23 of part 1 love causes children to break the fourth commandment and disobey their parents (p. 69). Love leads parents to kill children ('E viste nunca madre consentir en muerte de fijo or fija por non ser descubyerta, por quanto el fijo o fija le auía el tal pecado sentido o visto,' p. 71)? Envy sets women against female relatives ('E desta regla non saco madre contra fija, nin hermana, prima nin parienta contra parienta,' p. 133). Relatives kill each other over inheritances ('quel fijo desea la muerte al padre por ser él rey e ser señor, el hermano del rey desea a su hermano la muerte por suçeder en el reyno ... las mugeres desean a otras la muerte por herencias, por aver la fija a la madre, a la tía o a la ahuela,' pp. 290, 293). Martínez de Toledo certainly seems to agree with Averroës that crimes of passion between relatives (which even today account for a larger percentage of all crimes than most other causes) are more likely to serve as effective object lessons than crimes perpetrated by one enemy against another.

Rhyme. According to Hermannus's translation, images are not merely visual but aural as well (in fact they involve all five senses, as will be demonstrated later). Imagery and representation are composed of three qualities, writes Hermannus (Boggess, pp. 5–6): similar sound (*ex parte soni convenientis*), rhythm (*ex parte ponderis*), and resemblance of the thing itself (*ex parte ipsiusmet assimilationis*). And these three qualities are achieved in writing by means of rhyme (*ars consonandi*), metre (*ars metrificandi*), and vivid description (*ars componendi sermones representativos*). We have already seen how Martínez de Toledo applies the art of vivid description, but as Pérez Pastor and Gerli noted,[51] the archpriest is also fond of rhymed prose and alliterative word sequences. Here are two typical examples in the *Corbacho*, and an incomplete list of pages on which rhyming and alliterative sequences can be found: 'asý que de cras en cras vase el triste a Sathanás, e lo peor quel dezir es por demás' (p. 16); 'que mal de cada rato non lo sufre perro nin gato; dapno de cade dýa, sofrir non es cortesía; oy vna gallina e antier vn gallo, yo veo bien mi duelo, aunque me lo callo' (p. 119); and on pages 24, 29, 57–9, 65, 92, 109, 126–7, 129, 136, 138, 141–2, 145, 152, 160, 184, 204, 215, 219, 221–2, 266, 297, 307, 311–12. It is striking that comparatively little rhyming appears in the 'media parte'; one wonders whether this is because the middle part was supposed to be different, according to Hermannus, not only 'in ordine et loco sed in … bonitate' (Boggess, p. 25). Rhyme occurs in the *Corbacho* mainly in exempla and in refranes, but rarely in the serious doctrinal passages in which Martínez de Toledo seems to be attempting beautifully reasoned arguments. In the 'media parte,' for example, almost the only rhyme is in the exchanges between Fortune and Poverty in the exemplum borrowed from Boccaccio.

Animals. Perhaps the most frequent image used in the *Corbacho* is the comparison of sinful people to animals. Men are advised to flee from the unrestrained love of an inconstant woman as they would avoid a brute animal, poisonous beast, or rabid dog (p. 14). Men and women are compared pejoratively to wolves (pp. 55, 260, 291), birds (pp. 57, 151, 173, 184, 297, 311), goats (p. 60), asses (pp. 49, 61, 315), dogs (pp. 61, 91, 119, 126), camels (p. 82), frogs (p. 86), fish (pp. 99–9), fowl (pp. 98–9), cats (pp. 119, 170), spiders (pp. 126, 134), cattle (pp. 135, 149, 305), lions (pp. 160, 173), monkeys (p. 161), mules (p. 164), pigs (pp. 166, 218, 221), vixen (p. 184), and oxen (pp. 217, 220–1). These are all hortatory examples against vice, and even wise men like Solomon, Aristotle, and Virgil serve as negative models. Aristotle is described 'freno en la boca e sylla en el cuerpo, çinchado como bestia asnal' (p. 49: [PP]). Hermannus Alemannus mentions the importance of hortatory examples taken from the Bible, and he uses Joseph as an example of virtue (Boggess, pp. 40–3). Martínez de Toledo uses not only Solomon and David but, since it suits his purpose aptly, Nebuchadnezzar, who is described walking 'como bestia por los montes' (p. 235).[52] The arch-priest of Talavera leaves no room for doubt that his constant reference to the bestiality of human nature is authorized, in his opinion, by the Bible:

> Avn dize el mesmo Dauid en el salmo Dios de los dioses fabló, dize asý: el ombre como fuese en honra non touo entendimiento, e es comparado a las bestias e semejable e fecho a ellas. En otro logar dize fablando destos tales: como bestias, Señor, con el cabestro e con el freno, aprieta las quixadas [Tú] destas bestias tales, que se non quieren llegar a Ti; a los pecadores, Señor, dales muchos açotes e castígalos, e a los que en Ty esperaren de mucha misericordia e piedad serán en derredor çercados. Por ende no nos marauillemos sy por nuestros pecados e bestiedades Nuestro Señor mansamente nos açota. (p. 255–6; [PP])

The five senses. Closely related to images of animals are those that have to do with the five senses, especially with the sense of taste, or with eating and drinking. The link with animals is made by transferring the bridle image from animals to that of appetite, that is, from 'bestia desenfrenada' (pp. 14, 16, 20, 28, 55, 86, 89, 207) to 'desenfrenado apetito' (pp. 8, 10, 15, 40, 59, 62, 76, 89, 137, 184). Martínez de Toledo says the *Corbacho* is written 'especialmente para algunos que non han follado el mundo nin han beuido de sus amargos beurages nin han gustado de sus viandas amargas' (p. 2). He advises these people to restrain their tendency to excessive appetites and to cultivate instead a 'natural apetito' (p. 261). He reminds them that Eve's eating of the apple caused man's downfall (p. 163): He makes an easy shift from appetite for food and drink to appetite for the flesh ('delectaçión carnal,' p. 9; and 'apetitos ynçentivos de luxuria,' p. 39). Once a man has succumbed to an excessive carnal appetite, the archpriest warns, all five senses are destroyed ('El que locamente ama ... los çinco sesos corporales anulla,' p. 103).[53]

Fire. In the *Corbacho* fire can be a very useful substance, as valuable as faithful friends ('Agua, fuego nin dinero non es al ombre tan nesçesario como amigo fiel, leal e verdadero,' p. 14). But images of this virtuous, natural fire are rare, because the book is about vice. Emphasis is placed instead on the fire of lust ('amor desordenado en los coraçones con fuego [infernal que todo el cuerop inflamma],' p. 36, [PP] and 'aquel fuego maldito de luxuria,' p. 41). This image of lustful fire is linked to images about the five senses because such fire must be quenched, but not with wine, which excites heat ('Conuiene, pues, beuer e remojar

por apagar el tal fuego con cosas frias muchas vezes beuiendo,' p. 46];
and especially because inflamed lust causes a dangerous loss of appetite ('Cresçió su amor como fuego con estopas en tanto que ella cresçe
en amor, e pierde el comer, beuer e dormir e folgar,' pp. 206].[54] The biblical hortatory examples for this image are hell-fire itself ('las byuas
llamas del ynfierno,' p. 261) and the devil, who is closely related to it
('diablos ynfernales,' p. 261) and mentioned throughout the book.[55]

Women. From the categories analysed thus far a carefully woven
pattern of straightforward imagery is beginning to emerge, a pattern in
which animal imagery is linked to sensual imagery, which in turn is
linked to images about infernal fire. All of these images are made to
culminate in imagery about women. Old women well attired are like
monkeys ('paresçe mona desosada,' p. 161); other women are like
wolves (p. 55). Women, because of Eve, the biblical hortatory example,
are closely associated with both food and the devil (p. 164), and like
the devil are among man's three principal enemies ('¿Quántos enemigos
tiene el mezquino del ombre? El mundo, el diablo e la muger, e de más
la muger,' pp. 225, 107) Women, especially when irate, are associated
with infernal fire ('por aquella boca ynfernal ... non dexará de echar
fuego,' pp. 158–9). They gather around fires at winter time (p. 178),
burn the men who love them (pp. 184–5), and should themselves be
burned to death (p. 182) as they sometimes are (pp. 183, 219).

Since all categories of imagery are made to culminate in images
about women, the imagery about women is often given in the same
analogical structure that informs the book as a whole, that is, *a* is to *b*
as *c* is to *d*. For example, 'esperar firmeza (*a*) en amor de muger (*b*) es
querer agotar río cabdal (*d*) con cesta o espuerta o con muy ralo far-
nero (*c*),' p. 20]; or, separating virtuous women (*a*) from vicious ones (*b*)
is like separating gold (*c*) from dross (*d*) (p. 108). Similar four-part analogies about women are found on pages 64, 113, 120, 143 (two), 144–5,
147, 149, 162, 180, 210, 244. The analogy on page 244, in the important
'media parte,' is especially crucial to the argument of the book as a
whole. To those who would argue that it is the stars controlled by God
that impel men to 'loco amor,' and that this is therefore a strange God
who controls in this way, the archpriest replies that these men, who
cannot hope to find out all the secrets of the women who serve them,
should not hope to find out the secrets of God whom they serve. Men
as masters (*a*) cannot even discover women's secrets (*b*) therefore men
as servants (*c*) should not hope to discover God's secrets (*d*).

Sleep. Discussion of the previous six images leads us to an appreciation of the artistic necessity of the final section of the *Corbacho*, the
'demanda.' Whenever it was written, the epilogue remains of aesthetic

importance to the work as a whole because its imagery is entirely consonant with and acts as a crowning touch to the imagery in the rest of the work. Many of the images found throughout the work are mentioned also in the epilogue: drinking (pp. 328–9), fire (pp. 328, 330), the devil and animals ([‘asno’] p. 329). But the key to the imagery of the epilogue, and consequently to the raison d'être of the work as a whole, is sleep. In the rest of the work sleep is linked to the other categories of imagery through the images about the five senses: the lazy, lustful man (‘está con su coamante en la cama fasta mediodía, e a las vezes come e beue con ella en la cama dentro,’ p. 93); lust causes lack of sleep and lack of sleep, indigestion, and indigestion, in turn, debilitation of the body's strength (p. 47). Poverty conquers Fortune partly because the latter's stomach is full of sumptuous delicacies and partly because Fortune is fond of luxurious beds (‘Todo el estómago se la reboluió de cansançio por tornar lo que en él tenía, la Pobreza luego saltóle encima ... diziendo: doña traydora, non es todo delicados manjares tragar ... non es todo en camas deleytes folgar,’ p. 308).

In the *Corbacho*'s epilogue sleep is related, in a specific literary way, to truth and to images about truth as they appear in dreams and visions to persons who come perilously close to death.[56] Most of the elements of the literary dream tradition are mentioned by Martínez de Toledo: (a) approximate death (‘quede más muerto que no biuo,’ p. 329); (b) perspiration (‘sudando,’ p. 329); (c) the recognition of error or sin (‘conoscí el mal,’ p. 329); (d) the sort of twilight zone between sleeping and waking, between the reality of dreams and the reality of wakefulness (‘apenas conociera ... si era verdad o sueño,’ p. 329); and (e) the transformation of the person who experiences the vision (‘apenas conociera el que solía,’ p. 329). But the archpriest alters the tradition artistically. Whereas in Boccaccio's *Corbaccio*, for example, and in the writings of many other medieval writers, the dream is described at the beginning, and the bulk of the text consists of a description of the vision, in the *Corbacho* description of the dream is placed at the end, and the main body of the work is not about the vision itself, but about the lessons to be learned as a consequence of the vision.[57] Martínez de Toledo wishes to emphasize that his book, even though it was inspired by some of the lustful hazards of dreaming, is fact; he therefore reverses the traditional order.

The epilogue explains that the archpriest of Talavera had begun the work and was contemplating whether or not to continue it (‘Yo pues, forçado houe de ocupar mi entendimiento en diuersas e muchas ymaginaciones, si mejor me sería tal disfauor, hauiendo proseguir lo comiençado, continua[n]do ex proposito o nueuamente buscar paz e buena concordia de aquellas que siempre matan sin cuchillo,’ p. 328). With these thoughts heavily on his mind he went to sleep (‘Muy congoxado del pensamiento tal, retráxeme algund tanto al sueño natural,' p. 328). Now, even though this slumber was a 'sueño natural' and not one induced by overeating, it was nevertheless a serious mistake, according to the archpriest's own instructions, to fall asleep with women on his mind. The man who would avoid lust is firmly advised not to fall asleep thinking about women ('Primeramente, sy te viniere en la imaginación temptaçión deste pecado, non te aduermas en el pensar,' p. 40; and 'Pero sy estando en la cama tal escalentamiento te viniere, salta luego della e non te aduermas en pensar, sy non luego sal fuera,' pp. 41–2). It was only after the author awoke from the dream that he realized his lustful error ('Empero tal o qual mi sentido cobrado, sentí e conoscí el mal donde me venía ... temblaua, Dios lo sabe, que quisiera tener cabe mí compañía para me consolar. ¡Guay del que duerme solo!' pp 329–30). Having recognized his error the author moved swiftly to correct it. He instructed the lustful man to seek out someone to talk to ('Anda luego e busca persona tercera con quien fables de algún negocio,' pp. 40–1) and do something to rid his mind of its thought ('Sétymo e final, syempre faz alguna cosa por quitar to pensamiento de vanas imaginaçiones,' p. 43). The author decided to follow his own instructions and talk to his readers and finish the book he had started ('Por ende, pensé, siquiera, hermanos, por descanso y reposo de mí, de vos communicar del todo mi trabajo,' p. 330).

The epilogue, therefore, is artistically essential to the *Corbacho* as a whole, especially because it explains the book's existence as a cautious example of the vice the book itself condemns. It is by no means an unexpected ending, nor is it a joke or a retraction of what the rest of the book stands for.[58] At the transition points between each of the book's four main parts, the author has been preparing his readers for the epilogue by including himself among the lustful sinners.[59] Towards the end of part 1 he writes: 'Pero cs menester quel que reprehende reprensyón en él non aya. [E] como desto non me sienta yo libre, fablar poco e temeroso sabieza es' (p. 95; [PP]). At the end of part 1 he states: 'Tomé el enxiemplo de: a ty lo digo, nuera. De los viçiosos no saco a mí de fuera, biuiendo fasta que muera' (p. 109). Towards the end of part 2 he admits that 'nin otrosý yo querer dezir de los otros por que yo sea exento nin quito de culpa, antes confieso mi culpa e con vno de los que dixiere quiero ser contado por pecador e errado' (pp. 187–8). In preparation for part 3 he says: 'Asý que todos somos, segund más o menos, pecadores: sy dezimos que pecado non tenemos, nosotros engañamos a nos mesmos ... Por ende, contándome por vno, en el número de los que diré quiero ser el primero' (p. 189). And at the beginning of part 4: 'Dios Todopoderoso puede de ty *e de mí* ordenar contra tu calydad *e mía*, que avnque queramos [non podamos] vsar mal' (p. 229, my italics; [PP]).

The epilogue is therefore an explanation that the author wrote the book as penance for his sins. In the dream the angry women pummel the author, 'qual sea en penitencia de los males que hize e aun de mis pecados' (p. 329). He awakes, realizes his sin, and finishes the book as a means of resisting the dangerous temptation into which he himself had fallen. By his example, the author urges his readers to avoid vice; to achieve his purpose he uses throughout the work, including the epilogue, vivid, easily comprehensible images, according to the recommendation of Averroës ('Aben Ruys'), one of the many authorities mentioned in the book (p. 299). There can be no way of proving beyond a reasonable doubt the identity of the author of the epilogue, and an attempt to do so certainly was not the object of this section. Yet in the light of this analysis of the imagery and structure of the *Corbacho* there would seem to be a little less justification for doubting the caption that tells us that the epilogue was written by 'el autor,' presumably Alfonso Martínez de Toledo.[60] What can be concluded from this analysis is that the epilogue forms an essential, artistic part of the whole regardless of when it was written and by whom.

In terms of the traditions studied in the earlier chapters, *Buen amor* and the *Corbacho* show more affinity with the apocalpytic tradition than with the psalter tradition of the tradition or the Song of Songs. They have such apocalpytic elements as a concern for saving the soul of the reader, stress of virtue over vice, sections on confession (*Buen amor*) and the Ten Commandments (*Corbacho*), and denunciation of the sin of lust. These two works also use an important element of composition – the exemplum – that belongs to the tradition of wisdom literature, which is not discussed in this book except, by way of apology for its absence, in the concluding chapter. But the most significant development displayed by these texts, as far as literary composition is concerned, is their philosophical tone. Martínez de Toledo refers to his own work as a 'compendio' and to *Buen amor* as a 'tratado.' Indeed, it is the desire to prove a philosophical thesis, as it were, that distinguishes these works from the strong apocalyptic modes of composition that surround them. In the next chapter we shall turn to three key works that maintain both the aesthetic of contraries and the philosophical tone used by Juan Ruiz and Martínez de Toledo, but that vary these elements markedly and with great artistry. *Buen amor*'s 'sic et non' is employed in the concept of Fortune's wheel, and *Corbacho*'s syllogism (a is to b as c is to d) becomes a 'tratado,' in different senses of the word.

5 The Magic Wheel of Fortune

FOR BRUCE WARDROPPER

In this chapter aspects of the composition of three fifteenth-century works will be discussed, the *Siervo libre de amor*, *Cárcel de Amor*, and *Celestina*. These works have frequently been compared to each other in lengthy studies devoted to the sentimental novel and to the origins of the novel.[1] Therefore, in this chapter I will not attempt to make any startling new contribution to the understanding of the composition of the three works. Rather, I shall focus my remarks on how they use elements of composition already mentioned, especially confession and fortune. However, this focus leads to conclusions that may improve upon existing writings about the composition of the three late-medieval texts.

Siervo libre de amor

Juan Rodríguez de Padrón's *Siervo libre de amor* (*Siervo*) is a little masterpiece, if by masterpiece we understand a work that artfully alters most of the traditions it inherits while at the same time it charts courses for future traditions of literature. In less than thirteen manuscript folios, *Siervo* embodies mutated forms of all the traditions discussed in this book. The tiny work purports to be a treatise ('tratado') written by and about the narrator in the form of a letter to a judge, Gonçalo de Medina, at the latter's request. The letter tells in three main parts how the narrator, betrayed by a friend and jilted by his lover, contemplates suicide despite the advice of his personified Discretion. He is dissuaded from his suicidal path by his personified Understanding. After Understanding describes the hell of lovers to him, the narrator's spirit reminds him of the tragic story of two lovers, Ardanlier and Liessa, who had eloped in order to share their lives together away from the disapproval of their parents. Liessa is found at their hideaway by Ardanlier's father, King Croes, who kills her before the eyes of Lamidoras, Ardanlier's faithful tutor. Ardanlier returns and when he learns from Lamidoras what has happened, he dictates a letter to a French princess, Yrena, who, although her love for him is unrequited, has vowed to remain forever faithful. He charges Lamidoras to deliver the letter and then in despair kills himself on his sword. Yrena receives Lamidoras and vows to erect a temple to Ardanlier and Liessa at their hideaway. Lamidoras also visits a king of Europe who, upon hearing the tragic news, vows to take revenge on King Croes. Lamidoras and Yrena later die of grief at the hideaway temple, which becomes a spot that enchants generations of lovers who make pilgrimages to it, including the legendary Macías and the narrator himself. At the end of the recounting of the tale, the narrator awakes and makes a firm commitment to abandon the paths of requited and unrequited love, which he has pursued in the past, and seek out the path of neither loving nor being loved. As he contemplates this commitment, the narrator arrives at the seashore where a boat appears to him. Synderesis disembarks from the boat and asks the narrator to recount his adventures for her. At this point the narrative ends.

Siervo's link with the psalter tradition is clear and interesting: the text compares the sighs and complaints of lovers with the prayers (and, obviously, psalms) recited by the ancient fathers in the desert: 'Me hizieron retraher al templo de la grand soledat, en compañía de la triste amargura, sacerdotissa de aquella, donde, a la acostumbrada hora que los padres antigos en la esquividat del desierto se dan a la devota oración de plazer solitario, e acompañado de lágrimas gemidos e sospiros, todos los días remembrándome lo pasado, me daría a la siguiente contemplación.'[2] This association between prayers and lover's sighs is reminiscent of Boccaccio's reference (quoted in the chapter 1 of this book) to women who tell their paternoster beads in church when in fact their beads are really French chivralric stories and Italian love poems ('le su orazioni e i suoi paternostri sono i romanzi franceschi e le canzoni latine.')[3] In like manner, the story of Ardanlier and Liessa and the poems inserted in the narrative, are meant to be like set prayers and hymns that the narrator recites in the temple of love.[4] Of course, I do not mean to imply that Boccaccio's writings are a source for *Siervo*, which is a question that has given rise to much debate; I mean merely to begin to document the use in *Siervo* of the psalter tradition also used by Boccaccio and other writers.

Like the *Razón, Siervo* contains elements of allegorized lust, a widespread tradition rooted ultimately in the Song of Songs. Thus, when he finally decides to follow the right path, the narrator asks in vain where such a road can be found ('preguntava a los montañeros e burlavan de mí; a los fyeros salvajes, y no me respondían,' p. 107), and his words echo those of the Song of Songs (3:1–3; 5:6–7). Like the narrator of *Razón*, the narrator of *Siervo* has learned in a garden a lesson about true love and has decided to seek out the bridegroom of the Song of Songs and become a 'syervo yndigno del alto Jhesús' (p. 68). Like the *Razón*, *Siervo* makes poetic use of the stereotyped language of love, as even its title indicates.

From the apocalyptic tradition, *Siervo* borrows a reference to Ezekiel and Revelation for the epitaph on the tombs of Ardanlier and Liessa 'cuyos enteros cuerpos en testimonio de las obras perseveramos las dos rycas tumbas, fasta el pavoroso día que a los grandes bramidos de los quatro animales despierten del grand sueño, e sus muy puríficas ánimas posean perdurable folgança' (p. 102). These four animals that will make loud noises on the day of judgment ('el pavoroso día') are like the ones described in Ezekiel 1:5–14 and Revelation 4:6–9. It is perhaps significant that Jerome, in his commentary on Ezekiel interprets these four animals as reason, spirit, passion, and synderesis, or conscience, and that the narrator of *Siervo* uses the last of these, synderesis, as the name of the being who greets him at the end of the narrative and asks for an account of his adventures (p. 112).[5]

Synderesis is derived from a Greek verb that means to preserve, guard, or observe religiously; thus, as the word 'perseveramos' denotes in the epitaph, Yrena and other pilgrims preserved the memory of Ardanlier and Liessa as something divine or immortal; likewise, Synderesis appears to the narrator as his conscience, that very central part of his soul that preserves the likeness of his true God and reminds him of that likeness. We can be sure that Juan Rodríguez is thinking about the soul as he described the epitaph on the tomb of Ardanlier and Liessa because he relates the word 'animales' to the word 'ánima.' This animal-soul relationship is frequently made in commentaries on the visions of the four animals in Ezekiel and Revelation; Jerome, Origen, and Beatus, for example, discuss the meaning of the four animals in terms of the soul. Beatus explained: 'Animalia autem dicta sunt, quoniam propter animam hominis praedicatur evangelium Christi'; one of the animals took the shape of a man, which led commentators like Beatus to conclude that 'homo enim rationale est animal.'[6]

Yrena, of course, is mistaken in thinking that Ardanlier and Liessa have 'puríficas ánimas' that will be rewarded with 'perdurable folgança'; what she and other pilgrims of love, like the narrator, believe to be paradise is, actually, hell, as the narrator's Entendimiento tried earlier to tell him ('offreciéndote a las penas que alla sufren los amadores, aunque tu piensas que biuen en gloria,' p. 79). Thus, the vision of the shrine and tombs of Ardanlier and Liessa that the narrator has is a hellish vision of false glory; its counterpart is the true vision of Synderesis and her companions with which the narrative ends. It will be necessary to examine this final vision in greater detail in order to decide whether or not the narrative, as it has survived, is complete.

That Synderesis represents the central Godlike part of the soul is not accidental to the composition of *Siervo* because, in fact, the use of Synderesis varies another important element of the apocalyptic tradition – the debate between the body and soul. In the body-and-soul narratives discussed earlier the soul speaks to the body after death, when the one is separated from the other. The variant in *Siervo* permits the soul to speak to the body during life. To do this Juan Rodríguez takes the Aristotelian division of the soul into three parts (memory, understanding, and will), found also in other medieval Spanish works, and personifies each part;[7] for memory Rodríguez uses the heart, which was commonly believed to be the seat of memory. In fact, in *Siervo* the soul berates the body not after the narrator dies but at a point when he is very close to death ('E desý maltraýa el spíritu que en punto era a me dexar; culpava a mis cinco sentidos que andavan en torno de mí, dándolos fuertes gemidos,' p. 82). Other apocalyptic elements in *Siervo* include precise dates (for example, 'el día syguiente, primero del año,' p. 73), the virtues (for example, 'Prendí por señora ... la que es madre de todas virtudes,' p. 69), and repentance (for example, 'Buelta, buelta, mi esquyvo pensar, de la deciente vía de perdición,' p. 107).

From the 'sic et non' tradition the author employs in *Siervo* a variant of the philosophical treatise ('tratado') as well as the belief that one thing can more clearly be defined when it is juxtaposed with its contrary ('porque el más digno de los dos contrarios más claro viniese en vista del otro,' p. 69). And by the insertion of the 'estoria de dos amadores' as a crucial element of its structure, *Siervo* exemplifies the widespread tradition in medieval Spanish literature of one work being inserted into another, a tradition that will be discussed in the next chapter of this book.

Yet, although all these traditions are used artistically in *Siervo*, its own composition is quite different from that of any work analysed in the preceding chapters. The composition of *Siervo* involves a very clever combination of the Y of Pythagoras and the wheel of fortune. According to the Y of Pythagoras, as it has been interpreted and varied by many writers, including Plato, Dante, and Virgil, a person comes to a point in life, a juncture at which three distinct roads may be discerned: the road along which the person has been travelling, a road that leads to a bad end, and a third road that leads to a good end; thus, the three roads can be represented graphically by the letter Y.[8] Juan Rodríguez varies Virgil's version and states so explicitly: 'Piensas asý entrar esentamente en la casa de Plutón, dios infernal, segun hizo Eneas hyjo de la deesa, por cuyo mandado la sabia Sebilla le acompañava ... según dize vergilio, Eneydas' (pp. 78–9); here, the narrator has arrived at the juncture of the Y, and his understanding (Entendimiento) is trying to persuade him to not take the road that leads to lovers' hell. The three roads from which the narrator must choose are actually his own thoughts presented to him by three parts of his soul ('arribé con grand fortuna a los tres caminos, que son tres varios pensamientos,' p. 76). Just as the narrator is faced with a tripartite choice, so also many major statements and situations in the text offer at least three possible interpretations. Here are some examples.

The title of the work, *Siervo libre de amor*, is a clear reference to Paul's first letter to the Corinthians: 'Were you a slave ('servus') when called? Never mind. But if you can gain your freedom, avail yourself of the opportunity. For he who was called in the Lord as a slave is a freedman of the Lord. Likewise he who was free ('liber') when called is a slave of Christ' (7:21–2). This is why the narrator explains, in the crucial third section of the work, 'no soy siervo mas syrviente, / pues que libre fuy llamado ...' (p. 108). The meaning of the book's title, which critics have not explained adequately, therefore can be interpreted – in accordance with the three principal parts of the work – in three main ways: a slave who serves love of his own free will; a slave of love who is now free; and a servant (once a slave to love) who now serves Love (that is, Christ) of his own free will ('siervo yndigno del alto Jhesús,' p. 68).

One sentence of the narrator's letter addresses the judge, Gonçalo de Medina, in three distinct ways, as a superior ('mayor,' 'juez'), an equal ('eguales'), and a friend ('amigo'): 'Johan Rodríguez del Padrón, el menor de los dos amigos, egual en bien amar, al su mayor Gonçalo de Medina, juez de Mondoñedo, requiere dé paz y salut' (p. 67). Another sentence is deliberately constructed to keep turning upon itself as one of its polysemous meanings fades into another: 'Que en señal de amistad te escrivo de amor por mí que sientas la grand fallía de los amadores y poca fiança de los amigos; e por mí juzgues a ty, amador' (p. 68). Between the two persons referred to in the quoted sentence there can be said to be either love or friendship, or little loyalty ('poca fiança').[9] In another important example Ardanlier is faced at a crucial point in his life with a tripartite choice of living to take revenge on his father, or living for Yrena who loves him, or taking his own life for love of Liessa.

The three roads that explain the composition of the work at important places in the text are like spokes of the wheel of Fortune, or, as the author himself explains them, like three paths in the garden of Fortune ('Arribé con grand fortuna a los tres caminos, que son tres varios pensamientos que departen las tres árbores consagradas en el jardín de la ventura,' p. 76). The lover travelled along the road of requited love 'con grand fortuna' (p. 76), but when he arrived at the juncture in the Y and travelled down the road of unrequited love to lover's hell, he is described as 'INFORTUNÉ' (p. 77) and 'syn ventura' (p. 76). That the narrow road that *leads to* paradise is also within Fortune's wheel is no surprise, since it is not paradise itself but merely the road that leads to it; as Damon explains, Dante's journey up to paradise also takes him first, paradoxically, down through Hell.[10] Thus the composition of *Siervo* is most aptly described as the Y of Pythagoras circumscribed by the wheel of Fortune; in other words, the composition of the book, is like a Christianized version of the image of Ixion tied in punishment on a wheel of lustful fire and plagued by diabolical serpents in the garden of Fortune.

We can be sure that the author had in mind the story of Ixion because Ixion is mentioned in the same part of Virgil's *Aeneid* that contains the description of the Y of Pythagoras to which the narrative refers; because Ixion's story is similar to the narrator's experiences; and because the narrator's Entendimiento reminds him of the story of Ixion (p. 80). With confidence, therefore, the composition of *Siervo* can be shown graphically as ⊘ .[11]

Critics of *Siervo* have not described the composition of the work in terms of Ixion's wheel, as far as I know. They have been concerned mainly with attempting to answer an important question about the complete or incomplete nature of the narrative as it has survived in the unique manuscript. Two such recent attempts that contain a summary of the debate use very persuasive arguments to propose that *Siervo* is incomplete: the articles by Gregory P. Andrachuk, 'On the Missing Third Part of *Siervo libre de amor*,' and Javier Herrero, 'The Allegorical Structure of the *Siervo libre de amor*.'[12]

Both Andrachuk and Herrero believe that not only is the third part of *Siervo* missing but also they can prove what that third part should contain. They differ, however, about the contents of the missing part. Andrachuk claims that 'we might hypothesize the development of the missing Part Three in which Synderesis, having heard the author's story, invites the virtues to leave the ship and to accompany the author on the path to which she will direct him. This path, of course, is that which Rodríguez indicated at the beginning: the path of wis-

dom, followed by few because of its difficulty.' Herrero accepts Andrachuk's interpretation of Synderesis, but he concludes by defining more
precisely than Andrachuk the content of the missing part: 'We can
also claim to know what the content of the third part would be, had it
been written (or if it was written had it not been lost): the example of
Yrena's profession in a religious order provides, we know, the example
which the Author himself followed.'[13]

It seems by no means accidental that Juan Rodríguez puts both the
narrator and readers of his masterpiece at the same critical juncture –
the Pythagorean Y. Readers must judge for themselves whether the
book is complete, or almost complete though not really incomplete, or
incomplete because part has been lost or because the author did not
accomplish his plans for whatever reason. Yet Siervo is not 'hopelessly
contradictory,' as Herrero explained somewhat fearfully,[14] because the
narrator gives clear directions for his solution to the Pythagorean
dilemma.

Any complete narrative can be extended artistically in a way that
makes a prior version incomplete in the context of the new whole. Cervantes was a master at this technique, as we well know, and medieval
authors sometimes invited those who were willing and able to extend
their completed works. It is also entirely possible that a part of the
work has been lost, since Siervo appears at the end of the manuscript
without anything that can be called an explicit, or that can be compared with the elaborate incipit: 'Este es el primer titulo' (pp. 61–5).[15]

Until another version of Siervo or its alleged missing part is found, I
suggest that the known version be considered complete for the following reasons:

(1) The fact that Andrachuk and Herrero are confident that they
know what their missing part contains is evidence enough that an
artist as subtle as Juan Rodríguez did not necessarily need to complete
his Siervo to meet their needs; his hermetic, compact style in Siervo
has apparently told them everything they need to know.

(2) Andrachuk is not correct in his claim that 'all three sections
appear to be given equal value and representation within the structure' and 'Rodríguez' description of the theme of the work ... bears out
the belief that all the parts are of equal importance.'[16] Juan Rodríguez
does not say that the three parts of the work are equal. Rather he
states clearly that all are important ('principales') but all are different
('diversos,' 'varios'): 'Es departydo en tres partes principales, según tres
diversos tiempos ... e a tres varios pensamientos de aquellos' (p. 65).
He elaborates upon this difference further, pointing out that, in one
sense, one part is the opposite of the other two: 'Esta vía de no amar ni

ser amado no es tan seguida como la espaciosa de amar bien y ser amado, ni como la deciente de bien amar syn ser amado, por do siguendo más, por quanto van cuesta ayuso, en contrario de la muy agria de no amar ni ser amado, por la qual syguen muy pocos, por ser la más ligera de fallyr y más grave de seguir' (p. 66). Thus he leaves himself the artistic option of abbreviating the third part if he chooses to make brevity indicative of the difference to which he refers; but obviously he has other options as well.

(3) Gonçalo de Medina, the judge/equal/friend who requested the work, asked for an account of only *past* thoughts and deeds ('La muy agria relación del caso, los *pasados* tristes y alegres actos y esquivas contemplaciones e ynotos e varios pensamientos que el tiempo no consentía poner en efecto por escripturas, demandas saber,' p. 67). The relationship between this tripartite character and the 'tratado' he causes to be composed should stand close scrutiny. The word 'tratado' is used in the text in three senses (pp. 65, 68, 84) that seem to correspond to the threefold nature of the relationship between the narrator and his judge/equal/friend. To the equal, the 'tratado' is a philosophical treatise ('el siguiente "tratado,"' p. 65) with literary pretensions in the rhetorical style of Cicero, Homer, and others (p. 67), divided into three *main* parts ('departydo en tres partes principales').[17] The expressed aim of this literary philosophical discourse is to delight an equally cultured person with its rhetorical skill ('E ficciones digo el poético fyn de aprovechar y venir a ty en plazer con las fablas,' p. 68).

To the friend the 'tratado' is a manifestation of loyalty to a secret agreement or pact between friends or lovers ('por secreto y fiel tratado,' p. 84). The expressed aim of this loyal act (loyal, by the way, to the friend, but disloyal to the lover) is to teach by example: 'Por él te amonesto qué devas amar, o sy amas, perseverar; que en señal de amistad te escrivo de amor, por mí que sientas la grand fallía de los amadores y poca fiança de los amigos, e por mí jusgues a ty amador' (p. 68).

To the judge and superior the 'tratado' is a formal religious confession of thoughts and deeds whose expressed aim is to save the confessant from perdition by forcing him to obey his superiors ('E asý vergonçado, con la pena, del temor, escrivo a ty cuyo ruego es mandamiento e plegaria disciplina a mí, no poderoso de ty fuyr ... Ni porque mi tratado a mí se enderece en obras mundanas o en fechos de amores ... Esfuérçate en pensar lo que creo pensarás: yo aver sydo bien affortunado ... , por amar, alcançar lo que mayores de mí deseavan; que perdý, por amor, la principal causa de mi perdición,' pp. 67–8). Thus, Gonçalo de Medina is not only the friend and equal of the narrator but his inquisitor as well.

The role of inquisitor, as distinguished from that of judge or superior, is crucial to understanding of the development in Spain of what is commonly called the sentimental novel. As Henry Lea reminds us, 'the duty of the inquisitor, moreover, was distinguished from that of the ordinary judge by the fact that the task assigned to him was the impossible one of ascertaining the secret thoughts and opinions of the prisoner.'[18] This undertaking is very similar to that which Medina demands of the narrator ('esquivas contemplaciones e ynotos e varios pensamientos ... demandas saber,' p. 67). In terms of the history of literary composition in medieval Spain, one of the major elements of the so-called sentimental novel is a variant inquisitorial form of the confession, which was used differently by writers like López de Ayala in *Rimado*; the sentimental quality is the forced confession of intimate thoughts and sentiments, a form varied later by the author of *Lazarillo* and by Santa Teresa in her 'autohagiography.'[19]

The epistolary form that this confession takes is of long-standing tradition: 'A penitent, if there is sufficient cause, can write out the confession, in whole or in part, and hand it to the priest in the confessional ... and this apparently is sometimes done by women through sense of shame.'[20] (Note the use of 'verguença' and 'vergonçado' by the narrator in *Siervo*, p. 67). *Siervo* is not just a form of epistolary exchange between friends or the emancipation of Juan Rodríguez from the epistolary mould of Ovid's *Heroides*.[21] More precisely, *Siervo* is a copy of the written confession handed to an inquisitor, to which the author has added, for the benefit of the public, an introductory paragraph. Juan Rodríguez has masterfully varied Horace's famous 'prodesse atque delectare' by composing an epistolary treatise that seeks to delight a cultured peer and teach a friend and the public, and at the same time confess sins like his own.

Neither treatise nor confession requires that *Siervo* be any longer than it is. Both forms require details only about the past sins of the narrator and his present state of contrition and repentance; they cannot require the narrator to give details about the future which, as in Mena's *Laberinto*, can only be *glimpsed* from the point of view of the present. The narrator cannot be like Hercules, who is described by his Entendimiento as having conquered all three times – past, present, and future – in the form of the dog Cerberus (p. 78). Further, it can be deduced from the introduction to his public readers that the author expects most of them to be able to discern two of the main divisions of his complete work; only a select few, he seems to think, will understand the third main part, 'por ser la más ligera de fallyr y más grave de seguir' (p. 66).

(4) Evidence in the text makes it apparent that the author does not reveal everything to his public readers. What the public readers see is not what was handed to Gonçalo de Medina. Gonçalo de Medina may not have been handed the introductory paragraph written, as if afterwards, for the benefit of the public. As an equally cultured peer he may have been expected to understand the main divisions of the work without an introduction, and as a judge/inquisitor he certainly did not require such an introduction. The text does indicate that Gonçalo de Medina was handed a letter (from the narrator's lover) that was not shared with the public ('la grand señora, de cuyo nombre te dirá la su epístola,' p. 68).

The point is that Juan Rodríguez makes a distinction between an expansive and an hermetic style, in accordance with his audience. For the general public he includes an expansive introduction but leaves other pertinent matters to the reader's imagination; for the inquisitor, he includes, of necessity, a document that he withheld from the general public. Therefore, it is also very likely that he chose to withhold from the general public the judgment and response of Gonçalo de Medina and the consequences of that response, such as, for example, entry into a religious life, which is what Herrero claims the missing third part contains.[22] If it is proposed that the lover's letter is part of the missing portion of the work how and where the letter fits would have to be explained.

(5) Herrero is not correct in asserting that 'the allegorical structure of the *Siervo* proves conclusively that it contains only two complete parts.' Herrero's conclusion is based upon his misinterpretation of the role of Yrena and upon his incomplete understanding of her relationship to Synderesis, whom he does not identify precisely. For Herrero, 'Yrena's purified love for Ardanlier is the Christian self-sacrificing charity which moves her to dedicate her life to Vesta (a figure, here, for the Virgin Mary), to live in chastity, to profess in a religious order and to offer a life of penance for the salvation of a sinner's soul.' In fact, there is nothing strictly Christian about Yrena's love. Yrena never mentions Christ or Christianity; the religion she creates is, in Christian terms, an idolatrous religion that enshrines ordinary human beings and enchants its followers; the goddess she serves, Vesta, might well be chaste, but she is pagan, none the less, and certainly is not a figure for the Virgin Mary, since as will be explained, the allegorical structure of the text proves otherwise.[23]

Herrero claims that Yrena's love 'corresponds, obviously, to the Synderesis figure which closes the book and, as *penance*, opens the way to Yrena's purified and selfless charity.' But Herrero relies on Andrachuk as an authority for the identification of Synderesis as penance,'[24] and Andrachuk in turn cites Thomas Aquinas and Bonaventure. Nevertheless, a more apposite authority for Juan Rodríguez's allegorical use of Synderesis is neither Aquinas nor Bonaventure but St Jerome. In his commentary on the four animals of Ezekiel (the animals also used by Rodríguez) Jerome identifies Synderesis as the fourth part of the soul, Conscience, which exists outside of and above the other three ('Quartamque ponunt quae super haec et extra haec tria est, quam Graeci vocant *synteresin*, quae scintilla conscientiae in Cain [Adam] quoque pectore, postquam ejectus est de paradiso, non extinguitur; et qua victi voluptatibus, vel furore, ipsaque interdum rationis decepti similitudine, nos peccare sentimus').[25] Synderesis is, therefore, that Godlike spark of conscience that remains unextinguished to guide the sinner, lost in the darkness of his ways, to a safe port.

In order to understand the allegorical structure of the work better than the explanation of Andrachuk and Herrero allow, it is helpful to return to the main element of the work's composition – the Y of Pythagoras. The narrator of *Siervo* is pinned upon a deadly three-spoked wheel in the garden of Fortune; he is, like Ixion and Adam, stretched out upon the earth and sentenced to die for lust. He needs a guide if he is to escape his predicament. Once he chooses an appropriate guide, his work is, for all immediate extents and purposes, complete. But in order to understand his choice of a guide, we must appreciate how the narrator deploys what Damon felicitously calls a 'catenary' use of the Pythagorean Y.[26] Instead of bringing together his options for an appropriate guide in any one portion of his work, Rodríguez del Padrón spreads them out in three different sections – on page 79 where he described Charon, on page 101 where he depicts Yrena, and as an obvious culminating point, in his description of Synderesis, on pages 111 and 112.

The narrator's search for an appropriate guide takes place entirely within his own mind. It is important to note this because Herrero and Andrachuk seem to treat Synderesis as an entity apart from the narrator; but although Synderesis is personified, like other aspects of the narrator, it is a personification, nevertheless, of the narrator's own conscience, and not penance that comes in 'the battleship of the church.'[27] Just as the narrator's body wanders on land along three paths, so too the narrator sees in his mind's eye how souls float like a ship along three different waterways; and just as each ship is ferried by a different guide, so too each waterway represents the religious territory of a different goddess, 'señora,' or 'dueña.' Charon, in a small lighter, ferries the waterway on which souls serve Venus (pp. 79–81); Yrena, also in a small lighter, lands at Margadán, the seaport where the souls serve Vesta (pp. 100–1); and Synderesis, in a skiff from a large storeship, enters the temple of the narrator's body once more at the sea where souls who serve God are guided by the Virgin Mary, Stella Maris, ancient and former lover of the narrator ('antigua dueña,' pp. 111–12).[28]

The narrator sees clearly with his mind's eye that Charon would ferry his soul, like that of Ixion and others, to hell. He relives the story of Ardanlier in his mind in a dreamlike state very close to death ('El spíritu en punto era a me dexar,' p. 82), the state, as we have seen, in which other apocalyptic narrators often experience truth. Upon awakening from this state (p. 107) he visualizes clearly ('en las más altas árbores de mi escura maginança,' p. 111) his soul (in the form of a ship, which once belonged to the Virgin Mary, now draped in black to mourn her loss) approaching his body once more. The soul of the narrator (as ship) is armed with seven virtues, six of which have been forced to hide in the hold ('que todas fuesen so sotacubierta,' p. 112) while one of the them, Synderesis, sets out in a skiff to see whether it is safe for them all to reenter his body. Synderesis enters or comes close to his body ('decendió a la rrybera enverso de mí,' p. 112) and asks the narrator, as though he were a long-lost friend or relative, about his adventures ('vyno en demanda de mis aventuras,' p. 112). In reply the narrator recounts his experiences ('e yo esso mesmo en recuento de aquellas,' p. 112), letting his conscience, his Godlike spark, be his proverbial guide.

The narrator has seen clearly in his mind's eye that Yrena's penance, contrary to Herrero's claim, would lead his soul exactly where it led those of Ardanlier, Liessa, Lamidoras, Macías, and all the other pilgrims of the false religion of courtly love. Even the setting is carefully worked out by the author to match his Pythagorean image of Ixion's wheel: on the circular sea of love the author's Spanish soul rejects the waterway of its remote, pagan Roman past, rejects the waterway of French courtly love in its recent past and present, and chooses the waterway of its former Christian Gothic past (since the 'antigua dueña' and Synderesis appear in a ship styled after those of 'alta Alemaña,' p. 111).

(6) My sixth and final reason for considering *Siervo* complete, until evidence to the contrary is unearthed, is that a more fitting ending to the work would be hard to find, because the climactic vision of the sea is based upon Ezekiel's vision of the glory of God. We have seen in the story of Ardanlier how the author described Yrena's misuse of Ezekiel's four apocalyptic animals in an idolatrous way. Another part of Eze-

kiel's vision of the glory of God, in conjunction with the four animals, is an image of wheels. When Jerome translated Ezekiel's description of the wheels, he wrote, 'Et aspectus rotarum et opus earum quasi visio maris.'[29] Because of Jerome's translation, it was widely accepted that part of God's glory was like the shimmering surface of the sea. So, in *Siervo* the narrator, in search of the right path to God, climbs the tallest trees of his imagination (p. 111), from where he suddenly finds himself at the seashore, that is, as close to God's glory as can be expected.[30] His soul, draped in black, apparently had taken temporary refuge there (on the sea of part of God's glory) while it contemplated whether to leave his body permanently or return to it and fight its enemies. Having arrived, in his imagination, at the seaside, the narrator has reached an appropriate terminus for his contemplative terrestrial journey, and he brings his narrative not to its only possible end but an appropriate symbolic end, closer to the glory of God and to the salvation of his soul from perdition.

In sum, *Siervo* is a complete narrative composed on the structuring principles of the Pythagorean Y circumscribed by the wheel of Fortune, like Ixion on his wheel of punishment. All three main parts of the narrative referred to by the narrator (in an introductory paragraph intended to orient the general public) are present in the work. The first part begins immediately after the introduction and ends with an account of how the narrator's love affair came to an end (pp. 67–75). The second part begins, correctly, with the arrival of the narrator at the juncture of the Y, having traversed the path of requited love (p. 76); it ends when the narrator, now on the path of unrequited love, has replayed in his mind the exemplary story of Ardanlier and Liessa (p. 106), possibly with the words 'Aquí acaba la novella.'

The third part of the novel begins (p. 107) with the narrator's firm decision to seek out the 'muy agra senda.' This 'muy agra senda' actually begins when the creatures in the narrator's surroundings (the mountain-dwellers, the wild beasts, the birds) all ignore and mock him; it continues when a bird finally tells him, close to dawn, 'Servid al Señor' (p. 110). In response to the bird's wise message the narrator celebrates his own conversion ('mudado,' p. 111) by making out of one of Macías's courtly songs a contrafactum that now expresses happiness about his grief not at losing an earthly lover but at having deserted the Virgin Mary (p. 110–11). After he has finished this contrafactum the Virgin Mary appears to him (pp. 111–12), and the third and final part of the narrative concludes, just as the narrator's third contemplative path itself comes to a logical end at the seashore.

Cárcel de Amor

The fact that Juan Rodríguez del Padrón related the story of Ardanlier (as an explanation of a suicidal cult of love followed by pilgrims like Macías) proves that not all his contemporaries agreed with his rejection of secular love as an appropriate path to divine love. Parallels between Yrena's devotion and Christianity exist. Juan Rodríguez rejected those parallels. Other writers accepted them and wrote works that were apologies for a religion of secular love within the confines of Christianity. Such a work is the popular *Cárcel de Amor* (*Cárcel*) by Diego de San Pedro. Later, San Pedro described this work as 'salsa para pecar,' which shows that he was well aware that it could be challenged with orthodox Christian arguments.[31]

Cárcel purports to exist as a work written at the request of a dignitary ('vuestra merced') in a style more like one work by the same author and less like another of the author's works. The entire book is really an elaborate letter written to the dignitary, whom an editor of the letter identifies as 'Diego Hernandes, Alcaide de los Donzeles' (vol. 3, p. 79). This letter begins by addressing the dignitary as 'muy virtuoso señor' (p. 79) and ends, not unlike some letters, with an epistolary formula of dismissal ('donde quedo besando las manos de vuestra merced,' p. 176). In spite of its epistolary beginning and closing, it is clear from the text that this is not meant to be an ordinary letter, because its author invites its recipient to alter it ('También acordé endereçarla a vuestra merced porque la favorezca como señor y la emiende como discreto,' p. 80). In other words, this is an epistle, a self-conscious rhetorical exercise with literary and religious pretensions.

As we read the epistle it is important not to be unduly distracted by the editorial comments added by those who later reproduced it. For example, in my opinion too much emphasis has been placed on the so-called character whom an editor of the epistle has identified as 'el auctor.' It is important to remember that once this editorial 'auctor' is removed from the author's text, the 'auctor' correctly becomes the person writing to 'vuestra merced' a letter about his imagined experience. However, it would be naive to believe that this letter-writer is Diego de San Pedro himself, because it is clear that Diego de San Pedro was capable of recounting in a letter (for literary, rhetorical, and religious arguments) things he might have experienced only in his imagination as a fictional being, and not necessarily in his real life.[32]

We should be careful not to make inordinate claims for the title of the work, which the editor assures us is 'Cárcel de amor' (pp. 76, 176). This title is not altogether inappropriate for the work, and the phrase is taken directly from the author's text (p. 84). We know that San Pedro came to accept the title *Cárcel de Amor* because he refers in his poem 'Desprecio de Fortuna' to 'Aquella *Cárcel de Amor* que assí me plugo ordenar' (vol. 3, p. 276). But we cannot be sure that the title is what the author himself originally intended, or, if he was persuaded to name it so by his publishers, we do not know how seriously he considered it appropriate for the work.

We certainly ought not to deduce from the title, for example, that Leriano died in the 'Cárcel de Amor' described at the beginning of the work. The allegorical prison is transformed in the work when the author of the letter bears a hopeful response to Leriano ('y allegado a un alto donde se parecía la prisión, viendo los guardadores della mi seña ... en lugar de defenderse pusieronse en huida,' p. 112); Leriano dies in a bed in Susa ('su madre ... llegó a Susa,' p. 172). But before these details are further discussed, it would be well to summarize briefly the contents of the author's letter to 'vuestra merced'; the observations on *Cárcel*'s title serve to distinguish the letter itself from added editorial comments. Even if it can be proved that these editorial comments are the work of San Pedro (which I doubt), the remarks that follow remain essentially intact.

After recalling that 'vuestra merced' had requested that the work be written in a specific style related to two other works, the author of the letter goes on to explain what happened to him one winter's morning before dawn. In the deep, dark valleys of the Sierra Morena the correspondent sees a strange vision ('estraña visión,' p. 82) of a wild man named Desire who is taking a captive to the prison of Love. The captive, in mortal anguish, pleads with the correspondent to follow and help him. The correspondent decides to do as the captive has asked, but before the correspondent can get much information from him, Desire disappears mysteriously in the night. The correspondent decides to stay where he is rather than wander in unknown parts in the dark. At daybreak he finds himself on a steep mountain in Macedonia, before the prison of Love. In the prison he sees the captive, Leriano, who tells him his story.

Leriano, is a prisoner of love for Laureola, the daughter of the reigning king of Macedonia, Gaulo; the captive is the son of the Duchess Coleria and the late Duke Guersio. He asks the correspondent to inform Laureola of his condition and to seek a remedy for his lovesickness. The correspondent agrees and sets out to the royal court of Macedonia at Suria. With great difficulty the correspondent succeeds in persuading Laureola to write a reply to Leriano's letters, and especially to his decision to die unless Laureola reacts to his plight. When he receives Laureola's letter, Leriano changes his mind about dying and leaves the site of the prison of Love (now dissolved) and sets out for the royal court.

At court Leriano is welcomed enthusiastically by his fellow courtiers, received by Princess Laureola, and kisses her hand in obeisance. His friend (and rival for Laureola's love) Persio notices the emotional reactions of Laureola and Leriano as the latter kisses her hand. Out of jealousy Persio informs the king, falsely, that Leriano and Laureola are conducting a secret love affair. The king imprisons Laureola and orders Persio to accuse Leriano publicly of treachery. During the ensuing duel, the king spares Persio's life and robs Leriano of 'justice' as he is about to kill Persio.

Persio pays three false witnesses to cement his deception of the king, who exiles Leriano to Susa and condemns Laureola to die. When the diplomatic efforts of the correspondent fail to persuade the king to save Laureola's life, Leriano frees her by force and his men kill Persio. Leaving Laureola in the care of her uncle, he retreats to Susa where the king pursues him and lays siege to the city. Leriano is almost at the point of defeat when his men capture one of the false witnesses paid by Persio. Under threat of torture the false witness confesses and the king is persuaded to pardon Laureola and lift his siege of Leriano at Susa. However, since the king has forbidden Leriano to enter the royal court until passions have cooled, Leriano is unable to see Laureola. The text states that at this point Leriano returns to a lovesick state ('bolvióse a las congoxas enamoradas,' p. 148), which is not necessarily the same allegorical prison of Love that held him before.

Leriano then asks the correspondent to request that Laureola arrange to meet with him. Laureola steadfastly refuses, even after Leriano has informed her of his decision to die unless she accedes to his request. Leriano takes to his bed and refuses to eat or drink. Before he dies, a friend, Tefeo, tries to persuade him of the worthlessness of women, but Leriano replies with a lengthy religious defence of women. As Leriano lies dying, his mother arrives and makes an impassioned lament. Leriano reacts to his mother's lament by securing the secrecy of Laureola's letters (he has already declared publicly that he loves her), tearing up and drinking them. As he dies, Leriano's last act is to look at the correspondent and say, 'Acabados son mis males' (p. 176).

The role of the correspondent is a key element in the composition of *Cárcel*. At a commonplace time (before dawn in winter) the correspondent sees a vision that, in essence, summons him to go into Macedonia and help ('Caminante, por Dios te pido que me sigas y me ayudes en tan grand cuita ... Mi naturaleza es este reino do estás, llamado

Macedonia,' pp. 81–2, 88–9). It is difficult not to see in this initial situation a direct (even if inexact and varied) parallel between the correspondent and the apostle Paul who was also summoned in a vision into Macedonia to help ('And a vision appeared to Paul in the night: a man of Macedonia was standing beseeching him and saying, "Come over to Macedonia and help us." And when he had seen the vision, immediately we sought to go on into Macedonia, concluding that God had called us to preach the gospel to them,' Acts 16:9–10). The correspondent is, therefore, not an ordinary messenger but an apostle of a new gospel of love. His main role is to carry this gospel, as news, to Laureola ('No te pido otro bien sino que sepa de ti Laureola cuál me viste ...'; 'Mándasme, señor, que haga saber a Laureola cuál te ví ....'; 'Mucho te ruego ... que quieras levar a Laureola en una carta mía nuevas con que se alegre' (pp. 91, 93, 106–7).

Evidence exists that San Pedro intended to compose an apostolic epistle. In his *Sermón* (to which he refers in *Cárcel*) he conceives of a spurious work composed by an evangelist called 'Afición': 'Lastimados señores y desagradecidas señoras: las palabras que tomé por fundamento de mi intención, son escriptas en el Libro de la Muerte, a los siete capítulos de mi Desseo. Da testimonio dellas el Evangelista Afición' (vol. 1, p. 173). It is not necessary to assert that *Cárcel* is the 'Libro de la Muerte' referred to in San Pedro's *Sermón*; it suffices to note that the seminal idea (of an evangelist of love who gives testimony to a gospel of death), planted in the *Sermón*, comes to fruition, in whatever varied form, in *Cárcel*.

The gospel of love that the apostle witnesses and records is intended as not a replacement for Christianity but an acceptable part of it. The parallels with Christianity are not meant to be exact, and it will always be impossible to tell beyond a reasonable doubt to what extent they are sincerely Christian, or if they are the parodies of someone forced to accept Christianity – a 'converso,' or 'new Christian.'[33] Some of these parallels, sincere or ironic, may be mentioned. In addition to reflecting Paul's apostolic mission to Macedonia, Diego de San Pedro seems to be making use of his own apostolic name: Leriano's 'Cárcel de Amor' is founded, like the Christian church, upon a solid, hell-defying, death-defying rock. Leriano explains to the apostolic correspondent 'que aquella piedra sobre quien la prisión está fundada es mi fe, que determinó de sofrir el dolor de su pena por bien de su mal' (p. 89); the four pillars of this prison recommmend death as something beneficial for the captive ('que mejor le estará la dichosa muerte que la desesperada vida ... porque sin morir no pueda ser libre,' p. 90); and it is significant that Voluntad offers to be the key (to his prison) that vows never to yield before death ('Yo quiero ser llave de su prisión y determino de siempre querer,' p. 90).

Behind the iron gate of this hellish prison, Leriano sits chain-bound on a fiery throne, with a crown of iron thorns on his head (pp. 85–6). The rock, the defiance of death, the hellish ambience, the binding, the key, the suffering for a greater good, are all elements of the famous passage that has been used to explain the founding of the Christian church: '"And I tell you, you are Peter, and on this rock I will build my church, and the gate of Hell shall not prevail against it. I will give you the keys of the kingdom of heaven, and whatever you bind on earth shall be bound in heaven, and whatever you loose on earth shall be loosed in heaven." Then he strictly charged the disciples to tell no one that he was Christ. From that time Jesus began to show his disciples that he must go to Jerusalem and suffer many things ... and be killed' (Matthew 16:18–21).

Other parallels have been noted by Anna Krause and Bruce Wardropper: 'Como Cristo, hace posible su muerte. Como Cristo apura una bebida amarga – las cartas de Laureola hechas pedazos en una copa de agua –. Su madre llora el triste final. Pronuncia un consummatum est .... Las semejanzas entre la pasión de Cristo y la de Leriano se anticipan en la cárcel de amor: sufre "todos los males del mundo;" sobre su cabeza colocan una corona de puntas de hierro. Un negro (el Desesperar) le golpea.' For Whinnom 'These are not coincidences ... which need give us pause. Even when the tormented Leriano is crowned with a wreath of spikes ... the analogy cannot be fruitfully pursued: Leriano is not a figure of Christ.'[34] Leriano may not be intended as a figure of Christ, but his love, his life, and his death are clearly meant to be justifiable in Christian terms; Cárcel proposes a gospel of secular love consonant with the tenets of Christianity. San Pedro was aware, of course, that not all his Christian contemporaries would accept the orthodoxy of his proposition, which would be a good reason for his making the parallels between Leriano's passion and that of Christ somewhat less than exact.

The correspondent in Cárcel is therefore a Spanish apostle of a gospel of secular love who keeps his full testimony secret until he returns to Peñafiel. But what is the nature of the gospel of love for which this apostle has witnessed martyrdom? It is fairly clear how the prison of Love at the beginning and the death scene at the end are meant to be related to Christian love. But what does the balance of the narrative have to do with Christian love?

The narrative can be divided into three main parts according to the three principal locations of Leriano's adventures: a mountaintop prison somewhere in Macedonia, the royal court at Suria, and finally the city of Susa. At each of these sites Leriano's behaviour seems to be symbolic. In the prison of Love the main emphasis seems to be on Leriano's enchained heart ('Las cadenas que tenían en las manos son sus fuerças, con las cuales tiene atado el coraçón,' p. 90); 'Y ninguna destas cosas pudiera ver segund la escuridad de la torre, si no fuera por un claro resplandor que le salía al preso del coraçón, que la esclarecía toda,' p. 88). The text makes clear that there is no room in Leriano's heart for anything other than his own suffering ('Alguna parte del coraçón quisiera tener libre de sentimiento, por dolerme de ti segund yo deviera y tu merecías. Pero ya tu ves en mi tribulación que no tengo poder para sentir otro mal sino el mío,' p. 88).

This important detail – that Leriano loves Laureola with all his heart – offers the clue that his entire gospel of love, and hence *Cárcel* itself, is composed according to the great commandment found in Deuteronomy 6:5 and repeated variously in the synoptic gospels of Matthew, Mark, and Luke: 'And you shall love the Lord your God with all your heart, and with all your soul, and with all your might' (Matthew 22:37; Mark 12:30; Luke 10:27). Indeed, when his heart is freed from its chains, Leriano leaves the prison of Love and spends a few days regaining his bodily strength before leaving for the royal court at Suria ('Acordó de irse a la corte, y antes que fuesse estuvo algunos días en una villa suya por rehazerse de fuerças,' p. 113). There can be little doubt that during Leriano's stay at the royal court, the main emphasis of the narrative is on his might, his 'fortaleza;' Leriano defeats Persio in a duel and fulfils his vow to free Laureola in such a way as to make himself an eternal example of fortitude ('Por tu libertad haré tanto que será mi memoria, en cuanto el mundo durare, en exenplo de fortaleza,' p. 125).

At Suria, and in the two leagues between it and Susa, which formed the field of battle, Leriano serves Laureola with all his might. Once the king of Suria has lifted his siege of Susa and ordered that Laureola be returned to Suria and Leriano remain in Susa, the text indicates that Leriano has no further need of strength, and the emphasis shifts to things of the mind ('No podría ver a Laureola ... y viéndose apartado della, dexadas las obras de guerra, bolviose a las congoxas enamoradas,' p. 148). It is essential to note that the emphasis in this final section is not on Leriano's heart, as it was in the initial prison of Love, but on his mind and his soul. Leriano prepares his soul for death in the service of Laureola by neglecting his body and using his mind in her defence ('Huvo de venir a la cama, donde ni quiso comer ni bever ni ayudarse de cosa de las que sustentan la vida, llamándose siempre bienaventu-

rado porque era venida a sazón de hazer servicio a Laureola quitándola
en enojos ... Y como aquella enfermedad se havía de curar con sabias
razones, cada uno aguzava el seso lo mejor que podía .... "Las razones
mías ... te serán en exemplo para que calles.... Quiero mostrar quinze
causas ... veinte razones ... y diversos exemplos,"' p. 155–8). The
emphasis on mind in this final section is not accidental because,
although Deuteronomy 6:5 contains no direct mention of mind,
Matthew, Mark, and Luke all include the word *mind* in their versions
of this most important commandment of love. Leriano's mother confirms the composition of the narrative according to the great commandment of love: 'Ni te valió la fuerza del cuerpo, ni la virtud del
coraçón, ni el esfuerço del ánimo' (p. 174).[35]

Can the composition of *Cárcel* be defined more precisely than by
saying that it is an elaborate secular apostolic epistle structured
according to the great commandment of love? Several remarkable
attempts have been made to define the composition of *Cárcel* graphically. For Enrique Moreno-Báez, *Cárcel* is constructed like a gothic
cathedral; for Joseph Chorpenning, like a classical oration; for Dorothy
Severin, like a three-part sequence of a see-saw pattern in which Leriano and Laureola are either free or imprisoned. Keith Whinnom
regarded *Cárcel* as mainly a skilful medieval welding of set-pieces,
'bits,' into a coherent framework: 'San Pedro's achievement in welding
into a remarkably coherent work the various minor units (*narratio*, letters, speeches, *planctus*, harangue, *argumentatio*, etc.) has been under-
valued.' All of these analyses have merit, but I cannot agree with
Whinnom that 'it is implausible that San Pedro could have more than
one [of them] in mind.'[36]

Surely, as an artist composes a work, several graphic structures that
resemble each other will inevitably come to mind; for, as Aristotle
wrote about poetics, an eye for resemblances [plural] is a mark of
genius.[37] The work of the critic is, in part, to attempt to understand
the nature of the resemblances to which the work of the artist refers;
the critic's work is not, as Whinnom implies, to come to know the
hypothetical 'one' structure to which the critic limits the artist.

I am also somewhat sceptical about the significance of Whinnom's
claim that 'medieval works are notoriously "bitty,"' and that 'San Pedro
did not pay more attention than is usual in a medieval author to the
overall organization of his tale, and perceive and impose some pattern
upon it.'[38] In the first place, set-pieces, or bits, as Whinnom aptly calls
them, are no more peculiar to the medieval than to any other period:
set-pieces are as popular today as they ever were. In the second place,
San Pedro himself tells us that he took delight in composing his work

('Aquella Cárcel de Amor / que assí me plugo ordenar' (vol. 3, p. 276). The word *assí* can even be taken to mean that, for San Pedro, the composition of the work was both a delight and a labour of love during which the author felt as if imprisoned ('assí,' that is, like the 'Cárcel de amor'). It matters little here that 'me plugo' is also a colloquialism: many word-artists delight in playing with clichés.

The description of the 'cárcel de Amor' leaves little doubt that San Pedro is thinking of a church, as Moreno-Baéz suggests; and Leriano's defence of women at the end is somewhat like a sermon in its tone; but the remainder of the narrative, especially the duel and scenes of battle, is not especially churchlike. San Pedro is also thinking of an 'oración,' but as Chorpenning himself notes, 'the "oración" referred to is the *Sermón de amores*' which is not a classical literary oration composed according to Ciceronian precepts but, rather, a quasi-religious oration – a university sermon – clearly composed along the lines of the *artes praedicandi*. The religious (as opposed to classical) connotation of the 'oración' in *Cárcel* is confirmed by the use of the word elsewhere in the text to mean prayer ('Con las armas de la oración rogó a Nuestro Señor.... Ester ... por sus méritos y oración libró los judíos .... Cuando en mi oratorio me hallava rezando,' pp. 1698, 174). When San Pedro writes of a work in the style of an 'oración' that he sent to Doña Marina Manuel, the critic should remember the 'devota oración' that the narrator of *Siervo* says for his loved one (p. 75), which is like the prayers of Boccaccio's women who recite their paternoster romances in church.[39] This resemblance to the Italian women makes it less likely that *Cárcel* is composed according to the rules of classical oratory.

Whinnom analyses the rhetorical style of *Cárcel* impeccably. The leading critic of San Pedro's work notes the latter's favourite use of the aesthetic of contraries, such as 'a formula of preference, "this rather than that," ... *expolitio*, subdivision *aferre contrarium*, ... and denying the opposite of what he wishes to affirm ("not this but that")'; but he does not believe that the careful structure of the smaller units is reflected in that of the work as a whole. However, Severin's analysis, by far the most convincing, shows that the favourite use of contraries, which Whinnom finds in the small units, does indeed appear in the larger pattern of the work: 'Laureola's imprisonment is the price of Leriano's release, while Leriano's final state is the price for Laureola's release'; but what Severin calls, at Deyermond's suggestion, a '"see-saw" pattern' was perhaps better known to San Pedro as the wheel of Fortune.[40]

The wheel of Fortune, as a concept, accommodates the essential ideas of the patterns suggested by Moreno-Báez, Chorpenning, Whinnom, and Severin. The prison-house of Love at the beginning of *Cárcel* suggests both a church built upon a firm rock (Moreno-Báez) and the house of Fortune described in many other works as perched precariously upon the highest purgatorial mountaintop. The words that Leriano speaks and writes in this house of Fortune are, indeed, like prayers for his release. We can be sure that San Pedro meant to relate his 'cárcel de amor' to Fortune because he places Leriano's heart in chains in the 'cárcel'; later, the author was to explain the relationship between a heart in chains and Fortune: 'Los bienes ... son regidos sin ley alguna, tienen ... por madre a la Fortuna. Y aquestas riquezas ... como son amadas ... pueden ser llamadas cadenas del coraçón.'[41]

The aesthetic of contraries, which Whinnom finds favoured by San Pedro's style, and the 'altibajos' of Severin's see-saw are obviously accommodated by the reversals of the wheel of Fortune and need no further explanation. I should like to suggest, therefore, that the composition of *Cárcel* can be described more precisely than has been done before, as a narrative about a lover whose martyrdom upon the wheel of Fortune is recorded in an elaborate epistle by an apostle, according to the great commandment of a gospel of secular love.

But my simple description does not fully explain the workings of San Pedro's clever mind. The author of *Cárcel* obviously takes immense pleasure at playing with words and stereotyped ideas, as in, for example: 'Y como me vío venir ... conoció lo que era; y lo uno de la poca fuerça y lo otro de súpito bien, perdido el sentido cayó en el suelo de dentro de la casa. Pues yo, ... como llegué al escalera por donde solía sobir, eché a Descanso delante ... y subido a donde estava el ya bienaventurado ... pensé que iva a buen tiempo para llorarlo' (p. 112). The passage occurs at a point in the narrative at which Fortune has given a violent turn to her wheel: Leriano is being freed from the prison of love by Laureola's letter, and the use of the language of fortune ('súpito,' 'bien,' 'cayó,' 'sobir,' 'eché,' and 'bienaventurado') reflects this fact. But subtle surprises await us. Leriano, who should be climbing Fortune's wheel, is apparently so overcome by the sudden turn that he falls to the ground in a swoon; and the correspondent, who comes rejoicing, thinks for a moment that he has reason instead to weep. We find similar delightful ironies if we plot the ups and downs of Leriano's trajectory in the narrative.

We first meet Leriano in a vision in the deep, dark valleys of the Sierra Morena, and when we would expect him to descend even deeper into despair, we find him climbing until he reaches the top of a steep stairway; then, he is seated on a throne in a prison at the top of a mountain which seems to reach to heaven. Here in this mountaintop prison he is sad. Later, when he is happy and we should expect him to soar even higher, Leriano descends the mountain and enters the palace where he bows to kiss the hand of Laureola. From Suria we should expect Leriano to go downward after Laureola is imprisoned; instead we find him climbing the walls of Susa to defend the city against the king's siege. From the heights of Susa's fortified walls, we should expect Leriano to soar freely when Laureola is released; instead we find him lying in bed. From his deathbed, we would expect Leriano to go deeper, to his grave; instead, before he dies, he orders that he be seated upright ('Mandó que le sentasen en la cama, y sentado, bevióselas en el agua y assí quedó contenta su voluntad,' p. 176).

These ups and downs in Leriano's movements are not coincidences; the text advises us repeatedly that they are to be related to the wheel of Fortune. For example, after Persio has helped Fortune turn her wheel, the text records: 'Como la mala fortuna enbidiosa de los bienes de Leriano usase con él de su natural condición, diole tal revés cuando le vido mayor en prosperidad' (p. 116); and Leriano's mother, summarizing the cause of her son's death, blames Fortune more than any other cause ('Por cierto hoy quita la fuerça de tu fortuna los derechos a la razón, pues mueres sin tiempo y sin dolencia ... mas para librarte della [la muerte], ni tu fortuna quiso, ni yo, triste, pude,' pp. 173–4). It can be claimed fairly, therefore, that the wheel of Fortune is a pattern imposed upon the text of *Cárcel* by Diego de San Pedro. Moreover it might even be possible to begin to describe one of the multitudinous variants of the wheel of Fortune that San Pedro might have had in mind.

San Pedro is not using Ixion's wheel, as did Juan Rodríguez del Padrón in *Siervo*. In fact, the word 'rueda' is not used in the text of *Cárcel*; yet the word 'fortuna' was closely associated, especially in fifteenth-century Spain, with the word 'rueda' (which, by the way, is used by San Pedro in his poem *Desprecio de la Fortuna*). San Pedro seems to be thinking of the kind of wheel that appeared in a late ninth-century Spanish manuscript of St Gregory's *Moralia*, on which there is a monarch at each of the cardinal points.[42] Above or below the head of each monarch is written 'regno,' or 'regnavi,' or 'sum sine regno,' or 'regnabo,' according to the position (right-side up or upside-down) of each ruler's head. Correspondingly San Pedro seems to put four of the main characters of *Cárcel* at the cardinal points of Fortune's wheel. Leriano is, at the beginning of the narrative, in the pit of Fortune's wheel, 'sine regno.' Laureola, as heir to the kingdom of Macedonia, is not diametrically opposite to Leriano, but in the 'regnabo' position; she is close enough to Leriano to tempt him to reach out to her but nevertheless to be beyond his reach. King Gaulo, obviously, occupies the 'regno' position at the top of the wheel. The most likely candidate for the 'regnavi' position is Persio.

The text is not clear about Persio's position as it could be, and it would be unwise to insist on this point. However, Persio seems to be a character who has lost an opportunity for control of the country through Laureola's love, although he and his family are still very powerful. The correspondent reports that while watching Leriano and Laureola, Persio was 'trayendo el mismo pensamiento que Leriano traía' (p. 115); and Laureola's mother says of her, 'A todos eras agradable y a Persio fuiste odiosa' (p. 135), which could mean either that Persio hated Laureola or that Laureola was hateful to Persio. Persio and his family have so much control over the king that the latter imprisons his own daughter 'creyendo segund la virtud y auctoridad de Persio' (p. 114), and the family is able to persuade the king to spare Persio's life (p. 117); whereas not even his own wife nor his ecclesiastical advisors can persuade the king to spare his daughter's life. Even after the truth comes to light, the king still treats Persio's relatives with greater deference than they seem to deserve ('A Leriano mandóle el rey que no entrase por estonces en la corte hasta que pacificase a él y a los parientes de Persio,' p. 148).

At the narrative's beginning, therefore, the cardinal characters on the wheel seem to be as follows: King Gaulo is north at 'regno'; Laureola, east at 'regnabo'; Leriano, south at 'sine regno'; and Persio, west at 'regnavi.' (I give the directions for visual convenience in order to describe for the reader what happens when the wheel is turned.)

The wheel is first turned counterclockwise. When Leriano makes a triumphant entry into Suria (p. 113), the text says nothing about his paying homage to the king but gives minute details about what happens when he kisses Laureola's hand. With the attention of the entire court on the pair, Laureola moves for a fleeting moment to the 'regno' position, and Leriano, as her prospective husband, to the 'regnabo' position; consequently, the king and Persio are suddenly threatened with the 'regnavi' and 'sine regno' positions, respectively. The menace explains why Persio moves swiftly to restore his position and why the king orders him to accuse Leriano of treachery (p. 114): Leriano, as Laureola's suitor at 'regnabo,' is a political threat to the king. Persio's lie and the king's order send the wheel spinning two positions in counterclockwise direction: Laureola moves swiftly from 'regno' to prison in 'sine regno'; Persio, who is now in effective control of the king, moves to 'regno,' and the king to 'regnabo;' Leriano watches his fleeting moment of glory pass by as he lands at 'regnavi.' When Persio is killed and his lies are exposed, the wheel turns again in a counter-clockwise direction, moving the king back to 'regno,' Laureola to 'regnabo,' and Leriano to 'sine regno.'

Although Leriano dies 'sine regno,' the irony that has been described as affecting his trajectory comes once more into play at his death. At the beginning of the narrative, Leriano at 'sine regno' should have no crown on his head, but he wears a crown of iron thorns and is seated on a throne ('silla'). At the end of the narrative Leriano's deathbed becomes his throne, upon which he demands to be seated upright as he drinks a draught of passion to quench his desire and pronounces a Christlike dictum, 'Acabados son mis males.' The implication is that the wheel has turned once more counterclockwise: in a kingdom not of this world, Laureola, now partly inside the dying body of Leriano, moves to 'regno,' and Leriano to 'regnabo.' Although apparently inconsistent, these positions are correct because, in one clear sense, Laureola is still his reigning lord. The reader may not necessarily accept my interpretation of the wheel of fortune or place these characters on the wheel precisely as I have described, but I do ask the reader to accept the concept that Fortune is in some way operative in the text of *Cárcel de amor.*

Another noteworthy contribution to the composition of *Cárcel* should not be ignored. In 1966 Francisco Márquez Villanueva suggested that *Cárcel* ought to be read as a political novel about late-fifteenth-century Spain. Specifically, Márquez proposed that San Pedro was reacting in *Cárcel* against the Spanish Inquisition and its 'anti-converso' policies: 'Su modo de reaccionar ante la Inquisición ha de entenderse en el campo en que él quiso formularlo, que es el de la crítica de una medida de gobierno. San Pedro la considera instrumento tiránico e hipocrítica de una política anti-conversos.' One senses in Márquez's conclusions a desire, no doubt justifiable, to make a statement of righteous indignation against the Spain of 1966: 'Y así, por muy medieval y rey de baraja que pueda parecer ese padre de Laureola, no es sino prefigura y anticipo de todos los aspectos negativos del estado moderno.'[43] But this irresistible temptation to apply *Cárcel* to twentieth-century Spain should in no way detract from Márquez's suggestion that San Pedro has the Inquisition in mind. After rereading Márquez's article and *Cárcel* I do not now believe that the text of *Cárcel* supports his claims unequivocally, but for the following reasons I am certain that the matter ought to be pursued until it can be satisfactorily decided.

1. If we accept the proposition, suggested by the text, that San Pedro is thinking of the apostle Paul when he chooses Macedonia as an

appropriate setting, then we are faced with the fact that Paul, a Jewish convert to Christianity, was imprisoned in Macedonia for disturbing the city as a Jew when he was in fact a Christian (Acts 16:20). Paul's mission in Macedonia was to help new Christians.

2. The text of *Cárcel* does not permit us to decide unambiguously whether Macedonia is a Christian or a Jewish country. On the one hand, it can be argued that the Macedonia in *Cárcel* is a Christian country because it has a cardinal and prelates who advise the king. But on the other hand, the cardinal, who makes a long speech on behalf of this priestly group, says nothing that indicates that he is Christian. In fact, the only person in the narrative who identifies himself as Christian is Leriano, and from what he says we can assume that the people whom he addresses are also Christian ('En las autorizadas por santas, por tres razones no quiero hablar. La primera, porque lo que a todos es manifiesto parece sinpleza repetirlo,' p. 166). How are we to interpret 'todos'? Does the word mean all the people in Macedonia or does it refer only to those around Leriano's deathbed? We should bear in mind Diego de San Pedro's penchant (which he shares with the apostle Paul) for tailoring his words to suit the audience ('Para que toda materia sea bien entendida y notada, conviene que el razonamiento del que dize sea conforme a la condición del que oye.'[44] Is Leriano here addressing an audience of new Christians? If the world in which Leriano and his (new?) Christian sympathizers operate is a Christian world, then why is it governed by so many ancient Jewish laws which were altered or ignored by Christianity?

3. The law according to which Laureola is sentenced to death, the so-called law of Scotland ('ley de Escocia'), is an ancient Jewish law of chastity described clearly in Deuteronomy 22:20–1: 'But if the thing is true, that the tokens of virginity were not found in the young woman, then they shall bring out the young woman to the door of her father's house, and the men of her city shall stone her to death with stones, because she has wrought folly in Israel by playing the harlot in her father's house; so you shall purge the evil from the midst of you.' This is the law that apparently was altered by Christ when he said about the woman accused of adultery, 'Let him who is without sin among you be the first to throw a stone at her' (John 8:7). It is worth noting that the cardinal and the prelates, if they are Christian, do not refer to Christ's interpretation of the Jewish laws of chastity and adultery when the cardinal advises the king to spare Laureola's life.

4. The law according to which Persio condemns Laureola to death on the evidence of three witnesses, and the king promises to spare her life on the evidence of a single witness, is a Jewish law found in Deuteron-

omy 17:6: 'On the evidence of two witnesses or of three witnesses he that is to die shall be put to death; a person shall not be put to death on the evidence of one witness.' (Note that the last part of this verse is deliberately ambiguous, meaning both that a single witness cannot condemn a person to death *and* that a single witness can save a person's life.) This Jewish law is repeated later in Deuteronomy 19:15-21 in which the punishment for false witnesses, the *lex talionis*, is clearly defined: 'The judges shall inquire diligently and if the witness is a false witness and has accused his brother falsely, then you shall do to him as he had meant to do to his brother.' The laws of Macedonia in *Cárcel* thus coincide with the Jewish laws not only as to the number of witnesses required to condemn or liberate an accused, but also in so far as the false witnesses bribed by Persio are punished under the law of retaliation ('de los tres falsos hombres se hizo tal la justicia como fue la maldad,' p. 148). Again, it is noteworthy that the cardinal who appeals to the king for Laureola's life, if he was a Christian cardinal, does not refer to Christ's interpretation of the Jewish laws of witnesses in the same scriptural passage in which Christ also altered the law of chastity and adultery ('In your law it is written that the testimony of two men is true; I bear witness to myself, and the Father who sent me bears witness to me,' John 8:17-18). In fact, the text of *Cárcel* ignores Christ's interpretation of Jewish law and confirms the Jewish law that rules out the evidence of an accused person on his or her own behalf: 'The Pharisees then said to him, "You are bearing witness to yourself; your testimony is not true." Jesus answered, "Even if I do bear witness to myself, my testimony is true"' (John 8:13-14). Jesus's answer should be compared with Laurcola's first letter to Leriano: 'Porque si deste pecado fuese acusada no tengo otro testigo para salvarme sino mi intención, y por ser parte tan principal no se tomaría en cuenta su dicho' (p. 109). It is also remarkable that the laws of Macedonia, if they are Christian laws, do not reflect Christ's alteration of the *lex talionis* in Matthew 5:38-9: 'You have heard that it was said, "An eye for an eye and a tooth for a tooth." But I say to you, do not resist one who is evil. But if anyone strikes you on the right cheek, turn to him the other also.'

5. The laws according to which Leriano is sentenced to death at the beginning of the narrative (p. 90) are very similar to Jewish laws of idolatry given in the same passage in Deuteronomy that contain the law of chastity under which Laureola is condemned. Leriano follows a statue (carried by Deseo) up to a mountaintop altar with pillars. Jews were repeatedly forbidden to make or worship images, especially those on mountaintop altars of other nations, and in Deuteronomy 16:22

they are specifically warned against making pillars on such altars: 'And you shall not set up a pillar which the Lord your God hates.' The four pillars of Leriano's altar are his own Razón, Entendimiento, Memoria, and Voluntad. In accordance with Jewish law three of these witnesses condemn Leriano; the fourth, Voluntad, which could have saved his life, resolves instead to seal his fate. Leriano describes Amor as a just judge who applies a cruel law ('Pues oyendo Amor que quien me havía de salvar me condenava, dio como justo esta sentencia cruel contra mí,' p. 90). As a Christian, Leriano would have been free to follow a statue, for example, representing the Virgin Mary; as a Jew he could have been put to death for the same act (although, in fact, the death penalty for such an act was rarely carried out among Jews).

6. The laws of which Leriano and the cardinal remind the king, and to which the king himself refers, are Jewish laws. Leriano tells the king, 'Pues eres obligado a ser igual en derecho' (p. 120); the king confirms this law and adds that judges ought not to accept bribes: 'Igualmente se deve guardar el derecho, y el coraçón del juez no se ha de moveer por favor ni amor ni cobdicia, ni por ningún otro acidente' (p. 133). Chapter 16 of Deuteronomy also commands Jews to 'appoint judges and officers in all your towns ... and they shall judge the people with righteous judgment. You shall not show partiality; and you shall not take a bribe' (16:18–19).

In the next chapter of Deuteronomy verses 8 and 9 set out the law that compels Jews and Jewish leaders to seek the advice of priests for difficult matters: 'If any case arises ... within your towns which is too difficult for you, then you shall arise ... and coming to the Levitical priests, and to the judge who is in office in those days you shall consult them, and they shall declare to you the decision.' In *Cárcel*, the cardinal reminds the king that he would be acting in accordance with an ancient law if he were to take priestly advice: 'No a sinrazón los soberanos príncipes pasados ordenaron consejo en lo que huviesen de hazer ... y ... por seis razones aquella ley deve ser conservada' (p. 129–30). The king confirms the validity of the cardinal's reference to the law: 'No era menester dezirme las razones por que los poderosos deven recebir consejo, porque aquellas y otras que dexastes de dezir tengo yo conocidas' (p. 132). The cardinal and his prelates choose to ignore Christian interpretations and, like Levitical priests, adhere instead to Jewish laws. If the cardinal was Christian, he could, of course, have referred to Christ's strong support of Jewish law: 'Think not that I have come to abolish the law and the prophets; I have come not to abolish them but to fulfil them ... not an iota, not a dot, will pass from the law until all is accomplished' (Matthew 5:17–18). Christ's claim takes us back to the apparent fundamental ambivalence in the text of *Cárcel*: it seems impossible to tell unequivocally whether it is a Jewish or a Christian text.

7. The laws of duelling to which Persio and Leriano subject themselves reflect the ancient Jewish belief that God supports the righteousness of the representative of good, who will emerge victorious in a duel with the representative of evil. The most famous example of this belief is in the story of David and Goliath (1 Samuel 17), and the verbal exchanges between David and Goliath, although not written in 'carteles,' are not unlike the verbal exchanges between Persio and Leriano (p. 114–16, 1 Samuel 17:43–7).

Persio reminds Leriano of the latter's 'linpieza' and of 'la obligación de tu sangre' (pp. 114–15). The ambivalence of the text permits Persio's remarks to be interpreted in at least two ways. If Macedonia is a Christian country and Persio a devout 'old' Christian, the remark has to be taken ironically to refer to the Jewish ancestry of Leriano who is living among Christians. If Macedonia is a Jewish country and Persio a devout Jew fighting against a fellow Jew whom he considers a traitor because of his conversion to Christianity, again the remark is ironic since it implies that Jews are more rightly concerned with 'linpieza de sangre' than Christians should be. Further, if Leriano is a 'new' Christian fighting against a Jew before a Jewish king, the king's abrupt termination of the duel has a great deal of credibility. His reason for terminating the duel, namely, that in his opinion the witness of mankind is evidence that the law of God is not yet fulfilled ("que veo el testimonio cierto y el juizio no acabado,' p. 133), alludes overtly to the duel between Persio and Leriano and covertly to Christ's statement that he came to fulfil the law; in other words, the king's remark seems to emphasize a fundamental difference between Judaism and Christianity.

Besides, if the king is Jewish, he would know that he is not breaking Jewish law by stopping the duel; settlement by duel reflected Jewish belief, not Jewish law. As for Leriano, his insistence on justice by duel also reflects a belief that Christianity inherited from Judaism; so Leriano's actions are here consistent with his character as a ('new'?) Christian. It should be noted that Leriano, as a Christian, cannot be said to disapprove of some of the practices of the Inquisition since he agrees with the principle and practice of torturing false witnesses to exact confessions.

8. If Macedonia is a Christian country, why is Susa, one of its main cities (the city, by the way, to which Leriano is exiled), named after Susa, a capital of the Persian Empire, which Jews know as Shushan?

Jews read about Shushan during the feast of Purim, one of their most
important festivals, which celebrates the deliverance of the Jews of
Susa and all Persia from a nationally planned campaign to massacre
them. During the feast of Purim Jews read the scroll of Esther. We
know that Diego de San Pedro was thinking of the book of Esther as he
worked on *Cárcel* because Esther is one of the worthy women whom
Leriano cites as an example: 'Esther ... la cual por sus méritos y oración libró los judíos de la cativided que tenían' (p. 169).

9. The Christian reader of *Cárcel* will no doubt be reminded immediately of the passion of Jesus when Leriano drains his cup. But the
Jewish reader of the same passage will immediately recall verses 17
and 22 of Isaiah 51 (to which Christ referred as he remembered the cup
of affliction): 'Awake, awake, stand up, O Jerusalem, thou hast drunk at
the hand of the Lord the cup of his fury; thou has drunken the beaker,
even the cup of staggering and drained it .... Behold I have taken out
of thy hand the cup of staggering; the beaker, even the cup of My fury,
thou shalt no more drink it again.'[45] These words in Isaiah together
with the phrases in Deuteronomy (16:18–21:9) containing many of the
laws referred to in *Cárcel*, are the sections of the Bible read in the temple during a Haftarah. For Jews, this portion of Isaiah is an important
one. It is called a Haftarah of consolation, and is one of several read
after the Jewish feast commemorating the destruction of the Temple.
In other words, this portion of Isaiah is meant to console Jews with the
assurance that even if they are destroyed again they will rise from destruction as they did before.

When Leriano drains his cup, the Christian part of him remembers
Christ; when he *sits up* and drinks a 'cure' for his illness, the Jewish
part of him remembers the words of consolation of the prophet Isaiah
('Thou shalt no more drink it again; and I will put it into the hand of
them that afflict thee; that have said to thy soul: "Bow down, that we
may go over;" and thou hast laid back as the ground, and as the street,
to them that go over.... Arise, and sit down, O Jerusalem; loose thyself
from the bands of thy neck, O captive daughter of Zion,' Isaiah 51:22–
52:2). Much of Leriano's behaviour before he dies makes a kind of
sense in the light of these words of Isaiah, a sense that is lacking if the
scene is related only to the passion of Christ – the fact that he lies
down and then insists on being seated upright, that he has just
referred to 'Ester ... la cual ... libró los judíos de la captivided que
tenían' (p. 169), and that even as he dies, he is supposed to be regaining
emotional strength as his cup of affliction and misfortune is drained
and his illness is cured; ('bevióselas en el agua y assí quedó contenta

su voluntad,' p. 176). Even as Israel was twice destroyed and twice revived, so too this revival of Leriano is his second.

For a Jew, who would read this passage from Isaiah at least once every year after the feast of the Ninth of Av, the meaning of Leriano's deathbed scene, especially in Spain at the end of the fifteenth century, would have been inescapable. Even a 'converso' who no longer read this passage was likely to be well-acquainted with it, because either he used to read it as a Jew, or, as a Christian with or without Jewish roots, he would have had to know how Christ's behaviour was foretold in Isaiah.

10. In the light of the inherent ambivalence of the text of *Cárcel*, how seriously is the reader to interpret the first sentence of the narrative, which begins, 'Aunque me falta sofrimiento para callar, no me fallesce conoscimiento para ver' (p. 79)? Does the sentence mean that San Pedro had been forced to cultivate a style whereby what he implied is as important as what he said? Elsewhere he wrote: 'Pero Vosotras, señoras, rescevid en servicio no lo que con rudeza en el dezir publico, mas lo que por falta en el callar encubro.'[46] Are we to treat these words simply as topoi of modesty, or is San Pedro suggesting much more than modesty?

11. From the above reasons for pursuing the line of investigation suggested by Márquez Villanueva, one very tentative conclusion emerges, namely, *Cárcel* is an inherently ambivalent text that cannot be interpreted unequivocally as either Christian or Jewish. On the one hand, if the text is Christian, the book's statement seems to be that Macedonia, like Spain, is a country run by Christians who, when they sentence sincere Jewish converts to death or exile, act as harshly[47] as had the ancient Jews (Leriano is exiled from the royal court at the end of the book, and for him this exile is a sentence of death). On the other hand, just as the name Macedonia in the text can be a catchword for Spain, so too the words *cardinal* and *prelates* can be clues for Jewish Levitical priests mentioned in Deuteronomy, and Macedonia would be a Jewish country and the text a Jewish text. If the text is Jewish, then the book's statement seems to be that the Jewish kingdom of Macedonia, like the Jewish communities of Spain, treats 'conversos' as idolaters who have betrayed their obligation to their ancestral religion and lineage and, according to ancient Jewish law, deserve the sentence of death. In either Christian or Jewish interpretation of the text Leriano would be discouraged from marrying Laureola.

12. Could it be that Diego de San Pedro was clever enough to have imposed on the text of *Cárcel* both interpretations just described?

Could he have created a text that, when read from a Jewish point of view, would condemn a man to death for acts that for different reasons would condemn the man if the text were read from a Christian point of view? If *Cárcel* is indeed such a text, San Pedro has achieved a goal he repeatedly expressed as desirable, namely, to make his text adapt itself to his audience ('conformar mis palabras con vuestros pensamientos').[48]

13. It could be claimed that all of the above reasons involve the reading of an excessive amount of politics into an intimate sentimental narrative about love, honour, and religion.[49] But at the time of the composition of *Cárcel* love, honour, and religion were interrelated public sentiments of intense political urgency, which demanded the diplomatic mediation of some virtuous apostolic 'señor' if the wheel of Fortune were not to lock itself into a position of shallow triumph for some at the tragic expense of the life of others. *Cárcel* is a prayer for help.

Celestina

We do not need to know, for the purposes of this limited history of literary composition, if the text of *Siervo* was a source for the text of *Cárcel*. Without this knowledge we have described the different variants of the wheel of Fortune used in the composition of both works. In *Siervo* Juan Rodríguez places man at a central juncture of Fortune's wheel with a real choice of following either a road to destruction or a road to salvation. In *Cárcel* Diego de San Pedro places man in an irreconcilably chained position on the perimeter of Fortune's wheel, with no real choice but to make his inevitable destruction coterminous with his salvation; as Peter Dunn explains brilliantly, 'Leriano's alternatives are not real alternatives at all, before which rational choices might be made, but cruel paradoxes from which there is no escape.'[50] We come now, in this limited history, to a problematic hybrid text, Fernando de Rojas's *Celestina*, part of which acknowledges *Cárcel* as a source, and all of which deploys in its composition yet another variant of the wheel of Fortune.[51]

If *Siervo* describes intimately the inner machinations of arriving at a choice, and *Cárcel* the torture of living with an apparent choice that is paradoxically no choice at all, then *Celestina* describes inexorably what is bound to happen after a certain kind of choice has been made. The narrator of *Siervo* arrives, after much contemplation, at a decision to reject Yrena's idolatrous cult that worships secular lovers who are believed to be in paradise. In *Cárcel* Leriano dies with unshakable belief that his love for Laureola will lead him to God because Laureola's love is like the love of God; the correspondent assures Laureola:

'Mira en qué cargo eres a Leriano, que aun su passión te haze servicio, pues si la remedias te da causa que puedas hazer lo mismo que Dios; porque no es de menos estima el redemir quel criar, assí que harás tú tanto en quitalle la muerte como Dios en darle la vida' (p. 95). This passage from *Cárcel* makes its way into the text of *Celestina* when Melibea says to Celestina, 'Hazer beneficio es semejar a Dios, e el que le da le recibe, quando a persona digna dél le hace. E demás desto, dizen que el que puede sanar al que padece, no lo faziendo, le mata.'[52] In other words, Melibea already accepts, at the outset of Rojas's portion of the narrative, the basic idea that Laureola steadfastly rejects throughout *Cárcel*. In this sense *Celestina* begins where *Cárcel* ended.

For the narrator of *Siervo*, his lover is not God; for Ardanlier, Liessa is not God, and for Yrena, Ardanlier is not God; likewise, in *Cárcel*, for Leriano, Laureola, though godlike, is not God. But early in *Celestina* Calisto declares that Melibea is God: 'Por Dios la creo, por Dios la confiesso e no creo que ay otro soberano en el cielo, aunque entre nosotros mora' (vol. 1, p. 44). In this sense also *Celestina* begins where *Cárcel* ended.

When Leriano dies, his mother, in addition to confirming her belief that her son was God-fearing ('tú temeroso de Dios,' p. 173), expresses the idea that common people are not capable of feeling the kind of love for which he was dying ('Bienaventurados los baxos de condición y rudos de engenio, que no pueden sentir las cosas sino en el grado que las entienden; y malaventurados los que con sutil juizio las trascenden,' p. 173). This section of the lament of the Duchess Coleria is an open invitation to its literary-minded readers to compose a work that explores the nature and consequences of the feelings about love among 'los baxos de condición.' In this important respect too the *Celestina* begins where *Cárcel* ended: the characters of *Celestina* are meant, for the most part, to be 'baxos de condición,' with the important exceptions of Calisto and Melibea; even so, Calisto is no duke, and Melibea no duchess.

One should be careful not to claim too much for these resemblances between the texts of *Cárcel* and *Celestina*: the ideas were used widely. If, for example, Rojas did not insert these ideas into the first act which he said he found, the original author of the first act was responsible for two out of the three ideas: the exploration of love among the lower class, and the lover as God. This latter point is much harder to determine than the former, because Act 1 begins as though Calisto accepts that God exists apart from Melibea ('En esto veo, Melibea, la grandeza de Dios'). Did Rojas make the crucial change to the idea that 'Melibea es mi Dios'? Or did the original author let Calisto become mad after he was first rejected by Melibea? I do not know. However the text evolved, we have now to deal with a *Celestina* whose text extends the idea in *Cárcel* (and elsewhere, of course) that the lover is like God to an idea that the lover is God.

Celestina is structured in such a way that its principal characters are chained together on the rim of Fortune's wheel. When one of these main characters falls off the wheel, the others inevitably fall in swift consequence. Calisto gives Celestina a chain for her services in linking him, with skein and girdle, to Melibea. Calisto's servants covet this chain and kill Celestina for it; once Celestina dies so do the servants and Calisto and Melibea. That all these tragedies of love occur on the wheel of Fortune is reflected in many passages in the text. Celestina herself is made to describe her own downfall, and that of the entire world around her, in terms of Fortune's wheel ('¡Ay, quién me vido e quién me vee agora, no sé como no quiebra su coraçón de dolor? Yo ví, mi amor, a esta mesa donde agora están tus primas assentadas, nueve moças de tus días, que la mayor no passara de diezocho años e ninguna havía menor de quatorze. Mundo es, pase, ande su rueda, rodea sus alcaduzes, unos llenos, otros vazios. La ley es de Fortuna que ninguna cosa en un ser mucho tiempo permanesce: su orden es mudanças,' vol. 2, p. 43–4). Depictions of bodies around the rim of Fortune's wheel are not uncommon in medieval manuscripts; Rojas had simply to link the bodies to each other.[53]

Celestina seems to be composed around another great Commandment, the first, the most important commandment to religious Jews: 'You shall have no other gods before me.' In one of the many places where this commandment is repeated, there is a clear injunction against witchcraft and other forms of false prophecy, for which the punishment is death: 'There shall not be found among you ... anyone who practises divination, a soothsayer, or an augur, or a charmer, or a medium, or a wizard, or a necromancer. For whosoever does these things is an abomination to the Lord .... But the prophet who presumes to speak a word in my name which I have not commanded him to speak, or who speaks in the name of other gods, that same prophet shall die' (Deuteronomy 18:10–12, 20). This section of Deuteronomy was well known to San Pedro.[54]

Cárcel could well be a truly 'converso' text, in love with its Jewish ancestry as well as with its immediate necessity to be Christian. Could San Pedro's achievement have escaped Rojas? We must assume that someone who was capable of constructing the subtle ironies of *Celestina* was capable of recognizing similar ironies in the text of *Cárcel*. Russell's claim that 'Rojas era una figura de reconocida considera-

ción social cuya ortodoxia cristiana (lo mismo que la de su libro)
estaba fuera de toda sospecha' is true but incomplete.[55] It is true that
it would be imprudent to have a suspect defend a 'converso,' but it is
also true that a 'converso' was, by definition, suspect, or there would be
no need for the term – 'cristiano' would suffice, or 'judío.' And 'fuera de
toda sospecha' from whose point of view? If one were 'guilty' of revert-
ing to Judaism (or innocent for that matter), would one choose a purely
Christian lawyer or a lawyer much closer to one's situation?

To say that *Celestina* is an orthodox Christian text is true from a
Christian point of view; most Jews and, surely, some 'conversos' would
certainly find it hilarious that a Christian text should be composed
around the first Commandment, since from a strictly Jewish point of
view Christianity can be considered only idolatrous. Sempronio reacts
with infectious laughter ('Ha! ha! ha!' vol. 1, pp. 42–4), and there is
nothing distinctly Christian *in the words of his response* but much
that is essentially Old Testament and Jewish. The text of *Celestina*,
like the text of *Cárcel*, could very well be a Christian *and* a Jewish
text, depending on the reader. *Celestina* is a 'converso' text, a text composed so that its ironies convert themselves to the beliefs of the
reader, as San Pedro puts it, 'conformar mis palabras con vuestros pensamientos.'[56] Yet almost all of *Celestina* scholarship seems to assume
that all readers of the work were Christian, even though the book
might have been translated into Hebrew (even in Italy!) in the sixteenth century.

A key to the composition of *Celestina* lies in the very chasm of
inane differences between intuitive literary critics and legal-minded
historians, between legal-minded literary critics and intuitive historians. Research is only now beginning to demonstrate to what extent
the historical documents of the Inquisition are every bit as fictional as
works like *Celestina* are historical.[57]

In order to begin my arguments on *Celestina* I first had to write this
entire book. I knew that *Celestina* could not have been composed *in
vacuo* and I had to sort out for myself what it has to do with works in
Spain that precede it. For example, much has been written about the
composition of *Celestina* in terms of its relationship to Juan Ruiz's
Buen amor and the *Corbacho*. But it is now clearer to me that although
Celestina shares, with all other medieval Spanish works, variations of
the same common traditions, its own ironical structure is very different from, for example, the irony of *Buen amor*.

Let us say, for the purpose of this discussion, that Juan Ruiz directs
his work at good readers (A) and bad readers (B) about a certain sin,
luxuria (C); then we will have to say, tentatively, that Rojas directs his

work at Christian readers (A) and Jewish readers (B) about a sin, idolatry, (C). The crucial difference is that in Juan Ruiz, A and B agree with delight on the same interpretation of C as sin; in other words, religiously the text is static, and the reader chooses, according to his or her preference or ability, to heed for good, or exploit for evil, that same static text. With Rojas, however, the text is dynamic, so that although they remain delighted at Rojas's text, A and B are able to do so only because they interpret C in vastly different, even at times contrary, ways. This does not mean that the text of *Buen amor* is not subtle and polysemous, but it does mean that Rojas adds yet another level of irony on top of subtleties of the kind used by Juan Ruiz. *Buen amor* is essentially a Christian text, and for good or evil can be read only that way. Rojas, it seems, adds to the question of good or bad the crucial question of Christian or Jewish.[58]

To the Christian reader Calisto is, among other things, a courtly lover, heretic, and fool, and maybe a 'converso' as well. To the Jewish reader Calisto is, among other things, a courtly lover and idolater who goes 'a whoring after other gods,' a phrase that aptly describes the composition of *Celestina* and is repeated almost *ad nauseam* in the Jewish scriptures. Central themes of *Celestina* – ensnaring and marriage – are found, for example, in a single passage of Exodus: 'Take heed to thyself, lest thou make a covenant with the inhabitants of the land whither thou goest, lest it be for a snare in the midst of thee ... And thou take of their daughters unto thy sons, and their daughters go a whoring after their gods, and make thy sons go a whoring after their gods' (Exodus 34:12,16).[59]

Petrarch, the 'comedia humanística,' and courtly love are just a 'fermosa cobertura' for the ironical religious structure of *Celestina*. Bataillon thought along somewhat similar lines, but he looked ahead from Diego de San Pedro and Fernando de Rojas to writers like Montemayor, Villegas, and Garci Sánchez, whereas this chapter looks back and includes a writer (as an example of others) not known to be a 'converso.' Bataillon writes with the fine, understated sensitivity characteristic of his best style:

> Poetas hubo que se criaron, por tradición familiar, en la lectura de la *Biblia*, y que, por razón de su oficio dentro de la sociedad cristiana, ya clérigos, ya cantores, siguieron cultivándola ... El rápido éxito europeo de los dos primeros [Diego de San Pedro, Fernando de Rojas] ... hace sospechar que esta aportación de la península ibérica colmaba secretas aspiraciones de la época en

> general ... ¿Qué publica la imprenta de los Usque y Yom Tob
> Athias? ... En 1553, como era de esperar, la Biblia en español,
> obra imponente con la curiosa particularidad de que se hacen al
> mismo tiempo dos ediciones que difieren en variantes del texto
> y en los preliminares: una para uso de cristianos ... otra abierta-
> mente judía.[60]

This last point, about two editions of the Bible, one for Christians,
quite another for Jews, is circumstantial evidence in support of the
idea that Diego de San Pedro and Fernando de Rojas might have
thought of making their texts serve a similar dual purpose. The idea
was afloat in their time, not long after the writing of their masterpieces, if not before.

I shall end this chapter with some general remarks about the theme
that seems to be common to the three masterworks analysed as egre-
gious and convenient examples of countless others – the magic wheel
of Fortune in *Siervo*, *Cárcel*, and *Celestina* – a magic wheel because
clearly magic plays a functional role in all three works. The religion
instituted by Yrena and Lamidoras (in *Siervo*) that enchants pilgrims
like Macías and the narrator, and Leriano's gospel of love that enchants
him in a cathedral-like prison (in *Cárcel*) are the counterparts of Celestina's religion of diabolical magic arts. Russell is right about the centrality of magic. These religions of magic are also clearly and
consistently associated with Fortune. Gilman, therefore, is also right,
even if he states his case with infuriating creativity not always desirable (in the opinion of some) in a literary critic; right but like Russell,
like us all, not quite complete.[61]

I shall attempt to explain how both Gilman and Russell could be
right because I believe that the explanation has a great deal to do with
the subject matter of this chapter and this book. Gilman is correct, I
believe, when he sees a resemblance between the Inquisition and Fortune in fifteenth-century Spain, and when I read how he tries to prove
this resemblance, I *feel* that I am witnessing, in the words of the philosopher, a mark of genius. I say 'feel,' because when I read how Russell
proves that magic is a key factor in the structure of *Celestina* (at a
time when all my teachers were trying to persuade me that Freudian
psychology, not magic, was the key, as though Freud were not a kind of
witch doctor), I 'think' that I am in the presence of genius. But when I
read a beautiful, well-reasoned article about *feelings* (Wardropper's 'El
mundo sentimental,' referred to earlier – written at a time when virtu-
ally no other Hispanist was inspired to figure out the intimacy of a

masterpiece like *Cárcel de amor* – I understand, that is, I think *and* feel the force of genius, which explains why this chapter is dedicated to Bruce Wardropper.

To understand how Gilman is right, all we have to do is to examine one of the typical sentences of *The Spain of Fernando de Rojas*: 'In the Inquisitors the goddess Fortune had found willing and efficient human agents for her labor on earth.'[62] On page 130 of 'The "Conversos"' 'Earth' is capitalized, which makes me feel that the use of capitals in the sentence is not accidental: 'Inquisitors' means more than 'inquisitors.' I like 'Earth' better because then 'labor' connotes childbirth and fornication, and 'human agents' connotes 'alcahuetas'. This is what I mean by infuriating creativity; this Hispanist is no ordinary literary critic, he is a frustrated poet. Infuriating, because how on earth are we ever going to document a sentence like that? Are we supposed to send research assistants to the Spanish archives to see if they can dig up a memorandum from Fortune to Fulano saying 'The Inquisition wants YOU'? But let us treat the sentence as though it were literature, not history, or better, as literary history, and see what happens: let us substitute for 'Inquisitors' the words '*Siervo libre de amor, Cárcel de Amor*, and *Celestina*. The sentence would then read: 'In the *Siervo libre de amor, Cárcel de Amor*, and *Celestina* the goddess Fortune had found willing and efficient human agents for her labor on earth.'

The sentence suddenly becomes documentable if we can show that those three works are like 'Inquisitors.' And do not say to me that that was not what Gilman meant: poets often do not intend their text to mean what it says. Gilman is right, depending on whether his text is read as literature, history, or literary history. I consider it a positive contribution, not a scientific drawback, that *The Spain of Fernando de Rojas*, used sensibly for what it is, has 'as much validity as the reconstructions of a historical novelist.'[63] Students should not be protected from Gilman; they should be joyfully exposed to Gilman, so that the cream can more easily be separated from the crop. Those students who cannot use Gilman constructively will probably never grasp the subtleties of poets and platonic liars like Diego de San Pedro, Fernando de Rojas, and Juan Rodríguez del Padrón.

The reconstructed sentence presents no problem to document, since Lamidoras, Leriano, and Celestina herself can correctly be described as human agents, both willing and efficient, for the labour of the goddess Fortune on the planet Earth. But in what sense can the three works discussed in this chapter be called inquisitors? It is not enough to say that they all contain 'procesos' (*Siervo* is submitted to a 'juez,' *Cárcel* includes the trial of Laureola, and *Celestina* has the mock trial of the judge, which takes place in Calisto's head), because many other Spanish works also have themes like trials and fortune. The *Cid*, for example, has the trial of the Infantes de Carrión. It is the particular combination of common elements that makes these three works inquisitorial. For example, most critics would not seriously call the *Cid* essentially a 'tratado' about the king-vassal relationship, although some might. But our three sample works can be called 'tratados' in so far as they are philosophical inquiries into the nature of the relationship between variant forms of secular and religious love. When this aspect is supplemented with the confession of the narrator in *Siervo* to a judge who asks him to reveal his secret thoughts, the false witnesses in *Cárcel*, and in *Celestina* Calisto's debate about summary conviction and execution of prisoners by a judge whose motives, in Calisto's mind, are suspect, I believe that a strong case has been made for these works as metaphors for inquisitors; in each of the works main characters are accused of crimes, tried, and sentenced to death or penance. Further, there are elements of torture and confession: Ixion's wheel in *Siervo*, the false witnesses captured by Leriano's men in *Cárcel*, and in *Celestina*, perhaps (although one should not insist on it), the torturous confession of Melibea to her father before she commits suicide. Since all these inquisitorial processes are said repeatedly to have been facilitated by Fortune, why not agree with Gilman that, in the minds of fifteenth-century writers, Fortune is a metaphor for the Inquisition? After all, does it require such a big poetic leap to imagine that the wheel of Fortune can also be perceived as an inquisitorial wheel of torture?

But Gilman is not completely right, of course, if he means that this metaphor was peculiar to 'conversos.' Of our three works, limited though the sample is, one of the three writers, Juan Rodríguez del Padrón, was not a 'converso,' as far as we know, and there is sharp disagreement about the 'converso' status of Diego de San Pedro. Or, if we can find an inquisition in the *De Remediis*, was Petrarch also a 'converso'? True, the text of *Siervo* is not constructed with precisely the same kind of ambivalence as that of the other two texts; the irony of *Siervo* is closer to that of *Buen amor* than that of *Cárcel* and *Celestina*, and unless one caught on to the *contrafactum* at the end of *Siervo*, one could be led to believe that the narrator is still a disciple of the religion of Macías. There is, however, other evidence, if not in literature, then certainly in painting, that Spaniards other than 'conversos' used wheels of torture in their fifteenth-century works.

On the authority of C.R. Post, who knew a great deal about Fortune in European literature and also was a recognized expert on Spanish painting, we are assured that 'Spaniards ... have declared their medieval proclivity for forcing a composition into a formal design by using the wheel as a factor in the general pattern.'[64] Post was discussing depictions of the martyrdom of St Catherine by the brothers Francisco and Fernando Gallego. In a fifteenth-century tryptich on St Catherine's martyrdom, in the Old Cathedral of Salamanca, wheels of torture play a prominent role in the composition of two of the panels. The theme must have been a fairly popular one in the fifteenth century; it is found also in the work of an anonymous artist, in the collection of the Convent of St Mark in León.[65] It is highly unlikely that the Gallego brothers were 'conversos,' or that the anonymous painter of the wood panel in the Convent of St Mark was of Jewish descent. Painting was not encouraged among Jews. Language, however, and the interpretation of texts have always been a central part of the Jewish heritage; if 'conversos' excelled, it is perhaps natural that their excellence should have manifested itself in words.

It is not accidental that I have had to analyse the criticism along with the texts in this and other chapters, because in many ways a text reveals itself best through its criticism. As we try to understand the reality of medieval Spanish texts, let us also face our own reality. It is time it should be said: at our powerful university 'temples' we are the inquisition: we inquire after the facts. There will be accusers. But there are no crimes; there never were, only punishments. We have to be better mediators, better tutors than Lamidoras, better diplomats than Leriano's apostle, less perverse matchmakers than Celestina, so that our students make better lovers than Leriano, Calisto, and Juan Rodríguez because we have better represented beloved Spain and her beloved texts.

6 The Concept 'Book' and Early Spanish Literature

FOR ARMAND BAKER

Looking back at the works analysed in this book, it is fairly easy to notice that one of the most consistent techniques of composition in most of them is that of incorporating a foreign text, sometimes even in its entirety, into the work being composed. *Cid* incorporates the Rachel and Vidas episode; *Milagros* and the *Cantigas* are made up mainly of independent short narratives; the *Razón* includes a troubadouresque love song; *Alexandre* incorporates large sections of the *Alexandreis*; *Zifar* has the *Flores de filosofía*; *Rimado* borrows from the *Moralia*; *Laberinto* contains sections from the *Aeneid* and a large section based on Lucan's *Pharsalia*; *Syetes Virtudes* refers extensively to the *Divina commedia*; *Buen amor* has material from the *Pamphilus*; the *Corbacho* appropriates the debate between Fortune and Poverty; *Siervo* uses the story of Ardanlier and Liessa; and in *Celestina* the long first act is attributed to another author. The technique is far too common to pass unnoticed, and for this reason I have concluded that the 'book' itself is an important factor in literary composition in medieval Spain. In this chapter I shall offer one or two reasons that may help to explain the phenomenon, and then I shall try to describe some ways in which the composition of specific texts might be affected by other books.

I assume that one of the simplest explanations for this frequency of incorporation of foreign works is the apparent belief in the Middle Ages that the contents of a book was common property, belonging to no one in particular. And since literacy must have been a fairly uncommon achievement, it probably was a matter of pride to display in a book what its author had read. Still, since most books remained anonymous, a proud display of knowledge would avail a writer little unless readers knew the author. So the inclusion of someone else's work must have been not simply to display the writer's knowledge, but also, at least in some texts, to lend authority to the writer's message.

One of the main reasons for the phenomenon must be the centrality of a sacred text in the culture of the Christians, Jews, and Muslims who co-existed in Spain during the medieval period. In the religion of each of the groups the sacred text is a *book* revealed by God, a fact that lent an aspect of reverence, on a certain level, to all books. In Judaism and Christianity the revealed text itself consists of a number of independent books, thus making the idea of inserting books between other books a well-known and acceptable practice. Thus, when writers like Beatus of Liébana sought explanations for Ezekiel's vision of God as a wheel within a wheel, they thought of God's Book as a new testament inserted into an old one ('Ezeciel dicit: "rota in rota," id est, evangelium intra legem').[1] In the Koran the revealed text is a single unit that also consists of a series of revelations, the difference being that, unlike the Christian and Jewish texts, the revelations are made to the same person at different times; in this sense, works like *Milagros*, the *Cantigas*, and the *Conde Lucanor* are composed along the pattern of insertion found also in the Koran.

In all three religions the most important message of the revealed text is an apocalyptic message that includes repeated reference to a Book of Judgment that records all deeds of all persons for final sentence on the Last Day; in Judaism and Christianity the key apocalyptic texts contain references to other esoteric books and also, in Ezekiel and Revelation, to the eating of books.

Because of this centrality of a sacred text in the three cultures in Spain, the craft of making (as opposed to writing, or composing) books was of special importance, and some people who were engaged in the manufacture of books may also have been capable of writing their own. Even for an author who was not also a scribe or an employee of a scriptorium, the manufacture of books was likely to have had some effect, however slight, on the composition of his work, as it does even today in comparatively similar ways. It is difficult today, for example, to have accepted for publication an article that is longer than a certain number of pages. Other aspects of the book trade still have a decided effect on the writer as he works on a manuscript (and even after it has been accepted for publication), according to the requirements of the editor and the publisher.

I did not set out to write this book with the idea in mind that bibles were central to literary composition in medieval Spain, but it has turned out that the traditions I have discussed are all so closely connected with bibles that each can justly be called a biblical tradition. E.R. Curtius, a great scholar with a penchant for things classical as well as a knowledge of bibles, has noted the importance of the Christian Bible as a book that has influenced the composition of other books.

Curtius entitled a chapter of his *European Literature and the Latin Middle Ages* 'The Book as Symbol.' In this chapter Curtius demonstrates convincingly that 'the use of writing and the book in figurative language occurs in all periods of world literature but with the characteristic differences which are determined by the course of the culture in general.' In ancient Greek literature there are poems in praise of the tools writers used; for example, the calamus, the wax tablet, papyrus, and ink. Phrases like 'tabula rasa,' 'the Book of Life,' 'the Book of Nature,' 'complicabuntur sicut liber caeli' (Isaiah 34:4, 'The heavens shall be rolled together like a scroll'), and 'bibliales ... proscindere campos' ('to cleave the bookfields') attest to the widespread symbolic use of the book and the art of writing.[2]

This study is concerned with the book not so much as a symbol but rather as a structuring principle.[3] It is proposed that certain aspects of making books and the book trade in general may have influenced the structure of some works of medieval Spain. In this sense the study seeks to extend and complement the findings of Curtius with special reference to Spain; whereas Curtius refers to Góngora and Calderón, this study pays more attention to earlier authors, and has a different emphasis.

The basic unit of a medieval book was the quaternion, which was formed by folding a large sheet of paper or parchment twice to make a gathering of four folios, or eight pages. In Spain, the word 'cuaderno,' which is still used to mean notebook, was used by medieval writers to mean quaternion. Berceo described his predicament when a quaternion of the Latin manuscript he was adapting was lost: 'De quál guisa salió decir non lo sabría / Ca fallesció el libro en que lo aprendía / Perdiose un quaderno, mas non por culpa mía / Escribir aventura seríe grant folía.' Juan Ruiz, archpriest of Hita, explains how a king 'manda fazer libros e quadernos componer'; and Alfonso el Sabio, in a passage of the *Siete partidas* to be quoted below, gave instructions about the sale of 'quadernos.'[4] Indeed, the 'quaderno' was such a well-known item in medieval times that it would not be surprising to find that it may have influenced the structure of medieval Spanish writings.

The word 'cuaderno' is derived from the Latin numeral *quaterni, ae, a*, used normally in the plural to mean quaternary, by fours, or four at a time. This Latin numeral is also the root of 'quaderna,' an uncommon Castilian adjective, which is used in the important second stanza of *Alexandre* to describe the form of versification the poet has carefully chosen for his book:

> Mester trago fermoso, non es de joglaría
> mester es sen peccado, ca es de clerezía
> Fablar curso rimado per la quaderna vía
> A sillavas cuntadas, ca es grant maestría

Although there has been a great deal of criticism of this 'mester de clerezía,' Hispanists have not always been comfortable with the term 'quaderna vía.' The most successful interpretation of the term is the one offered by R.S. Willis, who found it 'tempting to see in the phrase, *quaderna vía*, a double play on words involving not only the quatrain as the road of the poem, but also the *quadrivium* ... as the symbol of the clerkly spirit and content of the poem.' Willis is correct, and although he does not refer to these texts specifically, there are descriptions of the quadrivium as 'ubi quatuor viae conveniunt' and 'quasi quadruplex via ad sapientiam.'[5]

But even if these texts explain the origin of 'quaderna vía,' they do not account for the specific application of the phrase by the author of *Alexandre*. Since 'quaderno' is so close to the original 'quaderna,' it may be plausible to propose that the author was thinking not only of quadrivium but specifically of quaternion when he uses (or perhaps even coins) the adjective 'quaderna' to mean quaternary, like a quaternion. If this meaning is acceptable, the phrase 'quaderna vía' can be translated 'the quaternary, or quaternion way.' The obvious question arises immediately: how exactly does the poet conceive of the 'mester de clerezía' as a quaternion? The easiest parallel seems to be that the four monorhymed lines of the 'mester de clerezía' are like the four folios of the quaternion. Another obvious parallel is that each line of the stanza consists of two hemistichs for a total of eight, just as each folio of the quaternion consists of two pages for a total of eight.

The verse form itself is not what is innovative about the stanza in question; critics have argued about its French or Latin origins and will continue to do so.[6] What is novel is the poet's conception of the verse form as something that is 'folded' like a 'cuaderno,' or quaternion. It is clear from the stanza quoted that the author of *Alexandre* intends the words of the second stanza to be interpreted in two senses. The phrase 'sen peccado' has a literal sense, *sensus literalis*: the 'mester' is 'sen peccado' or faultless because, as explained in the last line, the syllables are counted ('A sillauas cuntadas'); but 'sen peccado' has also a spiritual sense, *sensus spiritalis*, as explained by the phrase 'ca es de clerezía.' These two senses are meant to convey a single moral lesson which the poet summarizes in stanzas 2504–7 of the work: 'Acabada avemos, sennores, la estoria / Del bon rey de Grecia sennor de Babilonia. / Sennores, quien quisier su alma bien salvar / Deve en este siglo muy poco a fiar / ... / Alexandre que era rey de tan gran poder / Que mares nen tierra no lo podíen caber / En una fuessa ouo en cabo a caber / Que non podíe de término doze pies tener.'[7]

The poet is saying, in other words, that in the literal sense Alexander conquered the world, but in the spiritual sense he lost his soul. The single moral lesson to be drawn from these two senses, therefore, is that the person who wants to save his soul should not put much trust in this world. For the poet, this is the quaternion way to tell a story because a single moral is taught in two senses, just as a single sheet of paper or parchment is folded twice. The poet takes care to 'unfold' both senses of his story so that the reader can appreciate the whole moral.

It has been tempting to translate the phrase 'cuaderna vía' with the phrase 'fourfold way,' leading critics to think of the fourfold interpretation of the exegetical tradition – *sensus literalis* or *historicus, sensus tropologicus, sensus allegoricus,* and *sensus anagogicus*.[8] But it is clear that neither exegetical theory nor exegetical practice was uniform during the Middle Ages; and if some medieval writers in the rest of Europe, Dante among them, preferred the fourfold method of interpretation and composition, the writers of the 'mester de clerecía' in Spain preferred to fold one moral two ways. Berceo, for example talks only of two senses – the 'corteza' and the 'meollo' – and Juan Ruiz explains in one line that the 'fea letra' (*sensus literalis*) of his book conceals 'saber de grand doctor' (*sensus spiritalis*).

The Spanish method was based on the writings of ss Augustine and Gregory the Great, both of whom are mentioned by Berceo in his introduction to *Milagros*.[9] St Augustine referred to four topics of explication (*historia, aetiologia, analogia,* and *allegoria*) but the first three topics were subsumed under the first, leaving two senses only – the historical or literal, and the allegorical or spiritual.[10] By means of these two senses the Spaniards depicted a moral lesson in accordance with the recommendation of Gregory the Great: 'First we lay the foundations in history; then by following a symbolical sense, we erect an intellectual edifice to be a stronghold of faith; and lastly, by the grace of moral instruction, we as it were paint the fabric in fair colors.'[11] Gregory's *Magna Moralia*, from which the quoted excerpt was taken, was extremely popular in Spain, partly because it was written for a Spaniard, Leander of Seville. The *Magna Moralia* was even adapted in cuaderna-vía form and included in the *Rimado* of Pero López de Ayala.

The fourfold method of composition did not gain popularity in Spain in spite of the efforts of poets like Francisco Imperial, a contemporary

of Ayala, who tried to persuade the Spanish poets of the court of Juan
II to write in Dante's style. Ayala was a final reminder to the world
that Spanish poets favoured the quaternion way: a larger number of
lines of surviving medieval Spanish verse were written in cuaderna vía
than in any other single verse form. Although it cannot be claimed
that all the poets who wrote in cuaderna vía meant to compare this
verse form with the quaternion, it can be asserted that the author of
Alexandre made a comparison with the quaternion that fits most, perhaps all, of the works written in cuaderna vía.

An interesting precedent to the quaternion/cuaderna vía phenomenon may very well explain how the author of *Alexandre* generated
the comparison. In Roman times the concept *diptych*, which meant
originally anything folded in two, came to signify two leaves of ivory,
wood, or metal 'joined together by a hinge of some kind; the two inner
sides being covered with wax to receive the writing.' Later it occurred
to some poet that the writing itself should reflect the form of the thing
written upon, and the two-line verse poem, called distich, was conceived. The diptych was known to medieval Christians as a literary
form, as for example, in the popular *Disticha Catonis*, and also as an
artefact.[12] In the early Christian period the names of neophytes, bene-
factors, bishops, sovereigns, and dead parishioners were written on the
waxed inner portions of ecclesiastical diptychs; and during the late
Middle Ages the diptych was often used as a loose bookbinder in
which manuscripts of the Bible were placed.[13]

It is possible that the author of the cuaderna-vía poem *Libro de Apolonio* was thinking of a diptych made of lead when he mistranslated
his original Latin source to read 'Escriuyo en hun plomo con hun gra-
fio de azero.' The Latin source reads, 'Et facere loculum amplissimum
et carta plumbea obturari jubet eum inter iuncturas tabularum,' describing the making of a watertight coffin to hold the body of Luciana
who was believed to have died in childbirth at sea. 'Carta plumbea' was
intended in the original to mean a sheet of lead to seal the coffin, but
the cuaderna-vía poet interpreted the phrase to mean a writing
tablet.[14] The mistake seems to indicate that the Spanish writer was
familiar with the metal Roman diptychs and writing tablets used as
handbooks (a leaden handbook was sold in Rome as late as 1799).
Since the poets of the 'mester de clerecía' must have known the diptych as a handbook and as a verse form, it is not surprising that one of
them would have compared the cuaderna vía to the quaternion. The
quaternion is, in a real sense, composed of two diptychs.[15]

The quaternion was so important as a basic unit of all medieval
books that it influenced not only versification but composition as

well. During the rise of the universities in the thirteenth century, books were in such great demand and in such short supply that their sale had to be strictly regulated. A system was devised whereby the official university stationer and the scribes employed by him copied an original text and then divided the copy into *quaterni*. The student then rented a quaternion from the stationer and copied it; in this way several people could make copies of different parts of a book at the same time. The stationer became so essential to the system that the prices he could charge for the loan of a quaternion were fixed by law. Alfonso el Sabio mandated that the rector of the universities should supervise the pricing: 'Otrosí debe apreciar el rector con consejo de los del estudio quánto debe rescebir el estacionario por cada quaderno que prestare a los escolares para escrebir o para emendar sus libros.'[16]

A quaternion lent to a student was called a *pecia*, and at Bologna it consisted, by law, of '8 pages of two columns, each containing 60 lines, of 32 letters each.'[17] The regulation as to the precise number of letters was necessary because the number of words copied on a pecia could vary widely depending on the size of the scribe's lettering. In Paris, for example, where the laws governing peciae did not appear to be as strict as at Bologna, 'the number of lines in the *pecia* examined varied in one codex from 767 to 1,274, in another from 467 to 1,306 – the average being about 930.'[18]

The widespread practice of circulating books in quaterni explains how an entire quaternion could be lost from the manuscript that Berceo was adapting. It also explains one criterion that might have decided some of the divisions in Berceo's works. The *Vida de santo Domingo de Silos* is divided into three 'libros,' which contain 1,152, 988, and 968 lines, respectively; the *Vida de san Millán* also contains three books with 432, 848, and 680 lines, respectively; the *Sacrificio de la missa* contains 1,188 lines; the *Loores de Nuestra Señora*, 932; the *Duelo de la Virgen*, 840; and the *Vida de sancta Oria*, 820. These figures fall within the parameters for the number of lines – anywhere from 400 to 1,200 – in a pecia, but despite their wide range they permit the hypothesis that Berceo might have been working with Latin quaterni which he either amplified or abbreviated to suit his purposes.

The possible effect of the pecia on the composition of *Buen amor* is also intriguing. If Sáez and Trenchs are correct about the identity of the archpriest of Hita, Juan Ruiz may have left Spain around 1327 to attend university, perhaps at Montpellier.[19] The first version of *Buen amor* was completed in 1330, and consists, as Felix Lecoy has shown, of two main episodes around which smaller satellite compositions are arranged.[20] One of the main episodes is an elaboration of the Latin comedy *Pamphilus,* and the other is a version of a battle between Lent and Flesh, a popular theme in France at the time. Since the *Pamphilus,* which is 1,528 lines long in the archpriest's version, was 780 lines in the Latin version, and since the battle between Lent and Flesh is 992 lines long, it is tempting to speculate that the archpriest of Hita was working from two university peciae that he had acquired abroad.

The separation of a book into quaterni and the constant circulation of peciae on loan also tended to add much flexibility to the concept *book.* A book was conceived of as something that could be added to or subtracted from by the person who was collecting it in parts. A book was at once a prized possession because it was expensive, and at the same time something that had to be shared communally because it was scarce. In 1212 the Council of Paris regulated the loan of books with these words: 'We forbid monks to bind themselves by any oath not to lend books to the poor, seeing that such a loan is one of the chief works of mercy. We desire that the books of a community should be divided into two classes, one to remain in the house for the use of the brothers, the other to be lent out to the poor according to the judgement of the Abbot.'[21]

In Jewish communities in Spain 'the feeling was often forcefully manifested that books were objects of public interest and it was unethical for a private owner to refuse the loan of a book to a serious applicant.... A Rabbinic judge of the early fourteenth century was prepared to confiscate books which the owner declined to put into general circulation. He fined a recalcitrant person ten gold maravedis daily until he consented to the loan of his book.'[22] This concept of the book as communal property explains why some authors, Juan Ruiz, for example, preferred an openended structure for their compositions. Juan Ruiz's *Buen amor* can be said to begin and end at several places, and the author openly admits a reluctance to end his work definitively ('E con tanto faré / punto a mi librete, mas non lo cerraré,' ll. 1626cd). He also invites readers to add to his work ('qual quier omne que lo oya, si byen trobar sopiere / más aý añadir e emendar si quisiere,' ll. 1629ab). Although Berceo and other cuaderna-vía poets do not extend a similar invitation, their works end abruptly and would easily admit additions if more miracles or episodes were available.

Throughout the medieval Christian world the word *book* very often meant religious book as opposed to pagan book. The *Customs of Clugni* records that during the hours of silence 'the general rule, when asking for any book, was to extend the hand, making motions similar to those of turning over the leaves. In order, however, to indicate a pagan work, a monk was directed to scratch his ear as a dog does, because, says the regulation, unbelievers may well be compared to that animal.'[23] And as late as 1378, when the learned chancellor of Florence, Coluccio Salutati, asked the chancellor of Bologna, Giuliano Zonarini, to buy him a copy of Virgil, Zonarini refused. In Salutati's eloquent reply we learn the reasons for Zonarini's refusal: 'I wrote to you asking you to buy for me a copy of Vergil, and you reply reproving me for not occupying myself with quite different matters and calling Vergil – to quote your own words – a "lying soothsayer." You say that, since it is forbidden in the Canon Law to concern oneself with books of that sort, I ought not to burden you with such an errand, and you generously offer me a number of volumes of pious literature.'[24] In his defence of Virgil, Salutati referred to St Augustine who had proposed a solution to the Christian dilemma by arguing in his *De Doctrina Christiana* (book 4) that since rhetoric served both truth and falsehood, Christians should study the 'pagan' literature on rhetoric so as not to be left defenceless in the face of 'pagan' rhetorical arguments.[25]

The position of medieval Spain with regard to 'pagan' books is not yet quite clear and may never be satisfactorily clarified, because of a poor supply of surviving documentation. The investigations of Francisco Rico, Charles Faulhaber, and Janet Chapman seem to indicate that 'pagan' literature was even less popular in Spain than in the rest of Europe. Rico concludes his study of Latin letters in twelfth-century Galicia, León, and Castile with the fear that even the excuse that much has been lost does not alter the negative picture: 'Poco se escribió ... y bastante se habrá perdido; pero mucho me temo que lo mismo perdido arguye el escaso gusto coetáneo por la literatura.'[26] Faulhaber asserts that 'there are no intellectual centers in León or Castile comparable to those existing in the high Middle Ages in monasteries like Jarrow in England, Bobbio in Italy, St Gall or Fulda in Germany, Fleury or Corbie in France, or even Ripoll in Catalonia. In the later period ... the generality of Spanish schools ... are merely grammar or singing schools intent upon turning out clerics provided with the basic knowledge for caring for the religious necessities of their flocks.'[27] Chapman quotes three pronouncements of Spanish church councils in the thirteenth and fourteenth centuries in order to show that the Spanish clergy as a whole fell far short of the educational requirements their leaders repeatedly set for them: 'The *Siete partidas* at least confirm that the aim of the study was similar to that of other countries in western Europe, that is, the liberal arts were to be studied, but the information to be culled from the canons does not indicate a high level of intellectual attainment in the clergy in general, however high the intellectual aspirations of their leaders.'[28]

The findings of these critics cannot be faulted on the basis of the evidence available, and yet the available evidence does not always lead to logical conclusions.[29] If the *Danza* is to be trusted, for example, there may have been an appreciable difference in education between the average Spanish priest and the average Spanish friar. When Death calls him, the priest in the *Danza* protests that 'non quiero exebçiones nin conjugaciones, / con mis perrochianos quero yr folgar,' which seems to support the claim that priests were generally not keen on education. In contrast, in the same work Death describes the friar as a 'maestro famoso, sotil e capaz / Que en todas las artes fuestes sabidor.'[30]

Faulhaber's negative conclusions are based in part on the fact that he could find only thirty-seven copies of classical works in rhetoric up to the fourteenth century.[31] This is an astonishingly large number of manuscripts if one considers that for the same period only eleven Spanish manuscripts of the Latin Bible and fourteen of the vernacular Bible are extant.[32] Surely no one would argue that the Bible was not studied in Spain. Likewise, only two important collections of sermons of the period have survived, one in Catalan (*Homelies d'Organya*) and the Valencian sermons of Vicente Ferrer, but to say that sermons were not written in Spain during the thirteenth and fourteenth centuries would be absurd. It may very well be that the evidence that is now lacking disappeared at various times in Spain's history when it was safer to destroy books, including Bibles, than to keep them. But until evidence to the contrary is discovered, it remains safe to assume that when a medieval Spanish writer thought of the word *book*, he was most likely to conceive of a religious book. If this way of thinking is another indication of belatedness in Spain, it certainly is not, as Curtius reminds us, a sign of backwardness.[33]

It can be only natural that *book* in medieval Spain (perhaps more so than elsewhere) should be almost synonymous with *religious book*, since the Bible, or certain parts of it, played an important role in the daily life of Christians, Muslims, and Jews. One Jewish authority wrote in the fourteenth century that 'every Israelite is in duty bound to set apart a period every day and evening for study, whether he be poor or rich, sound in body or maimed in limb, young or old – aye, even the beggar who walks the streets.' 'Study' here meant religious study because 'nowhere in the Middle Ages did the educational system built up by the Jews make room for an extensive training in secular subjects.' The rabbi Shem Tob de Carrion, contemporary of Juan Ruiz, archpriest of Hita, exclaims in his *Proverbios morales* that 'non ha tan noble joya / nin tan buena ganançia, / nin mejor conpañón / comm' el libro.'[34] The 'book' here is the Torah. Muslims in medieval Spain called themselves 'the people of the book' and considered the provision of education a religious duty in order that the Koran could be read and studied.[35] Every upright Moor made an attempt to carry a copy of the Koran at all times.[36]

Among the Christians in Spain education gradually became almost coterminous with religious education. The following passage on rhetoric by Cassiodorus explains how a secular book was supposed to serve strictly religious purposes, according to the advice laid out by St Augustine in the *De Doctrina Christiana*:

> In his third book the aforesaid Fortunatianus has made mention of the orator's memorization and of his delivery and manner of speaking; the monk will derive a certain advantage from this book, since it seems not improper for him to adapt to his own uses that which orators have profitably applied to disputation. Duly cautious, he will pay heed to memorization, as applied to divine reading, when he has learned its force and nature from the aforementioned book; he will foster the art of delivery in reading the divine law aloud; and he will, moreover, preserve a careful manner of speaking, in chanting the Psalms. Thus, though he be somewhat occupied by secular books, he will be restored to holy work upon the completion of his instruction.[37]

Cassiodorus covers all five parts of classical rhetoric, and his explanation anticipates how classical education was to be developed into religious education; classical *inventio, dispositio*, and *elocutio* are to become Christian *disputatio*, and classical *memoria* and *pronuntiatio* are to be applied to Christian *lectio divina* and the chanting of the psalter. The most significant aspect of this development, for the purposes of this study, is that the need for the secular book in the study of literature was greatly diminished if not eliminated entirely. The Christian teacher would have no need for the secular Fortunatianus since the Christian Cassiodorus was more than adequate; and if Cassiodorus was not available, then Augustine, or Isidore, or any Christian encyclopaedic work would serve equally well. Original books on classical rhetoric, if they were necessary at all, would form a part of the library of the teacher, the collector, or the extraordinarily curious. The average student of the trivium needed only one basic text – the Bible, the *sacra pagina*.

In spite of the Bible's crucial importance to the trivium, studies of the influence of the Bible and biblical studies on early Spanish litera-

ture are few in number.[38] Hispanists continue to search for secular
models even though it is obvious that when writers like the authors of
Zifar, *Buen amor*, *Corbacho*, and *Rimado* thought of making a book,
they thought first of imitating a religious book. The Bible itself provided adequate examples to be imitated in all genres – epic, lyric, dramatic, and historical; but the teaching of the Bible soon gave rise to
new book words and new kinds of books. Words like *tractatus*, *glossa*,
and *compendium* are key words for the understanding of the Spanish
works mentioned in this paragraph. Martínez de Toledo, archpriest of
Talavera, refers to Juan Ruiz's *Buen amor* as a 'tractado,' but he calls
his own work, *Corbacho*, a 'compendio.'[39] The full implications of the
new terms on the works mentioned cannot be dealt with here, but
some aspects of the new terminology as it concerns *Buen amor* will be
explored.

Juan Ruiz, like many other cuaderna-vía poets, gave at the beginning
and at the end of *Buen amor* specific instructions for the understanding of his work. One set of instructions is found between lines 65a and
70d, immediately after the exemplum of the Greeks and the Romans.
Editors from Cejador y Frauca onward have had difficulty with this
passage, especially with stanza 70:

> de todos instrumentos yo libro so pariente;
> bien o mal, qual puntares, tal te dirá cierta mente
> qual tu dezir quisieres y faz punto y tente;
> ssy me puntar sopieres ssienpre me avrás en miente.

The interpretation that prevails is the musical one offered by Cejador
in 1913: 'Puntar, como *apuntar y contrapuntear*, y con esto se enten-
derá esta copla, que sin ello, fuera más oscura que la anterior,'; and as
late as 1970 the translators Mignani and Di Cesare confessed that 'the
meaning is somewhat obscure.'[40]

The archpriest of Hita must certainly be thinking of musical instruments in the quoted stanza, since he uses 'instrumentos' and 'punto' in
this sense again in lines 384b, 1227d, 1489b, 1513c, 1515ad, and
1228bc. But he must also be thinking of astrological as well as legal
instruments that were known to him. The word 'punto' is used in its
astrological sense in lines 130c ('desque vieron / los estrelleros / el
punto en que ovo de nascer') and 215d ('en fuerte punto te bý, la ora
fue mal dicha'), and as a book word in lines 1626cd and 1632c ('E con
tanto faré / punto a mi librete, mas non lo cerraré' and 'por ende fago
punto E cierro mi almario'). In fact it seems justifiable to propose that
the first meaning of the verb 'puntar' in stanza 70 is book related, and

only secondarily musical and astrological. The archpriest himself provides us with the key to this interpretation in lines 355ab ('por cartas
o por testigos o por buen instrumente / de público notario'). 'Instrumento' in this sense is a legal document that provides proof ('provada,'
l. 354d).

In stanza 70, which is also set in the context of proving truth from
falsehood ('verdat,' 'falssedat,' and 'juzgat,' ll. 69abc), the principal meaning is that Juan Ruiz's book is like a document of canon law. 'Puntar' in
this legal, book-related sense refers to the medieval university practice
of dividing textbooks on canon law into sections to be read by certain
dates. Destrez warns against confusing 'puncta' in medieval manuscripts with 'peciae': 'Il ne faut pas confondre non plus les indications de
pièces avec les *puncta* ... Les facultés de droit civil et canon divisaient
le texte que devaient enseigner les professeurs en un certain nombre
de *puncta*. Les professeurs étaient tenus de commencer l'explication
de chacune de ces sections ou *puncta* a une date déterminée et de
l'achever après un laps de temps strictement limité.' Destrez quotes
from a manuscript that uses the noun *punctum* in this book-related
sense: 'Hic finiuntur secunda puncta que leguntur mense novembris
... hic finitur quarta punctorum assignatio quae legitur in mense
genoarii.'[41]

Stanza 70 is not the only reference in *Buen amor* to university
books: an equally important passage towards the end of *Buen amor*
bears the title 'De commo dize el arcipreste que se ha de entender este
su libro' (stanzas 1626–34). The entire section is worthy of careful
analysis for its own sake, but stanzas 1631–2 are reproduced here
because they relate most closely to our topic:

> Ffiz vos pequeño libro de testo, mas la glosa
> non creo que es chica, ante es byen grand prosa,
> que sobre cada fabla se entyende otra cosa,
> sin la que se alega en la Rasón fermosa.
>
> De la santidat mucha es byen grand lyçionario,
> mas de juego E de burla es chico breviario,
> por ende fago punto E cierro mi almario,
> sea vos chica fabla, solás e letuario

As in other cuaderna-vía works mention is made (in line 1631c) of the
twofold method of interpretation: 'sobre cada fabla [*sensus literalis*] se
entyende otra cosa' [*sensus spiritalis*]; then the overriding moral purpose is clearly expressed throughout stanza 1632. Both stanzas are

riddled with special book words either in important rhyming positions or at the end of the first hemistich: 'libro de testo,' 'glosa,' 'prosa,' 'fabla,' 'Rasón fermosa,' 'lyçionario,' 'breviario,' 'almario,' and 'solás e letuario.' None of these words has caused problems to the editors of Buen amor, with the important exceptions of 'almario' and 'letuario.' Corominas, for example, explains, 'almario, "armario," aquí "colección de sus obras"'; whereas Willis translates 'almario' as 'cupboard,' and María Rosa Lida de Malkiel says simply 'armario.' In fact, 'armario' here is not an ordinary cupboard but a bookcase, 'armarium,' a word that is found in the Customs of Clugni to mean both bookcase and library.[42]

All editors understand 'letuario' to mean electuary, which is understandable, because Juan Ruiz uses the word in that sense in four places (ll. 1333d, 1334ab, 1338b). But it is clear that the scribes had trouble with the word Juan Ruiz wrote in line 1632d because the manuscript T, according to Criado de Val and Naylor, reads 'leutario.' There is no question that 'leutario' is a scribal error, and the easy solution would be to understand that the error is a misspelling of 'letuario.' But several factors militate against reading the misspelled word as 'letuario.' First, the three scribes copied 'letuario' four times each, for a total of twelve times, without making a mistake. (Criado de Val and Naylor say that manuscript S has 'leutario' in line 1334a, but this is a misreading of the manuscript which shows clearly the word 'letuario.')[43] Why then does one scribe suddenly write 'leutario'? It may be purely accidental, but it does arouse suspicion.

Second, Juan Ruiz uses the word 'soláz' at least twice with reference to books ('Que pueda de cantares un librete rimar / que los que lo oyeren puedan solaz tomar,' ll. 12cd; and 'Si queredes, señores, oir un buen solaz, / ascuchad el romance,' 14ab). But in Buen amor the word 'solaz' is never coupled with 'letuario' meaning sweetmeat or electuary. Third, since all the other words in rhyming position in stanza 1632 ('lyçionario,' 'breviario,' 'armario') refer to books, it is possible that Juan Ruiz intended the last rhyming word of the stanza to be a book word. Acceptance of the meaning of 'letuario' in line 1632d as electuary has seriously influenced the way in which numerous critics have judged the archpriest's book. Willis's assessment is representative of many others: 'So the "Book of the Archpriest," as it was known in the Middle Ages, ... was intended to be something sweet to the tongue, like an old-fashioned electuary.'[44] Consequently, if he did not write 'letuario,' it is essential to attempt to find out what Juan Ruiz might have written.

The archpriest of Hita obviously conceives of his book as a lectionary (l. 1632a), a word that in the early Middle Ages meant a book containing the biblical readings (*lectiones*) for the Mass. With the rise of the universities it came to also mean a lecture course book, that is, a book that contained the text and glosses for a university course on the Bible. Towards the end of the thirteenth century, the word *lectura* began to appear as a common synonym for *lectiones*, meaning lecture course.[45] Just as his 'lycionario' is derived from *lectionarius* and *lectiones*, Juan Ruiz probably wrote 'leturario' or 'lecturario' from *lecturarius*[46] and *lectura* as a synonym of 'lycionario' to mean a book containing a set of readings. Of the three scribes two must have replaced Juan Ruiz's 'leturario,' a technical book word they might not have known, with 'letuario,' a word with which they were familiar. A third scribe must have attempted to correct the original and made a mistake in the process, leaving us a tell-tale clue that something is amiss.

It now becomes clear that when the thought of writing a book occurred to him, Juan Ruiz decided to parody a religious university book. In 1322 the Council of Valladolid ordered that one out of every ten beneficed clerics should be sent to university. There must have been some resistance to this order, because in 1339 the archbishop of Toledo gave each church a fixed period of six months to comply with the demand.[47] It is tempting to speculate that the archpriest of Hita formed a part of the resistance. He may have gone to a university in 1327 for three years, but in 1329 he received a benefice in Toledo.[48] Did he go to university in 1327? Were his university studies interrupted? Were they an unpleasant experience for him? Juan Ruiz writes in lines 1135ab that he was neither a master nor a doctor ('Escolar so mucho rrudo, nin maestro nin doctor, / aprendí e sé poco para ser demonstrador'). Whatever the answers to these questions may be, it would seem that *Buen amor*, one version of which appeared in 1330 when its author was supposed to have completed his university training, was a deliberate attempt to ridicule the idea of university training for archpriests.

The diabolical lectionary of the archpriest is prompted by the implied question, 'Should certain priests be given higher learning? In answer to this question Juan Ruiz chooses a text which, as he says, is short – the story of the dispute betweeen the Greeks and Romans. As a parody the choice is brilliant. Not only does the dispute mock the three aspects of a university Bible course – *lectio*, *disputatio*, and *praedicatio* – but the story is also very much to the point since it deals with how the unlettered Romans came to be given learning. The gloss on this brief text is long and continuous, extending to line 1634d. The text and its gloss consist almost totally of irreligious material (in con-

trast to a normal university lectionary), and it demonstrates step by
step, 'punto por punto,' how a young man who has read Aristotle, Virgil, Ovid, and other 'pagan' authors becomes a disciple of Antichrist
and finally seduces the bride of Christ.⁴⁹ Juan Ruiz includes songs in
his lectionary because of the frequent practice of chanting *lectiones*,
especially the psalter, as implied in the word 'prosa' in line 1632b. He
includes exempla because, as Beryl Smalley explains, 'one type of lecture course resembles a collection of *exempla* or moral stories, strung
together on the thread of the text, and the thread is slender.'⁵⁰

At the beginning of his lectionary the archpriest places, perhaps
only in the 1343 version, a prologue in the form of a university sermon
because 'the commentator begins his explanation of each book by a
prologue ... [which] begins with a text of Scripture which either literally or spiritually applies 'to the book which we have in hand.'"⁵¹ *Buen
amor* seems to have been prompted by the *quaestio*,⁵² 'Should certain
priests be given higher learning?' because Juan Ruiz chose for his prologue the text, 'Intellectum tibi dabo, et instruam te in via hac qua gradieris,' (Psalm 31:8; literally, 'I will give you learning and will instruct
you in the way which you will go').

At the beginning and end of the diabolical lectionary the archpriest
places four sincere songs to the Virgin Mary, which contain twenty-
eight heavenly joys as an antidote to the fourteen carnal joys described in the lectionary. Thus the diabolical performance of the archpriest of Hita becomes understandable if the lectionary is seen as a
protest against the risk of exposing clerics to the 'pagan' influences of
a university atmosphere; especially when those clerics, like the ones
from Talavera, were already inclined towards carnal sin.⁵³ Like the
other cuaderna-vía poets, Juan Ruiz bases his moral on the literal and
the spiritual senses of his book. According to the literal sense the
young cleric acquired a great deal of 'pagan' learning as a disciple of
Don Amor, but in the spiritual sense he lost his soul and became a
chosen follower of Antichrist. The moral to be learned is that the
'buen amor de Dios,' as exemplified by the twenty-eight joys to the Virgin Mary, is to be preferred to the 'loco amor' of the devil as exemplified by the fourteen amorous episodes of the diabolical lectionary.

This chapter has attempted to show how certain concepts of the
making of books – the quaternion, the pecia, the punctum, and the lectionarius – have influenced the structure of some early Spanish
works.⁵⁴ It has shown that some of the originality of cuaderna-vía
poets like Berceo, and the authors of *Alexandre* and the *Libro de Apolonio* (who are believed to have imitated their sources closely), lies in
the fact that their art form is related to the quaternion. Juan Ruiz con-

tinued this cuaderna-vía/quaternion tradition, but he modified it by using university material, possibly peciae, to parody the lectionarius. He divides his lectionarius into puncta, according to university practice, and invites the reader to interpret his work correctly according to these puncta. The four songs (each about seven joys) to the Virgin, two at the beginning and two at the end of the work, provide a key to the puncta

> Por que Santa María, segund que dicho he,
> es comienço E fyn del bien, tal es mi fe,
> fiz le quatro cantares E con tanto faré
> punto a mi librete, mas non lo çerraré

The reader is supposed to weigh the twenty-eight joys to the Virgin against the fourteen amorous episodes and draw the obvious conclusion.

✦ Conclusion

FOR SYLVIA ZARETSKY

'College is for education:
knowledge is a different school.'

I have the impression that people still read books as they always have, sometimes avidly from cover to cover, sometimes impatiently jumping to the concluding chapter without having suffered through the body of the argument, at other times dipping into sections for reference or for entertainment, as travellers at a Cervantine inn might do when night has closed all doors. I also have the impression that books are still composed as they always were, more or less, that is, along lines similar to how they are read: sometimes with such intensity of form that to miss a section, a paragraph, a word would be to lose the sense of the whole; sometimes with such impatience that conclusions are arrived at before the whole structure has been carefully laid out; at other times in bits and pieces as delightful morsels of a delightful whole. Certainly books have been read and composed in many more ways than these, since there must be as many ways to begin and build and end a book as there are writers.

Yet, even if particular variations of reading and composing are infinite, my impression is that broader categories of readers and composers are more limited in number. I know, for example, that there is a category of reader and book reviewer who loses patience easily with an author (for reasons often justifiable) and jumps impatiently to a concluding chapter to form an opinion about the book under review; then the book is read, if at all, with preconceived notions about the conclusions. I know this category of reader exists, because on occasion I myself have been guilty of the offence. The matter of categories, therefore, is not a simple one, since all categories can and often do exist in the same reader or composer of books. There seems to be no individual or group method of beginning, building, and ending a book; rather, a variety of methods seems to co-exist in the same individual and group even as these methods vary in emphasis and focus from one individual and group to another. Categories exist, but they can in no way prove to be definitive.

They exist as heuristic tools that aid the critic but are always dispensable in the light of different perspectives.

Since methods are dispensable and often discarded by authors, I choose, among the many sensible ways of concluding a book, to discard the method I have been using thus far: I choose to conclude without carefully footnoted documentation and without due regard for research; I choose to conclude with apparent carelessness. I run the risk, of course, of having some justifiably impatient reviewer summarize the entire book as careless; so be it. After poring over so many complex medieval works, so many carefully written books and articles of criticism, I conclude that all my mountainous efforts may have produced a proverbial unmighty mouse. I am tired, and to me the results of my labours seem depressing. I need now to deceive myself with the fantasy that I am free to draw undocumented conclusions, that I have earned the right to make 'general remarks.'

My first category of general remarks has to do with things I have not done that obviously should be done.

We need a series of book-length studies composed along the lines of an article written by Yakov Malkiel explaining how María Rosa Lida de Malkiel worked. I know of a number of such articles and some books about Hispanomedievalists, usually written after their death as a tribute to their contribution to the profession. But it is time we also started studying such contributions while the scholar yet lives. It is time that we started to analyse methodically what medieval Hispanism has done for the last three or four hundred years, and, more importantly, how it has been done. What really happened, for example, to all those medieval manuscripts that passed through the hands of late-sixteenth-century pioneering scholars like Argote de Molina, Ambrosio de Morales, Pedro Ponce de León, Juan Bautista Pérez, and Miguel Ruiz de Azagra, and their circle of influential and powerful friends? Colin Smith is one of the few modern Hispanists who has expressed interest in print in this kind of question; I am thinking of an article about Argote de Molina and Herrera that he published about thirty years ago. This line of research would help us focus better on how we have inherited the texts we attempt to analyse; it might even provide us with texts now considered lost. What happened to medieval texts in the seventeenth century? Some critical editions trace the transmission of texts, but books like Mario Schiff's *La Bibliothèque de Marquis de Santillane* are not plentiful enough. We have scholars (like Charles Faulhaber) with skills for that kind of undertaking, who could help us see more clearly how medieval scholars worked, from Argote to Menéndez Pelayo, or Ramón Menéndez Pidal to Dámoso Alonso.

The immediate results of such an undertaking would be to tell us

how, as a profession, we have solved some important problems well, and
how we have focused other important problems badly. I have the impression (and it can only be an impression) that as a profession, medieval
Hispanism has moved from a national stage where a small select group
of scholars guarded textual secrets jealously and published results sparingly, to a more international stage where a larger group of scholars compared textual wares chauvinistically with the texts from other nations,
to a present stage where we have a very large and vigorous body of scholars competing ferociously to do everything at the same time. We need a
discipline, not merely a profession.

Even if I have dramatized the present state of affairs with exaggera-
tion, a healthy and sufficiently large group of Hispanomedievalists now
exists that we can afford to ask our historically minded experts to give
us a solid account of our past, present, and future capabilities, so that
individual scholars can better focus their efforts instead of wandering
from one 'style' or 'cult' of criticism to another. It is no longer necessary
for any Hispanomedievalist to bear the enormous burden of Menéndez y
Pelayo, Leo Spitzer, and María Rosa Lida de Malkiel, who obviously had
little choice but to think they had to do it all. To the question what has
this to do with this book, my answer is clear: this book would have been
one hundred times easier to write if I had not constantly had to dodge
through the crossfire of excellent critics shooting words at each other in
vastly different dialects of the same critical language.

The Castro/Sánchez Albornoz debate, the Pidal/Bédier debate, the
'juglaría'/'mester de clerecía' oral/written debate, the classical-
humanistic/didactic-religious debate, and the Spanish-original/European-
imitation debate are a few examples of important questions badly
focused. It is remarkable indeed that progress has been made in spite of
this uneconomical expense of energy. Maybe, when excellent Hispanists
were few, it was necessary to have an eminent historian like Sánchez
Albornoz argue with an excellent theoretician like Américo Castro, and
have two groups of lesser historical and theoretical minds fall in behind
them and wage war in print for decades. Now, surely, we can afford to let
the theoreticians theorize, the historians document, and the critics criticize, while the rest of us relax and enjoy the science of the arts of history, theory, and criticism. We can thus all conserve our energies for our
best abilities using sparingly and appropriately the fruits of experts in
areas related to our own.

Not everybody can be pan-Romanists in the noble tradition of Spitzer,
Curtius, and Auerbach. There is hardly any further need for another
book like María Rosa Lida de Malkiel's massive 750 pages on the originality of *Celestina*. Thanks to her solid foundation work – a laborious,

invaluable gift to Hispanism, as is the entire corpus of her production –
we can afford to parcel out our efforts with luxurious economy. Because
of all this badly aimed crossfire I have had to repeat unwillingly in this
book that the composition of such and such a medieval Spanish work
can be more precisely described; many critics were writing about the
composition of works when they had a lot of other important questions
on their minds. And for this same reason I have been able to make only a
beginning. Let me therefore list some of the specific tasks, related to the
subject of this book, that I should have done but could not do. I also
know that, happily, there are scholars much more capable than I to do
them.

Since biography is an obviously popular method of composition, there
should have been a chapter on the lives of saints. Bollandists like Dele-
haye have done marvellous foundation work in this area, and scholars
like Brian Dutton, Anthony Perry, and Jack Walsh have acquired skills
that will help us understand hagiographical composition. It might not be
a simple question of *imitatio Christi* once we get past the superficial
order of unusual childhood, wonder-working manhood, and miraculous
life after death.

There should definitely have been a chapter about wisdom literature. I
do not now know if the important *Libro de Apolonio* belongs to this proposed tradition of wisdom writings or fits more comfortably into the
hagiographical tradition. *Apolonio* seems like a curious combination of
enigma and commandment against incest, which might well link it (I am
guessing) with other works, like *Cárcel* and *Celestina*, composed according to specific commandments. I sense that *Apolonio* is a masterwork
but I have not had the time to let it tell me precisely what kind of mas-
tery of compositional elements is involved. However, other important
omissions from this book belong unquestionably to the tradition of wisdom literature: the *Conde Lucanor*, Shem Tob's *Proverbios morales*, Santillana's *Proverbios*, and all the exemplum collections. These works are
all a variant of apocalyptic literature in that they elaborate the element
of educating rulers to atone past sins and maintain present morality for
future redemption. The models of Spanish wisdom books include the
books of Proverbs, Ecclesiastes, Ecclesiasticus, and the Book of Wisdom;
like their models, the Spanish books draw upon a wealth of folklore
transmitted orally for centuries. Scholars like John Esten Keller and
Reinaldo Ayerbe Chaux have done us inestimable services in this area
and will no doubt continue to do so.

More work can be done on the element of wisdom in the composition
of works that belong more comfortably to other traditions. For instance,
in *Razón de amor* and *Libro de buen amor* (*Intellectum tibi dabo*) wisdom

helps to give the composition shape. Much deserved emphasis has been laid on the Christian aspect of these examples in their homiletic setting, and some attention has been paid to their transmission into Spain from their Arabic sources, but I suspect that we need to examine in greater detail the rich Jewish sources of exemplum material. For centuries Jews have put questions to their rabbis daily about the interpretation of their sacred laws, and the rabbis still reply, as they always have, with important anecdotal examples.

I read recently just such a commentary about the passage in Deuteronomy that orders Jews, if they have to disturb the nest of a mother bird sitting on her eggs, to make sure to let the mother fly free before they steal the eggs and the young. The verses in Deuteronomy were no doubt intended to discourage such disturbances of nature except in dire emergencies because surely no mother bird is liable to fly far enough away from her eggs and young to permit an orthodox Jew to comply with such a law. Like many such legal admonitions, the injunction ends with a formula, something like 'so that thy days may be long in the land which the Lord giveth thee.' Apparently some stickler for detail in the first century (there were structuralists then too), ignoring the context of emergency and the formula, saw fit to pose the following query to the famous Rabbi Akiba. 'What if,' the stickler said (I paraphrase from memory), 'a man should climb a lofty tower and chase the mother bird away, according to the commandment, and take the young ones and the eggs, but on the way down from the tower he should fall and die? How could it be that, even though he followed the commandment, his days were not prolonged? Where is the prolonging of days in this case?' 'In the life to come,' replied the Rabbi, undaunted, 'where everything goes well, without a hitch.'

I find the example not just delightful but also remarkable in that it teaches us that the anecdote might come as well from a less-learned questioner like Conde Lucanor as from a wise teacher like Patronio; it also tells us something (I am not sure what) about the relationship between the expansive example and its cryptic, more sentential accompanying reply. I have suggested that the examples in the *Zifar* about the whole friend and the half-friend, which play such a significant role in the beautiful but flawed composition of the work, belong to an extensive tradition of exempla about the 'heart' of the Judaeo-Christian Bible, namely, the commandment to 'love thy neighbour as thyself.' I suspect that we might learn much more about similar matters if we were to pay greater attention to the examples that abound in commentaries and *responsa* from Jewish law and lore.

Then, too, we might learn more about how these collections of wisdom literature were put together, more, that is, than the very vague ideas we now have that they are stacked together like set pieces of an anthology, in alphabetical order, according to the number of days, months, or weeks in a year. Rafael Lapesa has suggested in his book on Santillana that the *Proverbios* are arranged according to stages of a person's life, which, if it is true, would mark an interplay of the biographical and the wisdom traditions. Nicholas G. Round (*Belfast Spanish and Portuguese Papers*, p. 236) suggests more fanciful arrangements. Neither the Bible (which is a pervasively influential model in Spain and itself a collection) nor each of its separate books that are collections (for instance, Proverbs, Song of Songs), is carelessly arranged. Wherever the arrangement might have seemed careless, countless scholars throughout the centuries have invented ingenious ways to impose patterns; their ingenuity has created models of composition for subsequent writers. The Song of Songs is a prime example of this phenomenon, as I have tried to show in the chapter on the *Razón de amor*.

There should have been a chapter on the concept *genre* and its effect on what I have attempted in this book. I hint briefly in the introduction that genre fades in usefulness within the confines of this study, but that is obviously an oversimplification of the question. Using Wolfgang Kayser's definition of genre in his *Interpretación y análisis de la obra literaria*, a definition I find very hard to improve, I have discussed in this book, almost exclusively and with the possible exceptions of only *Celestina* and a brief discussion of *muwashshaha*s, narratives that belong to the epic genre. The dramatic genre is difficult to approach in this period, because of the paucity of texts; the lyric genre has survived mainly as bits and pieces between narratives, as for example, the *cantigas de loor* of Alfonso el Sabio, the lyrics of Juan Ruiz and Pero López de Ayala, and one or two songs in *Celestina*. I have tried to discuss the question of early Spanish lyric poetry in an article to be published in the *Dictionary of the Middle Ages*, a vast project partly sponsored by the American Council of Learned Societies. Nevertheless, it seems to me that in the light of the findings in this study, some convenient categories can be rethought and perhaps relabelled.

Is it more accurate to call Mena's *Laberinto de Fortuna*, for example, a literary epic than an apocalyptic narrative? And if we call *Laberinto* an apocalyptic narrative, then how comfortable do we feel using the same label for *Zifar*? Should we continue calling *Zifar* a chivalresque novel or a romance? What about *Alexandre*? Should we keep as many labels for the same work as are necessary? What kind of narrative is *Razón de amor*, a lyrical narrative about lust, as opposed to the *Cid*, which is an epic narrative, and the *Celestina*, which might be a dramatic narrative? And so on. I am not good at categorizing; and it has not been my purpose to answer questions about categories, because I know that we have expert categorizers, like Deyermond, who will tell me if the questions I have raised about genres are naïve or useful. What should we do, by the way, about scientific treatises like those of Alfonso el Sabio and Enrique de Villena? Are they not also literary in some important ways?

It did not even occur to me that I should write a chapter on more narrowly formal aspects like verse and prose styles. Why should I, when we have experts on prosody like Dorothy Clotelle Clarke, and on semantic usage like such linguistic giants as Margherita Morreale and Manuel Alvar who have acquired more knowledge in these matters than I could dream of hoarding in three long lifetimes? I might suggest, however, the need for two or three more formal aspects than the ones normally analysed. The question of chapter headings, incipits, explicits, and titles ought to receive more methodical attention from palaeographers and textual critics; so also should the question of the possible influence of making books upon the composition of the books themselves, which I skimmed only lightly in the previous chapter of this limited literary history.

The questions of sequels, of invitations to amend texts, of the insertion of texts within texts, could also stand further scrutiny, especially since there is hardly a text from the *Cid* to *Celestina* that might not have been altered in some discernible way. In the *Cid* it is the old question of the third 'cantar'; with *Corbacho*, the 'media parte' and the epilogue; with *Siervo*, the alleged missing part; and with *Celestina*, the problem of the first act and the additional acts. Then, too, there is the perennial problem, too easily forgotten at times on account of the painstaking work accomplished by brilliant philologists of the past, of the unsatisfactory state of some edited texts.

Maybe I should have written a chapter on the debate about oral/written composition. I trust the guidance we have had and will continue to have in this matter from such critics as John Miletich and Ruth House Webber, but I have some disturbing, perhaps also exciting, questions to ask these colleagues in the light of what I have learned in my analyses of medieval texts. Will my colleagues begin to take into account the enormous importance of the *chanting* of *written* texts in Christian, Jewish, and Islamic liturgies, especially since these texts are laden with formulas of all kinds, styles, and shapes? Do we not really need musicologists to figure out these problems? Should we not be training liturgists if we expect concrete answers to these problems about oral/written texts? Have we focused the question correctly? And so on.

We definitely need a new focus on the old debate about Spain versus the rest of Europe in literary skirmishes. The old approach was that Dante is better than Imperial and Mena, the *Roland* better than the *Cid*, Boccaccio better than the 'novela sentimental,' Jean de Meun comparable to Juan Ruiz, *Celestina* derived from the *comedia humanística*, *Razón de amor* dependent on the troubadour lyric, Chrétien de Troyes far better than the author of *Zifar*, Gautier de Châtillon more learned in classical material than the moralizing author of *Alexandre*. This outmoded approach has served its purpose and simply will not continue to suffice. My conviction is that by comparing roots with leaves we have missed the beauty of the trees in a European forest where Spanish trees, when judged by appropriate standards, are just as beautiful as French, Italian, and German ones. I do not mean to imply that this kind of international-border research should cease. I mean simply that we cannot hope to compare usefully until we have reached a certain level of comprehension of the local product. The argument that we will understand the local product more quickly by way of the foreign unquestionably is not valid and leads to complex distortions that impede constructive progress.

Much of the debate has no doubt been coloured by the so-called cultural belatedness of Spain, but Curtius made it quite plain that Spain's cultural belatedness in no way signifies a backwardness in the sense of either the new or the old progressivism. Some critics, bored by religious texts unless those texts show some appreciable trace of classical humanism, have permitted their conclusions and approaches to be prejudiced by their personal inclinations. This will not do because, for Spain, Curtius's approach will not suffice. The fact that seems to be emerging is that in many respects Spain was a medieval *leader* in literary composition *because* it was the hermeneutical centre of the world for the entire period covered by this book, and longer. Literary artists in Spain struggled on a daily basis with the same literary, hermeneutic problems that confront us today, and this struggle was made fiercer in Spain than in the rest of Europe by the rivalry of Christians, Jews, and Muslims for predominance, a rivalry that nowhere else was as intense as on Spanish soil.

The Jews, in particular, were far ahead in literary matters, in some respects, because they took the commandment seriously that *all* their children were to be educated in textual dilemmas. Whereas in Islam and Christianity education was mainly a matter of means, in Judaism it was, has always been, a question of legal, moral obligation. In Spain, the obligation for Jews was even greater than elsewhere because of the proximity of Islamic and Christian communities, sometimes sympathetic, often hostile; in the rest of Europe the alternatives for Judaism were different than those in Spain. Why should we be surprised, therefore, if we have to admit that the 'conversos' excelled at literature for special reasons? If they painted at all, they were bad painters, for the same reasons, and they certainly did not leave us great works of sculpture or magnificent edifices.

The 'conversos' were word artists of the highest calibre, all of them, from Pedro Alfonso to Fernando de Rojas. Not only did they have their own long-standing textual traditions to draw upon, which left them and their ancestors no choice but to be educated in literary matters, but also because, equipped with this liberating force – education – in the midst of servitude to Christan and Muslim masters, they had the option of mingling with their own the best literary achievements of their Muslim and Christian counterparts. What more ideal environment for literary artists: oppression and self-conscious tradition in a multicultural environment!

Although I am confident that my present inclinations on the question of the Christian, Jewish, and Muslim presence in medieval Spanish literature constitute another step towards the right direction, I am also sure that my suggestions on these matters are of necessity incomplete. We need socio-historical-minded experts with a firm background in the philosophy of literary forms to draw fresh inspiration from the rich foundation laid by scholars like Millás-Vallicrosa, Nykl, and Stern, in order to give us better answers about the social (rather than textual) history of literary composition in medieval Spain. All I can do is suspect, from my elementary close-reading of the texts, that intercultural factors are operative. I did not intend to pontificate about what Christian rosaries have to do with Muslim beads, what Jewish scrolls and Christian peciae have to do with Muslim calligraphy, what canon and Talmudic law have to do with Fiqh and Shariah, and what they all have to do with literary composition. I intended solely to state the obvious: for Christians, Jews, and Muslims the book and the interpretation of the book are matters of central, daily concern. My book has no hidden agenda. Its agenda was allowed to take its own shape as the book was written.

My second category of general remarks has to do with things I think I have accomplished. I proposed that the composition of the *Cantar de Mio Cid* ought to be considered as part of the psalter tradition because of several indirect references in the text to the Psalms, because of the significant role of the Virgin Mary, and because of the quotation from the Psalms on the last page of the manuscript. My proposal is not meant to deter the pace of research efforts to link the *Cid* to French epic poems; even if such a link was established, I doubt very much that it would affect seriously any of my suggestions in the first chapter. My impressions, at the moment, are that the *Cid* is a unique, sophisticated survivor of a long tradition of stringing psalmlike songs together, a tradition that preceded the *Cid* and is represented in a vastly varied form in the *Milagros* of Berceo and the *Cantigas* of Alfonso el Sabio.

In the first chapter I also make a fairly long excursus to explore the structure of masterworks by Boccaccio, Chaucer, and Marguerite de Navarre. This excursus helps to bolster the suggestions made in the chapter, and, more importantly, serves to support the conclusions made in chapter 5 about the function of prayers in *Siervo*, *Cárcel*, and to a lesser extent in *Celestina* where Calisto 'prays' for success in his affair with Melibea, and Celestina strings broken hymens (not hymns) as on a rosary.

In chapter 2, I prove conclusively, I believe, the much-debated question of the unity of the *Razón de amor*. In the process, I may have added force to what is already known about *contrafacta* and the widespread use in lyrical narrative verse of biblical clichés in simultaneously hieratic and demotic ways. Again, such subtlety presupposes a kind of knowledge of the Bible that many twentieth-century critics seem to have forgotten. We are dealing with a tradition, of which the *Razón* is an isolated example, that includes writers who knew extensive portions of the Bible (in some instances the entire Jewish Bible and its commentaries) by heart. Certainly these poets also knew troubadour lyrics, but, by comparison, their knowledge of the Bible, parts of which they repeated every day, was to them as natural as breathing.

Of some eleven texts examined in the chapter on the apocalyptic tradition I have been able to make an original contribution to the understanding of all, without exception. The concept of apocalyptic composition is, on the whole, a potentially useful addition to medieval-Spanish literary historiography. I sincerely attribute my contributions not so much to my own competence as to the phase through which Hispanism, as a profession, now seems to be passing.

Many minds are already set upon varying interpretations of Juan Ruiz's *Buen amor*, so that I hope to have persuaded very few with my analysis of the book's structure, especially since I have not changed the essence of the original article published in 1977. The same lack of expectations holds good for the study of the *Corbacho*, which was published in 1980. The most that I can hope to accomplish in chapter 4 is that, by juxtaposing these two studies, a few more people may be persuaded that in medieval Spanish composition there was such a thing as building with contraries and logic, and that this technique existed independently of the moral intent of the authors. These authors state openly that some people would prefer to exploit their books for purposes not recommended, whereas others would heed the warnings delivered by the authors with sternness as well as delight. Irony arises, especially in the work of Juan Ruiz, from the delight with which the author delivers the sincere warning, because he has chosen to emphasize good by dwelling on evil to ridiculous extents and for obviously exaggerated purposes. Piety is a boring teacher; sin makes good news and better disciples, but is still wrong; even Berceo knew that.

Martínez de Toledo, archpriest of Talavera, is a skilful writer and, as I have shown, a master of imagery. The lesson here is as much about approaches to texts as about their composition. One may hypothesize that if a text is masterfully composed, then an analysis should reveal that any of its elements (for example, title, plot, or characterization) says basically the same harmonious things about the composition of the work as a whole, but the element to which the author paid the most attention should definitely indicate clearly how the work was composed. I could have approached the composition of the *Corbacho*, as I did that of all the other works I have analysed, without asking methodical questions about imagery; since to me the text spoke most loudly about imagery, I decided to test the hypothesis on the archpriest's text.

The chapter on the magic wheel of Fortune was to me as engaging an undertaking as I intend it to be for my readers. In terms of graphic composition, it was one of the first chapters I sketched. Since I first started work on Imperial some seventeen years ago I have known, as everybody knew, that Fortune was an important concept in fifteenth-century Spain. I did not expect to find Ixion's wheel as a crucial element in *Siervo*, although I had silently suspected, since I read a paper some fifteen years ago in a graduate seminar at Toronto, that the Y of Pythagoras was functional in the work. It is pleasing to have solved the enigma of the title *Siervo libre de amor*. My analysis of *Cárcel de Amor* and, especially, of *Celestina* yielded unexpected pleasure; I had no idea that I would be able to describe what I suggest is their ironic 'converso' structure, which I had not known existed even as a working hypothesis. I feel somewhat confident about this discovery because I did not read Bataillon's 'Melancolía judía' until after I had written the analysis of both 'converso' texts. What a special delight to find circumstantial confirmation for my tentative suggestion in his more authoritative views! I think it a very special bonus that I should be able, in the process of analysing *Cárcel* and *Celestina*, to distinguish their peculiar irony, *en passant*, from that of *Buen amor* and the *Quijote*; even as hypotheses these distinctions excite me.

The chapter on the concept *book* is a provocative piece that has provided ideas for future projects; it is, in essence, the kind of work I love to do, in which I learn a lot and teach a little.

If I could, I would hand my text at this point to a socio-historical-minded critic who knows about the philosophy of forms, ask that critic to trust only my close-reading of the texts, and assign to him or her the task of trying to describe the heuristic model that my interpretation of the texts suggests. But instead I myself must attempt the task.

The first observation I should make is one that has already been made at several points in this book, but that, nevertheless, bears repeating: elements of all the traditions analysed in this book are present at all times in all texts. However, some traditions are dominant at all times (the apocalyptic tradition and the book tradition), whereas some traditions tend to recede in importance (the psalter tradition), and others tend to rise forcefully at a given period (the magic wheel of Fortune). The general shape of the model is, therefore, apocalypticism and books constantly dominant, with the remaining traditions receding and rising for reasons to be determined.

A specific shape for this temporary model is extremely risky to put into focus, since significant factors blur attempts at fixed outlines. The period being considered is too short to allow well-defined variants. Then, too, the traditions are related to each other in complex ways. Just one example of these interrelationships will suffice. Mena's *Laberinto* is an apocalyptic narrative, according to this book's definition of the term, which contains, as functional elements of its apocalyptic structure, magic and the wheel of Fortune, two elements also crucial to the composition of *Siervo*, *Cárcel*, and *Celestina*. To complicate matters further, *Siervo*, *Cárcel*, and *Celestina* contain apocalyptic elements, but in these works the elements are not arranged, as in *Laberinto*, in a way that they give primary meaning to the text as a whole. In other words, the texts have been correctly categorized in their respective traditions, in my opinion; still, a not insignificant area of overlap exists. Finally, important traditions, notably the lives of saints and the wisdom tradition, are missing from the model because they call for book-length studies in themselves.

Bearing the above severe limitations always in mind, I should proceed cautiously to delineate a model for a history of literary composition in medieval Spain. Using the problem of overlap as a convenient tool and not as a drawback, I would describe most of the thirteenth century as a period during which the traditions centred around the Virgin Mary (the psalter tradition and the Song of Songs) are dominant along with the lives of saints and other heroes; this makes historical sense because the cult of the Virgin enjoyed a special popularity during that time.

At the end of the thirteenth century and throughout the fourteenth, there seems to be a shift away from stringing and juxtaposing (hieratic and demotic, as in *Razón*) towards a more learned and philosophical direction. Aristotle plays an important role in *Alexandre*, is mentioned at several points in *Zifar*, and functions in *Buen amor*; important works not analysed in this book would also support this shift to learning and philosophy – the *Libro de Apolonio*, *Proverbios morales* of Shem Tob, and other works of the tradition of wisdom literature. Still, the concern with apocalypticism remains, as Derek Lomax demonstrates in an article, in *The Journal of Hispanic Philology*, about religious authors between 1295 and 1350. Nevertheless, the shift, under the surface of apocalypticism, from stringing and juxtaposing about the Virgin and various heroes, to learning and philosophy, also makes historical sense, since the period of the late-thirteenth and fourteenth centuries coincides with the increasing influence of universities in Spain. Whinnom suggests (in an article on the words 'autor' and 'tratado') that the disappearance of the word 'cuento' in the fifteenth century is astonishing. It is too early to suggest that 'cuento,' a word associated with stringing, disappears partly because stringing gives way to learning, philosophy, and words like 'tratado.'

From the end of the fourteenth and through the fifteenth centuries the picture is clearer: it shows the rise of the wheel of Fortune, linked with magic in the most skilfully composed texts. This shift also makes historical sense, since the period is marked by extraordinary political turmoil. So, if I were to describe, in imprecise and concise terms, the nature of literary composition in medieval Spain as represented by the major texts, I should say that it is a fundamentally biblical and apocalyptic phenomenon that, over a three-hundred-year period, varies from an advanced technique of stringing and juxtaposing texts together, to a philosophical technique of building texts dialectically, and ultimately to a highly sophisticated ironical technique of making a text alter its meaning.

INTRODUCTION

1 Alan Deyermond, *A Literary History of Spain: The Middle Ages* (London: Benn 1971); J.L. Alborg, *Historia de la Literatura española: edad media y renacimiento* (Madrid: Gredos 1972). See also Alan Deyermond, *Historia y crítica de la literatura española: edad media* (Barcelona: Crítica 1979).
2 P.E. Russell, *Temas de 'La Celestina'* (Barcelona: Ariel 1978); Dámaso Alonso, *Ensayos sobre poesía española* (Madrid: Revista de Occidente 1944); Joaquín Gimeno Casalduero, *Estructura y diseño en la literatura castellana medieval* (Madrid: Porrúa Turanzas 1974)
3 René Wellek and Austin Warren, *Theory of Literature* (New York: Harcourt, Brace, and World 1956), p. 253. During one of his trips to Albany as a visiting professor, Professor Wellek was kind enough to discuss with me briefly this portion of his epoch-making book. He told me that he was responsible for writing the section (of the joint venture with Professor Warren) that I cite here.
4 David Couzens Hoy, *The Critical Circle: Literature, History, and Philosophical Hermeneutics* (Berkeley: University of California Press 1978).
5 Ibid., pp. 43–8, quotation at pp. 47–8
6 Ibid., p. 67
7 Ibid., p. 116
8 E.D. Hirsch, *Validity in Interpretation* (New Haven: Yale University Press 1967), pp. 170–1, 169–70
9 Hoy, *The Critical Circle*, p. 113
10 Ian Michael, *The Treatment of Classical Material in the 'Libro de Alexandre'* (Manchester: Manchester University Press 1970), p. 9; Roger Walker, *Tradition and Technique in 'El Libro del Cavallero Zifar'* (London: Tamesis 1974), pp. 74, 77
11 Hans-Georg Gadamer, *Truth and Method* (New York: Seabury 1975), 154; Olga Tudorica Impey, 'La estructura unitaria de Razón de amor,' *Journal of Hispanic Philology*, 4 (1979), pp. 3, 20

12 James F. Burke, *History and Vision: The Figural Structure of the Libro del Cavallero Zifar* (London: Tamesis 1972); Thomas R. Hart, *La alegoría en el 'Libro de buen amor'* (Madrid: Revista de Occidente 1959), reviewed by María Rosa Lida de Malkiel in *Romance Philology*, 14 (1961), pp. 340–3
13 Tosefta Megilla, 3:21
14 Hoy, *The Critical Circle*, p. 39
15 R.G. Keightley, 'Models and Meanings for the *Libro del Cavallero Zifar*, *Mosaic*, 12 (1979), p. 55, n.3
16 Ibid., p. 72
17 For a more detailed distinction between allegory and symbol, see Paul Piehler, *The Visionary Landscape: A Study in Medieval Allegory* (London: Edward Arnold 1971). See also the review by Owen Barfield in *Medium Aevum* 42 (1973), pp. 84–91.
18 Jean Misrahi, 'Symbolism and Allegory in Arthurian Romance,' *Romance Philology*, 17 (1963–4), pp. 561, 569
19 Karl-Ludwig Selig, 'Don Quixote I/22: The Exploration of Form in Mini-Form,' in Américo Bugliani, ed., *The Two Hesperias, Literary Studies in Honor of Joseph G. Fucilla* (Madrid: Porrúa Turanzas 1977), pp. 349–57. I attended an NEH seminar directed by Professor Selig at Duke University during the summer of 1978. Professor Selig communicates an extraordinary connoisseur's feel for texts; the highlight of the seminar was a visit to the Rare Books Collection of the Duke University Library, where he seemed to savour the books and manuscripts he showed to us with sheer contagious delight. Now, as I write these lines, I realize to what extent my discussion of texts in this introduction is indebted to him. I cite him again in chapter 4, where I found support in his words for my approach to sources and traditions.
20 Mario J. Valdés, 'Heuristic Models of Inquiry,' in *Shadows in the Cave: A Phenomenological Approach to Literary Criticism Based on Hispanic Texts* (Toronto: University of Toronto Press 1982), p. 165
21 For a stimulating discussion of the mutual usefulness of formal analysis and hermeneutical interpretation, see Mario J. Valdés and Owen J. Miller, eds., *Interpretation of Narrative* (Toronto: University of Toronto Press 1978). On Ricouer's hermeneutical arch, see Hoy, *The Critical Circle*, p. 85ff.

CHAPTER ONE

1 A. Lucas, *Ancient Egyptian Materials and Industries*, 4th ed., revised and enlarged by J.R. Harris (London: Edward Arnold 1962), p. 41
2 Luis Pericot, 'Sobre algunos objetos de ornamentación del Eneolítico del Este de España,' *Revista de Archivos, Bibliotecas Y Museos*, 3 (1935), pp. 129–50. H. Giner de los Ríos, *Artes industriales desde el cristianismo hasta nuestros días* (Barcelona: Antonio López 1905), does not mention beads.

3 *Scriptorum Opus: Schreiber-Mönche am Werk. Prof. Dr. Otto Meyer zum 56 Geburtstag am 21 September 1971* (Wiesbaden: Richert 1971), p. 5, pl. facing p. 5, figs. 8–11. See also Virginia Wylie Egbert, *The Mediaeval Artist at Work* (Princeton: Princeton University Press 1967), pp. 28–9. An accurate description of this miniature is catalogued in the Princeton Index of Christian Art under the category 'Scene: Occupational: Bookmaking.' It is also described and reproduced by M.W. Evans in his *Medieval Drawings* (London: Hamlyn 1969), p. 20, and plate 1. The manuscript is in Bamberg, Staatliche Bibliotek, Patr. 5 (B. II), at folio ov°.

4 Lloyd Kasten and John Nitti, eds., *Concordances and Texts of the Royal Scriptorium Manuscripts of Alfonso X, El Sabio* (Madison: The Hispanic Seminary of Medieval Studies 1978), vol. 2, *Texts, Libro de las leyes*, p. 168, fol. 49v., lines 36–8. Cf. *Las siete partidas del Rey Don Alfonso el Sabio, cotejadas con varios códices antiguos por la Real Academia de la Historia* (1807; prt. Madrid: Ediciones Atlas 1972), tomo I, Partida Primera, titulo VI, ley XLIV, p. 285: 'Pero si el clérigo sabe bien escribir ó otras cosas facer que sean honestas, asi como escritorios o arcas, redes, cuevanos, cestos o otras cosas semejantes, tovieron por bien los santos padres que las podiesen facer et vender sin desapostura de su orden....'

5 *Las siete partidas* (1807; rpt. Madrid: Ediciones Atlas 1972), tomo II, Partida Segunda, título XX, ley V, p. 194

6 R.S. Willis, ed., *Libro de Alexandre* (Princeton: 1934; rpt. New York: Kraus 1965), st. 2

7 Herbert G. May and Bruce M. Metger, eds., *The Oxford Annotated Bible with the Apocrypha: Revised Standard Version* (New York: Oxford University Press 1965); all subsequent quotations from the Bible in English are taken from this edition. The French itinerant rabbi, Moses of Coucy, made an extensive revival tour of Spain, beginning in 1236, where he stirred masses in the Jewish communities to regain respect for the tephilin and the tallith.

8 Hayim Halevy Donin, *To Be a Jew: A Guide to Jewish Observance in Contemporary Life* (New York: Basic Books 1972), p. 159. Solomon Ganzfried, *Code of Jewish Law*, trans. Hyman E. Goldin (New York: Hebrew Publishing 1927), vol. 1, pp. 19–34: 'The numerical value of the letters of the word *tsitsis* is six hundred and taken together with the eight threads and five knots it makes a total of six hundred and thirteen (the number of the laws of the Torah)' p. 19.

9 Eithne Wilkins, *The Rose-garden Game: The Symbolic Background to the European Prayerbeads* (London: Victor Gollancz 1969), p. 206. Juan Ruiz, *Libro de buen Amor*, ed. R.S. Willis (Princeton: Princeton University Press 1972), st. 438

10 Millard Meiss and Elizabeth Beatson, *The Belles Heures of Jean, Duke of Berry* (New York: Brazilier 1947), fol. 192 v°. I am grateful to Ms Beatson for drawing this example to my attention, and for her kind assistance to me at the Princeton Index of Christian Art. C.R. Post, *A History of Spanish Paint-*

ing (Cambridge, Mass., 1941; rpt New York: Kraus 1970), vol. 8, pp 562–4, fig. 260; vol. 4, p. 570, fig. 228; vol. 3, pp. 3–5, fig. 249

11 For the history of the rosary see, in addition to Eithne Wilkins, *The Rose-garden Game*, the series of articles by Herbert Thurston, 'Our Popular Devotions: The Rosary,' *The Month*, 96 (1900), pp. 403–18, 513–27, 620–37; 97 (1901), pp. 67–789, 172–88, 286–304, 383–404; 100 (1902), pp. 189–203; Franz M. Williams, *The Rosary: Its History and Meaning*, trans. Edwin Kaiser (New York: Benziger 1953); M.M. Gorce, *Le rosaire et ses antécédents historiques, d'après le manuscrit 12483, fonds français de la Bibliothèque Nationale* (Paris: Picard 1932).

12 Wilkins, *The Rose-garden Game*, p. 42: 'A very old name for Hindu prayer-beads is *japamala*, which means "muttering-chaplet," but also "rose-chaplet," presumably because the beads were made of kneaded petals from *Hibiscus rosa sinensis*. The nuns of the Carmelite convent founded at Avila by St. Teresa the Great make rosaries of rose-petals, and the legends about the bestowal of the beads on St. Dominic include a story that they had the scent of roses, for the Virgin brought them from her rose garden, which is Paradise.' Professor Willis has suggested to me that Wilkins probably is not correct in claiming that rose-petals were used to make rosaries; the 'rose-chaplet,' he thinks, was made of rose hips. During a visit to Avila in 1981 I was able to buy a 'rose-chaplet' but I cannot determine whether Willis or Wilkins is correct. Similar rosaries were also on sale on the grounds of the Alhambra in Granada in 1981.

13 Lucia N. Valentine, *Ornament in Medieval Manuscripts* (London: Faber and Faber 1965), pp. 45–6, 83. On *Bible moralisée*, see Egbert, *The Mediaeval Artist*, fig. 9, p. 42, and pl. XI, p. 43. A remarkable example for a popular text is the twelfth-century depiction of the various tones of music on fol. 40 of Guido of Arezzo's *Micrologus de Disciplina Artis Musicae* Vienna, National Library, Codex 51). The tones are little rings threaded around a figure eight.

14 Wilkins, *The Rose-garden Game*, pp. 113, 145, 160, 174, and opposite pp. 80, 128

15 On Guido de Baysio see Filippo Liotta, 'Appunti per una biografia del canonista Guido da Baisio, arcidiano di Bologna,' *Studi Senesi*, 76 (1964), pp. 7–52.

16 W.W. Skeat, ed., *The Complete Works of Geoffrey Chaucer*, 2nd ed. (1899; rpt. Oxford: Clarendon Press, 6 vols., 1963), *Canterbury Tales*, vols. 4, 5, vol. 4, ll. 791–4; subsequent quotations from the *Canterbury Tales* are taken from this edition.

17 See M.H. Spielmann, *The Portraits of Geoffrey Chaucer* (London: Kegan Paul, Trench, Trübner 1900 for the Publications of the Chaucer Society, Series II, no. 31), esp. pp. 7, 9, 10, 11, 12, 13, 14, 16, 18, 19, reproduced without illustrations in *Chaucer Memorial Lectures*, ed. Percy W. Ames (London: Asher 1900; rpt. Fokroft 1973), pp. 111–41. Other fine reproductions are as follows: the Hoccleve and the National Gallery, in Derek Brewer, *Chaucer and His World* (London: Methuen 1978), reverse of frontispiece, and facing p. 110; of Harvard, in John Matthews Manly, *Some New Light on Chaucer*

(New York: Holt 1926), frontispiece; of BM Add. MS 5141, on the cover of Nevill Coghill, trans. *The Canterbury Tales* (Harmondsworth: Penguin Classics 1975). For a thorough discussion of the miniatures in the *Canterbury Tales* see the chapter on 'Illuminations' by Margaret Rickert in John M. Manley and Edith Rickert, *The Text of the Canterbury Tales* vol. 1 (Chicago: University of Chicago Press 1940), esp. pp. 583–90. The British Museum and National Gallery portraits were executed long after Chaucer's death, at the earliest in the sixteenth century, and it is possible that these two, as well as the Harvard portrait, derive ultimately from the Hoccleve original. Even if this were so it would not adversely affect the hypothesis proposed here, since Hoccleve, the beloved pupil of Chaucer, personally commissioned the portrait when the likeness of his master was still fresh in his mind:

> Althogh his lyf be queynt, the resemblaunce
> Of him hath in me so fresh lyflinesse
> That, to putte othere men in remembraunce
> Of his persone, I have heere his lyknesse
> Do make, to this ende, in sothfastnesse,
> That thei, that have of him lest thought and mynde
> By this peynture may ageyn him fynde
> (Hoccleve, *Governail of Princes*, stanza 714, cited in Skeat, ed., *The Complete Works of Geoffrey Chaucer*, vol. 1, p. lix)

See also Beverly Boyd, *Chaucer and the Medieval Book* (San Marino: Huntington Library 1973), pp. 37–45, 54.

18 Cited in Skeat, ed., *The Complete Works of Geoffrey Chaucer*, vol. 1, p. lix
19 The matin Psalms of the Ambrosian Psalter are divided into ten *decuriae* and are to be recited over a period of two weeks. For explicit details on the division of psalters, their types, and use see the magnificent reference work of Andrew Hughes, *Medieval Manuscripts for Mass Office: A Guide to their Organization and Terminology* (Toronto: University Press 1982), pp. 224–37, nos. 873–86; for the way in which psalms were sung, see pp. 23–43. Hughes underscores the widespread variations in liturgical practice throughout Europe, sometimes even between different churches in the same country. None of these variations affects the claims made in this study; what matters here is that the division of the psalter into three parts (and, in the case of Boccaccio, into ten) was well known.
20 Edith G. Kern, 'The Gardens in the *Decameron* Cornice, *PMLA*, 66 (1951), pp. 505–23; Marshall Brown, 'In the Valley of the Ladies,' *Italian Quarterly*, 18 (1975), pp. 33–52; Giuseppe Mazzotta, 'The *Decameron*: The Literal and the Allegorical, *Italian Quarterly*, 18 (1975), pp. 53–75
21 G. Boccaccio, *Decamerone*, ed. Vittore Branca (Florence: L'Accademia della Crusca 1976), p. 23; subsequent quotations from the Decameron are taken from this edition.
22 G. Boccaccio, *Corbaccio: a cura di Pier Giorgio Ricci, introduzione di Natalino Sapegno* (Torino: Enaudi 1977), pp. 73–4

23 Marguerite de Navarre, *L'Heptaméron*, ed. M. François (Paris: Garnier 1950), pp. 9–10

24 Ibid., p. 450, n.50

25 A.J. Krailsheimer, 'The *Heptaméron* Reconsidered,' in D.R. Haggis et al., eds., *The French Renaissance and Its Heritage: Essays Presented to Alan M. Boase* (London: Methuen 1968), p. 81

26 Aurelius Prudentius Clemens, *Peristephanon Liber*, ed. H.J. Thompson (Cambridge, Mass.: Loeb Classical Library 1953), vol. 2, vv. 208–9

27 For the different types of links between 'laisses' see Mildred K. Pope, 'Four *Chansons* de geste: A Study in Old French Versification,' *MLR*, 8 (1913), pp. 352–67; 9 (1914), pp. 41–52; 10 (1915), pp. 310–19; Jean Rychner, *La Chanson de geste. Essai sur L'art épique des jongleurs* (Geneva 1955); Angelo Monteverdi, 'La laisse épique,' in *La Technique littéraire des chansons de geste. Acte du colloque de Liège* (Paris 1959), pp. 127–40.

28 A.D. Deyermond, *Epic Poetry and the Clergy: Studies on the 'Mocedades de Rodrigo'* (London: Tamesis 1969), p. xviii

29 See John K. Walsh, 'Religious Motifs in the Early Spanish Epic,' *Revista Hispanica Moderna*, 36 (1970–71), pp. 165–72; Colbert I. Nepaulsingh, 'The Afrenta de Corpes and the Martyrological Tradition,' *Hispanic Review*, 51 (1983), pp. 205–21.

30 *Poema de Mio Cid*, ed. Ian Michael (Madrid: Clásicos Castalia 1976), l. 9. Subsequent quotations from the *Cid* are taken from this edition.

31 Alberto Colunga and L. Turrado eds., *Biblia Sacra Iuxta Vulgatam Clementianam* (Madrid: Biblioteca de autores cristianos 1977), Psalms 3–7, 9–12, 16, 24–7, 30, 34, 53–6, 58, 62–3, 68–70, 85, 91, 93, 108, 118 (vv. 89–96), 119, 122, 138–42. I cite the Psalms in Latin because this is the language in which they were memorized by Christians in medieval Europe; textual or conceptual echoes are more likely to be recognized if the Latin version is cited. I ask the reader who reads no Latin to consult an appropriate translation, bearing in mind that the Vulgate version has a slightly different numbering of the Psalms. All Latin quotations from the Bible are taken from this edition.

32 'Doors and Cloaks: Two Image-Patterns in the *Cantar de Mio Cid*,' *Modern Language Notes*, 94 (1979), pp. 366–77. Deyermond and Hook make note that 'door and gate imagery is frequent in the Bible,' (p. 376, n. 7F), and they quote Luke, Isaiah, Lamentations, and Ezekiel as examples, but make no reference to the Psalms.

33 These verses of Pslam 23 were especially appropriate for ceremonies welcoming dignitaries, like the *adventus regis*, for details of which see Ernst H. Kantorowicz, 'The "King's Advent" and the Enigmatic Panels in the Doors of Santa Sabina,' *The Art Bulletin*, 26 (1944), pp. 207–31.

34 H. Salvador Martínez, *El 'Poema de Almería' y la épica románica* (Madrid: Gredos 1975), pp. 224–5, 255

35 A.D. Deyermond,, 'Structural and Stylistic Patterns in the *Cantar de Mio Cid*,' in Brian Dutton et al., eds., *Medieval Studies in Honor of Robert White Linker* (Madrid: Castalia 1973), pp. 55–71 at p. 55

36 Some editors mention the Cid's devotion to the Virgin Mary, but they do
not elaborate on the implications of such devotion for the plot of the poem;
see, for example, Ramón Menéndez Pidal, ed., *Cantar de Mio Cid* (Madrid:
Espasa-Calpe 1944), vol. 1, p. 40, and Michael, ed., *Poema de Mio Cid*, p. 93,
n. 215, p. 98, n. 273.

37 Menéndez Pidal, *Cantar de Mio Cid*, vol. 1, p. 3, n. 2. I have checked Menéndez Pidal's reading of fol. 74 V° against the *Poema de Mio Cid. edición facsímil del Códice de Per Abat conservado en la Biblioteca national* (Madrid:
Dirección General de Archivos y Bibliotecas 1961), as well as against the
beautiful colour facsimile edition: *Poema de Mío Cid, edición facsímil del
manuscrito del Marqués de Pidal depositado en la Biblioteca Nacional*, 2
vols. (Burgos: Excmo. Ayuntamiento de Burgos, 1982). I thank Professor
David Hook for bringing the colour facsimile to my attention; in colour the
last page is much more legible than in the brown and white facsimile, but
nevertheless most of the writing on the page of the colour facsimile is
unclear, and the first half of the page seems to be severely discoloured,
probably from the use of chemicals on the parchment. I have had to rely on
Menéndez Pidal's transcription of this page, and on Ian Michael's (p. 55,
n. 65). It might be possible to recover the writing on this page with the use
of electronic cameras and digital image-processing as described in John
Benton, Alan Gillespie, and James Soha, 'Digital Image-Processing Applied
to the Photography of Manuscripts,' *Scriptorium*, 33 (1979), pp. 40–55, esp.
bibliographical n. 21, p. 47.

38 Kasten and Nitti, eds., *Concordances and Texts*, vol. 2, *Estoria de España* II,
p. 748, fol. 251r, ll. 52–6. It is of no consequence to this argument whether
these words were written under the reign of Sancho IV, or whether they
were included in the original text of the *Estoria de España*.

39 Michael, ed., *Poema de Mio Cid*, p. 55, n. 65

40 Thurston, 'The Rosary' (1900), p. 408

41 Menéndez Pidal suggests that these verses of Psalm 109 were copied 'acaso
pensando en el triunfo del Cid sobre sus enemigos' (vol. 1, p. 3, n. 2), but he
does not note their similarity to ll. 3114–16 of the *Cid*.

42 Gonzalo de Berceo, *Los milagros de Nuestra Señora*, ed., Brian Dutton (London: Tamesis 1971). All references are to this edition. Dutton identifies in
his notes all of these references to the Psalms except two: he omits 'salterio'
in 709b from his glossary (p. 255), and he does not relate the hymn 'Tibi
laus, tibi gloria' to Psalm 21:24, 'Qui timetis Dominum, laudate eum; uni-
versum semen Iacob, glorificate eum.' Cf. Daniel Devoto, ed., *Milagros de
Nuestra Señora* (Madrid: Castalia, Odres Nuevos 1957), p. 260. See also
Francis Gormly, *The Use of the Bible in Representative Works of Medieval
Spanish Literature (1250–1300)*, Studies in Romance Languages and Literatures, vol. 64, Microfilm Series, vol. 1 (Washington: The Catholic University
of America 1962), esp. pp. 4–26.

43 Berceo's style often has an epic ring reminiscent of the *Cid*: for example in
his repeated use of the epic formula 'plorar de los ojos' (sts. 301, 389, 398,
540, 541, 765, 770, 846), which, as has been suggested above, derives ulti-

mately from Psalm 6:7,8, and his use of other geographic formulas ('En Toleda la noble,' 413a, 'Colonna la rica,' 160a). Berceo obviously treats the Virgin Mary as an epic heroine of cosmic rather than merely terrestrial proportions; and one wonders if he was aware of the similarity to the *Cid* of some of the Latin material he was adapting; the hymn in honour of the Virgin (sts. 452–60), and Theophilus's prayer (sts. 781–6) are like Doña Ximena's prayer for the Cid; the bankrupt merchant of Byzantium seeks out a Jewish moneylender (sts. 636ff.) in a scene not unlike the Raquel and Vidas episode in the *Cid*; and some aspects of the robbery (by two Leonese thieves) of the nun and the image of the Virgin in 'La Iglesia Robada' (no. 25) remind the reader of the mistreatment of Doña Elvira and Doña Sol by the Leonese Infantes. Cf. Joaquín Artiles, *Los recursos literarios de Berceo* (Madrid: Gredos 1964), pp. 236–47. See also Brian Dutton, 'Gonzalo de Berceo and the *cantares de gesta*,' *Bulletin of Hispanic Studies*, 38 (1961), pp. 197–205.

44 See Thurston, 'The Rosary' (1900), pp. 624–9; Gorce, *Le rosaire*, pp. 23–4; Wilkins, *The Rose-garden Game*, pp. 31, 108; these historians omit a further influence; the Psalms themselves speak, at least twice, of an instrument of ten strings – 'in psalterio decem chordarum psallite illi' (32:2), and 'in decachordo psalterio' (91:4).

45 For example, Carmelo Gariano, *Análisis estilístico de los Milagros de Nuestra Señora* (Madrid: Gredos 1972), p. 187, points to 'la frecuencia del simbolismo cifrado en el cinco.' Gariano attributes the institution of the rosary devotion to Santo Domingo in Spain, a fact which the Bollandists and all serious historians of the topic have successfully disputed; only the most devoted Dominicans still hold strongly to what Gariano lists as simple fact, namely that the rosary is 'la devoción mariana más célebre, instituida en España en tiempos de Berceo por Santo Domingo ... santo de su orden en la campaña contra los albigenses' (p. 181). Gariano's statement must be compared with the following one written by Thurston in 'The Rosary' (1901) p. 67: 'The case against the commonly-received story of the origin of the Rosary falls naturally into two portions. The first consists of the negative argument, the absence, in other words, of any mention of St. Dominic's name in connection with this devotion for nearly two centuries and a half after his death. The second, which is more positive in character, finds a sufficient explanation of the so-called Dominican tradition in the popularity enjoyed by the revelation of Alan de Rupe at the end of the fifteenth century.' It seems prudent to suppose therefore, that although Berceo must have been familiar with various elements of the rosary tradition, including the use of beads, he did not know the devotion in the form later fixed by the Dominicans in the late fifteenth century.

46 This concern could not be only about the miracle in which it is expressed, since that miracle (Theophilus) is the longest in the book (163 stanzas). With regard to length, Berceo stops his work after 911 stanzas or 3644 lines, that is, only approximately one hundred lines less than the *Cid*. With regard to Berceo's choice of the monorhymed quatrain for his *Milagros*, it

should be noted that the most famous *rosaria*, the Marian psalters of Stephen Langton and Anselm of Canterbury, are written in monorhymed quatrains. I do not mean to claim that the *cuaderna vía* originated with the Marian psalters; I claim merely that Berceo's choice of strophe form is appropriate.

47 Thurston, 'The Rosary' (1901), pp. 392, 402. Williams, *The Rosary*, pp. 15, 30. Some critics of the *Cantigas* are aware that Alfonso is attempting to arrange his poems like a rosary, but they do not explain why every tenth *cantiga* is different, and not every eleventh like the modern rosary beads. Joseph T. Snow, for example, writes: 'there are nine miracles and a praise song and this forms the pattern of progression throughout the *Cantigas*. A comparison to rosary beads is doubtless intended' ('The Loor to the Virgin and Its Appearance in the *Cantigas de Santa María* of Alfonso X,' PH D diss., University of Wisconsin, 1972, p. 363).

48 Cantiga 111, lines 36–8. All quotations are from Alfonso X, O Sabio, *Cantigas de Santa Maria*, ed. Walter Mettmann, 4 vols. (Coimbra: Atlântida 1959–72), and will be cited in the text by *cantiga* and line numbers: e.g., c. 111, ll. 36–8.

49 Thurston, 'The Rosary' (1900), p. 520, n. 1; and Gorce *Le rosaire*, p. 28–9.

50 The five Psalms selected by the devotee are (1) Mary's psalm (the 'Magnificat,' Luke 1: 46–55, which though patterned upon Hannah's prayer in Samuel 2:10, also echoes Psalm 33:4 'Magnificate Dominum meum'); (2) Psalm 119 ('Ad Dominum cum tribularer clamavi'); (3(either Psalm 24 ('Ad te, Domine, levavi animam meam') or Psalm 27 'Ad te, domine, clamabo'), or Psalm 122 ('Ad te levavi oculos meos'); (4) Psalm 125 ('In convertendo Dominus captivitatem Sion'); and (5) Psalm 118:17–24 ('Retribue servo tuo, vivifica me'). The idea for the acrostic was probably suggested to the monk by the Psalms themselves since some Psalms are alphabetical acrostics (9, 24, 33, 36, 110, 111, 144). The longest Psalm (118) is subdivided according to the letters of the Hebrew alphabet; to get a Psalm that begun with the Latin letter 'R' the monk had to choose the section of Psalm 118 that corresponds to the Hebrew letter 'Ghimel.' This means that he probably recited Psalm 33 (instead of the 'Magnificat') and Psalm 24 (instead of Psalm 27 or 122) because 33 and 24 are acrostics.

51 Fidel Fita, ed., 'Biografías de San Fernando y de Alfonso el Sabio por Gil de Zamora,' *Boletín de la Real Academia de la Historia*, 5 (1884), p. 321

52 See Thurston, 'The History of the Rosary in All Countries,' *Scientific American Supplement*, 1370 (5 April 1902), pp. 21960–3; and for Paris see Etienne Boileau, *Règlemens sur les arts et mestiers de Paris redigés au XIIIe siècle*, ed., George B. Depping (Paris: Crapelet 1837), pp. 66–73, 97–9.

53 José Guerrero Lovillo, *Las Cantigas, estudio arqueológico de sus miniaturas* (Madrid: CSIC 1949), pl. 136. The Princeton Index describes the fourth panel as follows: 'Heads of 3 men, one wearing cap, and veiled woman wearing hat, appearing at windows of building in which men wearing hooded garment and merchant wearing pointed cap, R. hand indicating one of coins in 2 piles on counter behind which are 2 men, one with R. hand on column,

beside 2 men wearing caps, holding carpet or drapery behind counter on which are objects including caskets, rosary, chalices, candlesticks and cross.'

54 Julián Ribera y Tarragó, *El Cancionera de Abencuzmán: Disertaciones y opúsculos* (Madrid 1928), p. 55, n. 1; S.M. Stern trans., *Hispano-Arabic Strophic Poetry*, ed. L.P. Harvey (London: Oxford University Press 1974), p. 12, n. 1. For an annotated bibliography, see Richard Hitchcock, *The Kharjas*, Research Bibliographies and Checklists, 20 (London: Grant and Cutler 1977). The text of the *Kharjas* is problematic: see the recent articles by Alan Jones, 'Sunbeams from Cucumbers? An Arabist's Assessment of the State of *Kharja* Studies,' *La Corónica*, 10 (1981-2), pp. 38-53, James T. Monroe, '¿Pedir peras al olmo? On Medieval Arabs and Modern Arabists,' *La Corónica*, 10 (1981-2), pp. 121-47, and Samuel G. Armistead, 'Speed or Bacon? Further Meditations on Professor Alan Jones' "Sunbeams,"' *La Corónica*, (1981-82), pp. 148-55, and especially 'Pet Theories and Paper Tigers: Trouble with the Kharjas,' *La Corónica*, 14 (1985), pp. 65-70. J.M. Sola-Solé, *Corpus de poesía mozárabe* (Barcelona: Hispam 1973), numbers XXXVI, XLIII, and L, corresponding to García-Gómez numbers XI, XXXV, and II respectively.

55 S.M. Stern, 'An Arabic Muwashshah and Its Hebrew Imitations,' *Al Andalus*, 28 (1963), pp. 155-70, emphasis mine

56 Michael ed., *Poema de Mio Cid*, pp. 29-32. For an excellent thumbnail introduction to 'leixa-pren' see A.D. Deyermond, *A Literary History of Spain: The Middle Ages* (London/New York: Benn, Barnes and Noble 1971), pp. 15, 29, n. 28. John D. Fitz-Gerald, *Versification of the Cuaderna Vía as Found in Berceo's Vida de santo Domingo de Silos* (New York: Columbia University Press 1905), pp. 96; Gariano, *Análisis* pp. 87-93; Artiles, *Los recursos*, pp. 68-72, 82-6, 98-102

57 See Brian Dutton, 'Some New Evidence for the Romance Origins of the Muwashshahas,' *Bulletin of Hispanic Studies*, 42 (1965), pp. 73-81. Only 37 of the 420 *cantigas* edited by Mettmann contain no refrain or one with other than 2 or 4 lines.

58 Prudentius, *Dittochaeon or Tituli Historiarum*, trans. H.J. Thompson (Cambridge, Mass.: Loeb Classical Library 1953), vol. 2

59 In Phillip Ulstad, *Coelum Philosophorum seu Liber de Secretis Naturae* (London: Gulielmum Roillium 1572), pp. 432-553, at p. 434. See also the edition by Hieronymus Megiser, *Omnia, quae exstant, opera chymica* (Frankfurt: Ioachim Brathering 1603), p. 4: 'Istum autem librum nominavi Rosarium, eo quod ipsum abreviavi ex libris Philosophorum, quantum potui melius.'

60 Reproduced in José Manuel Bleucua, ed., *El Conde Lucanor* (Madrid: Castalia 1969), opposite p. 72

61 I shall deal with the composition of the *Cárcel de Amor* and *Celestina* in chapter 5. For Cervantes, see Karl-Ludwig Selig, 'Don Quixote I/22,' pp. 349-75, esp. p. 355, n. 9. I should like to thank Professors Alan Deyermond, Raymond Willis, and Louise Fainberg for reading a version of this chapter and sending me their comments.

62 Berceo, *Milagros*, ed. Dutton, 370d. Fita, ed., *Biografías*, p. 321

CHAPTER TWO

1 Alfonso X, O Sabio, *Cantigas de Santa Maria* ed. Walter Mettmann (Coimbra: Atlântida 1959), vol. 1, p. 173, no. 60

2 Moshe Ibn Ezra, Sîrēy ha-ḥol, Berlin, 1934, vol. 1, p. 4. The transliteration is mine, after the system used by J. Weingreen, *A Practical Grammar for Classical Hebrew*, 2nd ed. (Oxford: Clarendon 1959), p. 1. The translation is by David Goldstein, *The Jewish Poets of Spain, 900–1250* (Harmondsworth: Penguin 1971), p. 105. There are striking similarities between Ibn Ezra's poem and the *Razón*: the opening lines are practically the same, and the references to singing in a garden and to miracles are common to both poems. But this does not necessarily mean that one poem is a source for the other. Rather it might indicate that the first line of *Razón* was a common poetical opening in medieval Spain; songs sung in a garden and miracles are also frequently used in literature. I am grateful to Alicia de Colombí-Monguió and Alan Deyermond for their detailed and encouraging comments on a version of this chapter. Since these are leading experts on the *Razón*, I indicate in the notes where their remarks have caused me to clarify my meaning. They are, of course, not responsible for errors that persist in my text.

3 A. Morel-Fatio, 'Textes Castillans Inédits,' *Romania*, 16 (1887), pp. 364–82; R. Menéndez Pidal, '*Razón de amor* con los denuestos del agua y el vino,' *Revue Hispanique*, 13 (1905), pp. 602–18; Leo Spitzer, '*Razón de amor*,' *Romania*, 71 (1950), pp. 145–65; A. Pacheco, '*Razón de amor* o *Denuestos del agua y el vino?*' *Bulletin of Hispanic Studies*, 51 (1974), pp. 1–15, at p. 1: 'pero el espejismo del título, la innegable dualidad temática y distinta calidad artística de las dos partes del poema, y la simple inercia de la costumbre explican y justifican que haya todavía quienes mantienen el criterio de su primer editor.'

4 For Christian symbolism, Alfred Jacob, 'The *Razón de Amor* as Christian Symbolism, *Hispanic Review*, 20 (1952), pp. 283–301; for Cathar heresy, Enrique de Rivas, 'La razón secreta de la *Razón de amor*, *Anuario de filología*, 6–7 (1967–8), pp. 109–27; for grail legends Pachecho, 'Razón ...?; for the *Carmina Burana*, J. Holly Hanford, 'The Medieval Debate between Wine and Water,' *PMLA*, 28, new series 21 (1913), pp. 315–67; for troubadour poetry, Margo de Ley, 'Provençal Biographical Tradition and the *Razón de amor*,' *Journal of Hispanic Philology*, 1 (1976), pp. 1–17, and Alicia de Colombí-Monguió, '*Locus Amoenus* y vergel visionario en *Razón de amor*,' *Hispanic Review*, 42 (1974), pp. 173–83, 'Sentido y unidad de *Razón de amor*,' *Filología*, 14 (1970), pp. 1–48, and *De amor y poesía en la España medieval: Prólogo a Juan Ruiz* (México: Colegio de México 1976) esp. pp. 43–119. For linguistic arguments, Daniel N. Cárdenas, 'Nueva luz sobre "*Razón de amor* y denuestos del agua y el vino,"' *Revista Hispánica Moderna*, 34 (1968), pp. 227–41; for folk lyrics, Margaret Van Antwerp, '*Razón de amor* and the Popular Tradition,' *Romance Philology*, 32 (1978), pp. 1–17; for a recent assessment and annotated bibliography see Alan Deyermond, *Edad Media*, in Francisco Rico, ed., *Historia y crítica de la lite-*

ratura española, vol. 1 (Barcelona: Crítica 1980), 135–40, at p. 136: 'Aunque la *Razón* ha sido más estudiada que el resto de los debates poéticos españoles, queda mucho por hacer antes de que revele sus últimos misterios'; for a proposed relationship with one of Alfonso el Sabio's *cantigas,* see Roger M. Walker, 'Two Notes on Spanish Debate Poems,' in *Medieval Studies in Honour of R.W. Linker,* ed. Brian Dutton et al. (Madrid: Castalia 1973), pp. 177–84. For an attempt to prove the unity of the poem through formal structural analysis see Olga Tudórica Impey, 'La estructura unitaria de *Razón de amor, Journal of Hispanic Philology,* 4 (1979), pp. 1–24. Professor Impey's attempt fails because her insistence on the adequacy of the literal level of the poem prevents her from appreciating the subtle use of religious clichés by the author; she is therefore unable to make use of the biblical hermeneutic tradition to which the text makes clear, significant reference. For example, for Impey the debate between wine and water is merely a mundane argument that generates hatred and insults: 'Lejos de generar armonía, la mezcla genera odio e insultos' p. 20); thus, she interprets the powers attributed to wine as a 'perverso poder de envalentonar a los cobardes,' and does not appreciate the clear reference, on the spiritual, allegorical level, to the miracles of Jesus Christ as listed in the Bible. Impey seems to assume that the author was more acquainted with the poetry of courtly love than with the Bible; to the contrary the text of the *Razón* indicates that its author was well-enough acquainted with the Bible that he could use biblical clichés with great and subtle artistry. The ability to use biblical quotations cleverly was not uncommon among medieval authors, especially in Spain where learning was often coterminous with profound knowledge of the Bible, long parts of which many scholars knew by heart.

5 Colombí-Monguió, *De Amor y poesía,* p. 72

6 The importance of the Song of Songs in the development of medieval lyric has been neglected for some time, but recently some leading critics have been paying attention to the Song's influence; see, for example, Peter Dronke, 'The Song of Songs and Medieval Love-Lyric,' in W. Lourdaux and D. Verhelst, eds., *The Bible and Medieval Culture* (Louvain: University Press 1979), pp. 236–62. Hispanists have tended to pay attention to the Song mainly because of the Spanish mystics and the controversy around Fray Luis de León; hence works like Alexander Habib Arkin, *La influencia de la exégesis hebrea en los comentarios bíblicos de Fray Luis de León* (Madrid: Instituto Benito Arias Montano 1966). For the medieval period there is a poorly written thesis by Roger Duane Martin, 'The Influence of the Exegetical Tradition of the "Song of Songs" on the "Introduction" to the "Milagros de Nuestra Señora"' (University of Colorado 1974); poorly written because it makes no mention of Dutton's edition of the *Milagros,* nor of the *Razón de amor,* nor of seminal works like Z. García Villada, 'Antiguos comentarios al Cantar de los Cantares desconocidos e inéditos,' *Estudios eclesiásticos,* 7 (1928), pp. 104–13; Martin ignores the strong Jewish exegetical tradition in Spain and pays attention only to the Christian writers; and Martin also fails to establish that Berceo used the Song of Songs or its tradition. In

short, there is much need for a current assessment of the tradition of the Song of Songs in Spanish literature. See, also, Tony Hunt, 'The Song of Songs and Courtly Literature,' in Glyn S. Burgess, ed., *Court and Poet* (Liverpool: Francis Cairns 1981), pp. 189–95.

7 Rivas, 'La razón secreta,' p. 127: 'Uno, que para no dejar de señalarlo empieza su poema diciendo "Sancti spiritus adsid nobis gratia amen" cuando Berceo, Alfonxo X o Juan Ruiz abren sus obras poéticas con una invocación a la Virgen María.' Line numbers in this study refer to the edition by G.H. London, 'The *Razón de amor* and the *Denuestos del agua y el vino*,' *Romance Philology*, 29 (1965), pp. 28–47, except where stated otherwise.

8 Alberto Colunga and L. Turrado, eds., *Biblia Sacra Iuxta Vulgatam Clementinam* (Madrid: Biblioteca de Autores Cristianos 1977), Liber Sapientiae 1:5, p. 619. I cite this edition because the invocation of the *Razón* is in Latin.

9 For St Bernard: *Opera Bernardi* (London: Jacob Giunti 1544), *Super Cantica Canticorum*, sermon 1, fol. 122v., and Migne, *Patrologia Latina* (PL), vol. 183, col. 786. For Ibn Ezra: G. Genebrardo, *Canticum Canticorum Salomonis Versibus et Commentariis Illustratum* (Paris: Aegidium Gorbinum 1585), fol. 125. I do not refer to the work of Ibn Ezra and St Bernard as direct sources for the *Razón*, only as part of a tradition of understanding the Song of Songs which is reflected also in the composition of the *Razón*. Although I cite Ibn Ezra in a late (sixteenth century) Latin translation, I have also before me the edition (and translation) of a Hebrew version by H.J. Mathews, *Ibn Ezra's Commentary on the Canticles, After the First Recension* (London: Trubner 1874). Mathews believes (pp. vii–viii) that Abraham Ibn Ezra's commentary was written around 1140 in Italy, where the scholar was living after he left Spain. It would appear that there was greater need for Ibn Ezra's scholarship in other European countries than in Spain, where Ibn Ezra's knowledge was shared by a number of other Spanish Hebrew scholars; Spain was a leader in biblical scholarship in Ibn Ezra's time and before, so what he saw as an urgent need for biblical commentaries in Italy was more commonplace in his native Spain. I mean to imply that Ibn Ezra's knowledge of the Song of Songs, and his interpretation of it, were more easily available to a Spanish poet (like the composer of the *Razón*) than to a poet from the rest of Europe. European scholars like St Bernard drew upon a less rich hermeneutic tradition of the Bible than that which was accessible to their Spanish contemporaries.

10 Genebrardo, *Canticum Canticorum*, fols. 119–20

11 Cedric E. Pickford ed., *Cantique des cantiques* (Oxford: Oxford University Press 1974), p. 1

12 For 'tryança' see the excellent note by London, 'The *Razón de amor*,' p. 33, and the persuasive argument by Rivas, 'La razón secreta,' pp. 114–15, that it means 'desventura.' London documents 'triança' in the *Partidas* where it seems to have a negative connotation in that it is described as something clerics should avoid having with women. The last sentence of this paragraph of the text (p. 45) has been added in response to a request from Alicia de Colombí-Monguió that I attenuate the implication of strong relation

between the author of the *Razón* and Solomon: 'yo atenuaría la sugestión de conexión implícita entre el autor de la *Razón* y Salomón. Me parece algo arriesgada; cierto es que ambos amaron mucho a dueñas, pero de haber el poeta tenido en mientes tal sugerencia no creo que nos hubiese despistado tan pronto con eso del morar mucho en Lombardía para aprender cortesía.' It is not a question of 'despistar' but of varying the tradition to suit artistic purposes.

13 St Bernard's Sermon 23, in Migne, *PL*, vol. 183, col. 886. Impey, 'La estructura unitaria,' p. 6.

14 Christian D. Ginsburg, *The Song of Songs and Coheleth* (New York: KTAV 1970), p. 135, n. 7. The fact that the noonday siesta, like many of the other garden motifs, is a widespread practice in mediterranean cultures, probably accounts for the omission of the Song of Songs in serious studies of the theme. The main studies of the garden in Western literature either ignore the Song of Songs or make passing reference to it only. See, for example, E.R. Curtius, 'The Ideal Landscape,' in *European Literature and the Latin Middle Ages*, trans. W.R. Trask (New York: Harper & Row 1953), pp. 183–202; A. Bartlett Giamatti, *The Earthly Paradise and the Renaissance Epic* (Princeton: University Press 1966); Arturo Graf, *Miti, Leggende e Superstizioni del Medio Evo*, vol. 1, 'Il mito del paradiso terrestre' (New York: Burt Franklin 1971), pp. xi–238; Edith Kern, 'The Gardens in the Decameron Cornice,' *PMLA*, 66 (1951), pp. 505–23; Giuseppe Mazzotta, 'The *Decameron*: The Literal and the Allegorical,' *Italian Quarterly*, 18 (1975), pp. 53–73; Marshall Brown, 'In the Valley of the Ladies,' *Italian Quarterly* 18 (1975), pp. 33–52; Giusseppe Mazzotta, 'The *Decameron*: The Marginality of Literature,' *University of Toronto Quarterly*, 42 (1972), pp. 64–81, esp. pp. 67–8. See also Elizabeth Drayson, 'Some Possible Sources for the Introduction to Berceo's *Milagros de Nuestra Señora*,' *Medium Aevum*, 50 (1981), pp. 274–83; Drayson compares the *locus amenus* in *Milagros* with the one in *Razón*, at p. 281.

15 Margaret Van Antwerp, 'Razón de amor,' p. 7: 'With the detail of the hat – unique in an otherwise stereotyped medieval description of feminine beauty – the poet turns the reader back to his earlier, similarly unusual presentation of the vessel of wine.' Many of Van Antwerp's insights are correct and would have been sharpened had she referred to the Song of Songs; in addition to this one about the hat, see for example when she argues (p. 16) that the dove is symbolic of the damsel whom the poet has successfully hunted. This hunting metaphor harks back to Song of Songs 4:9 – 'Vulnerasti cor meum, soror mea sponsa; vulnerasti cor meum in uno oculorum tuorum'; the eyes are like doves, as repeated elsewhere in the Song. Alfred Jacob, 'The *Razón de amor*,' also noted that the hat was unusual but explained it 'as a Spanish tradition' (p. 292, n. 13). See also Colombí-Monguió, *De amor y poesía*, p. 83.

16 In his historical interpretation of the story ('Interpretatio altera historiae seu dramatis') Abraham Ibn Ezra states that the *Song* is the story of a young girl who falls in love with a shepherd whom she prefers even over the King:

'Puella parva admodum, cui nondum extabant ubera, custos vineae, contemplata Pastorem transeuntem, ipsum deperire et deinde amore sui sauciare coepit ... "Introduxit me rex in conclauia sua," magis te delectamur, quam quia induxit me rex in conclavia sua' (fol. 123). Ginsburg, *Song of Songs and Coheleth*, p. 46, strongly supports Ibn Ezra's interpretation. Alicia de Colombí-Monguió has pointed out to me that by showing similarities between the 'doncella' of the *Razón* and the bride of the Song, I risk robbing the *Razón* of coherence: 'si la doncella es semejante a la del *CC*, es difícil que sea también una encarnación de *luxuria*. Si la doncella no es la señora del heurto entonces tenemos dos mujeres que participan de paralelismo con la del *CC*. Los paraleismos que señalas entre la doncella y la del *CC* hacen muy difícil que el poeta haya querido darle connotaciones negativas, salvo que fuera torpe, y si encima de esta torpeza, nos desdobla el simbolismo en dos mujeres, se pierde toda coherencia simbólica ... Ojo: yo creo que el paralelismo con la esposa del *CC* existe, de donde dudo de la connotación lujuriosa, y de la dicotomía Doncella-señora del huerto.' The risk of incoherence and awkwardness to which Alicia de Colombí-Monguió correctly refers, confirms rather than denies the tradition to which the *Razón* belongs. Critics of the Song have always disagreed about whether it concerns one woman or several, and as I have said above, all critics agree on the Song's erotic content; they disagree only as to how this erotic content should be interpreted. The doubling of the women in *Razón* (doncella / señora del huerto) is not unlike the distinction between Ave and Eva; Eva has good qualities, but is also part of the evil cause of the Fall. The Song was often interpreted in terms of Genesis.

17 Although I quote the Vulgate version of the Bible in this study, I also consult other versions of the Bible available in Spain during the Middle Ages. The problem is succinctly stated by Dronke ('The Song,' p. 236) who reminds us that 'this is a problem that medieval literary scholars have never yet to [his] knowledge, broached ... For the medieval West, we must not simply assume the familiarity of Jerome's Vulgate version of the Song of Songs.' Whereas the Vulgate translates 'ubera' (breasts), scholars in Spain have always known this to be wrong; hence Ibn Ezra's translator interprets the Hebrew correctly 'qui meliores sunt amores tui' (fol. 123), which Mathews edits: 'Ki tobïm dodekha [miyayin]' and translates, 'For thy love gladdens the heart more than wine' (p. 9, Hebrew and p. 10 English). 'Tobïm means simply 'better,' so that a more precise translation would be 'For thy [sexual] love is better than wine.' Fray Luis de León, as late as the sixteenth century, also translates correctly 'son mas dulces que el vino tus amores.' On the Vulgate's error, see Ginsburg, *Song of Songs and Coheleth*, p. 130, n. 2: 'That this is a gross error is evident from the fact that a man and not a woman is here addressed.' On the widespread influence of the Spanish exegetes see Beryl Smalley, 'Hebrew Scholarship among Christians in XIIth Century England' (London: Shapiro Valentine 1939), lecture no. 6 read to the Society for Old Testament Study on 4 January 1939; and *The Study of the Bible in the Middle Ages* (Oxford: Clarendon Press 1941) esp. p. 122, 2nd ed.

(New York: Philosophical Library 1952) p. 150. Smalley admits not having paid as much attention to Spanish sources as she might have liked: 'Geographically, the book is limited to England, northern France, and the Rhineland where much the same educational system obtained' (p. lxi). 'Even here we have been obliged to neglect a very possible source, Ibn Ezra, for lack of time' (p. 126, n. 5, 2nd ed., p. 155, n. 1). The history of Spanish influence on biblical exegesis remains to be written. Existing books have a historical rather than literary focus, as, for example, the recent volume by Luis Suárez Fernández, *Judíos españoles en la edad media* (Madrid: Rialp 1980), esp. the bibliography, pp. 276–86. I have in mind a study, focused on medieval Spain, along the lines of Susan A. Handelman, *The Slayers of Moses: The Emergence of Rabbinic Interpretation in Modern Literary Theory* (Albany: SUNY Press 1982).

18 *Opera Bernardi*, sermon 49, fol. 159 p, and Migne, *PL*, vol. 183, col. 1016. The idea that love is wine is repeated by Bernard at the end of his sermon (no. 54) on *Song* 2:8.

19 I am aware that 'fin amor' is not necessarily always equivalent to 'amor purus' which, as Alicia de Colombí-Monguió shows (*De amor y poesía*, pp. 96–7), was sometimes identifiable with 'amor curialis.' However, these concepts were neither defined nor accepted by all medieval writers in the same way: 'while there does appear to exist in medieval literature a certain common core of ideas about love ... all attempts to define the phenomenon with any precision seem doomed to failure, in as much as rigid definition will relegate to an undefined limbo a large number of writers who are surely part of the tradition' (Keith Whinnom, *The Prison of Love* [Edinburgh: University Press 1979], p. xii.) If we assume that the poet of *Razón* was aware of this fluctuating state of affairs with respect to the meaning of terms like 'fin amor,' we should expect the text of *Razón* to reflect this reasonable assumption. In the *Razón*, 'fin amor' can be taken to mean carnal love, spiritual love, physical love that falls short of sexual consummation, or any mixture of these varieties. In the poem, no matter how 'fin amor' is understood, the distinction is between singing about something and actually participating in it, or singing about one thing and doing another. I choose the latter interpretation because it seems to fit the allegorical meaning of the rest of the narrative; but I do not deny other possibilities. I have added this explanation about my understanding of the term 'fin amor' at the strong suggestion of Alicia de Colombí-Monguió and Alan Deyermond.

20 Alan Deyermond has drawn to my attention the fact that Janet Chapman has noted that capabilities similar to the ones granted to wine in the *Razón* are accorded by Juan Ruiz to wine, money, love and death: see 'A Suggested Interpretation of Stanzas 528 to 549a of the *Libro de Buen Amor*,' *Romanische Forschungen*, 73 (1961), ppp. 29–39. One implication of Deyermond's comment is that since Chapman documents that in the *Libro de buen amor* love, wine, money, and death have similar negative effects, I ought to show how *Razón* is different (from *Libro de buen amor*) in its use of love and

wine for positive effects. This is not hard to do. As I note below, the poet of the *Razón* makes it quite clear that, in spite of Water's claims, he is not talking about any ordinary type of drunkards' wine, but of a special wine – 'qui de *tal* vino' (l. 13); it is also clear in the *Razón* (ll. 133–7) that Christ is made to enter the debate, something that does not happen in *Libro de buen amor* in a similar way. What Chapman's study does confirm, in terms of the contents of chapter 4 of this book, is that Juan Ruiz composed using the aesthetic of contraries to which I also refer: 'Some of the above stanzas are related by the common use of a stylistic formula which may be expressed: X makes Y become Z, where X represents the power of love, money, wine or death and Y and Z represent opposite qualities, statuses, abilities, disabilities and so on' (Chapman, 'A Suggested Interpretation,' pp. 29–30).

21 Alicia de Colombí-Monguió, *De amor y poesía*, pp. 116–17

22 See n. 7 above

23 Hanford, 'The Medieval Debate,' p. 359, end of first stanza. Long before St Bernard, ancient rabbis used Psalm 103:15 to justify the frequent use of wine in Jewish ritual. *Opera Bernardi*, sermon 23, fol. 138r, and Migne, *PL* vol. 183, col. 886.

24 Origen, for example, in his comment on Song 1:4 cites Wisdom in Proverbs 9:5: 'Supra jam diximus amicos sponsi, prophetas et omnes qui ministraverunt verbum Dei, ab initio saeculi intelligendos, ad quos recte vel Ecclesia Christi, vel anima verbo Dei adhaerens dicta ut se introducant in domum vini, id est, ubi sapientia miscuit in cratere vinum suum,' In *Cantica Canticorum, Liber Tertius*, in Migne, *Patrologiae graecae, Latine tantum editae*, vol. 1 (Paris: 1856), cols. 145–6.

25 The motif of falling ill is found in the Song, 2:5, 5:8. The curing properties of wine is accepted in many cultures: 'The ancients were in the habit of mixing wine with spices, to make it more stimulating and exciting. Wine thus mixed was called ... the *vinum aromatites* of the Greeks and Romans.' 'Wine, either pure or mixed, is often spoken of by the sacred and profane poets as delighting the hearts of both gods and men, and reviving their drooping spirits ... Hence Helen gave a bowl of mixed wine to her guests oppressed with grief, to raise their spirits (Hom. *Odyss.* IV. 220),' Ginsburg, *The Song*, pp. 177–8, 129.

26 The identification of ice with Satan is based on the commentaries to Job 38:29: 'De cuius utero egressa est glacies? Et gelu de caelo quis genuit?' On this text Gregory writes: 'etiam Satan in gelu et glacie nil obstat intelligi. Ipse quippe quasi de Dei utero glacies processit, quia a calore secretorum ejus, malitiae torpore frigidus, magister iniquitatis exivit' (*Moralium*, lib. 29. Migne, *PL*, vol. 76, col. 510). See also D.W. Robertson, 'The Doctrine of Charity in Medieval Literary Gardens,' *Speculum*, 26 (1951), pp. 24–49, esp. p. 33. The final paragraphs of Bernard's sermon (no. 54) on Song of Songs 2:8 describe the virtuous attributes of water as an agent which cools (but does not extinguish) carnal desires: this water is fear, or, the *beginning* of wisdom; these same paragraphs also establish in unequivocal terms the superiority of wine over water.

27 *Opera Bernardi*, sermon 33, fols. 148r–149v, and Migne *PL*, vol. 183, cols.
    955–6. On Sapientia and Scientia see Robertson, 'The Doctrine' pp. 26, 32.
    Alicia de Colombí-Monguió discusses the noonday devil in 'Locus amoenus'
    (pp. 177–8) and in *De amor y poesía* (pp. 76–7), and she cites the study by
    Joseph E. Gillet, 'El mediodía y el demonio meridiano en España,' *Nueva
    revista de filología hispánica* 7 (1953), pp. 307–15; but neither Colombí-
    Monguió nor Gillet mentions the tradition of the Song of Songs in this con-
    text. Alicia de Colombí-Monguió has, with her usual keen poetic percep-
    tion, drawn a most interesting point to my attention: 'Si la señora del
    huerto es Sapientia, está muy bien que sea cortesa e bela e bona pero sería
    imposible que Sapientia perdiera su sen. Nuevamente, implicaría una tor-
    peza de caracterización simbólica muy poco probable.' I write 'probably,' and
    I could concede that the 'dueña bela e bona' is not Sapientia without hurt-
    ing my interpretation severely. However, the reference to losing 'su *sen*,'
    which I had overlooked until Alicia de Colombí-Monguió drew it to my
    attention, confirms rather than denies the relationship with Sapientia –
    another demotic cliché put to hieratic use.
28 This theme will be examined more closely in the chapter on apocalyptic
    literature. See also Harriet Goldberg, 'The Dream Report as a Literary
    Device in Medieval Hispanic Literature,' *Hispania*, 66 (1983), pp. 21–31, and
    'The *Razón de amor* and *Los Denuestos del agua y el vino* as a Unified
    Dream Report,' *Kentucky Romance Quarterly*, 31 (1984), pp. 48–9.
29 Pacheco, 'Razón ... ?' p. 4: 'Debe notarse que, en algún momento que no se
    precisa, el vaso de vino ha sido destapado, pues en otro caso no se explica-
    ría que pudiera verterse en al agua derramada por la paloma.'
30 Leo Spitzer, 'Razón de amor,' p. 163
31 One would expect this kind of argument from the noontide devil about
    which St Bernard warned in his sermon on Song of Songs 1:6: 'Hence when
    this kind of noontide devil sets out to tempt a man, there is no chance what-
    ever of parrying with him; he will tempt and overthrow his victim by sug-
    gesting what appears to be good, by persuading him ... to commit evil
    under the guise of good, unless the sun from heaven shines into his heart
    with noontide brightness. The tempter really appears like noon, clothed in
    a certain splendor, when he comes with the suggestion of an apparently
    greater good,' *The Works of Bernard of Clairvaux*, vol. 3 (Kalamazoo: Cister-
    cian Publications 1976), pp. 152–3; *Opera Bernardi*, fol. 149 p., and Migne
    PL, vol. 183, col. 956. Water's argument is not exactly what Christ said, but
    a deceitful conflation of two different statements Christ is reported to have
    made in John 3:5 and in Matthew 5:9 (Water's claim is not based, by the
    way, on Mattahew 25:31, as Alfred Jacob claims in *Hispanic Review*, 20
    (1952), p. 301). In John 3:5 Christ is said to have told Nicodemus that
    'except a man be born of water and of the Spirit he cannot enter into the
    kingdom of God,' and in Matthew 5:9 Christ reportedly said, 'blessed are
    the peacemakers, for they shall be called the children of God.' By deliber-
    ately interpreting 'born of water and of the Spirit' as meaning 'children of
    God,' water not only twists Christ's words but defeats his own argument.

32 Morel-Fatio, 'Textes castillans inédits,' p. 378, and Menéndez Pidal who
edits the line 'de [mi] fazen el cuerpo de Jesu Cristo,' make this assumption.
33 'De fazerme el cuerpo de Jesu Christo,' if one accepts London's suggestion
(p. 44); or, 'just as it says in the scripture where the body of Christ makes
me,' if one accepts Morel-Fatio's reading of 'do' instead of 'de.' Note a similar
inversion of subject and verb in line 57: 'dizem un su mesaiero.'
34 'And great crowds came to him, bringing with them the lame, the maimed,
the blind, the dumb, and many others, and they put them at his feet and he
healed them, so that the throng wondered, when they saw the dumb speaking, the maimed whole, the lame walking, and the blind seeing,' Oxford
Annotated Bible, Matthew 15:30–4. Morel-Fatio (p. 378) and London (p. 45)
translate 'organar' as 'to sing,' citing Berceo as a reference. But it is clear
here that 'organar' means 'to function well,' that is, as any good instrument
functions.
35 Cf. Alfred Jacob who claims on the one hand that 'April is the last month of
Lent' (p. 284), and, on the other hand, that the drinking of the water represents baptism (p. 291). See also José Vives, ed., Concilios Visigóticos e
Hispano-Romanos (Barcelona, Madrid: CSIC 1963), pp. 528–9: 'De obserandis
[sic] ostiis baptisterii in initio quadregesimae.'
36 Some readers might consider it risky to assume that the explicit is part of
the debate that guarantees victory to wine. I see no such risk. There is no
rule, that I know of, that says that medieval poets could not make their
incipit and explicit integral parts of their narrative. And, even if such a rule
should ever be documented, I would suggest that we have, in the author of
the Razón, someone determined to defy that rule for the sake of artistic
ends. In my opinion, no part of the text of the Razón should be considered
external to the narrative.
37 Menéndez Pidal, 'Razón de amor,' pp. 605–6
38 I quote from the translation of the Koran by N.J. Dawood, 4th ed. rev. (Harmondsworth: Penguin 1974), 83: 22–8, p. 50; 76: 12–17, p. 18; 56: 15–23,
p. 110. The first three numbers refer to the chapter and verses to facilitate
reference to other versions. I have other versions and commentaries before
me, including A Comprehensive Commentary on the Quran: Comprising
Sale's Translation and Preliminary Discourse, With Additional Notes and
Emendations by the Rev. E.M. Wherry, 4 vols. (London 1896; rpt. New York:
AMS 1975). In an important, and interesting article, Norman Roth claims
that 'wine was not always considered a sin in Islam; even where it was, the
prohibition was frequently violated' ('"Deal gently with the young man":
Love of Boys in Medieval Hebrew Poetry in Spain,' Speculum, 57 [1982],
pp. 20–51, here at p. 29). Roth draws some interesting parallels between
wine and love, in this case homosexual love.
39 For a discussion of Paradise in the Koran see Sales and Wherry eds., 'Preliminary Discourse,' vol. 1, pp. 153–63. I am aware that E.R. Curtius (European Literature and the Latin Middle Ages) and, later, A. Bartlett Giamatti
have listed numerous passages from the classical Greek and Roman literary
tradition that resemble the semitic paradise. But one of the lessons in liter-

ary history to be gleaned from the foregoing analysis is that frequently with medieval Spanish literature the classical tradition, though essential, will not suffice. As long as hispanists confined their approach to the classical clues provided by Spitzer and to the European (as opposed to the Spanish) tradition of christianity as outlined by Alfred Jacob and Hanford (*Denudata veritate*, grail, troubadours), the *Razón de amor* refused to yield all its treasures and remained an enigma. I am also aware that Hanford (p. 365) conjectures that the wine and water debate may have originated in Germany, even though the *Razón de amor* is one of the earliest extant versions of the theme. Since wine is so central a religious substance to Christians, Moors, and Jews, there are equally valid reasons for conjecturing that the debate between wine and water might have originated in Spain. In addition to what has been said above it should also be noted that the Song of Songs is read in synagogues at Passover, that is, around April.

40 Morel-Fatio, 'Textes castillans inédits,' p. 380
41 Ibid., pp. 381–2
42 Ibid., pp. 380–1
43 Ibid., p. 380
44 The *Corbacho* also includes a passage about quenching the fire of lust, but not with wine because it excites heat. See Alfonso Martínez de Toledo, *Arcipreste de Talavera*, ed. C. Pérez pastor (Madrid 1901), p. 46.
45 Marqués de Santillana, *Poesías completas*, ed. Manuel Durán, 2 vols. (Madrid: Castalia 1980), here cited at vol. 1, p. 326, for sonnet 32, vol. 2, pp. 202, 195, for the 'Goços' and the 'Canonización,' and vol. 1, p. 165, for the 'Triunfete.' See also Rafael Lapesa, *La obra literaria del Marqués de Santillana* (Madrid: Insula 1957), pp. 236–7.
46 Cf. Lapesa, *La obra literaria*, p. 246: 'Como en toda la producción doctrinal de Santillana, los ejemplos de la antiguedad clásica confluyen aquí con los de la Biblia.' For the medieval love lyric see A.D. Deyermond, 'Pero Meogo's Stags and Fountains: Symbol and Anecdote in the Traditional Lyric,' *Romance Philology*, 33 (1979), pp. 265–83. Deyermond is aware of the importance of the Song of Songs for the motifs of the stags and fountains he traces in world literature: 'I do not propose to deal here ... with the Biblical analogues (especially those of the Song of Songs and the Psalms). It is not that I wish to minimize their importance, but rather that I have nothing to add to what has already been said by other scholars,' p. 280 and n. 46.
47 Fernando de Rojas, *La Celestina*, ed. J. Cejador y Frauca, vol. 1 (Madrid: Espasa-Calpe 1963), pp. 41, 44. For my use of this edition, see chapter 5. See also William D. Truesdell, 'The *Hortus Conclusus* Tradition, and the Implications of Its Absence in the *Celestina*,' *Kentucky Romance Quarterly*, 20 (1973), pp. 257–77.

CHAPTER THREE

1 Alfred Jacob, 'The *Razón de amor* as Christian Symbolism,' *Hispanic Review*, 20 (1952), p. 297

2 S.C. Cockrell, ed., *Old Testament Miniatures* (New York: Brazilier 1969), p. 126. These miniatures were probably painted in Paris around 1250. The manuscript that contains them was acquired in 1916, for the Pierpont Morgan Library, from the collection of Sir Thomas Phillipps.

3 Rene Ribeiro, 'Brazilian Messianic Movements,' in Sylvia L. Thrupp, ed., *Millennial Dreams in Action: Essays in Comparative Study*, (The Hague: Mouton 1962), pp. 55–6. William R. Alger, *A Critical History of the Doctrine of a Future Life* (Philadelphia: George W. Childs 1864)

4 For a discussion of these works see H.H. Rowley, *The Relevance of Apocalyptic: A Study of Jewish and Christian Apocalypses from Danniel to the Revelation*, new and rev. ed. (New York: Association Press 1963). For most of the texts see R.H. Charles, ed., *The Apocrypha and Pseudepigrapha of the Old Testament*, vol. 2, *Pseudipigrapha* (Oxford: Clarendon Press 1973). See also D.S. Russell, *The Method and Message of Jewish Apocalyptic 200 B.C.– A.D. 100* (Philadelphia: Westminster 1974), and James H. Charlesworth, ed., *The Old Testament Pseudepigrapha: Volume I: Apocalyptic Literature and Testaments* (New York: Doubleday 1983).

5 In the compilation of this list, I have relied mainly on Manuel C. Díaz y Díaz, *Index Scriptorum Latinorum Medii Aevi Hispanorum* (Madrid: CSIC 1959).

6 All references to Berceo's *Signos del Juicio Final* will be to the edition by Brian Dutton, *Obras Completas*, vol. 3 (London: Tamesis 1975), pp. 119–44, cited from now on as *Signos*. I have before me also the interesting popular edition by Clemente Canales Toro, Gonzalo de Berceo, *Signos del Juicio Final* (Santiago de Chile: Editorial Universitaria 1955), as well as the edition by Arturo M. Ramoneda (Madrid: Clásicos Castalia 1980), pp. 127–57.

7 James W. Marchand, 'Gonzalo de Berceo's *De los signos que aparescerán ante del Juicio*,' *Hispanic Review*, 45 (1977), pp. 283–95, here at p. 284

8 For Marchand, see ibid.; for Dutton, in addition to his introduction and annotation, see 'The Source of Berceo's *Signos del Juicio Final*,' *Kentucky Romance Quarterly*, 20 (1973), pp. 274–55. See also Joel Saugnieux, 'Berceo y el apocalipsis,' in Claudio García Turza, ed., *Actas de las III jornadas de estudios berceanos* (Logroño: Servicio de cultura de la Excima Diputación Provincial 1981), pp. 161–77.

9 Marchand, 'Gonzalo de Berceo's *De los signos*,' p. 294 and n. 323

10 Jean Longère, ed., *Liber Poenitentialis*, vol. 2 (Louvain: Nauwelaerts; Lille: Librairie Girard 1965), p. 149 and note a, and cf. Migne, *PL*, vol. 83, col. 901.

11 Rowley, *Relevance*, p. 129: 'This apocalyptic work [*The Testament of Abraham*] again has no background of crisis, and is couched throughout in terms of individual eschatology.'

12 T. Batiouchkof, 'Le débat de l'âme et du corps,' *Romania*, 20 (1891), pp. 1–55, 513–78

13 Rosemary Woolf, *English Religious Lyric in the Middle Ages*, (Oxford: Clarendon Press 1968), p. 91

14 It is sometimes too easily assumed that the Spanish versions of the debate have French origins. Even where this might be the case for individual ver-

sions, it must be remembered that the topic as a whole can be documented in Spain earlier than any existing Romance text; see José María Millás Vallicrosa, *La poesía sagrada hebraico-española*, 2nd ed. (Madrid: CSIC 1948), pp. 133, 312–16. Also, Batiouchkof notes the Talmudic roots of some aspects of the theme ('Le débat,' pp. 14, 45, 49, 557, 558), and it is well known that, in terms of Talmudic scholarship in the Middle Ages, Spain surpassed France.

15 I refer to these editions *Disputa*: Ramón Menéndez Pidal, ed., 'La disputa del alma y el cuerpo' *Revista de Archivos, Bibliotecas y Museos*, IV (1900), pp. 451–3; *Tractado*: Cyril A. Jones, ed., 'Tractado del cuerpo: e de la ánima' in 'Algunas versiones más del debate entre el cuerpo y el alma,' *Miscellanea di studi ispanici* (Pisa: Universita di Pisa 1963), pp. 110–34, here at l. 1; *Visión*: José M. Octavio de Toledo, ed., 'Visión de Filiberto,' *Zeitschrift für romanische Philologie*, 2 (1878), pp. 50–60, here at pp. 50–1; Escorial *Revelación*: José M. Octavio de Toledo, ed., 'Revelación de un hermitaño,' *Zeitschrift für romanische Philologie*, 2 (1878), pp. 63–9; Paris *Revelación*: José M. Octavio de Toledo, ed., 'Disputa del cuerpo e del ánima,' *Zeitschrift für romanische Philologie*, 2 (1878), pp. 63–9 printed alongside the Escorial *Revelación* cited above; *Dialogus*: 'Dialogus inter corpus et animam,' in Thomas Wright, ed., *The Latin Poems Commonly Attributed to Walter Mapes* (New York, London: AMS Press 1968), pp. 95–106, here ll. 1, 2, 5.

16 *Revelación*, ed. Octavio de Toledo, p. 63. *Disputa*, ed. Menéndez Pidal, ll. 5–6. *The Apocalypse of Paul*, in M.R. James, ed., *The Apocryphal New Testament* (Oxford: Clarendon Press 1966), pp. 525–55, at pp. 548–9; cf. Batiouchkof, 'Le débat,' p. 30. See also now the introduction and notes to Antonette di Paolo Healey, ed., *The Old English Vision of St. Paul* (Cambridge, Mass.: The Medieval Academy of America 1978).

17 *Disputa*, ed. Menéndez Pidal, l. 5–8; *Visión*, ed. Octavio de Toledo, p. 51, l. 4; *Tractato*, ed. Jones, l. 10

18 For questions of origin: Florence Whyte, *The Dance of Death in Spain and Catalonia* (Baltimore: Waverly Press 1931); Robert Eisler, 'Danse Macabre,' *Traditio*, 6 (1948), pp. 187–225; Mario Gennero, 'Elementos franciscanos en las danzas de la Muerte,' *Thesaurus*, 29 (1974), p. 181–5. For textual criticism: Margherita Morreale, ed., 'Para una antología de Literatura Castellana Medieval: La danza de la Muerte,' *Annali del Corso di Lingue e Litterature straniere*, 6 (1964), pp. 107–72; all *Danza* references are to this edition, although I am aware of the review of it by J. Sola-Solé in *Hispanic Review*, 34 (1968), pp. 538–60. I have before me the edition by C. Appel (*Beiträge zur romanischen und englischen Philolgie* [Breslau: Kommissionverlag von Preuss & Jünger 1902]), which Sola-Solé considers the best, as well as the edition by Sola-Solé (Barcelona: Puvill 1981). I have also before me the edition by Haydée Bermejo Hurtado and Dinko Cvitanovic, *Danza General de la Muerte* (Bahia Blanca: Cuadernos del Sur 1966), and the edition of the Seville 1520 version by José Amador de los Ríos, *Historia críitica de la literatura española* (Madrid 1865), vol. 7, pp. 507–40. Textual matters are also discussed by Sola-Solé in 'El rabí y el alfaquí en la Dança general de la

Muerte,' *Romance Philogogy*, 18 (1965) pp. 272–83, and 'En torno a la *Dança general de la Muerte*,' *Hispanic Review*, 36 (1968), pp. 303–27; L.P. Harvey, 'The *Alfaquí* in *La danca general de la Muerte*,' *Hispanic Review*, 41 (1973), pp. 498–510. For imagery: Roger Walker, '"Potest aliquis gustare quod gustatum affert mortem?" (Job VI, 6): An Aspect of Imagery and Structure in *La Danza General de la Muerte*,' *Medium Aevum*, 41 (1972), pp. 32–8; David Hook and J.R. Williamson, '"Pensastes el mundo por vos trastornar": The World Upside-Down in the *Dança general de la Muerte*,' *Medium Aevum*, 48 (1979), pp. 90–101: Julian Weiss, 'A Note on the Imagery in the *Dança general de la Muerte*,' *La Corónica*, 8 (1979), pp. 35–7. For reflection of contemporary society: A.D. Deyermond, 'El ambiente social e intelectual de la *Danza de la Muerte*,' *Actas del tercer congreso internacional de hispanistas* (Mexico: Colegio de Mexico 1970), pp. 267–76; Julio Rodríguez-Puértolas, *Poesía de protesta en la Edad Media castellana* (Madrid: Gredos 1968), pp. 37–9, 102–25, 283–6. See also Lucio Basalisco, 'Sulla *Danza de la Muerte*,' *Quaderni Ibero-Americani*, 49–50 (1976), pp. 37–46, and two recent articles by Geraldine McKendrick: 'The *Dança de la Muerte* of 1520 and Social Unrest in Seville,' *Journal of Hispanic Philology*, 3 (1979), pp. 239–59, and 'Sevilla y la *Dança de la Muerte* (1520),' *Historia, Instituciones Documentos*, 6 (1979), pp. 187–95. Joel Saugnieux, *Les danses macabres de France et d'Espagne et leur prolongements littéraires* (Lyon: Emmaneul Vitte 1972).

19 Bohigas, *Revista de Filolgía Española*, 20 (1933), p. 75–8, at p. 77. Eisler, 'Danse Macabre,' p. 211, n. 167

20 Morreale numbers the stanzas in Roman numerals and the lines in Arabic numbers, and I follow this system, used also by Appel.

21 Whyte, *The Dance of Death*, p. vii

22 Ibid., p. 3

23 Eleanor P. Hammond, *English Verse Between Chaucer and Surrey* (Durham: Duke University Press, and London: Cambridge University Press 1927), p. 127

24 Berceo, *Signos* (see n. 6), st. 20b. *Visión*, ed. Octavio de Toledo (see n. 15), p. 59. Escorial *Revelación*, ed. Octavio de Toledo, ll. 185–92; Whyte noted (*The Dance of Death*, pp. 15–16) the resemblance of this stanza of the *Revelación* to the *Danza*. For discussion of the estates with particular reference to Chaucer see Jill Mann, *Chaucer and Medieval Estates Satire: The Literature of Social Classes and the 'General Prologue' to the 'Canterbury Tales'* (Cambridge: Cambridge University Press 1973).

25 Berceo, *Signos*; Escorial, *Revelación*, ed. Octavio de Toledo, p. 69, l. 190. *Visión*, ed. Octavio de Toledo, p. 60

26 See the articles, cited above in note 18, by Hook and Williamson, Walker, Weiss, and Deyermond at p. 275.

27 Whyte, *The Dance of Death*, pp. 38–49. Bohigas, review of Whyte's book (see n. 19), p. 76. See Lecoy's review, 'Robert Eisler, "Danse Macabre,"' *Romania*, 71 (1950), pp. 408–12, at p. 412. W. Fehse, *Der Urspung der Totentanze* (Halle: Niemeyer 1907). Eisler, 'Danse Macabre,' *Traditio*, p. 194. Whyte, *The Dance of Death*, pp. 46–7. Leo Spitzer, 'La Danse macabre,' *Mélanges de*

linguistique offerts à Albert Dauzat par ses élèves et ses amis (Paris: D'Artery 1951), pp. 307–21. Hans Sperber, 'The Etymology of "macabre,"' in Anna Granville Hatcher and Karl-Ludwig Selig, eds., *Studio Philologica et Litteraria in Honorem Leo Spitzer* (Bern: Francke 1958), pp. 391–401; see also E.E. DuBruck, 'Another Look at "Macabre,"' *Romania*, 71 (1950), pp. 536–43, at pp. 538–9. Deyermond, 'El ambiente social,' cited above in note 18

28 I have been influenced in my remarks here by a stimulating lecture entitled 'Dance as a Celebration of Life,' given on 30 March 1982 by Dr Pearl Primus, Visiting Professor at the State University of New York at Albany. Dr Primus explained with remarkable effectiveness how all cultures react with dance to crucial points in the life cycle: germination, birth, initiation, marriage, and death; she is not responsible, of course, for any misapplication I may make of her remarks. I am especially grateful to Dr Primus for drawing the ghost dance to my attention. See also R.M. Utley, *The Last Days of the Sioux Nation*, (New Haven: Yale University Press 1963).

29 Whyte, *The Dance of Death*, p. vii

30 Antonio Machado, 'Una noche de verano,' *Campos de Castilla Poesías Completas*, 14th ed. (Madrid: Austral 1973), p. 134

31 For the deaths of Moses and Abraham: Whyte, *The Dance of Death*, pp. 54–5, Rowley, *Relevance*, pp. 128–9; for the Malak 'l Mauti: J.N. Lincoln, 'Aljamiado Texts: Legal and Religious,' *Hispanic Review*, 13 (1945), pp. 102–24

32 Cf. DuBruck, 'Another Look,' pp. 542–3.

33 The two stanzas that deal with the rabbi (LXXXII, LXXXIII) have received attention from those critics concerned with best readings of the text. Sola-Solé claims that the stanzas are a 'burda creación de un autor cristiano, conocedor mediocre de la Biblia' ('El rabí,' p. 274), because of the word 'Elohim,' which, he says, is never used in prayers in the synagogue. Sola-Solé's claim, on this point, is misleading. He is probably influenced by a desire to prove that attempts to read Judaism into *Danza general* are false: 'la falsa idea de que la *DM* es un producto del judaismo hispánico' (review of Morreale's edition, p. 360). But irrespective of the religious beliefs of the author of *Danza general*, the fact is that 'Elohim' occurs frequently in the Hebrew Bible to refer to the one and only God in whom Jews believe: Numbers 15:41; 25:5; 22:9, 11, 12, 20, 22, 38; Leviticus 22:33; Genesis 7:16, and elsewhere. In fact, 'elohim' appears so many times in Genesis that it is used by some biblical scholars to identify two authors in the first book of the Bible, according to the words used for God: 'Elohim' or 'Adonay.' Yehudah Halevi devoted an entire chapter of *The Kuzari* to explain the meaning of the word 'elohim,' summarizing at one point that 'no intelligent person will misunderstand the meaning conveyed by 'Elohim' (trans. Hartwig Hirschfeld [New York: Schocken Books 1974], p. 221). If the author of the *Danza general* was acquainted with elementary Jewish liturgical practice, he would not have put in the mouth of a rabbi the Tetragrammaton as Sola-Solé writes it (p. 275); he would have written either 'Elohim' or 'Adonay.' The form 'Elohim' or 'eloym' in line 569 is therefore correct; it is recited in the

synagogue, by the way, not only when chanted in the Torah but, for example, when the ancient prayer for travellers is recited and the phrase 'the angels of God' is used ('mal^eakhey Elohim,' J.H. Hertz, ed., *The Authorized Daily Prayer Book* [New York: Bloch 1982], pp. 1044–5). The conjunction 'and' ('e') in line 569 is also correct, and implies no 'contraposición ... entre Elohim y el Dios de Abraham,' as Sola-Solé claims (p. 274). The conjunction 'and' is found in the best known Hebrew prayer, the ancient 'Amidah,' which Jews have repeated thrice daily for centuries, and which is a central part of most Jewish services in the synagogue: 'Blessed art thou, O Lord our God *and* God of our fathers, God of Abraham, God of Isaac, *and* God of Jacob, the great, the mighty *and* revered God ...' [*Authorized Prayer Book*, p. 130–1]. This is the prayer which, almost certainly, the author of *Danza general* has in mind as he shapes the words of the rabbi; the phrase 'e Dios de Habrahan' gives the author away, as does the word 'beraha' in line 582; 'beraha' means 'blessing' or 'benediction,' and the Amidah consists of eighteen blessings (sometimes abbreviated to seven and recently expanded to nineteen), the first of which has the phrase 'God of Abraham.' The very first word of the Amidah (and one of the most repeated words in the entire Jewish liturgy) is 'baruch,' meaning 'Blessed,' as above 'Blessed art thou.' This means that, contrary to what Sola-Solé claims (p. 275), the reading of the Seville 1520 version of line 577 must be taken very seriously: 'Vos rabí baruc.' The person who reworked an earlier version to make the one dated 1520, or someone before that person, maybe even the original author, must have realized the play on words between 'baruc' in line 577 and 'beraha' in line 582 of the same stanza; both words have the same Hebrew root, in addition to their connection with the most famous Jewish prayer. This person, whether Jewish or Christian, is certainly not as crude ('burda') as Sola-Solé claims: the author of these two stanzas has at least an elementary knowledge of Jewish liturgical practice.

34 See, for example, A.C. Vega, ed., Apringuis Pacensis Episcopi, *Tractatus in Apocalypsin* (Escorial: Typis Augustinianis Monasterii Escurialensis 1941), p. 48; Marius Férotin, ed., *Apringius de Béja, Commentaire de L'Apocalypse* (Paris: Picard 1900), p. 52. Apringius' commentary was copied extensively, as authoritative, by Beatus, whose commentary was, in its turn, most widely read during the Middle Ages. For Beatus, see *Beati in Apocalipsin Libri Duodecim*, ed. Henry A. Sanders (Rome: American Academy in Rome 1930).

35 *Danza*, ed. Morreale, l. 435

36 Ian Michael, *The Treatment of Classical Material in the 'Libro de Alexandre,'* (Manchester: University Press 1970), p. 249. See also the excellent review article by R.S. Willis, 'The Artistry and Enigmas of the "Libro de Alexandre": A Review Article,' *Hispanic Review*, 42 (1974), pp. 33–42.

37 R.S. Willis, *The Relationship of the Spanish 'Libro de Alexandre' to the 'Alexandreis' of Gautier de Chatillon* (Princeton: Princeton University Press 1934; rpt. New York: Kraus 1965), pp. 66–70; Michael, *Treatment*, pp. 88–175. See also now Marina Scordilis Brownlee, 'Pagan and Christian: The

Bivalent Hero of the *Libro de Alexandre*,' *Kentucky Romance Quarterly*, 30 (1983), pp. 263–70.

38 P.A. Bly and A.D. Deyermond, 'The Use of *Figura* in the *Libro de Alexandre*, *The Journal of Medieval and Renaissance Studies*, 2 (1972), pp. 151–81, at p. 179 and n. 72.

39 For more information about these roles see A.R. Anderson, *Alexander's Gate, Gog and Magog, and the Inclosed Nations* (Cambridge, Mass.: Medieval Academy of America 1932); George Cary, *The Medieval Alexander* (Cambridge: University Press 1956, rpt. 1967), esp. pp. 133–4; Bernard McGinn, *Visions of the End, Apocalyptic Traditions in the Middle Ages* (New York: Columbia University Press 1979) esp. pp. 44, 70–3; María Rosa Lida de Malkiel, 'Alejandro en Jerusalén,' *Romance Philology*, 10 (1956–7), pp. 185–96.

40 Stanza references are to the composite numbers of the parallel edition by R.S. Willis (see n. 37).

41 I rely here mainly on Michael, 'Appendix 1: Division of the Libro de Alexandre into Episodes together with the Source References' (*Treatment*, pp. 287–93), especially on his definition of original 'to mean that the episode has no known source and appears to be original with the Spanish poet' (p. 287).

42 See Ian Michael, 'The Description of Hell in the Spanish Libro de Alexandre,' in Frederick Whitehead, ed., *Medieval Miscellany Presented to Eugene Vinaver* (Manchester: Manchester University Press 1965), pp. 220–9.

43 I give the reading here, as elsewhere, of MS P. MS O reads 'por vengar su despecho y por precio ganar,' but the preposition 'y,' from an apocalyptic standpoint, increases rather than removes the ambivalence.

44 Peter Comestor, *Historia Scholastica*, Migne, *PL*, vol. 198, col. 1456; see also Cary, *Medieval Alexander*, p. 292, n. 42. Other details included by the Spanish poet, the bear and the lion, may have come from biblical verses also associated with Alexander the Great: Daniel 7:1–28, the chapter about the four beasts – a bear, a lion, a leopard, and a ten-horned dragon. Alexander was usually associated with the fourth beast, the ten-horned dragon, but the Spanish poet seems to be amalgamating parts of the other animals to create an apocalyptic 'travesura' (stanza 153) that would instil fear in Dario.

45 Although in this final line MS O has a more apocalyptic, hence perhaps more authentic, ring than MS P, this adds nothing to the debate about authorship. Berceo, as we have seen, was an apocalyptic writer, but so might have been other contemporaries of his. It is also conceivable that Juan Lorenzo de Astorga or any other poet could have made a felicitous emendation to the last line of the original poem.

46 Michael (*Treatment*, pp. 263–6) has argued convincingly that 'el peor lugar' often means Hell. See also Alfonso's *Cantigas*, number 123, ll. 32, 51 (Mettmann, ed., vol. 2, p. 64).

47 See, for example, María Rosa Lida de Malkiel, *La idea de la fama en la Edad Media castellana* (Mexico: Fondo de Cultura Económica 1952), pp. 167–97, and Michael, *Treatment*, pp. 55–60.

48 I do not mean to imply here, or elsewhere, that the author of *Alexandre* knew the Koran or its commentaries.

49 See Niall J. Ware, 'The Date of Composition of the *Libro de Alexandre*: A Re-examination of Stanza 1799,' *Bulletin of Hispanic Studies*, 42 (1965), pp. 252–5, and Willis, *Relationship*, pp. 73–4. Ware's is an admirable attempt to solve the problem, but he is forced to assume things that might have been otherwise. There were many other chronologies in use besides Isidore's, on which Ware relies. Julian of Toledo counted 5325 years from the creation of the world to the birth of Christ (*Prognosticon PL*, vol. 96, col. 584), not 5196 years as Ware supposes after Isidore (p. 254). And, how do we know that medieval writers did not also make 'the common error of allowing for a non-existent year O' (p. 254)?

50 Willis was tempted by a similar speculation, but not for apocalyptic reasons: 'Or Alfonso el Sabio, descended from the Hohenstaufens through his mother, might, either as *infante* or new king, have been in the mind of the poet who was so evidently a partisan of the old imperial Latin–European tradition ... The suspicion also arises that the author might consciously or subconsciously have been resisting the cultural trend symbolized, though of course not initiated, by Alfonso with his learned Moslem and Jewish collaborators; and he thus might have executed his work as a bulwark against the tide: the old myth of Latin Visigothic Hispania opposing the emerging actuality of España,' "Mester de Clerecía." A Definition of the *Libro de Alexandre*, *Romance Philology*, 10 (1956–7), p. 223.

51 Antonio Ballesteros-Beretta, *Alfonso el Sabio* (Barcelona: Salvat 1963), pp. 153–74. The date 1256 is, for some critics, too late for the composition of *Alexandre*. For a recent summary of the problem of dating see the edition by Jesus Cañas Murillo (Madrid: Editora Nacional 1978), 19–25. I know of no definitive reason why *Fernán González*, which cites *Alexandre*, could not have been written after 1256. Willis suggests a date after 1248 for the composition of *Alexandre* in 'The Artistry,' *Hispanic Review*, 42 (1974), p. 36. María Eugenia Lacarra establishes that *Fernán González* could not have been written before 1264 because of the reference in stanza 3390a to 'aven-marinos': 'El Significado histórico del *Poema de Fernán González*,' *Studi Ispanici* (197(), 19–20. See also Emilio Alarcos Llorach, '¿Berceo, autor del *Alexandre*?' in *Actos de Las III jornadas* (cited above n. 8), pp. 11–18.

52 The recent 'reconstrucción crítica' by Dana A. Nelson is oriented more towards linguistic rather than literary annotation (Gonzalo de Berceo, *El Libro de Alexandre* [Madrid: Gredos 1979]). As I write, I have not seen the edition by Ian Michael announced in A.D. Deyermond, *Historia y crítica de la literatura española: edad media* (Barcelona: Crítica 1979), p. 133. Cañas Murillo cites numerous biblical references in his notes.

53 *Tractado*, ed. Jones (see n. 15), p. 15, l. 14. *Disputa*, ed. Menéndez Pidal, l. 5. *Visión*, ed. Octavio, l. 12

54 See María Rosa Lida de Malkiel, *La idea de la fama*, pp. 196–7; Michael, *Treatment*, pp. 108–11; and cf. Whyte, *The Dance of Death*, p. 59 and n. 25. Compare Cañas Murillo, ed., *Alexandre*, pp. 510, 514–15.

55 These computations are based on the editions of the Escorial manuscript by Erminio Polidori, ed., *Poema de Fernán González* (Taranto: Semerano 1962), and Ramón Menéndez Pidal, *Reliquias de la poesía épica española*, 2nd ed. (Madrid: Gredos 1980), pp. 39–176. All quotations from the poem refer to Menéndez Pidal's edition.

56 See, for example, J.P. Keller, 'The Structure of the *Poema de Fernán González*,' *Hispanic Review*, 25 (1957), 235–46; Joaquín Gimeno Casalduero, 'Sobre la composición del *Poema de Fernán González*,' *Estructura y diseño en la literature castellana medieval* (Madrid: Porrúa Turanza 1975), 31–64; and Graciela Brevedan, 'Estudio estructural del *Poema de Fernán González*,' PHD diss., University of Kentucky, 1977.

57 The interpretation of Gog and Magog changed as history changed. As A.R. Anderson explains, 'the term Gog and Magog has therefore become synonymous with barbarian, especially with the type of barbarian that bursts through the northern frontier of civilization. This frontier extends the whole length of the Eurasian continent from the Atlantic to the Pacific, from Spain to China,' (*Alexander's Gate* [see n. 39], pp. 3–14, at p. 8). Depending on the historical circumstances therefore, Gog and Magog was interpreted variously by apocalypticists as Scythians, Goths, Moors, Jews, Huns, Alans, Khazars, Turks, Magyars, Parthians, and Mongols. To the authorities cited by Anderson, St. Augustine should be added because he interprets Gog and Magog as the Goths and Moors in the *City of God* (20:11). Anderson (pp. 10–11) gives the relevant quotations from Isidore.

58 The texts are Ezekiel 38–39, especially 38:1–3, and Revelation 20, especially 20:7. For Apringius, see A.C. Vega, ed., *Apringii Pacensis Episcopi Tractatus in Apocalypsin* (Escorial: Typis Augustinianis Monasterii Escurialensis 1940), p. 62, and M. Férotin, *Apringius de Béja: son commentaire de l'Apocalypse* (Paris: Picard 1900), p. 67. Vega and Férotin cite and comment upon Isidore's reference to Apringius's authority on pages vii–ix and v–x, respectively, of their editions.

59 'Il faut ajouter que l'évêque catholique de Béja vivait sous la domination des Wisigoths Ariens, et cette circonstance explique suffisamment, nous semble t-il, le choix du livre sacré qu'il a pris pour texte de son commentaire ... le nom des Ariens ne se rencontre jamais sous sa plume,' Férotin, *Apringius*, p. xxii–xxiii.

60 Cf. Alonso Zamora Vicente, ed., *Poema de Fernán González*, 2nd ed. (Madrid: Espasa-Calpe 1963), p. 22. Zamora Vicente copies without comment or correction in a footnote to this line, a garbled passage from the 1541 edition by Florián de Ocampo of the *Cuarta Crónica General*. The passage refers to the prophecy of Jeremiah, not of Daniel, and the verse should read 'Vox in Rama, not 'Vox in Roma' (see Matthew 2:17–18, and Jeremiah 31:15).

61 Samuel G. Armistead, 'La perspectiva histórica del *Poema de Fernán González*,' *Papeles de Son Armadans*, 21 91961), pp. 9–18; G. Davis, 'National Sentiment in the *Poema de Fernán González* and in the *Poema de Alfonso Onceno*,' *Hispanic Review*, 16 (1948), pp. 61–8; María Eugenia Lacarra, 'El

significado histórico del *Poema de Fernán González*,' *Studi Ispanici* 1979, pp. 9–41. Louis Chalon shows that stanzas 34 to 104 of *Fernán González* ignore historical documents about Visigothic Spain: 'L'effondrement de L'Espagne visigothique et l'invasion musulmane selon le *Poema de Fernán González*,' *Anuario de estudios medievales*, 9 (1974–9), pp. 353–63.

62 For a convenient list of textual resemblances see the edition cited above (n. 60) by Alonso Zamora Vicente, pp. xiii–xv, and María Rosa Lida de Malkiel, *La idea de la fama*, pp. 201–7.

63 On the legend, see Cary, the *Medieval Alexander*, pp. 264–5, 350–1.

64 Lacarra, 'El significado,' p. 34: 'El autor no quiere incitar a los castellanos de su tiempo a la lucha contra el infiel, que en el momento en que escribe ha sido reducido a la impotencia.' She does not compare loss of life in *Fernán González* with *Alexandre* but with the *Cid*.

65 See also *Fernán González*, st. 488.

66 A.D. Deyermond, *Epic Poetry and the Clergy: Studies on the 'Mocedades de Rodrigo'* (London: Tamesis 1969), pp. 62–3; Lacarra, 'El significado,' pp. 11–14. Some critics have noticed the apocalyptic element in *Fernán González* but they do not link the work with the apocalypic tradition in Spain. Thus D.W. Foster noted that, in the text, Castile is the 'chosen land of the chosen people,' that the poet accommodates 'the Jewish theme of divine election' and underlines 'Spain's own "Babylonian"' captivity; but for Foster these themes are aspects of 'Christian allegory' (*Christian Allegory in Early Hispanic Poetry*, Studies in Romance Languages, no. 4 [Lexington: The University Press of Kentucky 1970], pp. 46–59). Likewise, Beverly West has recently noted that in the poem Fernán González is 'a messianic figure,' but for West, this portrayal of the hero if due to 'monastic influence'; see *Epic, Folk, and Christian Traditions in the Poema de Fernán González*, (Potomac: Studia Humanitatis 1983), pp. 112, 110.

67 See also *Fernán González*, st. 25.

68 Lacarra, 'El significado,' p. 14

69 All quotations are from the edition of *Zifar* by C.P. Wagner (Ann Arbor: University of Michigan Press 1929; rpt. New York: Kraus 1971), because it lists variants of the Paris manuscript and the Seville edition. Magog is alluded to in passing at p. 504, l. 5. For a summary of the contents of *Zifar* see C.P. Wagner, 'The Sources of *El Cavallero Cifar*,' *Revue Hispanique*, 10 (1903), p. 17. The need for a new edition has been attested to recently by Marilyn Olsen, 'A Reappraisal of Methodology in Medieval Editions: The Extant Material of the *Libro del cavallero Zifar*,' *Romance Philology*, 35 (1981–2), pp. 508–15, 'Three Observations on the *Zifar*,' *La Corónica*, 8 (1980), pp. 146–8, and in her edition of the Paris manuscript, Spanish Series, no. 16 (Madison: Seminary of Medieval Studies 1984) p.v. I have carefully checked all quotations in this section on the *Zifar* against Olsen's edition of P, and I have found no discrepancies between Wagner's edition and Olsen's except, of course, that Wagner's contains information on variant readings. It would have been easier to compare both editions if Olsen had numbered chapters and noted where her readings of P differed from Wagner's.

70 See, for example, Eliyahu Ashtor, *The Jews in Moslem Spain*, trans. A. and E. Klein, 2 vols. (Philadelphia: Jewish Publication Society of America 1973), vol. 1, p 383.
71 Cf. R.M. Walker, *Tradition and Technique in El Libro de Cavallero Zifar* (London: Tamesis 1974), p. 30: 'there could have been very few people in Spain in the fourteenth century who knew Syriac well enough to undertake a full-scale translation.' Walker states that '*caldeo*, strictly speaking, means' Syriac (p. 32) but he does not say whether he understands Syriac to refer also to Aramaic. He prefers to understand that *caldeo* means Arabic, since it 'can be used to mean both Syriac and Arabic' (p. 32). I agree with Walker 'that the *Zifar* author's claim that the ultimate source of his work is *caldeo* deserves much more serious attention than it has received in the past' (p. 33), but by *caldeo* I understand Aramaic, not Arabic. For the Council of Vienne and the University of Salamanca, see Hastings Rashdall, *The Universities of Europe in the Middle Ages*, eds., F.M. Powicke and A.B. Emden, 3 vols. (Oxford: Oxford University Press 1936), vol 2, p. 88, and vol. 1, p. 566n. It should also be remembered that some classical apocalyptic works (like Daniel, and parts of Esdras) were written originally in Aramaic.
72 Francisco J. Hernández, 'Ferrán Martínez, "Escrivano del Rey," canónigo de Toledo, y autor del *Zifar*,' *Revista de archivos bibliotecas y museos*, 81 (1978), pp. 289–325, at p. 290
73 Américo Castro et al., eds. *Biblia medieval romanceada* (Buenos Aires: Instituto de Filología 1927); O.H. Hauptmann, ed., *Escorial Bible, I.j.4; Pentateuch*, (Philadelphia: University of Pennsylvania Press 1953)
74 Walker, *Tradition and Technique*, p. 37
75 James F. Burke, *History and Vision: The Figural Structure of the Libro del Cavallero Zifar* (London: Tamesis 1972), pp. 41, 40, 118. Although Burke thought that 'redde quod debes' was not a biblical text, it is found in Matthew 18:28, but it does not have anything to do with redeeming a family inheritance there; rather it has to do with forgiving a burdensome debt. Burke was forced to come up with a text because he was convinced that *Zifar* is structured like a sermon. He chose a text to which the author of *Zifar* does not refer, and which in its own context is contrary to what is implied in *Zifar*. Whereas in Matthew 18 a burdensome pledge is to be forgiven by the creditor, in *Zifar* (and in Ezekiel 18) a pledge however burdensome is to be assiduously redeemed at all costs: 'e ciertas sy costas grandes fizo el Arcidiano ... lo enpleó muy bien ... asý commo lo deven fazer todos los omes' (p. 6, ll. 1–5). Literally, the pledges in *Zifar* that are to be restored are: the one Ferrán Martínez made to the Spanish Cardinal before he died, and the one Zifar made to his grandfather before he died; from these two pledges can be derived numerous other symbolic pledges in *Zifar* that characters owe to each other and to God.
76 This reference to eating 'upon the mountains' helps us to understand how skilfully the author of *Zifar* conflates his material. Zifar lost his son, Garfin, to a lioness at the side of a mountain (p. 85), after he had eaten a morning meal and was relaxing indolently in the lap of his wife. Subsequently,

he tells the *ribaldo* that he no longer eats in the morning (p. 123, l. 23), and he later teaches his sons to heed the advice of older wiser men because the young men eat in the morning (p. 327, ll. 5–15). The reference, to a young king whose advisers eat in the morning, is to Ecclesiastes 10:16, 'Woe to you, O land, when your king is a child, and your princes feast in the morning.' The reference, to a young king who takes the advice of young men over old, is to 1 Kings 12:6–15 where Rehoboam (after whom Roboán is named) is described ignoring the advice of elders. The text in Ezekiel that mentions eating on the mountains has to do with idolatry and the practice of sacrificing to many gods on hilltop altars; Zifar's ancestors, the lineage of Shem, were idolators. The author of *Zifar* has therefore subtly conflated texts from Ezekiel, Ecclesiastes, and 1 Kings to suit his purpose.

77 The 'tokaḥa,' or 'warning,' passage is part of what some biblical scholars call the 'holiness code.'

78 The anecdote is discussed by J.H. Hertz, ed., *The Pentateuch and Haftorahs* (London: Soncino Press 1980), p. 564.

79 Burke (*History and Vision*, pp. 101–2) discusses leprosy as a moral disease, but he does not mention Nasón's punishment by maiming in this connection, and he does not note the apocalyptic connection with Leviticus 19:16 and with Ezekiel 22:9.

80 Hernández, 'Ferrán Martínez,' pp. 293, 299–319, 319–25, 303

81 For the name Nasón, see also Numbers 1:7; 7:12,17; 10:14; Ruth 4:20; 1 Chronicles 2:10,11. One cannot rule out entirely the possibility of an ethnic stereotype in the name Nasón, which could refer to a large nose (cf. Quevedo's sonnet *A una nariz*: 'era Ovidio Nasón más Narizado … / las doce tribus de narices era').

82 For the derivation of Farán, see the posthumous article by María Rosa Lida de Malkiel (edited by Yakov Malkiel), 'Las sectas judías y los procuradores romanos. En torno a Josefo y su influjo sobre la literatura española,' *Hispanic Review*, 39 (1971), pp. 183–213, esp. pp. 186–7, n. 3; pp. 188–9, 194, 210–11. María Rosa Lida was probably aware that Josephus was not the only possible source for the passage from the *Zifar* since she calls the latter a 'curiosa reelaboración' of the former (p. 188).

83 Kenneth R. Scholberg, 'The Structure of the *Caballero Cifar*,' *Modern Language Notes*, 79 (1964), pp. 113–24; Walker, *Tradition and Technique*; Burke, *History and Vision*; R.G. Keightley, 'The Story of Zifar and the Structure of the *Zifar*,' *Modern Language Review*, 73 (1978); I agree with Keightley's division of the work into three, rather than four, main parts. See also the article by Marta Ana Diz cited below in note 88, the edition of *Zifar* by Cristina González (Madrid: Catedra 1983), and Cristina González, '*El caballero Zifar*' y el reino lejano (Madrid: Gredos 1984).

84 For interlacing, see Walker, *Tradition and Technique*, pp. 102–6; for preaching, see Burke, *History and Vision*, pp. 39–54 and passim, and also his 'The *Zifar* and the Medieval University Sermon,' *Viator* 1 (1970), pp. 207–21.

85 For an example of a body-and-soul narrative that uses the journey to Rome for penance in a Jubilee year, see the discussion of the *Romiatge del Ventu-*

ros *Pelegré* in Florence Whyte, *The Dance of Death*, pp. 60–7; see also *Alexandre*, stanza 200.

86 See p. 7, l. 15; p. 66, l. 18; p. 147, l. 20; p. 190, l. 3; p. 207, l. 22; p. 208, l. 1; p. 274, l. 11; p. 275; p. 276, l. 6; pp. 302–03; p. 323, l. 4; p. 339, l. 16; p. 341, l. 2; p. 359, l. 22; all of chap. 167; all of chap. 176; p. 403, l. 4; p. 412, l. 8; p. 475, l. 11; p. 489, l. 24; p. 499, l. 22; p. 516, l. 10.

87 Some critics might object that the King of Spain is nowhere addressed in *Zifar*. One reply to this objection is that it is quite unlikely that Zifar, an ancient Chaldean King, would have been able to give advice to his children about Jesus Christ. The anachronism, deliberately patent, invites the reader to compare Zifar with other kings. Any intelligent reader would have thought to compare Zifar with the king of his own country, even if only for the simple reason that they were both kings. About the name Zifar I am not sure that we fully understand it and other names in the book. Most of the work on names has been done by Burke, but he adopts a decidedly Arabic approach, which may be correct. It would be wiser, however, and perhaps more precise to take the author's clue and adopt an Aramaic approach to the meaning of the names in *Zifar*.

88 More recent attempts to explain the composition of *Zifar* include an article by R.G. Keightley, 'Models and Meanings for *Zifar*,' *Mosaic*, 12ii (1979), pp. 55–73. Keightley sets up a number of hurriedly constructed straw models for *Zifar* and blows them all apart in order to prove, it seems, that 'our personal responses are the product of our separate experiences and our individual devotions' (p. 72). He also reviews the books by Burke and Walker in *Romanistisches Jahrbuch*, 26 (1975), pp. 372–5. See also Marta Ana Diz, 'La construcción del *Cifar*,' *Nueva revista de filología hispánica*, 28 (1979), pp. 105–17, a superbly written formalist analysis of the structure of *Zifar*. Diz's analysis demonstrates how useful good structural analysis can be, and at the same time, how structuralism can be appreciably enhanced by a good hermeneutic approach. For example, Diz concludes by noting, correctly, the importance of the father/son relationship to the structure of *Zifar*: 'El Cifar presenta dos elementos que permiten reconstruir un círculo completo (padre-hijo-padre; maestro-discípulo-maestro),' p. 117. Thus far structuralism. What hermeneutics adds to this correct but incomplete analysis of the structure of *Zifar* is the precise location of this father/son teacher/student relationship within the apocalyptic tradition. In apocalyptic terms, the father/son relationship in *Zifar* can be understood as the need for a family's redeemer to correct the sins of the fathers of a prior generation and maintain the family's inheritance by passing on proper instruction to his sons and future generations. See also by Diz, 'El motivo de la partida del caballero en el *Cifar*,' *Kentucky Romance Quarterly*, 28 (1981), pp. 3–11, 'El mundo de las armas en el *Libro del Caballero Cifar*,' *Bulletin of Hispanic Studies*, 56 (1979), pp. 189–99, and 'El discurso de nobleza en el *Cifar* y la carta de Dido,' *Thesaurus*, 35 (1980), pp. 98–109; and on the prologue, Fernando Gómez Redondo, 'El prólogo de *Cifar*: Realidad, ficción y poética,' *Revista de filología española*, 61 (1981), pp. 85–112.

89 Bernard McGinn, *Visions of the End: Apocalyptic Traditions in the Middle Ages* (New York: Columbia University Press 1979), pp. 253, 254

90 All quotations and stanza numbers will be from the edition of Jacques Joset, *Pero López de Ayala, Libro rimado del palacio*, 2 vols. (Madrid: Alhambra 1978), here p. 23. Joset's numbering of the stanzas differs from that of Michel Garcia, *Libro de Poemas o Rimado de Palacio*, 2 vols. (Madrid: Gredos 1978) because he repeats a refrain at his stanza 776 and 778 which the manuscripts and Garcia omit. Forty-eight stanzas have been lost to missing folios; thus Joset arrives at 2170 stanzas in the following way: 2120 surviving stanzas plus two stanzas repeated at 776 and 778, plus 48 lost stanzas; Garcia numbers 2168. Garcia's edition is esepcially useful because it includes an edition of *Job* and the *Magna Moralia* according to manuscripts available to Ayala. For textual relationships between Gregory's *Magna Moralia* and López de Ayala see the articles of José Luis Coy, listed by Garcia (vol. 2, p. 392). See also the edition by Germán Orduna, *Pero López de Ayala, Rimado de Palacio*, 2 vols. (Pisa: Giardini 1981).

91 Joset, ed., *Libro rimado del palacio*, p. 23

92 *Zifar*, ed. Wagner, p. 275, l. 13; p. 258, l. 14

93 See E.B. Strong, 'The *Rimado de Palacio*: López de Ayala's Rimed Confession,' *Hispanic Review*, 37 (1969), pp. 439–51. Because he was not thinking in terms of the apocalyptic tradition, Strong finds a conflict in the composition of the work between the confession and the constant need to moralize. The confession itself can be said to begin at stanza 7, even though the section on the Ten Commandments begins at stanza 21. The first six stanzas of the work as an invocation to the Trinity. Strong was, of course, aware of the impact of the schism on López de Ayala: see 'The *Rimado de Palacio*: López de Ayala's Proposals for Ending the Great Schism,' *Bulletin of Hispanic Studies*, 38 (1961), 64–77.

94 Cf. *Zifar*, ed. Wagner, p. 327, l. 10.

95 For a discussion of these references to Job see Lawrence L. Besserman, *The Legend of Job in the Middle Ages* (Cambridge, Mass.: Harvard University Press 1979), pp. 33–5, 57–69, cited here at p. 58.

96 See also stanzas 1053, 1075, 1146, 1187, 1395–8, 1436, 1532, 1608.

97 Roger Boase, *The Troubadour Revival: A Study of Social Change and Traditionalism in Late Medieval Spain* (London: Routledge & Kegan Paul 1978), p. 161. The number 900 is cited by Boase on p. 3 and is based on information in J. Steunou and L. Knapp, *Bibliografía de los cancioneros castellanos del siglo XV repertorio de sus géneros poéticos*, 2 vols. (Paris: Centre National de la Recherche Scientifique 1975–8). Steunou and Knapp's work is now superseded by Brian Dutton et al., *Catálago-Indice de la poesía cancioneril del siglo XV*, Bibliographic Series, No. 3 (Madison: Hispanic Seminary of Medieval Studies 1982); Dutton's *Catálogo-Indice* lists 815 poets (p. viii).

98 Micer Francicso Imperial, '*El dezir a las syete virtudes*' y otros poemas, ed. Colbert Nepaulsingh, Clásicos Castellanos (Madrid: Espasa-Calpe 1977). Page and line numbers in parentheses refer to this edition only.

99 C.R. Post, 'The Sources of Juan de Mena,' *Romanic Review* 3 (1912), pp. 223–79, at pp. 268–9

100 Ibid., 268

101 Ibid., 272

102 See Miguel Pérez Priego, *Juan de Mena, Obra Lírica* (Madrid: Alhambra 1979), pp. 43–4, 268–75. The *Debate*, more commonly known as *Coplas de los siete pecados mortales*, has been edited recently (together with its continuation by Gómez Manrique) by Gladys M. Rivera, vol. 1 (Potomac: Studia Humanitatis 1982); Rivera is preparing a second volume with the continuations of Pero Guillén de Segovia and Fray Jerónimo de Olivares (vol. 1, p. ix).

103 I have reservations about whether the title of *Laberinto* is either authentic or appropriate, but a study of these reservations would be better placed in a history of medieval Spanish titles. Similar reservations can be expressed about titles such as Berceo's *Signos, Rimado, Buen amor, Razón*. It is well known that, at the end of the medieval period, the title of *Celestina* enters the artistic fabric of the work as a point of debate in the prologue; at the beginning of the medieval period titles have a different (at first glance less important) role.

104 María Rosa Lida de Malkiel, *Juan de Mena, poeta del prerenacimento español* (Mexico: Colegio de Mexico 1950), pp. 15, 534; her source study, 'El contenido episódico,' is at pp. 20–83.

105 Ibid., pp. 50–1

106 Rafael Lapesa, 'El elemento moral en el *Laberinto* de Mena: su influjo en la disposición de la obra,' *Hispanic Review*, 26 (1959), pp. 257–66

107 Joaquín Gimeno Casalduero, 'Notas sobre el *Laberinto*,' *Modern Language Notes*, 798 (1964), pp. 125–39, at pp. 128, 130

108 Philip O. Gericke, 'The Narrative Structure of *Laberinto*,' *Romance Philology*, 21 (1968) pp. 512–22, at p. 515

109 For Mena's explanation of the composition of the *Calamicleos*, see Juan de Mena, *La coronación*, Toulouse, 1489?, facsimile reproduction of the copy in the library of the Hispanic Society of America, Valencia: Artes Gráficas Soler, 1964, fol. iv. I am grateful to Professor Louise V. Fainberg for making a copy of this edition available to me.

110 Dorothy Clotelle Clarke, *Juan de Mena's Laberinto de Fortuna: Classic Epic and Mester de clerecía* (University of Mississippi: Romance Monographs 1971)

111 McGinn, *Visions of the End*, (see n. 89), pp. 20–1

112 Gericke, 'The Narrative Structure,' p. 513

113 Lida de Malkiel, *Juan de Mena*, p. 534

114 Clarke, *Juan de Mena's Laberinto de Fortuna*, pp. 11–40

115 All references to *Laberinto* are from the edition of Louise Vasvari Fainberg (Madrid: Alhambra 1976), reviewed by John G. Cummins in the *Bulletin of Hispanic Studies*, 56 (1979), pp. 58–9. I have other editions before me, including the one by Cummins (Madrid: Cátedra 1979) reviewed by Fainberg in *Hispanic Review*, 50 (1982), pp. 93–5.

116 Imperial, *Juan II* (see n. 98), ll. 2, 4; *Syete virtudes*, ll. 9–10, 13–14

117 Gericke, 'The Narrative Structure,' p. 515
118 Luis Beltrán, citing El Brocense in support, makes this point in 'The Poet, the King, and the Cardinal Virtues in Juan de Mena's *Laberinto*,' *Speculum*, 46 (1971), pp. 318–32, at p. 318.
119 Ibid., p. 321–2; Fainberg, ed., *Laberinto*, pp. 22–3. Beltrán, 'The Poet,' p. 330
120 John D. Sinclair, *Dante's Paradiso*, (Oxford University Press, 1939; rpt. New York 1969), p. 484
121 John Freccero, 'The Final Image: *Paradiso* XXXIII, 144,' *Modern Language Notes*, 789 (1964), pp. 14–27; see also Benvenuto da Imola's commentary on these pages in J.P. Lacaita, ed., *Comentum super Dantis Aldigherij* (Florence: Barbéra 1887), vol. 5, pp. 523–6.
122 See Edmond Faral, *Les arts poétiques du XIIᵉ et du XIIIᵉ siècle* (1924: rpt. Paris: Honoré Champion 1962), p. 87; and Giovanni Mari, 'Poetria et rithmica magistri Johannis anglici de arte prosayca metrica,' *Romanische Forschungen*, 13 (1902), pp. 883–965, at p. 900.
123 Berceo, *Signos* (see n.6), st. 55
124 In the Newberry Library and the library of the University of Michigan at Ann Arbor there are maps which once belonged to copies of a Beatus manuscript at Sever. I have seen a microfilm copy of one of the maps at the Newberry Library: 'S. Beati Liebanensis Mappam Mundi ad exemplar ecclesiae Sancti Severi quod nunc Parisiis asservatur primum integram edidit Conradus Miller, 1889 ... Nova editio n.p. 1929.' On the mapamundi in general see Lida de Malkiel, *Juan de Mena*, pp. 30–47.
125 *Alexandre* (see n. 37), sts. 276–94, 2508–13, 2376–85; *Zifar* (see n. 69), pp. 503–5
126 K. Kohler, The Apocalypse of Abraham and Its Kindred,' *Jewish Quarterly Review*, 7 (1895), p. 593.
127 Beltrán, 'The Poet,' p. 323. Fainberg ed., *Laberinto*, p. 26
128 Ibid., p. 325
129 Cited in ibid., p. 331, n. 15
130 Imperial, *Juan* II (see n. 98), ll. 118, 373, 373–4
131 Beltrán, 'The Poet,' p. 322. Fainberg, ed. *Laberinto*, p. 27
132 Gimeno Casalduero, 'Notas,' p. 127
133 Gericke, 'The Narrative Structure,' p. 521
134 Ibid.
135 For an interesting interpretation of the world 'labertino' as 'book,' and for some political observations correctly deduced from the work, see Alan D. Deyermond, 'Structure and Style as Instruments of Propaganda in Juan de Mena's *Laberinto de Fortuna*, '*Proceedings of the Patristic, Medieval* and *Renaissance Conference*, 5 (1980), 159–67.
136 Gericke, 'The Narrative Structure,' p. 514; cf. Lida de Malkiel, *Juan de Mena*, pp. 22–3

CHAPTER FOUR

1 *Cid* (see chap. 1, n. 30), l. 381
2 Juan de Mena, *La coronación* (see chap. 3, n. 109), fol. 1

3 Felix Lecoy, *Recherches sur le 'Libro de buen amor' de Juan Ruiz Archiprê-tre de Hita* with a New Prologue, Supplementary Bibliography, and Index by A.D. Deyermond (1938; Farnborough: Gregg International 1974), pp. xxi–xxii

4 Ibid., p. 352: 'A qui lit de bout en bout le *Libro de Buen Amor*, sans idée pré-conçue, il apparaît immédiatement que l'essentiel de l'ouvrage est consti-tuée par deux corps de récits indépendants, mais qui présentent, chacun de leur côte une unité de conception et de développement bien marquée ...'
For the adaptation of *Pamphilus* see G.B. Gybbon-Monypenny, "'Dixe la por te dar ensienpro": Juan Ruiz's Adaptation of the *Pamphilus*,' in G.B. Gybbon-Monypenny, ed., *'Libro de buen amor' Studies* (London: Tamesis 1970), pp. 123–47

5 R.M. Walker, 'Towards an Interpretation of the *LIbro de buen amor*,' *Bulletin of Hispanic Studies*, 43 (1966), p. 10

6 'Symmetry of Form in the *Libro de buen amor*,' *Philological Quarterly*, 51 (1972), p. 76.

7 Ibid., p. 74, n. 1; pp. 83–4.

8 Walker, 'Towards an Interpretation,' pp. 4, 10

9 Myers, 'Symmetry of Form,' pp. 79, n. 8, 83–4

10 Américo Castro, *The Structure of Spanish History*, trans. E.L. King (Prince-ton: Princeton University Press 1954), p. 393. María Rosa Lida de Malkiel, 'Nuevas notas para la interpretación del *Libro de buen amor*,' *Nueva revista de filología hispánica*, 13 (1959), p. 19

11 Castro, *Structure of Spanish History*, pp. 402–3

12 St Augustine, *Confessions* (Harmondsworth: Penguin 1961), Bk. 2: 2, p. 44; Bk. 2:5, p. 48

13 Ibid., Bk. 1:7, p. 27

14 Lida de Malkiel, 'Nuevas notas,' p. 23

15 Francisco Rico, 'Sobre el origen de la autobiografía en el *Libro de Buen Amor*,' *Anuario de estudios medievales*, 4 (1967), p. 312. See also G.B. Gybbon-Monypenny, 'Autobiography in the *Libro de buen amor*,' in the Light of some Literary Comparisons,' *Bulletin of Hispanic Studies*, 34 (1957), pp. 63–78

16 Leo Spitzer, 'En torno al arte del Arcipreste de Hita,' in *Lingüística e histo-ria literaria* (Madrid: Gredos 1955), pp. 129, 132. The original version of this article was published in German in 1936.

17 Otis H. Green, *Spain and the Western Tradition* (Madison: University of Wisconsin Press, 1968), vol. 1, p. 36

18 Edgar Paiewonsky Conde, 'Polarización erótica medieval y estructura del *Libro de Buen Amor*,' *Bulletin Hispanique*, 74 (1972), p. 332

19 Anthony N. Zahareas, *The Art of Juan Ruiz, Archpriest of Hita* (Madrid: Estudios de Literatura Española 1965), p. 44, n. 52; p. 45; p. 43, n. 50

20 Spitzer, 'En torno al arte,' pp. 117, 118, 123

21 Francis X. Weiser, *Handbook of Christian Feasts and Customs* (New York: Deus Books 1963), p. 139

22 Zahareas, *The Art*, pp. 6, 59–60. Paiewonsky Conde, 'Polarización,' p. 352

23 Paiewonsky Conde, 'Polarización,' p. 352. Spitzer, 'En torno al arte,' p. 129
24 Lida de Malkiel, 'Nuevas notas,' p. 20. Rico, 'Sobre el Origen,' p. 301. Deyermond, ed., *Recherches*, p. xxi. Ramón Menéndez Pidal, *Poesía juglaresca y
   orígenes de las literaturas románicas*, 6th ed. (Madrid: Instituto de estudios
   politicos 1957), p. 207; a section entitled 'El Buen Amor dentro de la literatura didáctica' was added to the original (1924) version, perhaps in response
   to the works of Felix Lecoy and Américo Castro. Green, *Spain and the
   Western Tradition*, vol. 1, p. 3. Paiewonsky Conde, 'Polarización erótica,' p.
   331.
25 All quotations are from the excellent edition of *Buen amor* by R.S. Willis
   (Princeton: Princeton University Press 1972).
26 Ms. Sheryl Postman presented a paper under my supervision to a graduate
   seminar on Medieval Spanish Poetry in which she proves that the description of the Archpriest fits not so much that of Apollo as claimed by
   Dorothy Clotelle Clarke (*Hispanic Review*, 40 [1972], pp. 145–59) but that
   of the God Pan. Since Pan was frequently associated with the devil in
   medieval writings, Ms. Postman's findings lend further support to my arguments in support of the diabolical nature of *Buen amor*.
27 *Milagros*, ed. Dutton (see Chap. 1, n. 42), pp. 151–2
28 Spitzer, 'En torno al arte,' p. 123
29 Colbert I. Nepaulsingh, 'The Rhetorical Structure of the Prologues to the
   Libro de buen amor and the *Celestina*,' *Bulletin of Hispanic Studies*, 51
   (1974), 325–34
30 Ian Michael, 'The Function of the Popular Tale in the *Libro de buen amor*,'
   in Gybbon-Monypenny, '*Libro de buen amor*' *Studies*, p. 215
31 Colbert I. Nepaulsingh, 'Sobre Juan Ruiz y las dueñas chicas,' *Cuadernos
   Hispanoamericanos*, no. 297 (March 1975), pp. 645–9
32 Castro, *The Structure*, p. 414. Menédez Pidal, *Poesía juglaresca*, p. 208. Lida
   de Malkiel, 'Nuevas notas,' p. 414. Deyermond, ed., *Recherches*, p. xxi
33 Nepaulsingh, 'The Rhetorical Strucutre,' p. 329
34 See this chapter, n. 21. Willis explains (p. xliv) how such a sermon recital
   might have lasted hours.
35 For a definition of *exsuperatio* and a more detailed demonstration of its
   function see my article, 'Sobre Juan Ruiz.'
36 The proceedings of the First International Congress on the Archpriest of
   Hita, *El Arcipreste de hita, el libro, el autor, la tierra, la época*, ed. Manuel
   Criado de Val (Barcelona: S.E.R.E.S.A. 1973), contain several articles that deal
   directly with the structure of the *Libro de buen amor*; the articles written
   by Castellanos, López Morales, Gariano and Michalski are relevant to this
   study. Only Michalski, however, comes close to the findings expressed in
   this article: he does emphasize the role of the Archpriest as a sinner and he
   sees the book itself as a hagiographical parody; he says nothing about the
   archpriest as devil and sees Trotaconventos rather than Doña Venus as the
   anti-type of the Virgin Mary. Moreover, Michalski thinks that there is a
   much closer link between the *Libro de buen amor* and the *Confessions of St
   Augustine* than has been realized, so that he seems to revive the traditional

search for a structural model. Since my article appeared in 1977, two books on the imagery in the *Libro de buen amor* have been published: Dayle Seidenspinner–Nuñez, *The Allegory of Good Love: Parodic Perspectivism in the 'Libro de buen amor,'* University of California Publications, Modern Philology, 112 (Berkeley: University of California Press 1981), and Gail Phillips, *The Imagery of the 'Libro de buen amor,'* Spanish Series, no. 9 (Madison, Wis.: Hispanic Seminary of Medieval Studies 1983). Both these studies tend to reinforce the attention I drew in 1977 to the role of the devil in the *Libro de buen amor* (see Seidenspinner-Nuñez, esp. pp. 48-53, and Phillips, esp. pp. 156–9). There have also been other articles on the *Libro de buen amor*, too numerous to list here, and a book-length structural analysis by Vittorio Marmo, *Dalle fonti alle forme: Studi sul 'Libro de buen amor* (Naples: Liguori 1983).

37 William F. Boggess, 'Averrois Cordvbensis Commentarium Medium in Aristotelis Poetriam' PH.D diss., University of North Carolina at Chapel Hill, 1965, pp. 20-1, 34-5, referred to in the text as Boggess and cited by page number only. In the manuscripts examined by Boggess the words attributed to Aristotle's original are distinguished from the commentary upon them, usually by putting the former in large letters. In my translations I indicate Aristotle's alleged words by placing the phrase [Aristotle said] within square brackets. I capitalize the first word of a sentence, where Boggess does not, and I have also modernized Boggess's orthography, changing 'v' to 'u' and 'y' and 'j' to 'i' where necessary. Words not attributed to Aristotle appear within parentheses in my transcription. The translations are mine, and I include them (even at the risk of annoying fluent readers of Latin) because of the technical nature of some key words and phrases which are not likely to be interpreted by all readers in the same way. For a translation that is at times somewhat less literal than my own see the one given by O.B. Hardison, Jr, in Alex Preminger et al., *Classical and Medieval Literary Criticism* (New York: F. Ungar 1974), pp. 349-82, referred to from now on in my text as Hardison and cited by page number only. I have paid close attention in my translation to the variant readings of the four Spanish manuscripts used by Boggess in his edition; none of these variants is significant in the passages quoted by me. Two Spanish manuscripts use *circumlocutio* as a synonym of *circulatio*, which is why I prefer to use 'circumlocution' in English, instead of 'circularity' or what Hardison calls in quotation marks 'indirectness.' A critical edition of Hermannus's translation based on all the extant Spanish manuscripts would be a desirable undertaking. Charles Faulhaber provides a list of the Castilian manuscripts in his 'Retóricas clásicas y medievales en bibliotecas castellanas' (*Abaco*, 4 [1973] pp. 151-300), but it should be remembered that he was concerned with Castile and did not enter other Spanish manuscripts such as the one in Valencia listed in George Lacombe et al., *Aristoteles Latinus, Pars Posterior* (Cambridge: University Press 1955), p. 861, and in L. Minio-Paluello, *Aristoteles Latinus* (Bruxelles-Paris: Desclée de Brouwer 1961), p. 131. I chose the Boggess edition instead of the one by Minio-Paluello (*Aristoteles Latinus, xxxiii, editio*

altera, de Arte Poetica, Bruxelles-Paris (?) 1968, pp. 41-74) mainly because Boggess gives variant readings from all four Spanish manuscripts whereas Minio-Paluello does not. Although the copy I used of Minio-Paluello's edition once read 'Bruxelles-Paris/Desclée de Brouwer' on the opening pages, it now bears glued pieces of paper covering those words and saying instead 'E.J. Brill/Leiden.' There are only slight orthographic differences between the Boggess and Minio-Paluello editions in those passages quoted in this study; these variants are cited at the end of the Latin quotations after the initials MP and the number of the page and line of Minio-Paluello's edition: in this quotation MP, p. 48, l. 35 vocabant; p. 53, l. 24 omits 'et': anima ut deinde.

38 I am indebted in my choice of words in this sentence to a remark made by Professor Karl-Ludwig Selig in another context, during his seminar on 'Ut Pictura Poesis' at Duke University in July 1978. Professor Selig is not responsible for any misapplication I may make of his remarks: he was not talking about Hermannus, nor about Martínez de Toledo.

39 On the popularity of the commentaries of Avverroës see, for example, G.H. Luquet, 'Herman L'Allemand,' *Revue de l'histoire des religions,* 44 (1901), pp. 407-22, esp. pp. 407, 412-13, 416-17; Harry A. Wolfson, 'Revised Plan for the Publication of a *Corpus* etc,' *Speculum,* 38 (1963), esp. pp. 88, 94, and by the same author 'The Twice-Revealed Averroës,' *Speculum* 36 (1961), esp. 382; P. Alphandéry ('Y a-t-il eu un Averroisme populaire?' *Revue de l'histoire des religions,* 44 [1901], pp. 395-406) limits Averroës' popularity to the schools; Boggess, p. xvi; Ernest Renan, *Averroës et l'Averroisme* (Paris, 1852), esp. pp. 173-77. For manuscripts of Averroës's commentary in Spain see, in addition to the above, G. Lacombe et al., *Aristoteles Latinus,* vol. 1 (Rome: La Libraria dello stato 1939), pp. 100-11, vol. 2 (Cambridge: University Press 1955), pp. 821-62, supplement by L. Minio-Paluello, (Paris, 1961); Boggess, pp. xvi-xxiii, xlviii-ix; Charles Faulhaber, 'Retóricas clásicas y medievales en bibliotecas castellanas,' *Abaco,* 4 (1973), pp. 151-300, esp. pp. 163-8. For Herman and Averroës, see now also Judson B. Allen, *The Ethical Poetic of the Later Middle Ages: A Decorum of Convenient Distinction* (Toronto: University of Toronto Press 1982).

40 Averroës's commentary, and earlier ideas similar to those expressed in Latin translations of it, may also help to solve some knotty problems in the works of other medieval writers on lust. As Robert Hollander explains, 'there is perhaps no more central and far-reaching problem confronting students of medieval literary texts, from about 1050 on, than the role of carnal love in these texts ... we may simply offer a partial list of major figures who would necessarily be involved in any "solution" of the problem: Chrétien de Troyes, Andreas Capellanus, Bernardus Silvestris, Guillaume de Conches, Alain de Lille, Guillaume de Lorris, Jean de Meun, Gino da Pistoia, Guido Guinzelli, Guido Cavalcanti, Dante Alighieri, Juan Ruiz, Francesco Petrarca, Giovanni Boccaccio, Geoffrey Chaucer' (*Boccaccio's Two Venuses* [New York: Columbia University Press 1977], pp. 117-18). Boggess (p. xi) explains how the terminology 'praise' and 'blame' was derived from

the Greek concepts of tragedy and comedy through the works of Abu Bisr and Averroës.

41 Alfonso Martínez de Toledo, *Arcipreste de Talavera*, ed. C. Pérez Pastor (Madrid: Sociedad de bibliofilos españoles 1901), p. 106. All references are to this edition and will be cited in my text by page number only.

42 I bear in mind the *caveat* made by Mario Penna concerning Pérez Pastor's edition (see *Arcipreste de Talavera*, ed. Penna [Torino, n.d.] esp. p. liv), and also the comments of Marcella Ciceri whose recent edition is referred to below in note 44. There is no room here to justify my selection by discussing the merits and demerits of the existing editions. Pérez Pastor puts in italics those words found in the printed editions that are lacking in the manuscript, and these words are indicated in my text thus: [PP], except for the epilogue (pp. 328–30) which is entirely in italics in Pérez Pastor's edition and which I treat as part of the whole text.

43 For the inclusion of the *Poetics* within the realm of logic see Boggess, p. xv, Hardison, pp. 341–4, and the works on Averroës cited in notes 39 and 45.

44 See E. Michael Gerli, *Alfonso Martínez de Toledo* (Boston: Twayne 1976), pp. 30–2, and the reference in his notes on page 154, for a discussion of the 'media parte.' Gerli's bibliography (pp. 175–8) is useful. Gerli admits that his discussion of the *Corbacho* in terms of a sermon is approximate rather than precise: 'Accordingly, the first part of the *Archpriest of Talavera* has every structural indication of being a sermon. Although it does not strictly follow the formal conventions of the university method, considered in its entirety it is developed along the lines of the art of preaching' (pp. 86–7). The *Corbacho* does contain numerous examples of oratorical techniques applicable to preaching, which is not unexpected, since its author was an archpriest; but overall structure of the *Corbacho* cannot be fully explained by means of either the popular or the learned sermon. I have shown elsewhere that the prologue (which together with the first 38 chapters, Gerli considers a sermon) answers precisely to an *accessus* ('Talavera's Prologue,' *Romance Notes* 16 [1974–5], pp. 514–18); and I try to describe above the logical structure of the four main parts of the work. I will discuss the epilogue below. Since Gerli states (p. 86) that the sermon ends with the word 'amen' at the end of chapter 38 of part 2, it should be pointed out that this 'amen' is the end of a prayer that forms the last sentence of this chapter: '... a Dios ruego ... que sea ...' (p. 107). Similar 'amens' are found at the end of prayers and curses throughout the text on pages 144, 148, 185, 217, 220, 221, 226, 259, 268, 284, 327. I am also aware of Marcella Ciceri's explanation (which appeared too late for Gerli to have mentioned) of 'media parte' as a scribal error for 'iiij^a': 'la "media parte" è evidente errore del copista che ha letto il numerale iiij^a come mj^a, interpretandolo come l'abbreviazione di "media"; in questo errore, o in altri simili è incorso infatti altre volte: c. 75 v. "lee el capitulo vasis e el capitulo non ergo que en esta manera ...;" c83r.: "fallaras esta conclusion en el capitulo vasis xxiij questa medio en el parrafo non ergo ..."; c.95v.; "rruy ql iiij° c°'; si tratta in tutti e tre i casi del *Decretum magistri Gratiani, pars secunda, Vasis,* c. 23.c xxiii; *qu.*4, che altrove cita

57 I do not mean to suggest that Boccaccio's work is a source for Talavera's. The best treatment of sources and influences remains that of Erich von Richthofen, 'Alfonso Martínez de Toledo und sein *Arcipreste de Talavera*,' *Zeitschrift für romanische Philologie*, 61 (1941), pp. 417–537. See also Arturo Farinelli, 'Note sulla fortuna del *Corbaccio* nella Spagna medievale' in *Festgabe für Adolfo Mussafia* (Halle: Niemeyer 1905), pp. 440–60. The question of the title or titles for the book remains unsettled. Gerli suggests that Talavera's title, *Arcipreste de Talavera*, is a 'homage to Ruiz's work' (p. 67). Other explanations of the title are conceivable. Martinez's 'Syn bautismo, sea por nombre llamado Arcipreste de Talavera' (p. 1) recalls the subtitle of Ovid's *Amores*: 'sine titulo.' The first three days of the *Decameron*, were also 'senza titolo,' as Robert Hollander has stated in his *Boccaccio's Two Venuses* (New York: Columbia University Press 1977), pp. 115, 235. For a discussion and bibliography of the words 'corbaccio' and 'corbacho,' see N.R. Cartier, 'Boccaccio's Old Crow,' *Romania*, 98 (1977), pp. 331–48. My conjecture for an English translation of both words is 'pizzle.'

58 Penna, ed., *Arcipreste de Talavera*, p. xlix: 'non è altro che uno scherzo.' Whitbourn claims that the epilogue is a retraction (*The 'Arcipreste de Talavera'*, pp. 58–63.

59 The inclusion of himself among the sinners cannot absolve the archpriest of Talavera of the charge of misogynism. With respect to this charge I find myself in mild disagreement with my kind and learned teacher who, years before my birth, asked the question: 'Ist der *Arcipreste de Talavera* ein frauenfeindlicher Traktat?' and answered it in part as follows: 'Alfonso Martínez war kein verknöcherter, böswilliger order rachsüchtiger Gegner des schwachen Geschlechts ... Darüber hinaus hat er uns eine Schilderung der kleinen und grossen Fehler der Frauen und Eigenschaften der in ihren Temperamenten verschiedenen Männer gegcben, die an Heiterkeit nichts fehlen lässt und an deren Abfassung Alfonso Martínez selbst des grösste Vergnügen gehabt haben mag' (E. Von Richthofen, Alfonso Martínez de Toledo und sein *Arcipreste de Talavera*, pp. 496, 500). Professor von Richthofen is here being as kind to Alfonso Martínez de Toledo as I have known him to be to students, colleagues and even to harsh critics of his own work. He emphasized to his graduate students that all critics should be taken seriously and treated with humanity rather than as enemies. After considering the Archpriest of Talavera's work seriously I have learned to sympathize humanely with his easy solution to man's shortcomings. But I find no humour in the view that, for example, even the cause of the crime of a necrophiliac male should be placed squarely, not on the man, but on the dead body of the woman: 'e avn después de muerta fue cabsa de la desonra del verdugo' (p. 72). The kindest statement that can be made about the *Corbacho* is that it is intended to deplore man's major weakness; the author was intelligent enough to find many ways of achieving this end; the fact that he chose to do it by denouncing women as the cause of what he perceives to be man's major weakness raises strong suspicions of misogynism. The author, of course, reserves the right to dissociate himself from the views expressed in his own work. Even in this case, where

the author inserts himself among those whom he reprehends, Alfonso Martínez can claim aesthetic distance. He can claim to be joking. But if it is a
joke, it is, nevertheless, a misogynistic joke.

60 Cf. Ciceri, ed., [Arcipreste, vol. 2, pp. 17–18] who believes that the epilogue
'presenta tratti non caratteristici, se non addirittura inabituali a Martínez,
come il tipo di datazione astrologico – burlesco.' I wish to thank the following people for their generous assistance in the preparation of this study of
the Corbacho: Professor Frank Carrino; the Southeastern Institute of Medieval and Renaissance studies; Mr. John L. Sharpe III, Curator of Rare Books,
Duke University; Professors Alan Deyermond, Margaret Egan, Frances
Exum, Sandra Foa, Eduardo González, Salvador Fajardo, Emilie Kadish, Karl-
Ludwig Selig. An abbreviated version of this section was read at a seminar
session of the annual meeting of the Modern Language Association of
America, December 1978.

CHAPTER FIVE

1 For a convenient list of works on the topic, see Dinko Cvitanovic, La novela
sentimental española (Madrid: Prensa española 1973), pp. 361–8. See, also,
Armando Durán, Estructura y técnicas de la novela sentimental y caballer-
esca (Madrid: Gredos 1973). Celestina is not usually discussed alongside
the so-called 'novelas sentimentales' except to illustrate the similarity of
certain themes, as for example in Peter G. Earle, 'Love Concepts in La Cárcel
de Amor and La Celestina,' Hispania, 39 (1956), pp. 92–6. In her analysis of
Melibea's character, María Rosa Lida Malkiel devotes a few pages to antecedents in the 'novela sentimental': La originalidad artística de la Celestina
(Buenos Aires: EUDEBA 1961), pp. 445–55, esp. pp. 452–5. For a recent bibliography, see Keith Whinnom, The Spanish Sentimental Romance, 1440-
1550: A Critical Bibliography, Research Bibliographies and Checklists, 41
(London: Grant and Cutler 1983).

2 All references are to the annotated edition by Francisco Serrano Puente,
with an introduction by Antonio Prieto (Madrid: Castalia 1976), here at p.
75. I occasionally change Serrano's punctuation and accentuation of the
text which do not always clarify its meaning; for example, the third line on
p. 67 should obviously read 'requiere dé paz.' There are sufficient lapses to
warrant a better edition to accompany Prieto's important introduction,
which expands upon the section of his Morfología de la novela devoted to
Siervo (Barcelona: Planeta pp. 242–70). I have also consulted the edition by
César Hernández Alonso, Juan Rodríguez del Padrón, Obras Completas
(Madrid: Editora Nacional 1982), pp. 153–208.

3 G. Boccaccio, Corbaccio: a cura di Pier Giorgio Ricci (Torino: Enaudi 1977),
p. 74

4 Cf the formal study, of the relationship between the poems and the prose,
of Olga Tudorica Impey, 'La poesía y la prosa del Siervo libre de amor,' in
Studies in Honor of John Esten Keller, ed. Joseph R. Jones (Newark, Dela-
ware: Juan de la Cuesta 1980), pp. 171–87. As is the case with her analysis

of the *Razón*, Professor Impey's strict adherence to structuralist analysis deprives her of the added richness that can be gained if one leaves the text to examine the tradition to which it refers. She concludes rigidly, 'Para comprender la primera "novela" sentimental castellana ... es necesario ... analizarla en sí misma y por sí misma' (p. 187). She also notes in passing (p. 180) the reference in *Siervo* to the Song of Songs, but she is not concerned with relating this to works like *Razón*, and thus misses a deeper appreciation of the composition of both works in so far as they both involve a quest, real or insincere, for the bridegroom (Christ) of the Song. Impey pays no attention to the emendations proposed by Jesús Ara, 'Sobre el texto de los poemas del *Siervo libre de amor,' Bulletin Hispanique*, 78 (1976), pp. 219–25. On the poems, see also César Hernández Alonso, *Siervo libre de amor de Juan Rodríguez del Padrón* (Valladolid: Universidad de Valladolid 1970), pp. 43–76.

5 See below for quotation and discussion of this passage in Jerome (Migne, *PL*, vol. 25, col. 22), and for an attempt to make more precise the interpretations of Synderesis by Andrachuk and Herrero. Olga Tudorica Impey discusses Synderesis in 'La poesía y prosa,' p. 181

6 Henry A. Sanders, ed., *Beati in Apocalipsin Libri Duodecim* (Rome: American Academy in Rome 1930), pp. 280, 286

7 See my discussion of the topos of the exordium that uses the three parts of the soul in the *Libro de buen amor*, the *Libro del cavallero Zifar*, and the *Leys d'Amors*, 'The Rhetorical Structure of the *Libro de buen amor* and the *Celestina,' Bulletin of Hispanic Studies*, 51 (1974), pp. 325–34, esp. p. 328.

8 Plato's version is found in the vision of Er described in his *Republic*, book x; for Dante's use of the Y see Phillip Damon, 'Geryon, Cacciaguida, and the Y of Pythagoras,' *Dante Studies*, 85 (1967), pp. 15–32; Virgil's version is in *Aeneid* VI, 540–3: 'hic locus est, partis ubi se via findit in ambas: /dextera quae Ditis magni sub moenia tendit, / hac iter Elysium nobis; at laeva malorum/exercet poenas, et ad impia Tartara mittit. Here is the place where the road parts in twain: there to the right, as it runs under the walls of great Dis, is our way to Elysium, but the left wreaks the punishment of the wicked, and sends them on to pitiless Tartarus' (H.R. Fairclough, trans., *Virgil, I Eclogues, Georgics, Aeneid I–IV*, [Cambridge, Mass.: Harvard University Press and London: Heinemann 1960], pp. 542–5).

9 This polysemous word play is reminiscent of one of the favourite techniques of Francisco Imperial; see, for example, the first stanza of *Syete Virtudes*, in my edition (Madrid: Espasa Calpe 1977), pp. 98–9 and the note to lines 1–8. With *Siervo* we seem to be at a point in the poetic manipulation of language equidistant from *Razón de amor* at the one end and the poetry of Góngora at the other. In *Razón*, key words seem to have one meaning in one (secular) context and the same meaning in another (religious) context; in Juan Ruiz's *Buen amor* key words mean one thing on one (literal) level and quite another opposite thing on a spiritual level; in *Siervo* the same key words have at least three different but related meanings on the same level.

10 Damon, 'Geryon,' p. 16
11 Virgil seems to confuse Ixion's punishment with that of Pirithous, and Juan
    Rodríguez must have used Ovid for details about Ixion not found in the
    Aeneid. However, a few lines after he mentions Ixion (Aeneid VI: 601), Virgil
    does refer to those who suffer punishment stretched out on the spokes of a
    wheel: 'radiisque rotarum / districti pendent' (Aeneid VI: 616-17). For other
    portrayals of Ixion on Fortune's wheel see C.R. Post, 'The sources of Juan de
    Mena, *Romanic Review* 3 (1912), p. 229, n. 22, and H.R. Patch, *The Goddess
    Fortuna* (Cambridge, Mass.: Harvard University Press 1927), p. 167.
12 Gregory P. Andrachuk, 'On the Missing Third Part of *Siervo Libre de Amor*,'
    Hispanic Review, 45 (1977), pp. 171-80. Javier Herrero, 'The Allegorical
    Structure of the *Siervo libre de amor*,' *Speculum*, 55 (1980), pp. 751-64
13 Andrachuk, 'The Missing Third Part,' p. 178. Herrero, 'Allegorical Structure,'
    p. 764 and n. 19.
14 Herrero, 'Allegorical Structure,' p. 757
15 I have not been able to examine the manuscript. It is regrettable that Prieto
    did not publish all the few pages in facsimile instead of just two of them.
    Although there is no explicit at the narrative's end, there is another docu-
    ment after it (p. 57) relating to María López.
16 Andrachuk, 'The Missing Third Part,' p. 172.
17 Herrero takes Prieto to task somewhat unfairly for dividing the work into
    four parts: 'it is surprising that Prieto asserts that the novel is divided into
    four parts when the author claims that 'El siguiente tratado es departydo en
    tres partes principales' (p. 751, n. 1). Herrero ignores the word 'principales.' I
    do not accept Prieto's division (see his p. 35), but I do agree with him that
    the work has four parts: an introduction plus three main parts. The Arci-
    preste de Talavera used the word 'principales' in a similar way in the intro-
    duction to his *Corbacho*: 'E va en quatro principales partes diviso' (ed. Pérez
    Pastor, p. 41). The most recent, and in many respects most thorough, discus-
    sion of the word 'tratado' is by Keith Whinnom, '*Autor* and *tratado* in the
    Fifteenth Century: Semantic Latinism or Etymological Trap?' *Bulletin of
    Hispanic Studies*, 59 (1982), pp. 211-18. Whinnom's article reached me after
    I had completed this chapter. The force of Whinnom's exploration of the
    semantic fields around the word 'tratado' confirms the necessity to examine
    the meaning of the word always in context and without predispositions
    about fixed meanings for it. I had decided to proceed in context without
    predispositions about 'tratado' before reading Whinnom's article. Whinnom
    documents many meanings for 'tratado,' but he does not deny 'that, in many
    contexts, *tratado* might properly be translated as treatise' (p. 215). I am also
    delighted, by the way, to read Whinnom's cautionary note (p. 215-16, no.
    34) about numerous medieval Spanish titles which we treat with more
    respect than they deserve. At several places in this book I have expressed
    the need for a comprehensive study of medieval Spanish titles.
18 Henry C. Lea, *A History of the Inquisition of the Middle Ages* (London:
    Macmillan 1922), vol. 1, p. 400. As Lea documents authoritatively (vol. 2,
    pp. 163-90), the inquisitorial process was not institutionalized in Castile

until after the publication of *Siervo*. Nevertheless, the procedure was well established in Aragon, in Italy, and elsewhere in Europe well before the time of Juan Rodríguez; it was therefore easy for him to have been acquainted with it. See also Edward Dudley, 'The Inquisition of Love: Tratado as a Fictional Genre,' *Medievalia*, 5 (1979), pp. 233–43; I thank Professor Dudley for sending me a copy of this article.

19 For an explanation of the neologism 'autohagiography,' see my '*El libro de la vida* de Santa Teresa de Avila,' *Homenaje a Manuel Alvar*, in press.

20 Henry C. Lea, *A History of Auricular Confession and Indulgences in the Latin Church* (1896; rpt New York: Greenwood 1968), vol. 1, p. 362. See also, John T. McNeill and Helena M. Gamer, *Medieval Handbooks of Penance* (New York: Octagon 1965), pp. 12–14.

21 Cf. Olga Tudorica Impey, 'The Literary Emancipation of Juan Rodríguez del Padrón: From the Fictional "Cartas" to the *Siervo libre de amor*,' *Speculum*, 55 (1980), pp. 305–16.

22 Herrero, 'Allegorical Structure,' p. 764

23 Herrero, 'The Allegorical Structure,' pp. 764, 762. Herrero relies, for his interpretation of Yrena's penance, on Edward Dudley, 'Court and Country: The Fusion of Two Images of Love in Juan Rodríguez's *El Siervo libre de amor*,' *PMLA*, 82 (1967), pp. 117–20. Dudley's study is an excellent introduction to a much needed analysis of the setting of the entire work. But since he analyses two images in the interpolated story of Ardanlier and Liessa his conclusions must be weighed against what holds true for analyses of the whole work.

24 Herrero, 'Allegorical Structure,' p. 762, n. 15; p. 764, n. 19

25 Jerome on Ezekiel in Migne, *PL*, vol. 25, col. 22

26 Damon, 'Geryon,' p. 15

27 Herrero, 'Allegorical Structure,' p. 764. Andrachuk, 'The Missing Third Part,' p. 177, n. 11

28 For Margadán, cf. the biblical Magadan in Matthew 15:39

29 Ezekiel 1:16: A more precise translation than Jerome's 'quasi visio maris' would have been 'like a beryl.' Juan Rodríguez was, most likely, using a version of the Bible derived from Jerome's Vulgate, but I wouild not be surprised if he knew a smattering of Hebrew and Greek; the name of Ardanlier's tutor, Lamidoras, has a consonantal pattern similar to the Hebrew verb 'limed' to teach; and Rodríguez uses the Greek word Synderesis in a way that shows his full awareness of its meaning. Jerome, of course, knew both Hebrew and Greek, and he is aware of altering the text of the Septuagint at this point: 'Opusque earum erat atque factura, quasi visio *tharsis*, quam nos in *mare* vertimus' (Migne; *PL*, vol. 15, col. 27)

30 For the narrator's climbing of trees, cf. Zacchaeus in Luke 19:2–4

31 Diego de San Pedro, *Obras completas*, vols 1 and 2, ed. Keith Whinnom, vol. 3, ed. Keith Whinnom and Dorothy S. Severin (Madrid: Castalia 1971–9); all references are to these editions by page number or volume and page, here vol. 3, p. 176. San Pedro's description of his *Cárcel* (*Obras completas*, vol. 3) as 'salsa para pecar' was made in his poem *Desprecio de la Fortuna*. *Cárcel*

was continued along more orthodox lines by Nicolás Nuñez who seems to have taken literally San Pedro's invitation to amend his work (see Keith Whinnom, trans., *Prison of Love, 1492, together with the Continuation by Nicolás Núñez, 1496* [Edinburgh: University Press 1979], and his *Dos opúsculos isabelinos: 'La coronación de la Señora Gracisla'* [BN ms. 22020] y *Nicolás Núñez, 'Cárcel de Amor,'* Exeter Hispanic Texts, xxii [Exeter: University of Exeter 1979], esp. pp. xliii–xliv, liv, 51–71, 85–92. Núñez's continuation is not analysed in this chapter, but it is another indication of the point made earlier (about *Siervo*) that any complete work might be expanded to form a new whole. Whinnom asks (*Prison*, p. xvi), 'to what extent did [Núñez's] messy and sentimental conclusion actually serve to popularize *Prison of Love* and make it acceptable?' Whinnom is by far the leading critic of the works of Diego de San Pedro; he brings the lucidity of his style to bear light on many thorny problems of San Pedro's text. I refer also, in addition to his editions cited in this note, to his 'Diego de San Pedro's Stylistic Reform,' *Bulletin of Hispanic Studies*, 37 (1960), pp. 1–15, as well as to his article and book about San Pedro cited below in note 33. In Whinnom's work on Diego de San Pedro I find much more with which I agree than disagree, and in the few instances where I differ, I could not have perceived my differences without the help of Whinnom's insights.

32 The distinction between 'reality' and 'imagination' is made here only for convenience; clearly, the world of the imagination is also real, and what we call reality is often illusory and fantastic. The editorial comments to which I refer in this paragraph are the incipit (vol 2, p. 79), the explicit (p. 176), and the subtitles in the text: 'comiença la obra' (p. 81), 'El preso al autor' (p. 88) etc., *all* of which can (and, perhaps should) be removed from the text, since there are all superfluous to a full understanding of it; they are, in fact, strange interpolations in an otherwise intelligible, though extraordinary, letter which, as stated above, begins and ends in accordance with normal epistolary practice. On the 'auctor' as 'ente ficticio' see Alfonso Rey, 'La primera personal narrativa en Diego de San Pedro,' *Bulletin of Hispanic Studies*, 58 (1981), pp. 91–102.

33 Whinnom is not convinced that Diego de San Pedro was a 'converso,; see his 'Was Diego de San Pedro a *converso*? A Re-examination of Cotarelo's Documentary Evidence,' *Bulletin of Hispanic Studies*, 34 (1957), pp. 187–200, and *Diego de San Pedro* (New York: Twayne 1974), pp. 19–22. The matter is still undecided, and I offer below reasons for continuing the line of investigation suggested by Francisco Márquez Villanueva, '*Cárcel de amor*, novela política,' *Revista de Occidente*, 2nd series, 14 (1966), pp. 185–200.

34 Bruce Wardropper, 'El mundo sentimental de la *Cárcel de Amor*, *Revista de Filolgía Española*, 37 (1953), pp. 168–93, at p. 176; cf. Anna Krause, 'El 'tractado' novelístico de Diego de San Pedro,' *Bulletin Hispanique*, 54 (1952), pp. 245–75, at p. 269. Whinnom, trans. *Prison of Love*, p. xvi

35 In terms of the history of literary composition in Spain after the medieval period, *Cárcel*'s use of the body analogy (heart, might, soul/mind) antici-

pates the *Quijote*. Cervantes divides the action of his masterpiece between adventures (might), love stories (heart), and discourses (mind); see my 'Cervantes, Don Quijote: The Unity of the Action,' *Revista Canadiense de Estudios Hispánicos*, 2 (1978), pp. 239–57. Laureola's acts, like don Quijote's, belie her feelings and her words. *Cárcel* is also an interesting work historically if its composition is compared with that of Santa Teresa's *Interior Castle*, and with Unamuno's masterpiece *San Manuel Bueno, Mártir* in which the role of Angela Carballino can be analysed in terms of that of the correspondent in *Cárcel*.

36 Enrique Moreno-Báez, ed., *Cárcel de Amor* (Madrid: Cátedra 1974); Joseph Chorpenning, 'Rhetoric and Feminism in the *Cárcel de Amor*,' *Bulletin of Hispanic Studies*, 54 (1977), pp. 1–8; Dorothy Sherman Severin, 'Structure and Thematic Repetitions in Diego de San Pedro's *Cárcel de Amor* and *Arnalte y Lucenda*,' *Hispanic Review*, 45 (1977), pp. 165–9. Whinnom, *Diego de San Pedro*, p. 115. Whinnom, trans. *Prison of Love*, p. xxx

37 S.H. Butcher, trans. and ed., *Aristotle's Theory of Poetry and Fine Art*, 4th ed. (New York: Dover 1951), p. 87

38 Whinnom, *Diego de San Pedro*, p. 114; *Prison of Love*, p. xxx

39 Moreno-Báez, ed., *Cárcel de Amor*, and Chorpenning, 'Rhetoric and Feminism,' p. 2. For Boccaccio, *Corbaccio*, pp. 73–4

40 Whinnom, *Diego de San Pedro*, p. 116; see also 'Stylistic Reform,' p. 11. Severin, 'Structure and Thematic Repetitions,' pp. 168, 167 n. 5

41 San Pedro, *Desprecio de la Fortuna*, *Obras completas*, vol. 3, pp. 287–8

42 M.W. Evans, *Medieval Drawings* (London: Hamlyn 1969), p. 27 and plate 40

43 *Cárcel de Amor*, novela política,' *Revista de Occidente*, 14 (1966), p. 198

44 San Pedro, *Sermón*, vol. 1, p. 173, n. 159. Cf. Regula Langbehn-Rohland, *Zur Interpretation der Romane des Diego de San Pedro* (Heidelberg: Carl Winter Universtats-Verlag 1970), p. 27 and n. 11. See also Whinnom's comments in *Obras* vol. 3, p. 81.

45 I cite the translation commissioned in 1908 by the Jewish Publication Society of America, *The Holy Scriptures According to the Masoretic Text* (Philadelphia 1980), here at vol. 2, pp. 1075–6. See also, J.H. Hertz ed., *The Pentateuch and Haftorahs*, 2nd ed. (London: Soncino 1980), pp. 836–7.

46 San Pedro, *Arnalte*, *Obras completas*, vol. 1, p. 87

47 Harshly: the word used in the text is cruel. Whinnom repeats that Wardropper and others are wrong to call Laureola cruel, but Laureola is made to describe herself that way: 'assí que es escusada tu demanda, porque ninguna esperança hallarás en ella, aunque la muerte que dizes te viese recebir, haviendo por mejor la crueldad honesta que la piedad culpada' (p. 153, and cf. Whinnom's remark at p. 42: 'no se trata de crueldad')

48 San Pedro, *Sermón*, *Obras completas*, vol. 1, p. 173

49 'We must be careful before we call a passionate romance a political novel. The *Cárcel de amor* can only be political in a way which is both excessively general and very peculiar, just as our modern romances of science fiction are scientific in a very broad and also a special way' (Peter Dunn,

'Narrator as Character in the *Cárcel de amor*,' *Modern Language Notes*, 94 (1979), pp. 187–99, at p. 189. Dunn's is a very perceptive structural analysis of *Cárcel*, but like most strictly formal approaches, it sticks too closely to the text instead of letting the text lead it, through references, to the rich hermeneutic world with which the text inseparably linked. Other readers, not nearly as strictly formal as Dunn, reach out beyond the text without paying careful attention to how the text is linked to the hermeneutical world around it. Thus, Bruno Damiani realizes that 'conversos' were liable to be special kinds of Christians who believed that '"el cristianismo comenzó con Jesucristo, un divino converso, y judíos conversos fueron sus apóstoles." Among the "conversos" of the time was the author of the *Cárcel de amor*, Diego de San Pedro' ('The Didactic Intention of the *Cárcel de Amor*,' *Hispanófila*, 56 [1976], pp. 29–43, at p. 31–2. In spite of this observation, Damiani proceeds to ignore the reference to 'judíos' in the Spanish aphorism he quotes about 'conversos,' and to read *Cárcel* as though it were, unequivocally, a Christian text with no Jewish roots whatever, as though Christianity, especially 'converso' Christianity, were easily divorceable from Judaism. 'This [didacticism] is particularly relevant to the *Cárcel de Amor*,' concludes Damiani, 'where allegory, religious analogies ... combine to create ... a symbolic and an exemplary model of Christian forebearance, benevolence, and compassion' (p. 43). Whinnom finds 'almost nothing to quarrel with' in Damiani's article ('*Autor* and *Tratado*,' p. 218, n. 39). Joseph F. Chorpenning ('Leriano's Consumption of Laureola's Letters in *Cárcel de Amor*,' *Modern Language Notes*, 95 [1980], 442–5) and E. Michael Gerli ('Leriano's Libation: Notes on the *Cancionero* Lyric, *Ars Moriendi*, and the Probable Debt to Boccaccio,' *Modern Language Notes*, 96 [1981], 414–20) discuss the final scene of *Cárcel* only from a Christian perspective even as they see fit to cite key texts from the Old Testament.

50 Dunn, 'Narrator as Character,' p. 192

51 Whinnom notes (pp. 80, 96, 131, 132, 174) some passages of *Cárcel* which are reflected in others in *Celestina*. Rojas is believed to have owned a copy of *Cárcel*.

52 Fernando de Rojas, *La Celestina*, ed. Julio Cejador y Frauca (Madrid: Espasa-Calpe 1963), vol. 1., p. 175. All references are to this edition, not because I consider it the best, but because it gives me a constant reminder of the hybrid nature of the text. Whinnom once wrote that 'The extraordinary fact is that the much-despised Cejador *Clásicos castellanos* edition is, in spite of its errors and eccentricities, probably the best version we have' ('The Relationship of the Early Editions of the *Celestina*,' *Zeitschrift für romanische Philologie*, 82 [1966], 22–40. Since Whinnom wrote these words a highly commendable edition has been published by Dorothy Severin (Madrid: Alianza 1976), and Whinnom himself has digested, in addition to Herriott, Miguel Marciales (see *Celestinesca*, 5, no. 2 [1981], pp. 51–3, and 6, no. 2 [1982], p. 45).

53 For human bodies around the wheel of Fortune, see H.R. Patch, *The God-*
   dess Fortuna (see n. 11), plates opposite pp. iii, 18, 32, 102, 112, 120 (plate
   7), 158 (plate 9), 164; see also George Cary, *The Medieval Alexander* (Cambridge: University Press 1967) opposite p. 194.

54 D.C. Clarke, *Allegory, Decalogue and Deadly Sins in 'La Celestina,'* (Berkeley: University of California Press, 1968), does not treat the commandments in sufficient detail.

55 P.E. Russell, *Temas de la Celestina* (Barcelona: Ariel 1978), pp. 370-1

56 San Pedro, *Sermón, Obras completas*, vol. 1, p. 173

57 See, for example, H.P. Salomon, *Portrait of a New Christian Fernao*
   Alvares Melo (Paris: Gulbenkian Foundation 1982). A colleague of mine
   once made me shatter, with laughter, the serenity of our academic halls
   when I asked him if he had read a certain novel. 'I do not read novels,' he
   replied, 'when I want to read fiction, I read history.' Cf. Keith Whinnom's
   point of departure as he extends the now famous (as well as poorly
   focused) Russell/Gilman debate: 'Historians, including literary historians,
   do well to stick to the documented facts, or they run some risk of turning
   into historical novelists,' 'Interpreting *La Celestina*: The Motives and the
   Personality of Fernando de Rojas,' in F.W. Hodcroft et al., eds., *Medieval*
   and Renaissance Studies on Spain and Portugal in Honour of P.E. Russell
   (Oxford: The Society for the Study of Medieval Languages and Literature
   1981), p. 53; and note, in the same volume, the point of departure of
   Gareth Davies for a study of '*La Araucana* and the Question of Ercilla's
   Converso Origins' (pp. 86-108, at p. 86): 'Nevertheless, the sceptical
   approach is itself open to the charge that it seeks to accept only documentary proof as evidence, whereas in fact historians are constantly
   obliged to draw conclusions from an array of circumstantial evidence ...
   that carries conviction only because the individual pieces, inconclusive
   in themselves, cluster around one point.' Whinnom, in apt tribute to Russell, seeks to do to Rojas what Russell sought to do to Cervantes, that is,
   emphasize his flaws: 'One of the greatest obstacles to proper interpretation of *Celestina* is surely the presupposition that it is a masterpiece
   without flaws ... And we shall make very heavy weather of understanding
   the book if we cannot conceive of a flawed author, an author whose logic
   is inconsistent' ('Interpreting *Celestina*,' pp. 66-7, and compare what Russell says about Cervantes and the *Quijote*, cited below in note 58).

58 Not much later, Cervantes was to add, on top of the subtleties of Juan
   Ruiz and Fernando de Rojas, the Muslim factor, to create, in his *Quijote*,
   Spain's greatest masterpiece, and one of the best in all the world; but that
   is the subject-matter of another book, tentatively entitled: 'Three Spanish
   Masterpieces: the *Libro de buen amor*, *Celestina*, and *Don Quijote*.' Cf.
   P.E. Russell: 'Certainly, on its most obvious level, the lesson which Cervantes seems to want to teach seems rather pathetic to the modern
   reader. We scarcely need, these days, to be warned against Quixotism. At
   the same time we have become more aware of the serious defects which

exist in *Don Quijote* as a work of art – defects which seem, in the main, due to its author's uncertainty as to what he was about, and to his hyper-sensitivity to the possibility of adverse criticism' ('The Art of Fernando de Rojas,' *Bulletin of Hispanic Studies*, 34 [1957], p. 160). Cervantes's mistakes are not nearly as awkward and artless as Russell supposed in 1957: Cervantes weaves a classic Persian carpet with its inevitable flaw, as I have begun to show in 'La aventura de los narradores del *Quijote*,' *Actas del Sexto Congreso Internacional de Hispanistas* (Toronto, 1980), pp. 515–18. When Russell classes himself with the modern reader who 'detects an agnostic turn of mind in the scepticism of Rojas' (p. 160), he might be confusing Rojas's opinions with those of the characters of *Celestina*, and he might also be projecting modern religious beliefs onto a late fifteenth-century 'converso' text. Cervantes, much closer to the text of *Celestina*, probably understood it a lot better than Russell as a 'libro ... divi- / si encubriera mas lo huma-.' Cervantes attributes his polysemous description of *Celestina* to a spurious poet who wrote verses in praise of the divinely human old Christian called Sancho Panza. For one simple example of the Muslim factor imposed deliberately by Cervantes on the text of the *Quijote*, see the treatment of Zoraida in terms of Islamic attitudes toward the Virgin Mary as described, for example, in Juan Mohamed Abd-El-Jalil, 'El Islam ante la Virgen María,' *Arbor*, 19 (1951), pp. 1–27; see also my 'Cervantes, Don Quijote: The Unity of the Action,' *Revista Canadiense de Estudios Hispánicos*, 2 (1978), pp. 248–9.

59 For the theme of ensnaring, see A.D. Deyermond, 'Hilado-Cordón-Cadena: Symbolic Equivalence in *La Celestina*,' *Celestinesca*, 1 (1977), pp. 6–12. For marriage, D.W. McPheeters, 'Una traducción hebrea de la *Celestina* en el siglo XVI,' *Homenaje a Antonio Rodríguez Moñino*, vol. 1 (Madrid: Castalia 1966), pp. 399–411. McPheeters does not explain the theme of marriage fully (pp. 408–11); for Christians like Novizzano it is a question of marriage, but for Jews like Tsarfati it is not just marriage but especially inter-marriage, not just anti-feminism but 'whoring after other gods.'

60 Marcel Bataillon, 'Melancolía renacentista o melancolía judía,' in *Estudios hispánicos: Homenaje a Archer M. Huntington* (Wellesley, Mass.: Wellesley College 1952), pp. 30–50, at pp. 45, 48

61 Russell, 'La magia, tema integral de *La Celestina*,' in *Temas*, pp. 243–76. Stephen Gilman, 'The "Conversos" and the Fall of Fortune,' in *Collected Studies in Honour of Americo Castro's 80th Year* (Oxford: Lincombe Lodge Research Library 1965), pp. 127–36; Gilman, *The Spain of Fernando de Rojas* (Princeton: Princeton University Press 1972)

62 Gilman, *The Spain*, p. 173

63 Whinnom, review of Gilman, *The Spain of Fernando de Rojas, Bulletin of Hispanic Studies*, 52 (1975), p. 160.

64 C.R. Post, *A History of Spanish Painting*, vol. 4 (Cambridge, Mass.: 1933; rpt. New York: Kraus 1970), p. 104; see also vol. 3, p. 186.

65 For reproductions of these paintings see Alfonso Rodríguez G. de Ceballos, *Las catedrales de Salamanca* (Madrid: Everest 1978), pp. 44–5, and

Museo Provincal de Arqueología y Bellas Artes, Convento de San Marcos: Guía del visitante (León, 1975), p. 16.

CHAPTER SIX

1 Beatus, *Beati in Apocalipsin Libri Duodecim*, ed. Henry A. Sanders (Rome: American Academy in Rome 1930), pp. 306, 314
2 Ernst Robert Curtius, *European Literature and the Latin Middle Ages*, trans. Willard R. Trask (New York: Harper & Row 1963), pp. 303, 310
3 I am grateful to Professors Raúl Castagnino, Alan Deyermond, Robert Hollander, and Harlan Sturm who made encouraging remarks about this section; they are, of course, not responsible for its errors.
4 Gonzalo de Berceo, *Vida de santo Domingo de Silos*. ed. Brian Dutton (London: Tamesis 1978), st. 751. Juan Ruiz, *Libro de buen amor*, ed. R.S. Willis (Princeton: Princeton University Press 1972) st. 142; all quotations from *Buen amor* in the chapter are taken from this edition.
5 R.S. Willis, '"Mester de Clerecía," A Definition of the *Libro de Alexandre*,' *Romance Philology*, 10 (1956–7), p. 217. For evidence of discomfort see John D. Fitz-Gerald, *Versification of the Cuaderna Via as found in Berceo's 'Vida de santo Domingo de Silos'* (New York: Columbia University Press 1905), p. xii. A basic bibliography is listed in Alfredo Carballo Picazo, *Métrica española* (Madrid 1956), p. 147. See also A.D. Deyermond 'Mester es sen peccado,' *Romanische Forschungen*, 77, 1965, pp. 111–16. For descriptions of 'quadrivium,' see Du Cange, *Glossarium mediae et infimae latinitatus* (Paris: Librarie des sciences et des arts 1937–8), p. 587.
6 See, for example, Felix Lecoy, *Recherches sur le 'Libro de buen amor' de Juan Ruiz Archiprêtre de Hita*, with a New Prologue, Supplementary Bibliography, and Index by A.D. Deyermond (Farnborough: Gregg International 1974), p. 50.
7 Stanza references are from R.S. Willis's edition, *The Relationship of the Spanish 'Libro de Alexandre' to the 'Alexandreis' of Gautier de Chatillon* (see chap. 3, n. 37).
8 See, for example, George T. Northup, *An Introduction to Spanish Literature*: 3rd ed. Revised and Enlarged by Nicholson B. Adams (Chicago: University of Chicago Press 1971), p. 59. Fitz-Gerald is intrigued by 'the odd use of the word *vía* in the term *cuaderna vía*. We might be tempted to translate the term by the "four track" system, if that phrase were not so brazenly modern and Philistine' *Versification*, p. xii, n. 1. Aníbal Biglieri has asked me if my interpretation of the term 'cuaderna vía' calls special attention to the word 'vía.' I do not think so, because the word 'vía' was used by 'cuaderna vía' poets in the same two senses as the word 'way' is used in English today: Juan Ruiz uses 'vía' repeatedly to mean 'road,' *sensus literalis* (422d, 648c, 687a, 1313b, 1451d), and to mean 'plan' or 'method,' *sensus spiritalis* ('et instruam te in via hac qua gradieris'). Berceo also uses 'vía' in these two senses (see, for example, *Vida de santo Domingo*, p. 314, and p. 8).

9 Gonzalo de Berceo, *Los milagros de Nuestra Señora*, ed. Brian Dutton (London: Tamesis 1971), 26c

10 Harry Caplan, 'The Four Senses of Scriptural Interpretation and the Medieval Theory of Preaching,' *Speculum*, 4 (1929), p. 285.

11 Ibid. p. 284. Cf. the reference made by Juan Ruiz to 'firme hedificio' in the prologue to *Buen amor* (Criado de Val and Naylor, eds. [Madrid: C.S.I.C. 1965, p. 7]. Both Gregory and Juan Ruiz are probably elaborating on Ephesians 2:19–21, where Paul writes 'sed estis ... superaedificati super fundamentum apostolorum, et prophetarum, ipso summo angulari lapide Christo Iesu: in que omnis aedificatio constructa crescit in templum sanctum in Domino'; and on 1 Corinthians 3:;9–11: '... De aedificatio estis ... Fundamentum enim aliud nemo potest ponere praeter id quod positum est, quod est Christus Iesus.'

12 W.S. Brassington, *A History of the Art of Bookbinding* (London: E. Stock 1894), p. 47. The author of the *Disticha Catonis* ed. Marcus Boas (Amsterdam: North Holland Publishing Co. 1952) states that his method is 'sensu uno jungere binos' ('to join two things in one sense,' or 'to join two senses in one,' Book 4, p. 49).

13 Brassington, *Art of Bookbinding*, p. 56.

14 C.C. Marden, ed., *The 'Libro de Apolonio,' an Old Spanish Poem*, vol. 1, Elliot Monographs in the Romance Languages and Literatures, no. 6 (Baltimore: Johns Hopkins Press 1917), 282c and p. xlviii

15 For the leaden handbook, see Brassington, *Art of Bookbinding*, p. 43. On the popularity of the cuaderna vía, see John K. Walsh who suggests that it was so popular that it might have been parodied by Juan Ruiz: 'Juan Ruiz and the *mester de clerezía*: Lost Context and Lost Parody in the *Libro de buen amor*,' *Romance Philology*, 33 (1979–80), pp. 62–86.

16 Alfonso x, El Sabio, *Las Siete Partidas* (1807; rpt. Madrid: Ediciones Atlas 1972), vol. 2, pp. 345–6

17 Robert Steele, 'The Pecia,' *Library*, 1930, p. 231. See also the classic study by Jean Destrez, *La Pecia dans les manuscrits universitaires du XIII* et du *XIV* siècle (Paris: Editions Jacques Vautrain 1935). Destrez explains that the word *pecia* begins to be used interchangeably with *quaternus*, and that both words are sometimes used loosely to mean 'notebook,' from the second half of the fourteenth century: 'peu a peu, le sens special du mot *pecia* se perd et ... dans la seconde moitié de XIV* on trouve quelquefois le mot *quaternus* employé à la place du mot *pecia* et aussi le mot *pecia* employé dans le sens de cahier (*quaternus ou sexternus*),' p. 14; Graham Pollard, 'The Pecia System in the Medieval Universities,' in M.D. Parkes and Andrew Watson, eds., *Medieval Scribes, Manuscripts and Libraries: Essays Presented to N.R. Ker* (London: Scolar Press 1978), pp. 145–61.

18 Steele, 'The Pecia,' p.XX

19 Emilio Sáez and José Trenchs, 'Juan Ruiz de Cisneros (1295/1296–1351/ 1352) autor del *Buen Amor*,' in M. Criado de Val, ed., *El Arcipreste de Hita, el libro, el autor, la tierra, la época* (Barcelona: S.E.R.E.S.A. (1973), p. 366. But see, now, the important article by Francisco J. Hernández, 'The Vener-

able Juan Ruiz, Archpriest of Hita,' *La Corónica*, 13 (1984), pp. 10–22. Hernández takes pains 'to make clear ... that there is no connection between this Juan Ruiz and [the] Juan Rodríguez de Cisneros' for whom Sáez and Trenchs claimed authorship of the *Libro de buen amor* (p. 10).

20 Lecoy, *Recherches*, p. 352

21 G.H. Putnam, *Books and Their Makers during the Middle Ages* (New York: Hillary House 1962), vol. 1, p. 138

22 A.A. Neuman, *The Jews in Spain* (New York: Octagon 1969), vol. 2, pp. 95–6

23 Putnam, *Books*, vol. 1, p. 63

24 Coluccio Salutati, 'Letter to Guiliano Zonarini, Chancellor of Bologna,' trans. E. Emerton, in *Humanism and Tyranny* (Cambridge: Harvard University Press 1925), p. 291

25 Emerton, *Humanism*, p. 292. For a summary of the debate on Christian and pagan literature see J.J. Murphy, 'Saint Augustine and the Debate about a Christian Rhetoric,' *Quarterly Journal of Speech*, 46 (1960), pp. 400–10.

26 Francisco Rico, 'Las letras latinas del siglo XII en Galicia, León y Castilla,' *Abaco: Estudios sobre literatura española*, 2 (1969), p. 89

27 Charles Faulhaber, *Latin Rhetorical Theory in Thirteenth and Fourteenth Century Castile* (Berkeley: University of California Press 1972), p. 27

28 Janet A. Chapman, 'I lerned never rethoryk': A Problem of Apprenticeship,' in *Medieval Hispanic Studies Presented to Rita Hamilton* (London: Tamesis 1976), p. 23

29 The weak case for 'pagan' literature in Spain was outlined by Juan Pérez de Guzmán in 'El libro y la biblioteca en España durante los siglos medios,' *La España Moderna*, 202 (October 1905), pp. 111–52: 'hay que hacer notar que todos estos libros no eran litúrgicos, y que a veces en estas donaciones se intercalaban libros preciosos de la alta literatura romana,' p. 113. Peter Linehan documents the deep-seated resistance by Spanish clerics to education in *The Spanish Church and the Papacy in the Thirteenth Century* (Cambridge: University Press 1971), esp. pp. 12, 29–31, 237.

30 Carl Appel, ed., 'Die Danza general nach der Handschrift des Escorial neu herausgegeben,' *Beitrage zur romanischen und englischen Philologie* (Breslau: Kommissionverlag von Preuss & Junger 1902), lines 377–8, 449–50, pp. 24, 26. Cf. Margherita Morreale, 'Para una antología de la literatura castellana medieval: la Danza de la muerte,' *Annali del corso di lingue e letterature straniere*, 6 (1964), pp. 142, 146; Morreale edits line 377 to read 'Non quiero exorçismos nin conjuraciones,' but she also notes, questioningly, that 'si se conserva *exebçion* ... habría que admitir también *conjugaçion* ... ¿Podría se[r] un chiste acerca de la aversión del cura por los latines?';

31 Faulhaber, 'Retóricas clásicas y medievales en bibliotecas castellanas,' *Abaco*, 4 (1973), p. 154.

32 Samuel Berger, *Histoire de la Vulgate* (1893; rpt. New York: Burt Franklin

n.d.), pp. 8–28, 391–3. For the fourteen vernacular manuscripts see Margherita Morreale, 'Vernacular Scriptures in Spain,' in *The Cambridge History of the Bible*, ed. G.W.H. Lampe, vol. 2 (Cambridge: University Press 1969), p. 466; see also in this volume of the *Cambridge History*, Raphael Loewe, 'The Medieval History of the Latin Vulgate,' esp.pp. 120–9.

33 Curtius, *European Literature*, p. 542: 'Spain's cultural 'belatedness' of course in no sense signifies a "backwardness", in the sense either of the old or the new progressivism.' See also Manuel C. Díaz y Díaz, *Libros y librerías en la Rioja altomedieval* (Lograño: Servicio de Cultura de la Excma. Diputación Provincial 1979), esp. pp. 269–74, 'Libros Perdidos.'

34 Neuman, *The Jews in Spain*, vol. 2, pp. 69, 73. Agustin García Calvo, ed., *Don Sem Tob, Glosas de Sabiduría* (Madrid: Alianza 1974), p. 92. See also Manuel Carrión, 'A propósito del elogio al libro de Don Sem Tob de Carrión,' *Revista de archivos, bibliotecas y museos*, 82 (1979), pp. 449–60.

35 Vincente de la Fuente, *Historia de las universidades, colegios y demás establecimientos de enseñanza en España* (1884: rpt. Frankfurt: Verlag Sauer & Auvermann 1969), vol. 1, p. 33

36 Juan Pérez de Guzmán, 'El libro,' p. 146: 'Todo moro procuraba llevar siempre consigo en la escarcela su *korán*, encerrado dentro de una *bolsa*.'

37 Leslie W. Jones, trans., *An Introduction to Divine and Human Readings by Cassiodorus Senator* (New York: Columbia University Press 1946), pp. 157–8

38 The work accomplished so far is due mainly to the efforts of Margherita Morreale who writes, for example, 'El estudio de las fuentes eclesiásticas, particularmente la Biblia, y de la tradición viva nos provee como de una caja de resonancia para muchos vv. del *LBA*," in 'J. Corominas y el "Libro de buen amor,"' *Hispanic Review*, 37 (1969), p. 161. Professor Morreale supervised the thesis written by Sister Francis Gormly which was published in book form and is perhaps the only monograph on the topic: *The Use of the Bible in Representative Works of Medieval Spanish Literature 125--1300*, Studies in Romance Languages and Literature, vol. 64, Microfilm Series, vol. 1 (Washington: The Catholic University of America 1962), reviewed by Diego Catalán, 'La Biblia en la literatura medieval española,' *Hispanic Review*, 33 (1965), pp. 310–18. For a bibliography, see the one provided by Professor Morreale in the *Cambridge History of the Bible*, ed. Lampe, pp. 533–5.

39 J. González Muela, ed., *Alfonso Martínez de Toledo: Arcipreste de Talavera* (Madrid: Castalia 1970), p. 41

40 Julio Cejador y Frauca, ed., *Juan Ruiz, Arcipreste de Hita, Libro de buen amor*, 2 vols. (Madrid: Clásicos Castellanos 1913), vol. 1, p. 34. Rigo Mignani and Mario A. Di Cesare, trans., *The Book of Good Love*, (Albany: State University of New York Press 1970), p. 339.

41 Jean Destrez, *La Pecia*, p. 14.

42 Joan Corominas, ed., *Juan Ruiz, Libro de buen amor* (Madrid: Gredos

1967), p. 600. R.S. Willis, ed., *Juan Ruiz, Libro de buen amor* (Princeton: Princeton University Press 1972), p. 436. *Juan Ruiz, Libro de buen amor,* ed. María Rosa Lida de Malkiel (Buenos Aires: Losada 1941), p. 172. For the *Customs of Clugni,* see John Willis Clark, *The Care of Books* (Cambridge: Cambridge University Press 1901), pp. 36, 67. Professor Derek W. Lomax has kindly pointed out to me that 'the word *armarium* is used, apparently independently, by both Rodrigo Jiménez de Rada and the author of the Latin chronicle of the Kings of Castile to describe the archive of the cathedral of Burgos (*De rebus Hispaniae,* IX,5, and for the Latin Chronicle: ed. G.D. Cirot [Bordeaux: Feret 1913], p. 91).'
43 Criado de Val and Naylor, eds., *Buen amor,* p. 426
44 Willis, ed., *Buen amor,* p. xix. If the Archpriest did write 'letuario,' he would have been using that word especially in a book-related sense, not merely as an ordinary irreverent electuary. In several passages of the Bible, books and words are described as being sweet to the taste; in Psalms 118:103, in a verse that discusses the acquisition of understanding, words are described as sweeter than honey: 'Quam dulcia faucibus meis eloquia tua! super mel ori meo'; in Proverbs 16:24 pleasant words are like a honeycomb: 'Favus mellis composita verba'; and in Revelations 10:10 (a verse which seems to cite Ezekiel) a little scroll is eaten and it is sweet to the mouth and bitter in the stomach: 'Et accepi librum de manu angeli, et devoravi illum: et erat in ore meo tamquam mel dulce, et cum devorassem eum, amaricatus est venter meus.' Indeed, the relationship can be considered trite, since books and words and all things that are eaten have in common the tongue which either pronounces or tastes them. It will always be subject to doubt whether or not the archpriest had such a biblical theme in mind when he wrote the word at the end of line 1632d. However, we know from line 1632a that the author conceived of the book as a lectionary, which makes 'leturario' a plausible reading at 1632d. Of course, Juan Ruiz was capable of suggesting a lectionary that was, like an electuary, sweet to the taste; he might have chosen an appropriate word that would imply both a kind of book and a sweet taste.
45 Beryl Smalley, 'The Bible in the Medieval Schools,' in the *Cambridge History of the Bible,* ed. Lampe, p. 203. See also by the same author, *The Study of the Bible in the Middle Ages* (Oxford: Clarendon 1941' 2nd ed. New York: Philosophical Library 1952), esp. chaps. 1, 2, 5, from which material was absorbed for various points made in this study.
46 Du Cange lists *lectorarius* as a synonym of *lector* (see n. 5).
47 Faulhaber, *Latin Rhetorical Theory,* p. 34
48 Sáez and Trenchs, 'Juan Ruiz de Cisneros,' pp. 366–7, but bear in mind the recent discovery of Francisco Hernández, 'The Venerable Juan Ruiz.'
49 For an elaboration of this statement see this writer's study of 'The Structure of the *Libro de buen amor,*' *Neophilologus,* 61 (1977), pp. 58–73, now incorporated in chap. 4 of this book.
50 Smalley, 'The Bible in the Medieval Schools,' p. 213

51 Smalley, *The Study of the Bible*, p. 176, 2nd ed., pp. 216–17
52 He uses the word in st. 1153: 'Decretales mas de ciento, en libros E en questiones.'
53 Linehan demonstrates that the two most important issues of church reform in Spain, even as late as Juan Ruiz's lifetime, were education and concubinage (*The Spanish Church*, pp. 237–9). It must have been infuriating to a reformer like Cardinal Albornoz to have an archpriest, Juan Ruiz, publish a work that compounds the issue by demonstrating that educational reform leads only to a greater desire for concubinage.
54 For more bibliography about the making of ancient books, see Svend Dahl, *History of the Book* 2nd ed. (Metuchen, N.J.: Scarecrow Press 1968); M.A. Hussein, *Origins of the Book* (Greenwich, Conn.: New York Graphics Society 1972); H.D.L. Vervliet, ed., *The Book through 5000 Years* (London and New York: Phaidon 1972), and the pertinent sections of the *Annual Bibliography of the Book*, also edited by Verliet. Since material in this study first appeared in 1978, a number of articles have been published which deal with some of the points I have attempted to make. The most noteworthy of the articles include John Ahern, 'Binding the Book: Hermeneutics and Manuscript Production in *Paradiso* 33,' *PMLA*, 97 (1982), pp. 800–9; Nicasio Salvador Miguel, 'Mester de Clerecía: Marbete caracterizador de un género literario,' *Revista de literatura*, 42 (1979), pp. 5–30; Francisco López Estrada, 'Mester de Clerecía: las palabras y el concepto,' *Journal of Hispanic Philology*, 3 (1978), pp. 165–74; Gisela Beutler, 'Enigmas y adivinanzas sobre el libro, la pluma y otros utensilios para escribir: estudio sobre su origen, sus metáforas, su estructura,' in *Homenaje a Fernando Antonio Martínez: Estudios de lingüística, filosofía, literatura e historia cultural* (Bogotá: Instituto Caro y Cuervo 1979), pp. 1–39; Francsico Rico, 'La clerecía del mester,' *Hispanic Review*, 53 (1985), pp. 1–23, 127–50. There is also now the excellent research tool by Andrew Hughes, *Medieval Manuscripts for Mass and Office* (Toronto: University of Toronto Press 1981), which contains much valuable information on how lectionaries and other liturgical books were put together. I have also noted that Marilyn Olsen has applied ideas about the *pecia* system to her edition of *Zifar*, Spanish Series, no. 16 (Madison: Seminary of Medieval Studies), pp. vi–viii.

INDEX

UNIVERSITY OF TORONTO ROMANCE SERIES

UNIVERSITY OF TORONTO ROMANCE SERIES

UNIVERSITY OF TORONTO ROMANCE SERIES

UNIVERSITY OF TORONTO ROMANCE SERIES

UNIVERSITY OF TORONTO ROMANCE SERIES